Adult Career Development

Concepts, Issues, and Practices

Second Edition

Editors: H. Daniel Lea
Zandy B. Leibowitz

THE NATIONAL CAREER DEVELOPMENT ASSOCIATION

1992

A Publication of
THE NATIONAL CAREER DEVELOPMENT ASSOCIATION

Copyright 1992 by **The National Career Development Association,** a
division of the American Association for Counseling and Development

ISBN: 1-55620-095-1

Copies can be ordered from:

Publication Sales
AACD
5999 Stevenson Avenue
Alexandria, VA 22304

Preface

The National Career Development Association is proud to present the second edition of this important work on adult career development. The response to the first edition was gratifying to the Association, to the editors, and to the authors. It was your response that led directly to the decision to produce a second edition. In this edition the same team of editors, Danny Lea and Zandy Leibowitz, continued their excellent work of identifying authors who were able to provide the most thoughtful and current expression of theory and practice in the important area of adult career development.

Knowledge of the importance of adult career development has grown over the past two decades as we have seen rapid changes in the world affect all our lives. Changes in technology have added new occupations and reformed existing ones. At the same time, for some adults this change has meant displacement from jobs they expected to hold throughout their working lives. The very map of the world has continued to be re-shaped bringing economic opportunities to some and hardships to others. Market highs and lows have affected long-held assumptions about career paths as many workers at all organizational levels have found themselves in—or out of—flatter and thinner organizations. Better knowledge of healthful living and medical advances have increased the life span and thereby raised new questions for many about the meaning of work and income in the second half of life.

We can expect the pace and quality of external change to continue. What neither we nor our clients can predict is how the world will change or how these changes will affect each person's life-career. It is with the belief that counselors and other career development professionals can help people as they encounter life's challenges and opportunities, that this book is offered by NCDA.

The association remains grateful to Danny Lea and Zandy Leibowitz for their enthusiasm, their hard work, and this generous gift of their time and talents. We thank, as well, each of the authors and the Media Committee, chaired by Arnold Spokane, for their contributions of energy and expertise. We know you will appreciate the knowledge you will gain from this work.

Deborah P. Block, Ph.D.
President
NCDA

Acknowledgments

Adult career development is a concept whose time has come, as evidenced by the popularity of the first edition of this book. This second edition seeks to retain and build upon the strengths of the first. As in the first edition, the rich diversity of the field of adult career development is represented by both the chapter topics and authors.

The chapters retained from the first edition have been updated and revised. In addition, this second edition has three chapters which did not appear in the first edition. Arnie Spokane contributes a chapter on career counseling and intervention theory which complements Schlossberg's chapter on adult development theory and Minor's chapter on career development theory. Robert Carter and Donelda Cook contribute a chapter about the career paths of visible racial/ethnic groups. It addresses the career development issues of Black, Latino, Native American, and Asian-Americans in a way that respects the individuality of each group and that of the individuals within each group. Geri Horton and Dennis Engels contribute a chapter focused on the needs of one of the fastest growing groups—the older, mature worker. As is the first edition, this book will probably be most frequently read as a book of readings. Also, despite the rich diversity of the field, some theories and concepts have had universal impact across the field. Consequently, some redundancy has been permitted across the chapters.

Special thanks to the NCDA Board of Directors, Media Committee, and staff for their patience and support throughout the publication process for both editions of this book. The 36 authors who contributed to this second edition deserve most of the credit for its success. Without their unselfish contributions, this book could not have happened. Also, thanks to Conceptual Systems Inc. who permitted the editors to devote considerable time to this publication during the past two years.

As was the first edition, this book is dedicated to our families who have been very tolerant of our personal ongoing searches for the answer to the question, "what do you want to be when you grow up?"

—Danny and Zandy
Silver Spring, Maryland
December, 1991

Table of Contents

Introduction

JUST WHEN I THOUGHT I HAD THE ANSWERS . . . THE QUESTIONS CHANGED

Elusive answers . . . frustrating questions . . . the essence of adult career development. All of us grew up with the perpetual question, "What do you want to be when you grow up?" Most of us have struggled with the answer. Some of us may have managed to find a career niche for ourselves through trial and error or even luck, but the answer may have been only temporary. In adult career development, the only constant seems to be change. Most of us will face two to three career changes in our lifetime. The once-and-forever career choice is becoming a myth due to rapidly changing technological, organizational, and personal realities.

With change a certainty in adulthood, how do providers of adult career development services help adults face and negotiate change? This book was written to help answer that question. It covers a range of concepts, theories, and, particularly, strategies for working with adults.

This book is intended for anyone charged with the responsibility of providing career services to adults—career counselors, human resource specialists, or graduate students in the field. The book can be read from cover to cover or as a reference for certain key issues and topics. The one disclaimer that seems appropriate is that by including a cross section of views and writings, we're sure that we've excluded some others. Thus, the book must serve as a selected, certainly not a comprehensive, view.

At present, adult career development practice is best characterized by diversity. The organization of the content of this book reflects this diversity. Adult career development is a variety of ideas (*Section I: Theories and Concepts*), used in a variety of approaches (*Section II: Strategies and Methods*), for a variety of people (*Section III: Target Populations*), and in a variety of places (*Section IV: Settings*). In order to handle this diversity we need to prepare ourselves (*Section V: Training Programs*), establish our effectiveness and accountability (*Section VI: Evaluation*), and anticipate the future (*Section VII: Future Trends*).

Likewise, the authors represented have a variety of conceptual orientations and methodologies and have worked with diverse populations in a variety of settings. Each was asked to address three specific questions:

1. What theories, concepts, or models have you found useful in understanding your topic?
2. What are the relevant issues surrounding your topic?
3. What are the practical implications of these concepts and issues?

We hope that what is written will be used as food for thought and practice.

SECTION I:

THEORIES AND CONCEPTS

A VARIETY OF IDEAS . . .

CHAPTER 1

Adult Development Theories: Ways to Illuminate the Adult Experience

Nancy K. Schlossberg
Department of Counseling and Personnel Services
University of Maryland
College Park, Maryland

Adult development theories provide a lens through which to view adults in relation to their work. Adult development theories are presented not only to explain the role of work in adults' lives but to amplify the knowledge gained from the field of career development. This article describes four adult development perspectives and their implications for practitioners in their work with adults.

FOUR PERSPECTIVES ON ADULTHOOD

Adult development theorists view the adult experience from different perspectives. For example, one group explains adulthood within the cultural context. A second group focuses on the psychological developmental stages of the individual. A third group discusses the adult experience in terms of transitions. A fourth group examines continuity and change over the life span.

Cultural Perspective

Theorists who focus on the cultural context—social environment— believe that, given a particular environment, individual life stories will be predictable and similar. For example, the life stories of bakery workers throughout France indicate similar family lives, health, and activities outside of work. Bertaux (1982) explained this similarity in terms of bakery production structure, not in terms of psychological tendencies. Bakery workers have long hours, at least 9 hours per shift 6 nights a week, and their work time begins around 3 a.m. and continues until noon. This work pattern affects their social life, sex life, and energy levels.

Another example of viewing adulthood within the cultural context is Rosenbaum's (1979) theory that midlife crises can be predicted from examining the impact of organizational structure rather than the aging process. His research indicates that promotion chances in organizations increase until age 35 to 40 and then decline. Specifically, promotion chances for those with baccalaureate degrees reach a peak (over 60%) at age 35 and then decline abruptly during the next 5 to 10 years (less than 20%). Midlife crises become predictable from the extreme decline in promotion chances for those individuals. Because the popular press attributes midlife crises to the psychological effects of aging, Rosenbaum's views demonstrate how the cultural perspective deserves notice.

In addition, Kanter (1977) also attributed human problems to the organizational structure rather than to intrapsychic issues. She believes that the structure of work systems and the resulting work environments are largely responsible for the behaviors people engage in at work and outside. For example, she argues that to understand secretaries' behavior it is important to examine how organizations define and structure secretarial work and reward commitment to employers. Interviewing individual secretaries is not the way to gain this understanding.

Developmental Perspective

The most widely read group of theorists explain adult behavior in terms of age and sequential stages of development. For example, Levinson, Darrow, Klein, Levinson, and McKee (1978) divided adult behavior into six age-related sequential periods:

- leaving the family—late adolescence to about age 22;
- getting into the adult world—early to late 20s;
- settling down—early 30s to early 40s;
- becoming one's own person—age 35 to 39;
- making a midlife transition—early 40s; and
- restabilizing and beginning middle adulthood—middle and late 40s.

Levinson et al. (1978) emphasized similarity in the adult experience. They believe that young people have dreams about what they will become. Mentors help them implement their dreams. Then in midlife people begin to evaluate their lives in terms of their early dreams. It is important to note that Levinson's sample, although extensively interviewed, consisted of only 40 men.

Other theorists postulate that adults pass through developmentally sequenced stages that are not based on chronological age. Some people move through the stages swiftly, whereas others become arrested at one stage and never move forward. Important in this group is Erikson (1950), who described a predictable eight-stage progression in ego development. Each stage is characterized by a crucial issue that must be successfully resolved before the individual can move on to the next stage. The adult stages involve issues of: identity (Who am I?); intimacy (Can I be committed and close to others?); generativity (Can I nurture others?); and ego integrity (Am I satisfied with my life?).

3

Vaillant (1977) identified career consolidation as an additional developmental stage in Erikson's progression. This evolved from a longitudinal analysis of advantaged men who progressed through Erikson's basic stages. Vaillant found that those men who were able to achieve intimacy were able to deal effectively with their careers and then nurture younger men in their career quests. In other words, the career consolidation stage occurs between Erikson's intimacy and generativity stages. Vaillant found the same progression through Erikson's stages when he examined longitudinal data on inner city men.

Gould (1978) explained the stages of adult development as the progressive struggles for freedom from the internal constraints of childhood. He perceives people at all ages as being "stuck" and needing help with the underdeveloped aspects of self. Gould's theory on the struggle for freedom from childhood constrictions and belief that maturity arrives after age 50 are similar to Erikson's view that successful aging requires resolving crucial issues. Yet Gould conceives of a continuous process of developing some aspect of self, whereas Erikson believes the resolution of each crisis is the completion of a developmental stage.

Still other theorists view adult development as moving from the simple to the complex. For example, Kohlberg's (1970) moral development and Loevinger's (1976) ego development theories described adults as progressing from dependency on outside authority and others' judgments to a higher stage of responsibility for consequences of their own actions and a tolerance for ambiguity. For example, two couples are facing parenthood for the first time. One couple might deal with this experience by relying on pediatrician's fiats, whereas partners of the other couple might rely on their own judgment as to the best course of action. According to the developmental view, the second couple has reached a higher, more complex developmental stage.

Another developmental perspective stems from Jung's work as corroborated by Fiske (1980) and Gutmann (1987). This view compared men and women and discovered that as men aged they began to place more value on expressive and interpersonal goals, whereas women began to direct their interests outward and to become more concerned with contribution to society. In other words, men began to turn inward or become more introspective as they aged, and women began to turn outward or become more involved in the external world. When comparing the developmental stages of men and women, the effect is of "crisscrossing trajectories" where successive stages reflect different developmental changes and scheduling.

Most of the research behind the theories mentioned in this section has focused primarily on men; yet the application of these theories has been considered useful for both men and women. Gilligan (1983) challenged this application. She believes that even when differences between men and women are pointed out, they are presented in terms of deficits. A woman lacks a penis, an occupation, or an education. She also contends that most developmental theorists have dealt with individual progression through various stages with a focus on achievement and work. There is little concern for love. Gilligan (1982) identified different issues as being central to the development of women. They are issues of attachment,

4

caring, and interdependence. Her work involved extensive interviews with women at decision points in their lives. Her findings seem to have important implications for women.

Gilligan's (1982) results indicate that a woman's moral development begins with a concern for survival, moves to a concern with responsibility (not hurting others), and finally becomes a concern for meriting equal care for self. Renegotiation of interdependence over time is a critical issue of adult development for women. Whether this renegotiation takes place between parents and children, teachers and students, therapists and clients, or researchers and subjects, it is a continuous process for women. Gilligan asserts that maturity is different for women than for men and that these differences must be built into current models of adult development. No longer can the view be of the "heroic individual" marching predictably up the sequential stages. Instead the view is of the individual renegotiating interdependence and caring. The metaphor changes from one of stairs to one of widening circles of attachment.

Transitional Perspective

Nearly all cultures celebrate rites of passage for birth, puberty, marriage, death, and other major life events. One way to look at the adult experience is through these events or transitions.

Cultural norms sometimes dictate age-appropriate behavior when there is little biological basis for that behavior (Neugarten, Moore, & Lowe, 1965). In fact, most of us hold rather rigid views about what constitutes appropriate behavior for people at different ages. For example, societal norms prescribe at what age people should take jobs, marry, have children, and retire. In fact, if an individual experiences an event at an age different from that prescribed by our culture, it may be considered "off-time" and the person may have more difficulty with the transition as a result. The extent to which these ideas prevail was investigated in studies by Neugarten and her associates. They found that at least 80% of their sample of "normal, middle-class Americans" believed that the best age for men to marry is between 20 and 27 and for women between 20 and 22, and that people should retire between ages 60 and 65. Such norms as these constitute our "social clock."

Today the prescriptions for and predictability of age-appropriate behavior are lessening (Neugarten et al., 1965). Because people are living longer, the postparental period has lengthened considerably. At the same time many young people are attending college and going on to graduate or professional school and delaying their "economic maturity." Patterns for women have changed radically. More young women are now employed full-time. Many middle-aged women are returning to the labor force after their children leave home. In addition, child-rearing practices are changing. Fathers are beginning to share with their working wives the responsibility for parenting. Couples are also marrying later and more are deciding not to have children.

Lowenthal and Pierce (1975) discussed major life events or transitions in their longitudinal study, *Four Stages of Life*. They focused on four transitional groups of men and women in the San Francisco area: grad-

5

uating high school seniors, newlyweds, middle-aged parents, and pre-retirement couples. At the start of the study each group was on the threshold of a major transition. The researchers found that the groups differed considerably in their general outlook on life, the stresses they faced, and in their attitudes toward those stresses. They concluded that it is less important to know that a person is 40 years old than it is to know that the person is 40 with adolescent children, recently divorced, and about to enter the work force. It is clear that the transition itself is more important than the age of the individual. For example, men facing retirement after an active work life encounter many of the same problems whether they retire at age 50, 60, or 70. Newlyweds of any age are engaged in similar tasks of bonding, discovery, and negotiation. In short, life events or transitions are more important than chronological age in understanding and evaluating behavior.

Lowenthal and Pierce (1975) also highlighted the different ways men and women handle transitions. Women generally have less positive self-images than men, feel less in control of their lives, and are less likely to plan for transitions. At the same time their affective lives are richer and more complex and they have a greater tolerance for ambiguity. Men's life styles become less complex as they grow older and shed roles and activities. Women, on the other hand, have a simplistic pattern as high school seniors and middle-aged women and a complex pattern as newlyweds and before retirement. This is due to the complexity of playing many roles and engaging in many activities in the later transitional stages. Also, highly stressed men in the older groups tend to deny stress, whereas women tend to be preoccupied with stress.

Schlossberg (1984; 1991) developed a model to examine how transitions affect an individual's life and how the individual copes with transitions. Her model incorporates both anticipated and unanticipated transitions. Anticipated transitions are expected events that have a "likelihood of occurrence for the individual" (Brim & Ryff, 1980, p. 374) and that can be rehearsed. Some examples include an expected promotion, scheduled retirement, or a planned career change. Unanticipated transitions are the "nonscheduled events" that are not predictable. These usually "involve crises, eruptive circumstances, and other unexpected occurrences that are not the consequence of life-cycle transitions" (Pearlin, 1982, p. 179). "Events of this type in the occupational arena are being fired, laid off, or demoted; having to give up work because of illness, . . . being promoted, and leaving one job for a better one. Divorce, separation, . . . premature death of spouse, . . . [and] illness or death of a child represent such events in the parental arena" (Pearlin, 1982, p. 180).

After considering transitions and their impact, the second part of Schlossberg's (1984) model focused on the process of assimilating transitions. During this process the individual moves from being enveloped by the transition to eventual integration. For example, the individual is no longer the graduate, but someone who has graduated. The third part of the model identifies variables in three clusters that influence the ease with which the transition is assimilated—first, the characteristics of the transition: timing, source, and duration; second, the characteristics of the individual: coping and ego strength; and third, the characteristics of the environment: the individual's support and options. This eclectic model is substantiated with data from three major studies to date: the impact of geographical moving on men and women (Schlossberg, 1981); the experience of men whose jobs were eliminated (Schlossberg & Leibowitz, 1980); and the identification of transitions by clerical workers (Schlossberg & Charner, 1982). The model incorporates both a sociological perspective of identifying anticipated transitions or rites of passage and a psychological perspective of examining the individual's response to anticipated and unanticipated transitions.

Life Span Perspective: Continuity and Change

The adult experience incorporates both continuity and change. Theorists who examine adulthood from this perspective consider the continuous aspects of the adult experience; change over the life span; variations in how groups experience adulthood; and the socioeconomic, racial, and ethnic differences.

Brim and Kagan (1980, p. 13) described the life span development approach as "an emergent intellectual movement, responsive to the possibility of change, currently trying to select its major premises, to gather new facts, and to conceptualize the developmental span without using chronological age categories." This is in distinct opposition to theories involving adult stages because "stages cast development as unidirectional, hierarchical, sequenced in time, cumulative, and irreversible— ideas not supported by commanding evidence."

In examining the life span, Neugarten (1982) emphasized the trend toward variability or individual fanning out. For example, 10-year-olds are more similar to each other than are 60-year-olds. The research on aging consistently shows that people grow old in very different ways. The striking variations among groups and the idiosyncratic sequences of life events make individuals between 60 and 80 years old highly unique. Today with changing life patterns, the life course is fluid. It is marked by many role transitions, proliferating timetables for role entries and exits, and dissimilar age-related roles.

The Grant Study (Vaillant, 1977) covered 35 years for over 200 men. Most of the sample had high ability levels and were from high socioeconomic backgrounds. When the study began the men were college sophomores. This study also corroborates the individuality and variability in the adult experience. The purpose of the study was to predict what sophomores would do with their lives. When all the data were in, it became clear that people's futures are shaped by the quality of their sustained relationships with others, not by childhood traumas, and that the course of life has surprising outcomes.

Conclusions

Each theorist provides valuable insight, but as Pearlin (1982) stated, "There is not one process of aging, but many; there is not one life course followed, but multiple courses. . . . There is not one sequence of stages, but many. The variety is as rich as the historic conditions people have faced and the current circumstances they experience" (p. 63). Then too, similar events have different effects on different people because of variations in coping responses. "All in all, it seems untenable to speak of either ages or life stages as though they are made up of undifferentiated people following a uniform life course" (p. 71).

Pearlin (1982) cautioned not to glorify one stage and dramatize another. The fascination with the midlife crisis is a case in point. Crisis can occur at any period. In fact, young adults experience more strains than other age groups. Yet the media and some scholars continue to dramatize crisis in midlife, the inevitability of which is not corroborated by hard data.

Indeed, Pearlin's cautionary note regarding ages and stages should be our concern about any theoretical perspective. Overemphasizing any particular life event, period, or transition categorizes people as if they were all the same. Yet adults come in all shapes and sizes, with widely differing personalities, perceptions, and life experiences. Of course, the setting and historical period must be considered as well as the particular transitions an individual has experienced. However, never discount the variety of experience and the individual's uniqueness in interpreting and reacting to life.

The major reason why four perspectives and many theorists have been presented here is to point out that the answers to adult development questions will differ according to the perspective employed. Theoretical perspective determines whether one explains adult career behavior through the historical or cultural period in which the adult lives, through the developmental unfolding of individual lives over time, or through the expected and unexpected transitions adults experience.

IMPLICATIONS FOR PRACTICE

The central issue for practitioners is translating theories into effective practice. To do that, strategies will be explicated for each perspective: cultural, developmental, transitional, and life span (see Table 1).

Cultural Practices

Practices stemming from the cultural perspective involve changing or modifying the system. For example, Rosenbaum (1979) pointed out the dangers of counseling employees to adjust to work situations that might be harmful to self-esteem and sense of control. Energy would be better spent on reorganizing organizational career systems. Rosenbaum makes several specific policy recommendations based on his analysis of organizational promotional practices. For example, he suggests promoting older individuals as their family responsibilities lessen.

Kanter (1977) corroborated Rosenbaum's position by juxtaposing two types of reform. For example, offer secretaries assertiveness training so they can stand up for their rights. At the same time, change the reward system for secretaries so their promotions and salary increases are dependent on their performance rather than on their loyalty to a particular boss. In other words, she advocates changing the system rather than the

Table 1

The Adult Experience: Perspectives, Concepts, and Practices

Perspectives	Concepts	Practices
Cultural:	*Bertaux* • Life stories depend on work structure *Rosenbaum* • Career mobility results from organizational structure • Midlife crisis is a sociological phenomenon *Kanter* • Individual progress is determined by opportunity structure	Change or modify system Examples: • Hire and promote older individuals • Gear admissions and financial aid to older part-time individuals
Developmental: Age/Stage	*Levinson et al.* • Invariant sequence of developmental methods • Life structure • Dream, mentor • Polarities *Erikson* • Unfolding of life and resolving of inner issues • Hierarchical stages *Gould* • Release from childhood assumptions • Tinkering with inadequacies *Perry, Loevinger, Kohlberg* • Hierarchical sequence • Sequence in ego development and moral development	Design programs for people at different stages Examples: • Programs for returning students, preretirees Design programs for people who process work differently Examples: • Differential teaching, advising, and counseling Assess congruence of supervisor, supervisee along dimensions of personality, learning style, achievement Sensitize faculty, counselors, and others to age, social class bias

(Table 1 continued)

Perspectives	Concepts	Practices
Transitions: Life Course/ Life Span/ Life Events	*Fiske, Gutman* ● Men and women express the dormant part of themselves at midlife *Gilligan* ● Critique of models based on men and applied to women ● Hierarchical models obscure other voices ● Widening circles of attachment ● Renegotiation of interdependence over time *Neugarten, Moore, Lowe* ● Socially created rather than biologically determined transitions *Lowenthal (Fiske), Chiriboga, Thurnher* ● Life span ● Stage not age ● Coping with transitions; balance of resources to deficits ● Sex differences *Schlossberg* ● Types of transitions: anticipated, unanticipated, nonevents ● Coping moderators: transition, environment, self ● Transition process: over time, for better or worse *Pearlin* ● Coping, not life events, is central issue ● Classification of life strains and coping responses	Design programs for people in similar transitions ● Support from others who have successfully negotiated the same transition ● Provide cognitive map ● Offer programs at several times: before, during, after transition Teach individual coping skills ● To change situation ● To modify meaning of situation ● To relax

Life Span:
Continuity
and Change

Neugarten
- Capacity of individual to select, ignore, or mod-ify socializing influence
- Fanning out and variations
- Fluid life span

Vaillant
- Early trauma not predictive of later behavior

Pearlin
- Variability
- Differential distribution of strains by sex, age, different patterns of coping

Brim, Kagan
- Orientation (not yet theory) toward constancy and change
- Discontinuities rather than sequencing are studied
- Importance of variability based on cohort, sex, age, social class

Multiple programs for larger population
- Individual and group programs
- Media
- Other

individual secretary. System modification can have an enormous effect on individual career development.

Developmental Practices

Kammen (1979) explained why the age and stage theories are so popular. "We want predictability and we desperately want definitions of 'normality' " (p. 64). The most popular developmental perspective in the press is that of regular stages with identifiable issues and tasks (Levinson et al., 1978). This view would offer different programs for people by age. Administrators and employers would differentiate among groups in that way. For example, today many write about the adult learner as an entity; yet the developmental perspective emphasizes that the adult employee or learner of 25 has very different concerns from the adult learner of 60.

Another developmental perspective claims that people process the world differently: some in either/or terms and others in complex ways. This implies that faculty, supervisors, and managers should engage in differential training depending on stage complexity. In other words, two employees who are regularly late are not the same and would respond differently to different types of supervision. One employee may need clear rules and clear consequences. The other may need more autonomy in setting hours and controlling work destiny.

Knefelkamp and Slepitza (1976) took Perry's cognitive developmental scheme (Perry, 1970) as a springboard for their work. Perry's model outlines in sequence the ways in which students intellectually process the world. Knefelkamp and Slepitza adapted the Perry model to career development. They developed ways to train career counselors to work differently with people at different levels of maturity. They challenged the assumption that all people seeking career advice about obtaining a first job, a promotion, a pay raise, or retirement plans are similar. They found that some need concrete suggestions whereas others need help in creatively exploring numerous possibilities.

The proliferation of measurement tools to assess workers' characteristics attests to the interest in differential treatment of workers. Some instruments differentiate learning styles of employees and students (Kolb, 1981). Others measure achievement styles (Lipman-Blumen & Leavitt, 1977). Still others measure ways people approach the world (i.e., Myers, 1962). These measures are increasingly used in business and industry to help managers understand the importance of individual differences and the concept of team building. Thus, developmental differences are receiving some attention in practice today.

Transition Practices

All through life people are involved in transitions, many of them relating to work. Even when the transition seems personal (i.e., illness of a spouse), it may have work implications. There seems to be a ripple effect of transitions from one arena of life to others. Weiss (1976) classified transitions in three categories: crisis, transitions, or deficit.

12

The first category, crisis, Weiss (1976) described as a sudden, severely upsetting situation of short duration that requires mobilization of energies and resources. An example of a crisis would be the sudden onset of a major illness or an accident. People in crisis are frequently emotionally numbed; their feelings are suspended. For individuals experiencing a crisis, support seems to be the only effective help. The helper, professional or nonprofessional, must communicate empathy, understanding, and a readiness to help the individual through the crisis. Such support is also helpful to those in transition states and deficit situations, but there individuals can benefit as well from other kinds of help.

When the crisis passes, the situation either returns to normal or results in change. The individual with the illness either returns to health, is permanently invalided, or dies. In the invalid case, the individual enters a transition state. This period is marked by relational and personal changes. It includes coping with upset, grief, and other disruptive emotions and finding new sources of support. It is also a time of confusion and uncertainty as the person attempts to rearrange his or her life. People in early transition are particularly likely to benefit from counseling because the decisions made at this point can affect the rest of their life course.

The end of a transition state is usually marked by a new life organization and personal identity. The new situation is either satisfactory or unsatisfactory. If it is unsatisfactory, the individual enters a deficit situation. For example, a widow may find that she has continuous difficulty in raising dependent children by herself. In contrast to a short-lived crisis, a deficit situation tends to be long-lasting. People in deficit situations may have stability even though their situation is unsatisfactory. Short-term help is of little value to them. They need a continuing, problem-focused support system. For instance, the widow may require continued help with her problems as she tries to raise children on her own.

People in transition must find new ways of managing their lives. Thus, cognitive information or materials to help them understand the new situation may be of help. For instance, the new widow may need help in managing finances or in locating child-care services. In addition, people in transition may be grappling with emotions that they do not understand. Therefore, they may benefit from cognitive materials that help them understand their emotions. Support groups may also be beneficial. The bereaved may find that the old social network gradually disappears and that social isolation sets in. Meeting with others in the same situation may have practical as well as psychological value. In this group setting, mutual problems and possible solutions can be shared.

In the work setting, people experience crises such as being fired, transitions such as moving into management or retiring, and deficits such as being demoted or plateaued. Organizations have now begun to develop programs for people in these transitions. They realize that supporting employees will be mutually beneficial to the individuals and the organization.

Pearlin's (1982) research demonstrated that men and women cope with transitions by either changing the situation, modifying its meaning, or relaxing in the face of stress. This information offers direct program possibilities. Counselors can design workshops to help people learn the

13

three major coping strategies (i.e., mediation, stress management, or relaxation). Rather than focusing on one strategy, multi-strategy workshops can be developed. Pearlin states that no single magic coping strategy exists. Effective copers use multiple strategies depending on the nature of the transition.

Life Span Practices

Life span orientation suggests that individuals deal with certain issues differently throughout life. For example, these issues might be relating to people, concern with self, or decision making. Both elementary school children and people in retirement homes make decisions. The content and quality of the decision making might vary. Life span perspective shows the benefits of discovering life skills and developing programs to train people in these skills.

A life span scholar of a different orientation might suggest that the variety of individual patterns makes categorization impossible. Therefore, multiple and multi-strategy programs are needed. For example, adults "plateaued" in a work setting may feel distraught at remaining there for the rest of their lives. These individuals could obtain help from a variety of programs such as individual counseling, a group support system, an internship involving trying something new within the organization, or a computer-based career guidance program. In other words, what works for one person might not work for everyone. Furthermore, what works for an individual at one time in his or her life might not be the most helpful strategy over time.

Conclusion

The utility of an eclectic perspective can be seen through an example of elderly parent care. Practitioners could work with an individual family or groups of families about appropriate arrangements. On the other hand, they could focus on changing funding for residential homes for ill older people or on reforming nursing homes and their image. If the transition were a heart attack, they could work with the spouses of heart attack victims, or they could design preventive programs, such as exercise and jogging programs, for the work setting to help ward off heart attacks.

In some programs helpers deal directly with the individual (i.e., the retiree, the abused, the new parent, the newly disabled). In other programs helpers deal with a significant other (i.e., the spouse of the newly disabled, the adult children of the aging person, the abuser). In addition, some programs deal with the system in which the individuals and significant others operate (i.e., an organization's retirement plan, a state's policy on housing for the elderly).

In short, the optimal plan is one in which all aspects of an issue can be addressed simultaneously. In that way practitioners can help the individual in transition as well as help cause change in the system to enable people to achieve their potential. Yet often, depending on resources, the decision must be made to work with the individual, the group, or the system. One particular goal must be identified.

The practitioner's orientation will influence both the analysis of and intervention plan for any issue. An example would be Rosenbaum's (1979) employees at the midcareer transition. If the helper sees the promotion issue as the individual's responsibility, the suggested intervention might be therapy or retraining. If the promotion issue is viewed as a function of the group, suggested interventions might be job redesign or skill training. Finally, if the promotion issue is seen as resulting from the organizational climate, the suggested intervention might be a new promotional system for older workers. In reality, all three sets of interventions may be needed.

Thus, evidently at least four different perspectives exist to explain the adult experience. Each perspective holds implications for practice. There is something to be learned from all four views. It is important to look at all perspectives and generate a variety of practices to help people better understand their careers.

REFERENCES

Bertaux, D. (1982). The life course approach as a challenge to the social sciences. In T.K. Haraven & K.J. Adams (Eds.), *Aging and life course transitions: An interdisciplinary perspective* (pp. 127–150). New York: Guilford Press.

Brim, O.G., & Kagan, J. (Eds.). (1980). *Constancy and change in human development.* Cambridge, MA: Harvard University Press.

Brim, O.G., Jr., & Ryff, C.D. (1980). On the properties of life events. In P.B. Baltes & O.G. Brim (Eds.), *Life-span development and behavior: Vol. 3* (pp. 368–388). New York: Academic Press.

Erikson, E. (1950). *Childhood and society.* New York: Norton.

Fiske, M. (1980). Changing hierarchies of commitment in adulthood. In N.J. Smelser & E.H. Erikson (Eds.), *Themes of work and love in adulthood* (pp. 238–264). Cambridge, MA: Harvard University Press.

Gilligan, C. (1982). *In a different voice.* Cambridge, MA: Harvard University Press.

Gilligan, C. (1983, May). *Challenging existing theories: Conclusions.* Paper presented at Eighth Annual Conference for Helpers of Adults, University of Maryland, College Park.

Gould, R. (1978). *Transformations.* New York: Simon & Schuster.

Gutmann, D.C. (1987). *Reclaimed powers.* New York: Basic Books, Inc.

Kammen, M. (1979). Changing perceptions of the life cycle in American thought and culture. *Massachusetts Historical Society Proceedings, 91,* 35–66.

Kanter, R.M. (1977). *Men and women of the corporation.* New York: Basic Books.

Knefelkamp, L.L., & Slepitza, R. (1978). A cognitive-developmental model of career development: An adaptation of the Perry Scheme. *The Counseling Psychologist, 6* (3), 53–58.

Kohlberg, L. (1970). Stages of moral development as a basis for moral education. In C. Beck and E. Sullivan (Eds.), *Moral education* (pp. 23–92). Toronto, Canada: University of Toronto.

Kolb, D.A. (1981). Learning styles and disciplinary differences. In A.W. Chickering, *The modern American college* (pp. 232–255). San Francisco: Jossey-Bass.

Levinson, D.J., Darrow, C.M., Klein, E.B., Levinson, M.A., & McKee, B. (1978). *The seasons of a man's life.* New York: Knopf.

Lipman-Blumen, J., & Leavitt, H.S. (1977). Vicarious and direct achievement patterns in adulthood. In N.K. Schlossberg & A.D. Entine (Eds.), *Counseling adults* (pp. 60–76). Monterey, CA: Brooks/Cole.

Loevinger, J. (1976). *Ego development: Conceptions and theories.* San Francisco: Jossey-Bass.

Lowenthal, M.F., & Pierce, R. (1975). The pretransitional stance. In M.F. Lowenthal, M. Thurnher, & D. Chiriboga (Eds.), *Four stages of life: A comparative study of men and women facing transitions* (pp. 201–222). San Francisco: Jossey-Bass.

Myers, I.B. (1962). *Manual: The Myers-Briggs Type Indicator.* Princeton NJ: Educational Testing Service.

Neugarten, B.L. (1982, August). *Successful aging.* Paper presented to the annual meeting of the American Psychological Association.

Neugarten, B.L., Moore, J.C., & Lowe, J.C. (1965). Age nouns, age constraints, and adult socialization. *American Journal of Sociology, 70,* 710–717.

Pearlin, L.I. (1982). Discontinuities in the study of aging. In T.K. Haraven & K.J. Adams (Eds.), *Aging and life course transitions: An interdisciplinary perspective* (pp. 55–74). New York: Guilford Press.

Perry, W., Jr. (1970). *Intellectual and ethical development in the college years.* New York: Holt, Rinehart & Winston.

Rosenbaum, J.E. (1979). Tournament mobility: Career patterns in a corporation. *Administrative Science Quarterly, 24,* 220–241.

Schlossberg, N.K. (1991). *Overwhelmed: Coping with life's ups and downs.* New York: Dell Books.

Schlossberg, N.K. (1984). *Counseling adults in transition.* New York: Springer.

Schlossberg, N.K., & Charner, I. (1982). *Development of a self-help instrument for coping with change.* Project in process.

Schlossberg, N.K., & Leibowitz, Z.B. (1980). Organizational support systems as a buffer to job loss. *Journal of Vocational Behavior, 17,* 204–217.

Vaillant, G.E. (1977). *Adaptation to life.* Boston: Little, Brown.

Weiss, R.S. (1976). Transition states and other stressful situations: Their nature and programs for their management. In G. Caplan & M. Killilea (Eds.), *Support systems and mutual help: Multidisciplinary explorations.* (pp. 213–232). New York: Grune & Stratton.

CHAPTER 2

Career Development Theories and Models

Carole W. Minor
Faculty in Counseling
Northern Illinois University
DeKalb, Illinois

For almost a century theories that explain career behavior and prescribe interventions have been formulated, discussed, and researched. These theories have developed chronologically from a prescriptive model of matching individuals with jobs (Parsons, 1909), through stage models of career choice and career development (Ginzberg, Ginsburg, Axelrad, & Herma, 1951; Super, 1953), to more specific explanations of factors involved in career choices and adjustment (Holland, 1973, 1985; Krumboltz, 1979; Roe, 1956). This discussion is organized around the following assumptions (see Figure 1):

1. Career development is a continuous process over the life span.
2. Career development involves both career choice and career adjustment issues.
3. Both career choice and career adjustment involve content and process variables.
4. Theories tend to focus on either the content or the process of career choice or adjustment.

DEVELOPMENTAL FRAMEWORK

Developmental career theories provide a useful framework from which to view all other theoretical work. Historically, prior to the early 1950s, there was little career theory per se. In the first decade of this century, Frank Parsons (1909) developed a process of vocational guidance—an intervention model—which underlies most career guidance practice to this day. He stated that vocational guidance consisted of three steps:

First, a clear understanding of your aptitudes, abilities, interests, resources, limitations, and other qualities. Second, a knowledge of the requirements and conditions of success, advantages and disadvantages, compensation, opportunities, and prospects in different lines of work. Third, reasoning on the relationships of these two groups of facts. (Parsons, 1909, p. 5)

Figure 1
The Process of Career Development Over the Life Span

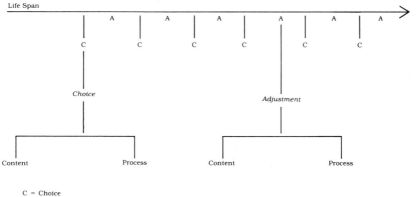

C = Choice
A = Adjustment

E.G. Williamson (1939) amplified and improved Parsons' intervention model, stating its assumptions. Other forces, including the increasing sophistication of the methods of differential psychology, improved the practice of what was known as vocational guidance. However, until the early 1950s both the general public and professional practitioners viewed occupational choice as a once-in-a-lifetime event. At some particular point individuals chose to enter occupations and generally continued in them for their entire productive lifetimes.

In the early 1950s two career theories proposed a different view.

Ginzberg

Ginzberg, Ginsburg, Axelrad, and Herma, in 1951, described a career theory contending that:

1. Decision making is a process that occurs from prepuberty to the late teens or early 20s.
2. Many decisions are irreversible.
3. The resolution of the choice process is a compromise.

In 1972 Ginzberg revised his model to focus on the continuation of the career choice process throughout the life span. He revised his ideas as follows:

1. Occupational choice is a process that remains open as long as we make decisions about work and career.
2. Early decisions have a shaping influence on career, but so do continuing changes of work and life.
3. People make decisions with the aim of optimizing satisfaction by finding the best possible fit between their needs and desires and the opportunities and constraints in the world of work. (p. 173)

18

His recent writings (Ginzberg, 1984) support this reformulation with the addition of one point: "Occupational choice is a lifelong process of decision making for those who seek major satisfactions from their work. This leads them to reassess repeatedly how they can improve the fit between their changing career goals and the realities of the World of Work" (p. 180).

These changes that Ginzberg has made in his ideas over the past 35 years exemplify the changing view of occupation and career in our society. This view has probably resulted from increases in our knowledge of the adult work experience and actual changes in our society in terms of stability of occupations and career patterns. For example, the idea of person/environment fit is important in each of Ginzberg's statements. However, it progresses from the idea that the resolution of the choice process is a compromise between what one would like and what is available (static choice) to the idea that choice is a lifelong process, for those who seek major satisfaction from work, of compromise between their own changing goals and the new realities of the work place (dynamic choice).

Super

Super (1953) presented a theory that was much more explicit and extensive. It was based in part on the early work of Charlotte Buehler (1933) in Vienna. Super's original propositions with more recent updates and modifications appear below.

1. People differ in their abilities, interests, and personalities.
2. They are each qualified, by virtue of these characteristics, for a number of occupations.
3. Each of these occupations requires a characteristic pattern of abilities, interests, and personality traits, with tolerance wide enough to allow some variety of occupations for each individual and some variety of individuals in each occupation.
4. Vocational preferences and competencies, the situations in which people live and work and hence their self-concepts, change with time and experience, although self-concepts, as products of social learning, are increasingly stable from late adolescence until late maturity, providing some continuity in choice and adjustment.
5. This process of change may be summed up in a series of life stages (a maxicycle) characterized as a sequence of growth, exploration, establishment, maintenance, and decline. These stages may in turn be subdivided into (a) the fantasy, tentative, and realistic phase of the exploratory stage and (b) the trial and stable phases of the establishment stage. A small (mini) cycle takes place in the transition from one stage to the next or each time an individual is destabilized by a reduction in force, changes in type of personnel needs, illness or injury, or other socioeconomic or personal events. Such unstable or multiple-trial careers involve new growth, reexploration, and reestablishment (recycling).

19

6. The nature of the career pattern—that is, the occupational level attained and the sequence, frequency, and duration of trial and stable jobs—is determined by the individual's parental socioeconomic level, mental ability, education, skills, personality characteristics (needs, values, interests, traits, and self concepts), career maturity, and the opportunities to which he or she is exposed.

7. Success in coping with the demands of environment and of the organism in that context at any given life-career stage depends on the readiness of the individual to cope with these demands (that is, on his or her career maturity). *Career maturity* is a constellation of physical, psychological, and social characteristics; psychologically, it is both cognitive and affective. It includes the degree of success in coping with the demands of earlier stages and substages of career development, and especially with the most recent.

8. Career maturity is a hypothetical concept. Its operational definition is perhaps as difficult to formulate as is that of intelligence, but its history is much briefer and its achievements even less definitive. Contrary to the impressions created by some writers, it does not increase monotonically, and it is not a unitary trait.

9. Development through the life stages can be guided, partly by facilitating the maturing of abilities and interests and partly by aiding in reality testing and in the development of self-concepts.

10. The process of career development is essentially that of developing and implementing occupational self-concepts. It is a synthesizing and compromising process in which the self-concept is a product of the interaction of inherited aptitudes, physical makeup, opportunity to observe and play various roles, and evaluations of the extent to which the results of role playing meet with the approval of superiors and fellows (interactive learning).

11. The process of synthesis of or compromise between individual and social factors, between self-concepts and reality, is one of role playing and of learning from feedback; the role may be played in fantasy, in the counseling interview, or in real life activities such as classes, clubs, part-time work, and entry jobs.

12. Work satisfactions and life satisfactions depend upon the extent to which the individual finds adequate outlets for abilities, needs, values, interests, personality traits, and self-concepts. They depend upon the establishment in a type of work, a work situation, and a way of life in which one can play the kind of role that growth and exploratory experiences have led one to consider congenial and appropriate.

13. The degree of satisfaction people attain from work is proportional to the degree to which they have been able to implement self concepts.

14. Work and occupation provide a focus for personality organization for most men and many women. For some persons this focus is peripheral, incidental, or even nonexistent and other foci, such as leisure activities and homemaking, may be central. (Social traditions, such as sex-role stereotyping and modeling, racial and ethnic biases, and the opportunity structure, as well as individual

differences, are important determinants of preferences for such roles as worker, student, leisurite, homemaker, and citizen.) (Super, 1990, pp. 206–208)

More recently, Super (1976, 1990) has discussed the roles people play at different times in their lives and the theaters in which these roles are played.

A significant contribution of Super and Ginzberg and their colleagues was the idea that career development and even career choices were the result of a process rather than being a point-in-time event. They also presented the idea that career choices and career development could be described by means of stages. These developmental stages are considered to be hierarchical, sequential, and qualitatively different.

The reader will note similarities in Super's and Ginzberg's stages and in their more recent formulations, particularly Super's proposition 11 and Ginzberg's proposition 3 (revised).

Career Stages Theory

Gene Dalton, Paul Thompson, and Raymond Price (1977) developed a model that describes the career stages of professionals in organizations. Although limited in the population it describes, the model does make a significant contribution to the understanding of successful careers in organizations. Basically, four stages illustrating the progression of successful professional careers in organizations are described.

Stage I. In stage I the individual is newly hired in the organization. The central activities of this stage are learning about the work of the organization, doing routine work under the close supervision of someone more experienced, helping, following directions, and so forth. The others in the organization view this individual as a learner or "apprentice." The major psychological issue to be dealt with in this stage is dependence—following orders and being successful at routine work. The major task of this stage is accepting the routine work and doing it well, while demonstrating the ability and initiative to progress to the stage of independent contributor.

Stage II. The primary activity in this stage is being responsible for projects from conception to completion—doing all the work oneself. In this stage, one is viewed as a colleague, an independent contributor. The major psychological issue to be dealt with is independence. The task of this stage is to develop an area of expertise and become skilled and respected in it. Some individuals tend to want to move through this stage too quickly, without fully laying the groundwork for the next stage by developing a high level of expertise in the work of the organization.

Stage III. This stage involves taking responsibility for the work of others. It may be in the form of line management, informal group leadership or mentoring, or influencing groups through expertise, ideas, and suggestions. An individual in this stage is involved in training, supervising, and interacting with other parts of the organization or with other organizations. He or she is seen by others as an expert, a leader in the field, and sometimes a mentor to individuals in stage I. Many individuals do not move beyond this stage, but remain productive in this stage for the remainder of their careers.

Stage IV. The final state is one that few reach. Tasks of this stage involve policymaking and shaping the direction of the organization. This person moves to delegate responsibility for the day-to-day work of the organization. This person "sponsors" individuals by creating experiences in which they can learn what is necessary to move up in the organization. The two major psychological issues of this stage are giving up the control of the day-to-day operations—delegating that responsibility—and exercising power. One of the major responsibilities of individuals in this stage is to exercise power for the benefit of the organization and the individuals in it.

Thus Dalton and associates take up where Ginzberg and others left off in describing what happens to an individual after an initial occupational choice is made. They amplify the tasks and experiences of Super's establishment and maintenance stages. Although they do not discuss this directly, the assumption is that individuals changing occupations—the midlife career changers, for example—would have to recycle earlier stages, although they may progress through the stages much more rapidly than before.

Similarly, the latest work of Super (1990) suggests that although indeed he still believes there is a "maxicycle" over the life span, there can also be a number of "minicycles" during which the individual recycles through the stages.

This cyclical approach seems to be the most applicable to present-day career stages. The work of all the stage theorists may be viewed as presenting a maxicycle over the life span, but also describing the minicycles of career change as it occurs in our society today. Figure 2 can be seen as describing this maxicycle. It should not be considered restrictive, but as possibly including several minicycles.

Figure 2
Developmental Stage Models

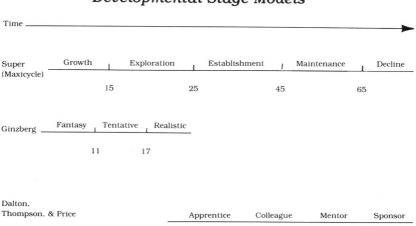

A significant limitation of all developmental career theories as well as of almost all other career theories is that the supporting research has been done almost exclusively on men. Super (1957), Zytowski (1969), and others have done research on career patterns of women as differentiated from those of men. The differences they found, however, have not been attended to in theory building. Gilligan (1982, 1988) found that moral development of women was different from that of men. It is reasonable to assume that career stages, as well as patterns, may also be different for women. It is inappropriate to use models developed on men to categorize the development of women. Inevitably, under those models women may be found lacking, when actually they are only different. Recently developed models of influences of women's career decisions are presented in the section describing career choice content and process theories.

John Crites (1981) added to the developmental view of career the idea that career choice can be viewed in terms of process and content. That idea provides the last level of organization for the model for understanding career theory (Figure 1).

In summary, this section has discussed the assumptions, propositions, and evolution of the developmental view of careers. The following sections will provide some details as to how that developmental process operates. They will address what theory and research tell us of career choice and adjustment in terms of content and process.

CAREER CHOICE CONTENT THEORY

Career choice content theories predict career choices from individual characteristics. For example, Ann Roe (1956, 1990) postulated that the type of parental environment in which an individual is reared predicts occupational choice. John Holland (1985) predicted occupation from personality type using a six-category typology. Some sociologists have predicted occupational choice from demographic variables such as age, sex, and socioeconomic status. Trait-factor interventions are based in part on career choice content theories.

Holland

John Holland (1973, 1985) has developed the most heavily researched and widely used career choice content theory. The ideas that led to the development of the theory grew out of his experience as a military interviewer during World War II. After interviewing hundreds of young inductees who needed to be assigned a military occupational specialty (a job), he began to see patterns in what these individuals were saying about themselves, their interests, and their skills. These patterns were the beginnings of his personality typology.

The four primary assumptions of Holland's theory are:

1. In our culture, most people can be categorized as one of six types: realistic, investigative, artistic, social, enterprising, and conventional.

    The *Realistic* type likes realistic jobs such as automobile mechanic, aircraft controller, surveyor, farmer, electrician. Has mechanical abilities but may lack social skills. Is described as conforming, materialistic, modest, frank, natural, shy, honest, persistent, stable, humble, practical, and thrifty.

The *Investigative* type likes investigative jobs such as biologist, chemist, physicist, anthropologist, geologist, medical technologist. Has mathematical and scientific ability but often lacks leadership ability. Is described as analytical, independent, modest, cautious, intellectual, precise, critical, introverted, rational, curious, methodical, and reserved.

The *Artistic* type likes artistic jobs such as composer, musician, stage director, writer, interior decorator, actor/actress. Has artistic abilities: writing, musical, or artistic, but often lacks clerical skills. Is described as complicated, idealistic, independent, disorderly, imaginative, intuitive, emotional, impractical, nonconforming, expressive, impulsive, and original.

The *Social* type likes social jobs such as teacher, religious worker, counselor, clinical psychologist, psychologist, psychiatric case worker, speech therapist. Has social skills and talents, but often lacks mechanical and scientific ability. Is described as convincing, helpful, responsible, cooperative, idealistic, sociable, friendly, insightful, tactful, generous, kind, and understanding.

The *Enterprising* type likes enterprising jobs such as salesperson, manager, business executive, television producer, sports promoter, buyer. Has leadership and speaking abilities but often lacks scientific ability. Is described as adventurous, energetic, self-confident, ambitious, impulsive, sociable, attention-getting, optimistic, popular, domineering, and pleasure-seeking.

The *Conventional* type likes conventional jobs such as bookkeeper/stenographer, financial analyst, banker, cost estimator, tax expert. Has clerical and arithmetic ability, but often lacks artistic abilities. Is described as conforming, inhibited, practical, conscientious, obedient, self-controlled (calm), careful, orderly, unimaginative, conservative, persistent, and efficient.

2. There are six model environments: realistic, investigative, artistic, social, enterprising, and conventional.
3. People search for environments that will let them exercise their skills and abilities, express their attitudes and values, and take on agreeable problems and roles.
4. Behavior is determined by the interaction between personality and environment. (Adapted from Holland, 1985b, p. 2–4)

Several elaborations need to be made on these points. First, the instrument that Holland developed to measure his personality types is called the Self-Directed Search (SDS) (Holland, 1985a). Upon completion of this instrument, an individual has devised a three-letter code composed of the first letters of his or her three most important personality types. This is called the individual's "Holland code."

Holland has assessed individuals who have entered or plan to enter many occupations and has defined the occupational environment by the predominant three-letter code in that environment. In this way an individual may look into an Occupations Finder and find listed occupations that are related to his or her Holland code. This correspondence is a most useful tool for career counselors. It has now been extended to relating Holland codes to each occupation listed in the *Dictionary of Occupational Titles* (Gottfredson & Holland, 1989).

Holland states that people search for environments in which they can express their personalities. He does not state that individuals will be more successful or satisfied in congruent environments, although this is the assumption from which most counselors operate when using Holland's theory.

Several other important concepts Holland uses are calculus, congruence, consistency, differentiation, and identity. He states that the relationships within and between types or environments can be ordered according to a hexagonal model (see Figure 3). He calls this concept, *calculus*. Using the hexagonal model, *congruence* is defined as close correspondence between the individual's personality type and the environment. The degree of congruence is determined by the closeness of the individual and occupational types on the hexagon. For example, a social person in a social environment represents a high level of congruence; a social person in an enterprising or artistic environment represents a lower level of congruence; a social person in a conventional or investigative environment even less; and a social person in a realistic environment represents the lowest level of congruence.

Consistency is also defined by distance apart on the hexagon: the closer the codes, the more consistent they are. For example, SEA is composed of types adjacent on the hexagon and has a high degree of consistency. ACR is composed of types that are opposite or nonadjacent and are in the most inconsistent category. Individuals with inconsistent codes tend to have difficulty finding occupations in which to express all facets of their personalities.

Differentiation refers to the degree to which a person or an environment is well defined—that is, different from the other types or models. Individuals who are young and/or inexperienced tend to have low differentiation. This concept is related to that of identity. *Personal identity* is defined as having a clear and stable picture of one's goals, interests, and talents.

One of the reasons for the widespread use of Holland's theory is that he has developed two instruments, the Vocational Preference Inventory and The Self-Directed Search, to measure personality types and to relate them to specific occupations. The Self-Directed Search, in particular, has been attractive to practitioners as well as easy to use in research. Other instruments, including the highly respected Strong Interest Inventory and, most recently, the Armed Services Vocational Aptitude Battery, have used Holland's typology as an organizing tool.

Another reason for the widespread use of Holland's typology is that the overwhelming body of research it has stimulated generally supports the theory (Holland, Magoon, & Spokane, 1981). In general, individuals do tend to seek environments similar to their personality types, and there is some evidence that adults changing occupations do seek more congruent environments.

Roe

Anne Roe developed a theory that predicts occupational choice from childhood relationships with parents. Her goal was to explain the origin

Figure 3

A Hexagonal Model for Defining the Psychological Resemblances Among Types and Environments and Their Interactions.

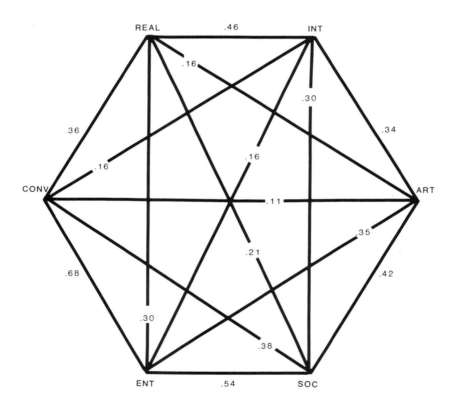

From *An Empirical Occupational Classification Derived From a Theory of Personality and Intended for Practice and Research* (p. 4). ACT Research Report No. 29, 1969, Iowa City: The American College Testing Program. Copyright 1969 by ACT. Reprinted by permission.

of interests and needs. Her ideas were based on Maslow's (1954) concept of basic needs arranged in a hierarchy of prepotency. That hierarchy arranged in order from most to least potent is: (a) the physiological needs, (b) the safety needs, (c) the need for belongingness and love, (d) the need for importance, respect, self-esteem, and independence, (e) the need for information, (f) the need for understanding, (g) the need for beauty, and (h) the need for self-actualization.

Roe stated that: "In our society there is no single situation that is potentially so capable of giving some satisfaction at all levels of basic needs as the occupation" (1990, p. 69).

To study occupations, Roe first developed a classification scheme based on the primary activities of occupations. She developed a continuum based on the nature and intensity of interpersonal relationships required in the occupation. The resulting eight occupational groups are (1) service, (2) business contact, (3) organization (managerial), (4) technology, (5) outdoor, (6) science, (7) general culture (preservation and transmission of the culture), and (8) arts and entertainment. She also classified the levels of responsibility of occupations. The levels are: (a) professional and managerial (independent responsibility), (b) professional and managerial (lower levels), (c) semiprofessional and small business, (d) skilled, (e) semiskilled, and (f) unskilled.

Roe hypothesized three categories of parental behavior toward children: (1) emotional concentration on the child (overprotective or overbearing), (2) avoidance (emotional rejection or neglect), and (3) acceptance (casual or loving). These types of childhood environments were then related in a predictive way to occupations categorized as either oriented toward persons or not toward persons. Later she expanded her dimension of classification of occupations to a two-dimensional system (Roe & Klos, 1972). One axis is orientation to interpersonal relationships—orientation to natural phenomena, and the other is orientation to purposeful communication—orientation to resourceful utilization. Her picture of occupational classification is symbolized as a truncated cone with the eight occupational groups spaced around the circle with wider divisions at the highest levels and narrowing spacing as the levels progress downward.

Although Roe's propositions are intuitively sensible and her classification system useful, there is little empirical support for her propositions. Roe herself stated that in the attempts to find a direct link between parent-child relations and occupational choice, "the results have been consistently negative" (1990, p. 86). The only support comes from a few studies of specializations within occupations or occupational fields.

Roe's contribution may be seen in part as an expansion of the earlier developmental work (Ginzberg et al., 1951, Super, 1957) in describing the process of career choice. She described the limitations of heredity and the influence of interaction with the environment, and tried to specify the character of that interaction. Even though research provides little support for her ideas on ways that interaction takes place, it does not mean that the interaction does not take place. In fact, more recent research indicates that parental expectations do influence both educational and occupational choices. (Conklin & Dailey, 1981; Lavine, 1982).

More recent and more applicable propositions (Holland, 1973, 1985) are similar to Roe's classification of occupations and levels. Thus, although her specific propositions have, in general, not been supported, her general ideas have stimulated research and thinking that have advanced the formulation of career theory.

Psychodynamic Theory

Bordin (1990) presented a psychodynamic model of career choice as a synthesis of previous applications of psychodynamic theory to career choice. The basis of this model is that ". . . the participation of personality in work and career is rooted in the role of play in human life" (p. 104).

Bordin's propositions are:

1. This sense of wholeness, this experience of joy is sought by all persons, preferably in all aspects of life, including work.
2. The degree of fusion of work and play is a function of an individual's developmental history regarding compulsion and effort.
3. A person's life can be seen as a string of career decisions reflecting the individual groping for an ideal fit between self and work.
4. The most useful system of mapping occupations for intrinsic motives will be one that captures life-styles or character styles and stimulates or is receptive to developmental conceptions.
5. The roots of the personal aspects of career development are to be found throughout the early development of the individual, sometimes in the earliest years.
6. Each individual seeks to build a personal identity that incorporates aspects of father and mother, yet retains elements unique to self.
7. One source of perplexity and paralysis at career decision points will be found in doubts and dissatisfactions with current resolutions of self. (p. 105)

The predictive aspects of this theory include the emphasis on needs and satisfactions that are developed at an early age. These are shaped by early experiences, identifications with mother and father, and sex role socialization (all of these being overlapping factors). Knowledge of these needs and satisfactions predicts how they will be acted out in the work place. For example, individuals whose needs are satisfied by the role of nurturer will go into nurturing occupations.

This theory also incorporates the ideal of development, but it is primarily predictive. Its usefulness is in developing the notion that the part of our lives called work can satisfy some (but not all) of our psychological needs. It also does a good job of describing career choices in the context of a larger theory of personality and development.

As far as practical applications go, there are no instruments that effectively make these predictions for an individual. In usual practice based on psychodynamic theory, those applications are identified directly by the individual therapist and depend on the skill and knowledge of the therapist.

Sociological Theory

Sociological research into occupational choice uses basically demographic variables to predict types of occupations entered. Its emphasis is on factors that are beyond the control of the individual, such as parent's (father's) occupation and education and labor market conditions. The categories of occupations studied are defined by occupational status.

There are several major foci of the sociological study of individuals and occupations. One is the area of status attainment. This line of research relates father's education and occupation to son's educational and occupational attainment. Blau and Duncan (1967) developed a model that indicates that father's education and occupation predicts son's education and that all three of those predict the son's occupational status. Other research by Sewell, Haller, and Portes (1969); Sewell, Haller, and Ohlendorf (1970); and Clarridge, Sheehy and Hauser (1977) followed a population of Wisconsin residents from youth to middle age. They found that both family status and mental ability predicted occupational achievement through influence on significant others, career plans, and educational level.

Status attainment research has been done on differences among the majority group (white men), and minority groups. Differences in income are larger between men and women than between whites and other races (Bridges, 1982; Corcoran & Duncan, 1979; Hartman, 1976; Mincer & Polacheck, 1974; Treiman & Hartman, 1981). Bielby and Baron (1986) found that within some firms job segregation by sex is nearly complete, with corresponding differences in pay grades. Being of a racial minority or a woman, then, would predict lower educational level and occupational status than for a comparable white man.

Another area of sociological research in occupations has to do with social and economic systems. Blau, Gystad, Jessor, Parnes, and Wilcock (1956) developed a model that incorporates social structure (values, stratification, demography, technology, and type of economy), physical conditions, historical change, socioeconomic organizations, and immediate job requirements and characteristics as predictors of occupational entry. They described parallel determinants of biological attributes and personal qualifications and information about particular occupations that also influence occupational entry. Others have studied occupational aspirations and entry as a function of local labor market conditions, availability of information, and role models related to specific occupations and cultural restraints that narrow the consideration of potential occupations (Asbury, 1968; LoCascio, 1967; Schmeiding & Jensen, 1968).

Accident theory, or the effects of chance on vocational choices, has been discussed by Bandura (1982), Caplow (1954), Miller and Form (1951), and others. Basically, this is the idea of "being in the right place at the right time," of meeting an individual who has an important influence on one's career, of being born at a certain demographic time when there are few or many jobs or into a family with certain socioeconomic values, and geographical location. Although "chance," thus described, certainly plays a part in everyone's life, other theories incorporate these and other variables related to occupational choice (Krumboltz, 1979). Thus chance on its own cannot be examined as an explanation of career behavior.

29

Although there is not just one sociological theory of career choice or development, sociological research predicts occupational choice primarily in terms of status, using such variables as father's education and occupation, educational level, race, sex, and influence of significant others. Accident theory also falls into this category.

CAREER CHOICE CONTENT AND PROCESS THEORY

Krumboltz

John Krumboltz (1979) developed a theory of career decision making that is an application of social learning theory. This theory incorporates both the content and process aspects of career choice. It also explains some concepts discussed more generally in other theories, such as accident theory from the sociological perspective and the development of the personality types from Holland's typology. This theory attempts to specify all of the "accidents"—they are described as genetic endowments and special abilities, environmental conditions and events, and learning experiences. John Holland (1983) said that this theory ". . . fills in the cracks in my typology." It explains how interest and personality patterns develop, an issue not addressed by Holland.

Krumboltz (1979) specified influences on career decision making, outcomes of interactions among influences, a set of theoretical propositions, and a description of the process of career planning and development.

Influences on career decision making. Four influences on career decision making are described. First are genetic endowments, such as race, sex, physical appearance and characteristics, and special abilities which include intelligence, musical and artistic abilities, and muscular coordination.

Environmental conditions and events also influence career decision making. They include such factors as job and training opportunities; labor laws and union rules; amount of rewards for various occupations; catastrophic events such as earthquakes and floods; natural resources; technological developments; social organization and government policy; and family, educational, and community influences.

Learning experiences are the third category of influences. Krumboltz divides them into instrumental and associative learning experiences. Instrumental or direct learning experiences occur when an individual acts on the environment to produce consequences (operant conditioning model). That is, one or more of the events or conditions previously described interacts with a particular problem or stimulus presented to an individual. The individual responds and receives consequences (feedback, praise, reward, punishment, etc.) from the environment. The skills necessary for career planning and educational and job performance are learned through these direct experiences.

Associative learning experiences are basically the development of attitudes, feelings, and positive or negative occupational stereotypes through observation of the behavior or responses of others. This is done via a classical conditioning model—a previously neutral stimulus is paired with a positive or negative response and the neutral stimulus (e.g., occupational title) stimulates a positive or negative response.

The fourth influence on career decision making is task approach skills. These skills are developed as a result of the previous three influences. Task approach skills are a set of skills and attitudes that influence career planning behavior as well as occupational performance. They include specific occupational and other skills, values, and work habits.

Outcomes of interactions among influences. As a result of interactions among the preceding four factors, three outcomes can be described. The first is the development of self-observation generalizations. These are a set of generalizations (such as, "I am good at telling funny stories") individuals make about themselves as a result of past learning experiences. They may not remember the actual experiences but do remember and generalize the feedback they received in those types of experiences. Self-observation generalizations may or may not be accurate. They can be identified and organized by means of interest inventories.

The second outcome is the development of task approach skills. They are developed as a result of learning experiences. One of the more significant of these is the person's view of whether or not individuals can influence their own environments. If individuals have a number of experiences in which they attempt unsuccessfully to influence their environments, they develop the idea that "fate," not their own actions, is controlling their lives.

The final outcome of these interactions is action. Krumboltz's theory focuses primarily on entry behavior, that is, entering into an occupation or a training program for an occupation.

Theoretical propositions.   Krumboltz's propositions state that:

1. An individual is more likely to enter an occupation if he or she (a) has been positively reinforced for activities related to that occupation, (b) has seen a valued model be positively reinforced for activities related to that occupation, (c) has been positively reinforced by a valued person who advocates that he or she engage in that occupation, or (d) has been exposed to positive words or images relating to that occupation.
2. A person is less likely to engage in an occupation or its related training and activities if he or she (a) has been punished or not reinforced for engaging in related activities, (b) has observed a valued model being punished or not reinforced for those activities, or (c) has been reinforced by a valued model who expresses negative words or images related to the occupation.
3. An individual is more likely to learn appropriate career decision making skills if he or she (a) has been reinforced for those activities, (b) has observed a model be reinforced for those activities, and (c) has access to people and other resources with necessary information.
4. An individual is less likely to learn the skills necessary for career decision making if he or she (a) has been punished or not reinforced for such behaviors, (b) has observed a model be punished or not

31

reinforced for those behaviors, or (c) has little or no access to people or other resources with the necessary information.

5. An individual is more likely to enter an occupation if that individual (a) has recently expressed a preference for that occupation, (b) has been exposed to learning and employment opportunities in that field, and (c) has learned skills that match the requirements of the occupation.

6. An individual is less likely to enter an occupation if the individual (a) finds the cost of preparation to be greater than the eventual return or (b) is denied access to the minimum resources necessary for entering the occupation.

Krumboltz views the career planning and development process as an interdependent sequence of learning experiences that follows the above-stated rules. Although he describes this as a lifelong process of each experience building on the last, he stops short of describing "development" as a process that could be composed of discrete, hierarchical, sequential stages.

This theory provides an explanation of the mechanics of all the career choice content and process theories. The addition of some of the developmental concepts and some propositions regarding work adjustment could make it a more comprehensive career theory.

Models Including Variables Important to the Career Choices of Women

Several models have been developed more recently which incorporate variables that have been shown to influence women's career decisions (Astin, 1984; Farmer, 1985; Gottfredson, 1981; Hackett & Betz, 1981). Each explains the process of the development of career choice content and makes predictions using that content.

Hackett and Betz

Hackett and Betz (1981) developed a model which explained factors in the development of self-efficacy expectations in women—that is, how women view their ability to perform certain tasks and be successful in certain activities. They discussed three ways in which women are socialized to feel successful in different tasks than men. Young girls are encouraged to have more involvement in domestic and nurturing activities and less involvement in sports, mechanical activities, and other traditionally male activities. This leads them to feel more successful and comfortable at domestic and nurturing activities and less comfortable in most other activities. Young women still have a predominance of role models in traditional roles and occupations. They tend to have a lack of exposure to female role models representing the full range of career options. Thus, they develop stronger feelings of self-efficacy regarding traditional roles and occupations. Women of all ages tend to experience a lack of encouragement, sometimes active discouragement, to engage in nontraditional roles and pursuits. This gives them a lower sense of self-efficacy toward nontraditional roles and occupations. These socialization experiences lead to predictions that women will predominately choose traditional roles and occupations.

Gottfredson, also in 1981, described the mechanism by which women determine a range of acceptable occupational alternatives. She stated that self-concept (having the components of gender, social class, intelligence, interests, and values) interacts with occupational images (sex type, prestige level, and field) to determine occupational preferences. These preferences, together with perceptions of job accessibility (opportunities and barriers), determine a range of acceptable occupational alternatives. This model highlights the significance of the sex role socialization of the individual, the perceived sex type (appropriateness of one sex or the other) of the occupation, and the perceptions of opportunities or barriers to women or women's career choices. It also specifies the role of feedback from the environment in the development of women's perceptions of themselves, of occupations, and of barriers or opportunities in the environment. She also notes that many of these perceptions are developed at a very early age.

Astin (1984) proposed a model of career choice and work behavior that includes the influence of work motivation, sex role socialization, and the structure of opportunity. She indicates that sex role socialization takes place at play, in the family, at school, and at work. It interacts with the structure of opportunity, including the distribution of jobs, sex typing of jobs, discrimination, job requirements, the economy, family structure, and reproductive technology. This interaction is influenced by the three basic motivators for work (survival, enjoyment of the work, and a sense of contribution) and plays a part in determining individual expectations, which also influence career choice and work behavior.

Farmer (1985) presented a model of career and achievement motivation. She described three aspects of career motivation—aspiration, level of occupation chosen; mastery, motivation to accomplish challenging, short term tasks; and career, the degree of commitment to the long range prospects of the career. She suggested that three groups of factors influenced this motivation: personal variables (academic self esteem, success attributions, intrinsic values, and homemaking orientation), background variables (sex, social status, school location, race, age, math, and verbal abilities), and environmental variables (parental support, teacher support, and support in the environment "for women working").

The contribution of these models is that they take into account variables, heretofore unspecified, that are important influences on the career choices of women. The gender and socialization issues important to women are generally important to men also. Therefore these models can be applied to men as well as women.

CHOICE AND ADJUSTMENT PROCESS THEORY

The work of David Tiedeman and his associates over the years describes the processes of career choice and adjustment. Originally, Tiedeman and O'Hara (1963) described a model that was directional (though not irreversible), developmental (based on the ideas of Erik Erikson), and somewhat similar to that of Super (1953) in that it specified a series of stages individuals progress through over the life span. They formulated a model that described an individual's process of career choice and implementation (see Figure 4).

The first phase, anticipation, consists of four stages prior to entry into an occupation. Exploration is a period of somewhat random behavior in which the individual interacts with the environment and receives feedback. It is a period of collecting observations about that interaction (differentiation) and incorporating that information into the ego identity (integration). Crystallization begins as these observations begin to form patterns (e.g., "I like to work with my hands" or "I am good at influencing other people"). Choice is the process of using those observations to make a tentative choice and to begin to act upon it. Clarification is the period of preparation for entry into the occupation during which the choice is reconsidered and specializations are considered.

The second phase is called implementation. Induction, the initial stage, is the first entry into a job in the field. It is a period when the individual

Figure 4

A Career Decision Making Model Adapted from Tiedeman and O'Hara's Paradigm of the Processes of Differentiation and Integration in Problem Solving.

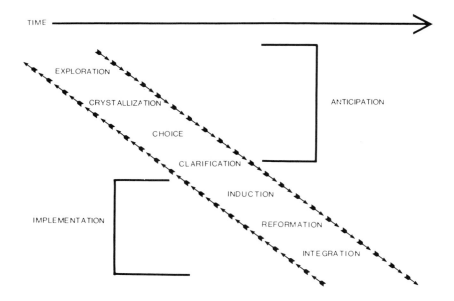

From *Career Development: Choice and Adjustment* (p. 40) by D.V. Tiedeman and R.P. O'Hara, 1963, New York: College Entrance Examination Board. Copyright 1963 by CEEB. Adapted by permission.

is primarily conforming to the organization and learning how to be successful. The second stage, reformation, happens after the individual gains credibility in the organization. The individual is then able to influence the organization to make changes deemed necessary. Finally, there develops a balance, integration, between the organization influencing the individual and the individual influencing the organization. This is a period of relative satisfaction that lasts until something happens to change the balance. At that time the individual may begin the cycle again or return to any of the other stages, as indicated by the two-way arrows in the model. Tiedeman and O'Hara also described the process by which an individual progresses through the stages. The core of their formulation was that an individual develops an ego identity though the processes of differentiation and integration.

Differentiation is the process of differentiating oneself from the environment, that is, observing different outcomes of one's own behavior as well as that of others. This process goes on continuously as individuals interact with the environment and observe the consequences. This information is personalized and integrated into the ego identity. Thus, new information that results from interaction of the person and the environment is constantly being incorporated into and changing the ego identity.

More recently Tiedeman and Miller-Tiedeman (1990) defined a two-dimensional model that further amplifies the anticipation phase of the original model. This model is based on the idea that the ways an individual views decision making is a function of how far the individual has advanced in his or her career. An important way of measuring this advancement in the career process is the language individuals use to describe their careers.

They defined two perspectives from which individuals describe their careers—personal reality and common reality. Common reality is a notion similar to societal, parental, or other external expectations: "they" expect me (all men) to be able to support a family. Personal reality is what feels "right" or good to the individual, irrespective of outside expectations. It is similar to the notion of internal locus of control. Recognizing and acting on one's personal reality is the goal of interventions based on the Tiedemans' model.

Another idea important to the recent work of David and Anna Tiedeman is "life as career" (1983). That is, the notion that each individual's life is his or her career; that individuals make choices about how they will create or "construct" their careers (or spend their lives); and that the goal for the individual is to integrate all aspects of life by becoming empowered to act on his or her personal reality (Miller-Tiedeman, 1988, 1989).

CAREER ADJUSTMENT CONTENT THEORY

Much work that is not usually noticed by counselors has been done in the area of work adjustment and job satisfaction. Work adjustment has been defined as success (or "satisfactoriness") and satisfaction on the job. Success is typically operationally defined by longevity on the job and by supervisory ratings. Satisfaction is typically measured by asking the individual whether he or she is satisfied on the job.

A key factor in work adjustment is the match between the expectations of the organization and the expectations of the employee. Dawis, England, and Lofquist (1964) developed a number of propositions in their theory of work adjustment. Their basic points are:

1. Work adjustment is composed of satisfactoriness and satisfaction.
2. Satisfactoriness is determined by the relationship of the individual's abilities and the requirements of the work place, assuming the individual's needs are being met by the organization's reward system.
3. Satisfaction is determined by how well the reward system of the organization meets the individual's needs, assuming the individual's skills meet the organization's requirements.
4. Satisfaction and satisfactoriness have moderating effects on each other.
5. Tenure is a function of satisfactoriness and satisfaction.
6. The fit between the individual (needs and skills) and the environment (requirements and rewards) increases as a function of tenure.

More recently, the fit between organizational and individual expectations has been specified as important in the process of the individual joining the organization. This is sometimes called the "psychological contract" (Argyris, 1960; Levenson, 1962).

Berlew and Hall (1966) and later Kotter (1980) developed two sets of dimensions on which individuals and organizations have expectations. The first dimension is composed of areas in which individuals have expectations of receiving and organizations have expectations of giving. These areas are:

1. a sense of meaning or purpose in the job;
2. personal development opportunities;
3. the amount of interesting work that stimulates curiosity and induces excitement;
4. the challenge in the work;
5. the power and responsibility in the job;
6. recognition and approval for good work;
7. the status and prestige in the job;
8. the friendliness of the people, the congeniality of the work group;
9. salary;
10. the amount of structure in the environment (general practices, discipline, regimentation);
11. the amount of security in the job;
12. advancement opportunities; and
13. the amount and frequency of feedback and evaluation. (Morgan, 1980, p. 65)

Areas in which organizations have expectations of receiving and individuals of giving are:

1. performing nonsocial job-related tasks requiring some degree of technical knowledge and skill;
2. learning the various aspects of a position while on the job;

3. discovering new methods of performing tasks; solving novel problems;
4. presenting a point of view effectively and convincingly;
5. working productively with groups of people;
6. making well-organized, clear presentations both orally and in writing;
7. supervising and directing the work of others;
8. making responsible decisions without assistance from others;
9. planning and organizing work efforts for oneself or others;
10. utilizing time and energy for the benefit of the company;
11. accepting company demands that conflict with personal prerogatives;
12. maintaining social relationships with other members of the company outside of work;
13. conforming to the folkways of the organization or work group on the job in areas not directly related to job performance;
14. pursuing further education on personal time;
15. maintaining a good public image of the company;
16. taking on company values and goals as one's own; and
17. seeing what should or must be done and initiating appropriate activity. (Morgan, 1980, p. 65)

The clearer both parties are about expectations in each of these areas, the easier it is to make appropriate judgments about individuals joining organizations. Unclear expectations or a change from either the individual or the organization without a comparable change in the other can upset the balance and cause dissatisfaction and unsatisfactoriness. A check on the expectations of these dimensions can be of great assistance in problem identification when counseling dissatisfied workers.

INTEGRATION AND IMPLICATIONS

By combining elements of all these theories, a number of statements can be made that are useful to counselors who seek to develop interventions for adults.

1. Individuals regard their careers differently and emit different career-related behaviors at different times in their lives.
2. Choices of occupational field and specific jobs at specific times are influenced by and can be predicted from certain individual characteristics. These characteristics include sex; race or ethnic group; intelligence and achievement; special skills and talents; ability to relate to people; individual needs, values, and goals; and personality type.
3. Choices of occupational field and specific jobs are also influenced by factors external to the individual. These factors include the reinforcement received from parents in career-related activities, community influence, family requirements and values, the economic and social conditions of society, opportunities for learning, availability of information, and historical events.

4. The process of making choices about occupational fields or specific jobs follows the general pattern of exploration, crystallization, choice, and clarification.

5. The process of making adjustments to those choices follows the general pattern of induction, reformation, and integration of the needs of the individual with the needs of the organization.

6. Adjustment to the consequences of occupational or specific job choices depends on factors in the work environment and on characteristics of the individual. The most powerful of these factors is the magnitude of the discrepancy between what the individual expects to find in terms of work requirements and rewards, and what the environment provides.

7. Satisfaction and success in an occupational field or in a specific job depends on the person/environment fit. That is, individuals must have opportunities to express their values and interests in their work and play roles and perform activities that they deem appropriate for themselves.

8. Satisfaction in a specific job comes from receiving feedback on successful performance of tasks or activities the individual considers important.

9. The individual's occupational career is very much a part of the individual's life career. The interactions of occupational and family life cycles, life style, leisure, and other issues cannot be separated. They must be considered together in career planning.

10. Individuals can be assisted in making choices and planning their careers by helping them understand their own characteristics as described in item 2 above, by helping them understand the work environment and other external forces described in item 3 above, by providing access to information and appropriate training, and by assisting in the consideration of the impact of occupational and job choices on other aspects of their lives.

11. The goals of career counseling are:
    - to enable clients to have sufficient information about their own characteristics; about training, assistance, and other resources available; about occupations and their characteristics; about potential barriers and how to deal with them; and about ways to use that information in decision making; and
    - to enable them to view themselves as having the ability to make their own choices and to act on their "personal reality."

CONCLUSION

This discussion has described career theories in light of their contribution to the current state of knowledge of career development and behavior. A model for organizing current knowledge was presented and a summary of the most prominent career theories and their implications was described. An attempt has been made to identify areas of overlap as well as areas in which each theory makes unique contributions.

It is hoped that this model will be useful in application of these theories to facilitate the career development of adults.

REFERENCES

Argyris, E. (1960). *Understanding organizational behavior*. Homewood, IL: Dorsey Press.

Asbury, F.A. (1968). Vocational development of rural disadvantaged eighth grade boys. *Vocational Guidance Quarterly, 17*, 109–113.

Astin, H.S. (1984). The meaning of work in women's lives: A socio-psychological model of career choice and work behavior. *The Counseling Psychologist, 12*, 117–126.

Bandura, A. (1982). The psychology of chance encounters and life paths. *The American Psychologist, 37*(7), 747–755.

Berlew, D.E., & Hall, D.T. (1966). The socialization of managers: Effects of expectations on performance. *An Administrative Science Quarterly, 10*, 207–223.

Bielby, T. & Baron, N. (1986). Men and women at work: Sex segregation and statistical discrimination. *American Journal of Sociology, 91*, 759–799.

Blau, P.M., & Duncan, O.D. (1967). *The American occupational structure*. New York: Wiley.

Blau, P.M., Gustad, J.W., Jessor, R., Parnes, H.S., & Wilcock, R.C. (1956). Occupational choice: A conceptual framework. *Industrial Labor Relations* (rev. ed.), *9*, 531–543.

Bordin, E.S. (1990). Psychodynamic model of career choice and satisfaction. In D. Brown and L. Brooks (Eds.), *Career choice and development* (2nd ed., pp. 102–144). San Francisco: Jossey-Bass.

Bridges, W.P. (1982). The sexual segregation of occupations: Theories of labor stratification in industry. *American Journal of Sociology, 88*, 270–295.

Buehler, C. (1933). *Der menschliche Lebenslauf als psychologisches Problem*. Leipzig: Hirzel.

Caplow, T. (1954). *The sociology of work*. Minneapolis: University of Minnesota Press.

Clarridge, B.R., Sheehy, L.L., & Hauser, T.S. (1978). Tracing members of a panel: A seventeen-year follow-up. In K.F. Schussler (Ed.), *Sociological methodology* (pp. 185–203). San Francisco: Jossey-Bass.

Conklin, M.E., & Dailey, A.R. (1981). Does consistency of parental educational encouragement matter for secondary school students. *Sociology of Education, 54*, 254–262.

Corcoran, M.E., & Duncan, G.J. (1979). Work history, labor force attachment, and earnings differences between the races and sexes. *Journal of Human Resources, 14*, 3–20.

Crites, J.O. (1981). *Career counseling: Models, methods and materials*. New York: McGraw-Hill.

Dalton, G., Thompson, P., & Price, R. (1977). Career stages: A model of professional careers in organizations. *Organizational Dynamics, 6*, 19–42.

Dawis, R.V., England, G.W., & Lofquist, L.H. (1964). A theory of work adjustment. *Minnesota Studies in Vocational Rehabilitation*, no. 15. Minneapolis: University of Minnesota Industrial Relations Center.

Farmer, H.S. (1985). Model of career and achievement motivation for women and men. *Journal of Counseling Psychology, 32,* 363–390.

Gilligan, C. (1982). *In a different voice.* Cambridge, MA: Harvard University Press.

Gilligan, C. & Attanucci, J. (1988). Two moral orientations: Gender differences and similarities. *Merrill-Palmer Quarterly, 34,* 223–237.

Ginzberg, E. (1972). Restatement of the theory of occupational choice. *Vocational Guidance Quarterly, 20*(3), 169–176.

Ginzberg, E. (1984). Career development. In D. Brown and L. Brooks (Eds.), *Career choice and development* (pp. 169–191). San Francisco: Jossey-Bass.

Ginzberg, E., Ginsburg, S.W., Axelrad, S., & Herma, J. (1951). *Occupational choice: An approach to a general theory.* New York: Columbia University Press.

Gottfredson, G.D. & Holland J.L. (1989). *Dictionary of Holland occupational codes.* (2nd ed.) Odessa, FL: Psychological Assessment Resources, Inc.

Gottfredson, L.S. (1981). Circumscription and compromise: A development theory of occupational aspirations. *Journal of Counseling Psychology Monograph, 28,* 545–579.

Hackett, G., & Betz, N.E. (1981). A self-efficacy approach to the approach to the career development of women. *Journal of Vocational Behavior, 18,* 326–339.

Hartman, H.I. (1976). Capitalism, patriarchy, and job segregation by sex. *Signs, 1,* 137–169.

Holland, J.L. (1973). *Making vocational choices: A theory of careers.* Englewood Cliffs, NJ: Prentice-Hall.

Holland, J.L. (1983). In C. Minor & F. Burtnett (Producers). *Career development: Linking theory with practice.* (Videotape). Arlington, VA: American Association for Counseling and Development.

Holland, J.L. (1985a). *The self-directed search professional manual.* Odessa, FL: Psychological Assessment Resources, Inc.

Holland, J.L. (1985b). *Making vocational choices: A theory of vocational personalities and work environments.* (2nd ed.). Englewood Cliffs, NJ: Prentice-Hall.

Holland, J.L., Magoon, T.M., & Spokane, A.R. (1981). Counseling psychology: Career interventions, research and theory. *Annual Review of Psychology, 32,* 279–305.

Kotter, J.P. (1980). The psychological contract: Managing the joining up process. In M.A. Morgan (Ed.), *Managing career development* (pp. 63–72). New York: Van Nostrand Reinhold.

Krumboltz, J.D. (1979). A social learning theory of career decision making. In A.M. Mitchell, G.B. Jones, & J.D. Krumboltz (Eds.), *Social learning and career decision making* (pp. 19–49). Cranston, RI: Carroll Press.

Lavine. L.O. (1982). Parental power as a potential influence on girls' career choice. *Child Development, 53,* 658–663.

Levenson, H. (1962). *Men, management, and mental health.* Cambridge, MA: Harvard University Press.

LoCascio, R. (1967). Continuity and discontinuity in vocational development theory. *Personnel and Guidance Journal, 46,* 32–36.

Maslow, A.H. (1954). *Motivation and personality.* New York: Harper & Row.

Miller, D.C., & Form, W.H. (1951). *Industrial sociology.* New York: Harper & Row.

Miller-Tiedeman, A. (1988). *Lifecareer: The quantum leap into a process theory of career.* Vista, CA: Lifecareer Foundation.

Miller-Tiedeman, A. (1989). *How not to make it . . . and succeed: Life on your own terms.* Vista, CA: Lifecareer Foundation.

Mincer, J., & Polacheck, S.W. (1974). Family investment in human capital: Earnings of women. *Journal of Political Economy, 82,* S74–S108.

Morgan, M.A. (1980). *Managing career development.* New York: Van Nostrand Reinhold.

Parsons, F. (1909). *Choosing a vocation.* Boston: Houghton Mifflin.

Roe, A. (1956). *The psychology of occupations.* New York: Wiley.

Roe, A., & Lunneborg, P. (1990). Personality development and career choice. In D. Brown and L. Brooks (Eds.), *Career choice and development* (2nd ed., pp. 68–101). San Francisco: Jossey-Bass.

Roe, A., & Klos, D., (1972). Classification of occupations. In J.M. Whitely and A. Resnikoff (Eds.), *Perspectives on vocational development.* Washington, DC: American Personnel and Guidance Association.

Schmeiding, O.A., & Jensen, S. (1968). American Indian students: Vocational development and vocational tenacity. *Vocational Guidance Quarterly, 17,* 120–123.

Sewell, W.H., Haller, A.O., & Ohlendorf, G. (1970). The educational and early occupational attainment process: Replications and revisions. *American Sociological Review, 45,* 1014–1027.

Sewell, W.H., Haller, A.O., & Portes, A. (1969). The educational and early occupational attainment process. *American Sociological Review, 34,* 89–92.

Super, D.E. (1953). A theory of vocational development. *American Psychologist, 8,* 185–190.

Super, D.E. (1957). *The psychology of careers.* New York: Harper & Row.

Super, D.E. (1976). *Career education and the meanings of work.* Washington, DC: U.S. Government Printing Office.

Super, D.E. (1990). Career and life development. In D. Brown and L. Brooks (Eds.). *Career choice and development* (2nd ed., pp. 197–261). San Francisco: Jossey-Bass.

Tiedeman, D.V. (1983). In C. Minor & F. Burtnett (Producers). *Career development: Linking theory with practice.* (Videotape). Arlington, VA: American Association for Counseling and Development.

Tiedeman, D.V., & Miller-Tiedeman, A. (1984). Career decision-making: An individualistic perspective. In D. Brown and L. Brooks (Eds.), *Career choice and development* (pp. 281–310). San Francisco: Jossey-Bass.

Tiedeman, D.V., & O'Hara, R.P. (1963). *Career development: Choice and adjustment.* New York: College Entrance Examination Board.

Treiman, D.J., & Hartman, H.I. (Eds.). (1981). *Women, work, and wages: Equal pay for jobs of equal value.* Washington, DC: National Research Council, National Academy of Sciences.

Williamson, E.G. (1939). *How to counsel students.* New York: McGraw-Hill.

Zytowski, D.G. (1969). Toward a theory of career development for women. *Personnel and Guidance Journal, 47,* 660–664.

CHAPTER 3

Career Intervention and Counseling Theory for Adults: Toward a Consensus Model

Arnold R. Spokane
College of Education
Lehigh University
Bethlehem, Pennsylvania

Imagine, if you can, that you are a practicing career counselor some time in the future. You sit down with an individual or a group of clients, or you begin a semester-long class for college students or adults or a consultation with a group of line managers. You have a clear idea about what you want to accomplish, and as your client's story unfolds you draw on the wealth of relevant published research, theory, and case material to form an immediate understanding of the problem the client is facing. The research over the past 20 years or so has been so clear that you can be reasonably sure that the outcome will be positive for this client. Moreover, you have evidence that suggests several specific techniques with enough demonstrated effectiveness to work with this client. If one of these techniques fails, you select a backup strategy or combine two strategies to attain the proper effect. The scientific and technical sophistication of the instruments you use is the envy of modern psychology. In short, you are the consummate professional who draws upon a sound scientific base with consistent results.

Sound far fetched? Not at all! We are fast approaching this juncture in the career field. If our clinical practice and understanding is simply blended with the advances of the past 20 years of research and theory, we need not suffer further from the absence of a valid intervention model (Holland, 1984), and we need not bootleg ill-fitting models from other disciplines. A consensus model of the career intervention process may now be possible. As Gelso & Fassinger noted (1990), we are among the most mature, advanced, and rigorous specialists in the counseling field.

In D. Lea & Z. Leibowitz (Eds.). *Adult Career Development* (2nd ed.). Alexandria, VA: National Career Development Association, in press.

A long string of independent reviews of career intervention research confirm that career assistance has beneficial effects (at least as effective as psychotherapy and sometimes more so) on a wide array of outcome measures (Holland, Magoon, & Spokane, 1981; Krumboltz, Becker-Haven, & Burnett, 1978; Myers, 1986; Osipow, 1987a; Oliver & Spokane, 1988; Rounds & Tinsley, 1984; Spokane & Oliver, 1983). We also know that more intensive treatments with greater numbers of sessions (e.g., semester-long classes) have greater effects on client outcomes than less intensive interventions. We have parent disciplines (e.g., career development theory, decision theory, psychometric theory, information processing, and social cognition theory) just as medicine has parent disciplines, but we also have an independent and coherent core. My experience over the past 20 years and a recent informal survey of APA and NCDA members (Spokane & Hawks, 1990) suggests that we agree on how we practice, even if some healthy arguments remain about abstract ideas of what the core is, why we do what we do, and why what we do works.

It is not necessary to emulate the field of psychotherapy by developing separate models based on individual theories before developing consensus models from the data at hand (Goldfried, 1980). The elucidation of several of these conceptual models may, however, serve to improve and/or speed the development of a consensus model. Crites (1981) took such an approach in his groundbreaking volume on career counseling, in which he reviewed client-centered, behavioral, developmental, and cognitive approaches to career counseling and then expounded an ecclectic model. A similar tack is being taken by Walsh & Osipow (1990) in an edited volume on career counseling.

We might begin progress toward a consensus model by examining the common elements in career counseling models, and then working to clarify and strengthen those common elements in practice. This convergent approach emphasizes our considerable similarities, rather than focusing on the differences between career practice models. We do not suggest that the same treatment is appropriate for all types of career problems. There do appear to be some differential effects for treatments with clients who have personality style differences (Kivlighan et al.); however, research on these attribute-treatment-interactions (Fretz, 1981) has not yet yielded stable, replicable attribute treatment interactions of sufficient magnitude that we could make exact diagnoses and follow them with specific treatment recommendations. It is not clear whether we will ever be able to make such diagnostic decisions with confidence. We do know that more intensive interventions are more effective (Oliver & Spokane, 1988). The client may choose to invest more or less energy, time, and emotional involvement in a career intervention, and should be permitted to select an intensive intervention or a less intensive intervention in an informed manner. Discussions with colleagues in the Division 17 Special Interest Group on Careers (SIG) at National Career Development Association Meetings and at American Society for Training and Development gatherings suggest many more similarities than differences among career professionals in their actual approach to practice. The various models of career practice being described now are probably more hypothetical than real—i.e., their differences are exaggerated to delineate a distinctive approach to career practice.

This chapter summarizes the elements of a broad consensus career intervention model which is different from psychotherapy in important ways, but which shares some assumptions and practices. Career interventions differ from psychotherapy in the considerable influence that social constraints have on the career counseling process; the fundamental belief that the client and counselor hold about the general benefits of person-environment fit or congruence as a goal; the increased use of therapeutic structure during career intervention; and the combination of continuous and discontinuous decisions involved in career choice. The consensus model of career intervention acknowledges these unique qualities of career intervention. The model, which emphasizes the client's rather than the counselor's process, is applicable in dyadic encounters, group career counseling with some modifications, classes, consultation and prevention, and, to a degree, computer interventions. A more complete explanation of this position can be found in Spokane (1991).

Toward a Broad Definition of Career Intervention

Two schools of thought exist about the nature of career interventions. The first school employs the term career counseling to refer to dyadic encounters and, perhaps, to group career counseling, which it considers to be a variant of psychotherapy (Rounds & Tinsley, 1984). Proponents of this restrictive definition argue, with some justification, that it will be difficult to study, understand, and improve career counseling if too wide and confusing a variety of activities is considered. Progress according to this position will result when we understand the underlying processes involved in dyadic career counseling and perfect our diagnostic systems, much as psychotherapy research has attempted to understand its curative process and validate a diagnostic system.

The second school defines a career intervention as any attempt to assist an individual in making improved career decisions through such means as workshops, classes, consultation, prevention, etc. This broader definition of career intervention includes many different kinds of activities, and it may be difficult, using this inclusive definition, to understand the processes underlying the effectiveness of an intervention (Lunneborg, 1983; Rounds & Tinsley, 1984). It is possible, however, to view career interventions on a continuum from the most counselor and client intensive dyadic interventions to the least intensive alternative treatments such as brief inventories and informational interventions (Spokane, 1990). If, as expected, research reveals that the client processes underlying all these approaches are similar, then the broad definition of career intervention will be most useful. If different mechanisms are found to be responsible for the beneficial effects of dyadic as opposed to classroom encounters, then a psychotherapeutic interpretation of career counseling may be most appropriate.

Restoring Morale and Mobilizing Constructive Behavior: The Essential Client Processes in Career Intervention

Most types of career interventions involve two independent client processes. The first is the general restoration of the client's morale and, in particular, the activation of hope that a reasonably fitting career option might be found. The second process is the mobilization of constructive client behaviors to implement the option under consideration. Presentation of reasonable options without mobilization leaves the client in an incomplete state and risks the erosion of the plausibility of the options derived by the first process. Mobilization without reasonable options results in misdirected, random, or self-defeating behavior and/or continued confusion on the part of the client.

Figure 1 portrays the range of constructive and non-constructive attitudes, emotions, and behaviors possible in the face of a career decision situation. The goal of any career intervention is to move the client from nonconstructive or even destructive behavior to more constructive alternatives. The four boxed-in entries in Figure 1 represent critical positions

Figure 1
Critical, constructive client behaviors, emotions, and attitudes in the face of career decisions.

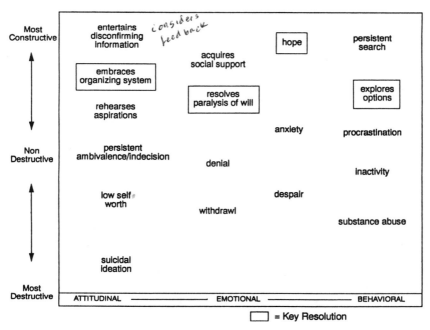

Reprinted with permission from A. R. Spokane, *Career Intervention*, Englewood Cliffs, NJ: Prentice Hall, 1991.

45

in the shift from destructive to constructive client behaviors in the domains that have repeatedly been shown to constitute critical client variables in career intervention (Holland, Magoon, & Spokane, 1981; Kirshner, 1988).

The first column on the left in Figure 1 illustrates the range of cognitive reactions a client might experience during a career intervention. It shows the range from the most destructive suicidal ideations through the critical step of embracing an organizing system or schema for understanding the self and the world of work. Osipow (1987b) found that a general lack of structure was the primary element in career indecision, and clinical experience suggests that most clients will report some degree of confusion. Having an organizing framework for understanding the self, filtering information about the world of work, and arriving at a reasonably fitting set of career options is crucial to the ability to retrieve and absorb occupational information. The second column in Figure 1 illustrates the acquisition of social support, and the third column illustrates the gain avenue involved in the experience of hope and the general restoration of morale (Holland et al., 1981). Finally, Figure 1 illustrates the range of constructive and destructive behaviors in which a client might engage when presented with a career situation. These behaviors range from drug abuse, inactivity or ambivalence, to persistent exploratory activity, which has been found to result in more congruent occupational choices (Grotevant, Cooper & Kramer, 1986).

The Nature of the Career Intervention Process

Most career clients seem to benefit when certain specific elements are present in the intervention. The following six postulates constitute a testable model of the career intervention process:

Postulate 1. Effective career intervention will instill in the client a sense of hope that a reasonably fitting career option can be found and implemented.

Postulate 2. The goal of career intervention is to mobilize persistently constructive behaviors, attitudes, and emotions that will increase the likelihood of implementing a chosen career option.

Postulate 3. Effective career intervention will provide the client with a clear framework, either self-derived or counselor-imposed, that contains an intellectual or cognitive schema or structure for understanding the world of work and the client's role in selecting and implementing an occupational choice.

Postulate 4. Multidimensional fit (ability, interests, sex role, and prestige) should guide exploratory behavior, except where expressed and measured interests disagree, in which case expressed interests should direct exploration.

Postulate 5. A limited number of personality variables (e.g., sociability, decisional style) should guide the selection of an intervention mode for a given client. Specifically, the stronger the level of client personality integration, the less intensive the intervention need be.

Postulate 6. Anxiety will follow a sine curve during career intervention, beginning high, then dropping, and subsequently rising again. This anxiety can serve as a motivator or an inhibitor of constructive career behavior, depending on the client's ability to convert the anxiety into constructive behavior, attitudes, and emotions. Moderate levels of anxiety probably facilitate mobilization, whereas anxiety levels that are too high or too low are likely to inhibit mobilization.

There is some consensus about the phasic nature of career intervention beginning with Crites' (1981) three-stage model.

Table 1 depicts a three-phase model of the career intervention process (beginning, activation, completion), and specifies the therapeutic tasks, techniques, and client reactions during each of the three phases and related subphases. The beginning phase contains three subphases (opening, aspiring, loosening) during which the therapeutic context is established, and the client rehearses career aspirations (Holland et al., 1981). The counselor uses structure, acceptance, fantasy, and reflection, and, according to the model, the client experiences first relief, then excitement, then anxiety. During the second or activation phase, which contains three subphases (assessment, inquiry, commitment), the therapeutic tasks include facilitating the acquisition of a cognitive structure, mobilizing behavior, and managing anxiety. It is during this activation phase that the counselor and the client formulate hypotheses for testing. During the completion phase closure is achieved, and periodic re-contact is encouraged to maintain the self esteem enhancing effects of the counseling experience (Janis, 1983; Meichenbaum & Turk, 1987).

It now seems evident that a sine-shaped anxiety curve generally pertains during career interventions (Spokane, Fretz, Hoffman, Nagel, & Davison, 1990), and that anxiety starts high, drops, and then rises again as the client moves into the activation phase. Figure 2, from Spokane (1991), depicts this sine curve and the typical counselor use of decreasing structure during a career intervention. The sine curve, if confirmed in subsequent studies, suggests that counselors should be more sensitive to the ebb and flow of anxiety across sessions, and adapt or at least prepare clinically for the presence of increasing anxiety during the activation phase.

The feasibility inquisition. In workshops, groups, and classes as well as in dyadic counseling, this observed increase in anxiety results in dropout levels as high as 50% (Oneil, Ohlde, Barke, Gelwick, & Garfield, 1980; Zager, 1982). Commonly, also, a phenomenon dubbed the "feasibility inquisition" (Spokane, 1991) occurs in response to this anxiety. The client, as the activation phase approaches, becomes acutely aware of the social constraints operating on his or her particular career choice, and becomes convinced that a reasonably fitting option cannot be implemented. The client presents this fear, often in a very disguised manner, to the counselor. If the counselor ignores or brushes aside the inquisition the client may re-present the fear, but eventually, if the feasibility inquisition is not attended to directly, the client will simply despair, lose hope and morale, and may drop out or simply lose faith in the possibility of a positive outcome from the career intervention. Clients are rarely direct in expressing this inquisition, but there are few clients who do not feel the fear that a reasonable solution cannot be found or that, if found, it might not be implementable. The naïve counselor

Table 1

Three-phase model of career intervention process.

Phase	Beginning			Activation			Completion	
Sub-Phase	Opening	Aspiring	Loosening	Assessment	Inquiry	Commitment	Execution	Follow-through
Principal Therapeutic Task	Establish Therapeutic Context	Client Rehearsal of Aspirations	Perception of Incongruence	Acquisition of Cognitive Structure	Mobilize Constructive Behavior	Manage Anxiety	Persistent Search	Consolidate Gain
Counselor Process	Set Expectation	Activate Hope	Identify Conflicts	Hypothesis Generation	Hypothesis Testing	Hypothesis Sharing	Resolve Conflicts	Closure
Counselor Technique	Structure/ Acceptance	Fantasy	Reflection/ Clarification	Test/ Interpretation	Probing/ Leading	Reassurance	Reinforce-ment	Periodic Recontact
Client Process	Acquire Structure	Experience Hope	Accept Conflict	Generate, test, and receive hypotheses			Act on valid hypothesis	Retest Hypothesis
Client Reaction	Relief	Excitement	Anxiety	Progress/ Insight	Self-Efficacy-Control	Compromise	Withdrawal/ Adherence	Satisfaction/ Certainty

Adapted with permission from A.R. Spokane, *Career Intervention*, Englewood Cliffs, NJ: Prentice Hall, 1991.

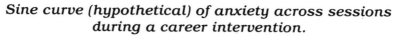

Figure 2

Sine curve (hypothetical) of anxiety across sessions during a career intervention.

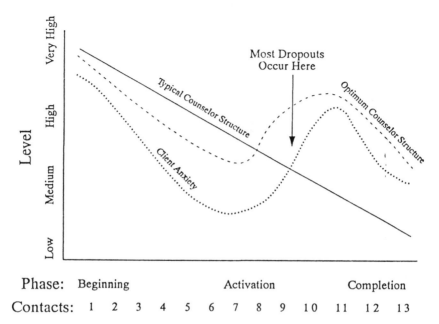

Reprinted with permission from A. R. Spokane, *Career Intervention*, Englewood Cliffs, NJ: Prentice Hall, 1991.

who accepts the client's pessimistic scenario may not be able to generate what counselors in a recent survey called faith or belief in the outcome (Spokane & Hawks, 1990).

Intervention techniques. Two primary techniques are heavily employed in career intervention (Spokane & Hawks, 1990). These are guided fantasy, as described by Morgan & Skovholt (1977), and Skovholt, Morgan, & Negron-Cunningham (1989), and skills analysis—the systematic review of the client's work-related skills. Except for studies on the use of interest inventory feedback, there exist few well-controlled studies evaluating the effectiveness or proper use of techniques in career intervention. Several recent volumes, however, contain examples of these techniques, and studies of specific techniques are certainly possible now.

In sum, the most effective career interventions result in restoration of the client's morale and mobilization of persistently constructive behaviors, attitudes, and emotions. Clients are portrayed as personal scientists who formulate and test hypotheses about their career world, and use the counselor as a sounding board to facilitate input for the hypothesis testing process. Anxiety drops in the beginning phases of a career intervention, but climbs during the activation phase, an occurrence which can result in a form of client self-protective resistance called the feasibility inquisition. This inquisition requires sensitive handling of client emotions during the intervention and recognition that the client's process is rarely linear. Several specific ingredients in a career intervention (rehearsal, information, assessment, and job search) are essential in promoting gain and are discussed below.

The Client As Personal Scientist

Rehearsal of aspirations. The most popular intervention technique is the guided fantasy and its variations (Morgan & Skovholt, 1977; Skovholt, et al., 1989). The fantasy is a form of cognitive rehearsal of aspirations which catalyzes the client's scientific process by forming an identity filter with which to screen and evaluate subsequent information. Fantasy techniques used early in the career intervention process can "kick start" the exploratory process and, used later during the intervention, can lower anxiety attached to decision-making and job search.

Information. Occupations, and especially professions, are protected by successively impenetrable layers of information which serve as social constraints limiting entry to that occupation (Bucher, 1979). The social psychology of information acquisition, retrieval, and processing is an important but neglected area of career intervention research theory and practice. Three independent research programs by Krumboltz and colleagues (e.g., Krumboltz & Schroeder, 1965); Bodden and colleagues (e.g., Bodden, 1970; Neimeyer & Ebben, 1985); and Blustein and colleagues (e.g., Blustein & Strohmer, 1987) recognize the importance of this area and appear to be converging in the portrayal of the client as a naïve scientist (Kuhn, 1989) who formulates hypotheses about occupations, and then seeks out confirming or disconfirming information to test those hypotheses.

Information is more than a simple collection of facts (Rusalem, 1954), and it is the psychosocial aspects of career information which are most influential in career choice (Samler, 1961). Occupational information exists along a continuum from most near (or proximal) to the client, to the closest to the real work world (or distal to the client). Clients begin proximally with an internal search and then move distally, exploring some aspects of occupations (Blustein et al., 1989; Gati & Tikotzki, 1989), and ignoring others; selecting some occupations for further exploration and discarding others. The full consideration of negative or disconfirming information about options is more important in the quality of decisions than is confirming information. However, research on social cognition continues to support the observation that confirming information is much more likely to be considered in a decision than is disconfirming information.

Assessment. Assessment has many purposes, but the principle purpose is to provide input for use in formulating and testing hypotheses about the suitability and availability of options. Several assessment and classification systems exist, including behavior–analytic systems which identify those specific target behaviors necessary for success in career

50

choice and adjustment, and then examine the client's assets, deficits, and excesses in an attempt to facilitate desired target behaviors. Developmental career assessment is a comprehensive evaluation of the client's career skills and attitudes as they relate to effectively resolving the tasks characteristic of the client's developmental stage. Ability-focussed assessment attempts to determine an ability/effort range in which the client can concentrate exploratory efforts. Person–environment systems, characterized by Holland (1985), attempt to ascertain the general congruence between the client's interests and the requirements of jobs under consideration. Lastly, problem-focussed assessment identifies the range of possible adult career problems and attempts to narrow the focus of the problem for direct intervention.

These several diagnostic systems are only partially developed (Rounds & Tinsley, 1984) and are now being applied in the design and evaluation of career treatments (Kivlighan, Hageseth, Tipton, & McGovern, 1981). The large number of inventories available for use (see Table 2) still have as their principal purpose the provision of feedback to the client to increase the client's sense of vocational identity, reduce anxiety, identify reasonably fitting options, and mobilize constructive behavior. Each of these inventory classes has special purposes or provides somewhat different input and feedback to the client. For complete details of these instruments and related instruments the interested reader is referred to Kapes & Mastie (1988).

Exploration. An important but underemphasized aspect of career intervention is the career search. Generally, informal methods are used more frequently than formal methods and, in some circumstances, may be more effective (Becker, 1977). Heavily structured methods of job search training and intervention ranging from interview skills training (Hol-

Table 2
Thirteen Classes of Vocational Instruments for Use in Career Intervention

Class 1: Criterion-based Interest Inventories, College-bound
Class 2: Criterion-based Interest Inventories, Non-college
Class 3: Homogeneous, Self-guiding Interest Inventories
Class 4: Homogeneous, Hand or Machine-scored Inventories
Class 5: Career Maturity Measures
Class 6: Decisional Status Measures
Class 7: Personal Agency Measures
Class 8: Vocational Card Sorts
Class 9: Measures of Personal Style, Values, and Needs
Class 10: Work Sample Batteries
Class 11: Ability Measures
Class 12: Measures of General Personality
Class 13: Measures of Work Environment and Job Satisfaction

landsworth, Dressel, & Stevens, 1977; Speas, 1979) to the more comprehensive Job Club method (Azrin, Phillip, Thienes-Hontos, & Besalel, 1980) have recently been found to be consistently successful with a wide array of clients. This crucial aspect of the completion phase of the career intervention process deserves more attention than it currently receives from counselors and researchers alike.

Effective intervention with adults requires more attention to information acquisition and job search. The counselor may need to provide considerable structure during the completion phase by arranging interviews, teaching interview skills, and providing extra social support.

Testing the Consensus Model

This paper describes a process-oriented model of career intervention that draws on the considerable scientific literature of the past 25 years. It is clear that career counseling and various other career interventions are moderately effective across a broad range of clients and outcome measures. The task for career counselors and researchers now is to combine their talents, insights, and skills to produce a new generation of career intervention research that will be an exciting blend of case study approaches and traditional group data analyses. The findings from these studies could be applied directly to career practice, and would exemplify the assertion by Krumboltz et al. (1978) that the best research results in a direct alteration of the way counselors practice.

The consensus model describes two essential elements in the client's process (hope and mobilization) and discusses the counselor's role in facilitating the scientific inquiry that occurs during an effective career intervention. A three-phase model of the career intervention process is described (beginning, activation, completion). This model is heavily used in practice and should be examined in empirical studies. The measures, techniques, and sophistication are available to begin the next generation of career process research and to evaluate the proposed model.

REFERENCES

Azrin, N.H., Philip, R.A., Thienes-Hontos, P., & Besalel, V.A. (1980). Comparative evaluation of the job club program with welfare recipients. *Journal of Vocational Behavior, 16,* 133–145.

Becker, H.J. (1977). *How young people find jobs.* Tech. Rep. Center For Social Organization of Schools, Johns Hopkins University, Baltimore, MD.

Blustein, D.L., & Strohmer, D.C. (1987). Vocational hypothesis testing in career decision-making. *Journal of Vocational Behavior, 31,* 45–62.

Bodden, J.L. (1970). Cognitive complexity as a factor in appropriate vocational choice. *Journal of Counseling Psychology, 17,* 364–368.

Bucher, R. (1979). Social structural constraints in career decision making occupational hurdles. In J.D. Krumboltz, A. M. Mitchell, & G.B. Jones (Eds.), *Social learning and career decision making* (pp. 116–133). Cranston, RI: Carrol Press.

Crites, J.O. (1981). *Career counseling models, methods, and materials.* New York: McGraw-Hill.

Gati, I., & Tikotzki, Y. (1989). Strategies for collection and processing of occupational information in making career decisions. *Journal of Counseling Psychology, 36,* 430–439.

Gelso, C.J., & Fassinger, R. (1990). Counseling psychology, theory research and interventions. *Annual Review of Psychology 44,* 355–386.

Goldfried, M.R. (1980). Toward the delineation of therapeutic change principles. *American Psychologist, 35,* 991–999.

Grotevant, H.D., Cooper, C.R., & Kramer, K. (1986). Exploration as a predictor of congruence in adolescent's career choices. *Journal of Vocational Behavior, 29,* 201–215.

Holland, J.L. (1984). A celebration of the career point of view [Review of *Handbook of vocational psychology*]. *Contemporary Psychology, 29,* 862.

Holland, J.L. (1985). *Making vocational choices: A theory of vocational personalities and work environments* (2nd ed.). Englewood Cliffs, NJ: Prentice-Hall.

Holland, J.L., Magoon, T.M., & Spokane, A.R. (1981). Counseling psychology: Career interventions, research, and theory. *Annual Review of Psychology, 32,* 279–305.

Hollandsworth, J.G., Dressel, M.E., & Stevens, J. (1977). Use of behavioral versus traditional procedures for increasing job interview skills. *Journal of Counseling Psychology, 24,* 503–510.

Janis, I.L. (1983). The role of social support in adherence to stressful decisions. *American Psychologist, 38,* 143–160.

Kapes, J.T., & Mastie, M.M. (1988). A counselor's guide to career assessment instruments (2nd ed.). Alexandria, VA. National Career Development Association.

Kirschner, T. (1988). *Process and outcome of career counseling: A case study.* Unpublished doctoral dissertation, University of Maryland, College Park.

Kivlighan, D.M., Jr., Hageseth, J.A., Tipton, R.M., & McGovern, T.V. (1981). Effects of matching treatment approaches and personality types in group vocational counseling. *Journal of Counseling Psychology, 28,* 315–320.

Krumboltz, J.D., Becker-Haven, J.F., & Burnett, K.F. (1979). Counseling psychology. *Annual Review of Psychology, 30,* 55–602.

Krumboltz, J.D., & Shroeder, W.W. (1965). Promoting career planning through reinforcement. *Personnel & Guidance Journal, 11,* 19–26.

Kuhn, D. (1989). Children and adults as intuitive scientists. *Psychological Review, 96,* 674–689.

Lunneborg, P.W. (1983). Career counseling techniques. In W.B. Walsh & S.H. Osipow (Eds.), *Handbook of Vocational Psychology: Vol. 2.* (pp. 41–76). Hillsdale, NJ: Lawrence Erlbaum.

Meichenbaum, D., & Turk, D.C. (1987). *Facilitating treatment adherence: A practitioner's guidebook.* New York: Plenum.

Morgan, J.I., & Skovholt, T.M. (1977). Using inner experience: Fantasy and daydreams in career counseling. *Journal of Counseling Psychology, 24,* 391–397.

Myers, R.A. (1986). Research on educational and vocational counseling. In A.E. Bergin and S.L. Garfield (Eds.), *Handbook of psychotherapy and behavior change.* (3rd ed.) 715–738. New York: Wiley.

Neimeyer, G.J., & Ebben, R. (1985). The effects of vocational interventions on the complexity and positivity of occupational judgments. *Journal of Vocational Behavior, 27,* 87–97.

Oliver, L.W., & Spokane, A.R. (1988). Career counseling outcome: What contributes to client gain? *Journal of Counseling Psychology, 35,* 447–462.

O'Neil, J.M., Ohlde, C., Barke, C., Gelwick, B.P., & Garfield, N. (1980). Research on a workshop to reduce the effects of sexism and sex role socialization on women's career planning. *Journal of Counseling Psychology, 27,* 355–363.

Osipow, S.H. (1987a). Counseling psychology: Theory, research, and practice in career counseling. *Annual Review of Psychology, 38,* 257–278.

Osipow, S.H. (1987b). *Career decision scale: Manual.* Odessa, FL: Psychological Assessment Resources.

Rounds, J.B. Jr., & Tinsley, H.E.A. (1984). Diagnosis and treatment of vocational problems. In S.D. Brown and R.W. Lent (Eds.), *Handbook of counseling psychology* (pp. 137–177). New York: Wiley.

Rusalem, H. (1954). New insights on the role of occupational information in counseling. *Journal of Counseling Psychology, 1,* 84–88.

Samler, J. (1961). Psycho-social aspects of work: A critique of occupational information. *Personnel and Guidance Journal, 39,* 458–465.

Skovholt, T.M., Morgan, J.I., & Negron-Cunningham, H. (1989). Mental imagery in career counseling and life planning: A review of research and intervention methods. *Journal of Counseling and Development, 67,* 287–292.

Speas, C.M. (1979). Job-seeking interview skills training: A comparison of four instructional techniques. *Journal of Counseling Psychology, 26,* 405–412.

Spokane, A.R. (1991). *Career intervention.* Englewood Cliffs, NJ: Prentice Hall.

Spokane, A.R. (1990). Self-guided interest inventories: The self-directed search. In E. Watkins, & V. Campbell (Eds.), *Testing in counseling practice.* Hillsdale, NJ: Lawrence Erlbaum.

Spokane, A.R., Fretz, B., Hoffman, M.A., Nagel, D., & Davison, R.M. (July 1990). Preliminary findings on the impact of career counseling on career adjustment and mental health status. Paper presented at The International Congress of Applied Psychology, Kyoto Japan.

Spokane, A.R. & Hawks, B.K. (1990). Annual review: Career practice and theory, 1989. *The Career Development Quarterly, 39,* 98–128.

Spokane, A.R., & Oliver, L.W. (1983). The outcomes of vocational intervention. In W.B. Walsh & S.H. Osipow (Eds.), *Handbook of Vocational Psychology: Vol. 2.* (pp. 99–136). Hillsdale, NJ: Lawrence Erlbaum.

Walsh, W.B., & Osipow, S.H. (Eds.) (1990). *Career counseling: Contemporary topics in vocational psychology,* Hillsdale, NJ: Lawrence Erlbaum.

Zager, J.J. (1982). *Self-esteem enhancement as an intervention for career indecision.* Unpublished doctoral dissertation. University of Maryland, College Park, MD.

SECTION II:

STRATEGIES AND METHODS

A VARIETY OF APPROACHES . . .

CHAPTER 4

Principles of Program Development for Adult Career Development Programs

H. Daniel Lea
Conceptual Systems, Inc.
Silver Spring, Maryland

Zandy Leibowitz
Conceptual Systems, Inc.
Silver Spring, Maryland

Successful program development in adult career development settings requires a person with the following qualities:

40% willingness to learn
10% commitment
10% expertise
10% courage
10% emotional endurance
10% pragmatism
10% sense of humor

In short, program developers are, first and foremost, learners. Program development is an experiential learning process in which program developers discover how to provide the most relevant services to both program users and sponsors. The program is the product of this learning process.

"Experts" do not make good program developers because experts feel they have the answers to clients' problems and needs. Good program developers never assume they know the answers. However, they do know questions—questions that will help them learn how to effectively meet clients' needs.

MODEL OF ADULT CAREER PROGRAM DEVELOPMENT

There are five basic questions that the program developer—as learner—must answer. These are:

- What needs to be done?
- What is possible?
- What is realistic?
- What steps need to be taken?
- What needs to be retained/what needs to be changed?

These questions form the basis for the five-stage model of adult career program development described in this chapter. Table 1 outlines the model.

This model incorporates Kolb's learning style concepts (Kolb & Plovnick, 1977; Kolb, 1984). Kolb conceives of learning as a four-stage cycle: experience serves as the basis for observation and reflection; observations serve as the basis for theory formation; and finally, theories provide input for decision making and problem solving. The model also incorporates principles of effective career development systems (Leibowitz, Farren, & Kaye, 1985).

Elaboration of each program development stage will be organized around the following questions:

1. What is the learning objective for the program developer at this stage?
2. What program development activity will lead to this learning?
3. What learning behaviors are most useful at this stage?
4. What role do potential program users and program sponsors play in the process?
5. If effective learning takes place, what is the desired end result at this stage?
6. What are the practical issues and implications that need to be considered at this stage of program development?

The final section of the chapter will examine how the inherent strengths and weaknesses of characteristic individual learning styles of program developers can affect the program development process.

STAGE I: DATA GATHERING

Description

The primary learning objective of Stage I is to find an answer to the question, "What needs to be done?" In other words, "What do the people you wish to serve by the program need?" In addition, "What do the sponsors of the program need from the program?" Answers to these questions are usually provided by carrying out a needs assessment. Needs assessments can range from highly sophisticated survey techniques to structured interviews, even to include informal hallway chats. Regardless of technique, all are data generating and data gathering procedures with the primary purpose of helping the program developer become thoroughly acquainted with the environment and people who potentially may be served by the program. Needs assessments also serve to provide involvement and commitment of the people who will subsequently be served by the program.

57

Table 1
Stages of Program Development

Program Development Stage	Learning Objective	Program Development Activity	Learning Style	User/ Sponsor Role	Desired End Result
Stage I: Data Gathering	What needs to be done?	Needs assessment	Divergent	Resource	Needs data-base
Stage II: Conceptualization	What is possible?	Visioning/ model building	Assimilative	Translator	Theoretical program model
Stage III: Design	What is realistic?	Strategy design	Convergent	Reality check	Program strategy
Stage IV: Implementation	What steps need to be taken?	Logistical action planning	Accommodative	Catalyst	Logistical action plan
Stage V: Evaluation/ Redesign	What needs to be retained/ what needs to be changed?	Evaluation-based redesign	Assimilative/ all styles	Source of feedback	Ideas for improvement

Kolb's *divergent* learning style includes the key behaviors that program developers use in Stage I. According to Kolb, divergent learning requires an openness to concrete experience and reflective observation of that experience. In program development, there has to be some method of generating data from concrete experience and observing and recording that data. Any interaction with a potential client population or program sponsor provides the opportunity for generation of needs data. Consequently, it is pretty difficult to make mistakes in this phase of program development unless there is isolation from the people the program is supposed to serve. However, mistakes can be made in the second aspect of divergent learning. Often, time is not taken to think about what is heard or experienced, thus preventing the data from sinking in as a learning experience.

The program developer cannot successfully meet the learning objective of this stage without assistance. There must be involvement of potential program users and sponsors. Both are *data resources*. Potential users are the foremost experts in terms of their own needs. In addition, sponsors can identify what they will need to realize to justify supporting the program.

As an end result of this stage the program developer has a substantive database from which to visualize a program. Good program developers may not always have answers, but the right questions asked in this phase will provide a sound program start.

Issues, Implications, and Other Assorted Practical Tips

- There is no best method of data generation and gathering. Sometimes data generated in a friendly chat over a cup of coffee can be as valid and reliable as that produced by the most rigorous scientific methods. Never underestimate the power of good communication skills.
- Combining several assessment methods—if possible—is usually more useful than emphasizing one. Surveys, interviews, observations, and direct experience all have their strengths and problems.
- When does one stop gathering data and move on to the next stage? Move on when you feel you can do a fair job of walking in the users' and sponsors' shoes.
- Use conceptual tools to raise hypotheses, then use concrete data to validate/invalidate these hypotheses. Holland's personality/environmental types (Holland, 1973), Deal and Kennedy's organizational cultures (Deal & Kennedy, 1982), Super's developmental tasks (Super, Crites, Humme, Moser, Overstreet & Warnath, 1957), Dalton, Thompson and Price's career stages (Dalton, Thompson, & Price, 1977), and Crites' model of career maturity (Crites, 1973) are examples of practical models that can be quite useful at this stage if used as sources of questions rather than definitive answers.
- Identify problems of the program sponsor that may be solved by the program. What will the sponsor get out of the program—*both now and in the future*? There are few totally altruistic program sponsors.
- Identify potential obstacles and resources; these can take the form of people or things.

59

- Balance the energy and resources committed to data collection with those expended for the entire program. Don't spend 90% of your time and money on Stage I, with only 10% to allocate to subsequent steps.
- One never feels one has enough data. Do the best you can in the amount of time you have and move on to the next stage. The entire program development process will generate data. The stages of program development are not mutually exclusive.

STAGE II: CONCEPTUALIZATION

Description

The primary learning objective of Stage II is to conceptualize an answer to the question, "What is possible?" In other words, "What programmatic options can I visualize that would address the needs of both program users and sponsors?" The program development activities of this stage involve visioning and model building. Visioning involves that difficult-to-describe, creative, cognitive activity that has been called "forming a dream" (Levinson, Darrow, Klein, Levinson, & McKee, 1978). It is not totally fantasy-based because the stimulus for visioning is data-based. The reality data that were collected in Stage I provide the context for a vision. Model building gives form and substance to the vision. Model building goes one step beyond visioning and translates that vision into a concrete, tangible, theoretical blueprint. Visioning and model building involve a complementary melding of creativity and logic.

Kolb's *assimilative* learning style incorporates the primary behaviors that program developers use in Stage II. According to Kolb, assimilative learning requires reflective observation and abstract conceptualization. In Stage II of program development, the creative activity of visioning or dreaming is given form by the logical theorizing of model building. A good program developer at this stage utilizes two very different but complementary types of behavior. Visioning is not limited by the restrictiveness of logic. However, logic provides an element of discipline to creativity.

The activities of Stage II are primarily the responsibility of the program developer. Certain creative individuals from among potential program users and sponsors may be useful to this stage, but the program developer should be very selective. Many program users and sponsors are too close to reality to be helpful at this stage. They will "yes, but . . ." every creative idea to death! Where assistance can be rendered is in the latter phases of Stage II when the theoretical program model must be translated into language that is readily understood in the environment in which the program will be implemented. What is acceptable is often merely a matter of semantics. One of the authors, who had to implement a career development program in an organization composed largely of career plateaued employees in the latter stages of their careers, was able to gain acceptance of the program by changing the name of the program from career development to career assistance. What was different? The difference was semantics. Career "development" in that environment meant vertical mobility, which was viewed—correctly—as unrealistic. "Assistance" had no restrictive connotations and consequently allowed for the consideration of various other career options such as job enrichment and lateral mobility.

As a product of Stage II the program developer will have a theoretical program model. This structure will be the foundation and underpinnings from which numerous program strategies can emanate in the next stage of program development.

Issues, Implications, and Other Assorted Practical Tips

- McCaskey's concept of directional planning (McCaskey, 1977) provides some useful concepts for the visioning and model building of Stage II. McCaskey contends that planning in an ambiguous environment largely involves defining a direction and a domain. Some questions to consider, based on this model, include:
  —What is your vision of the possible objectives the program may address? (direction) What are the "musts" the programs has to address and the "nevers" of which the program should steer clear? (domain)
  —In your program model, what is the primary mission? (direction) What are the primary program functions and the interrelationships of those functions? (domain)
- What is needed is not always popular nor readily accepted by program users or program sponsors. Program credibility must first be established. In such cases, the program developer is best advised to *formalize what is desired* and *subtly incorporate what is needed*.
- If you expect support, do not speak in foreign tongues. Translate your program model into language that users and sponsors can understand.

STAGE III: DESIGN

Description

The primary learning objective of Stage III for the program developer is to answer the question, "What is realistic?" In other words, "What program approaches have the highest likelihood of success given the environment in which the program must be implemented?" Also, "What program strategies will have the highest benefit-to-cost ratio?" The program development activity that characterizes this stage is strategy design. Whereas Stage I and Stage II provided a data-based conceptual design, Stage III defines what is going to be done. Strategy design involves more than just the definition of activities. It also includes definition of how and in what sequence those activities will fit together to translate the theoretical model into concrete action.

Kolb's *convergent* learning style characterizes the primary behaviors that program developers use in Stage III. According to Kolb, convergent learning requires abstract conceptualization and active experimentation. The task involves translating a theoretical model into behavioral strategies. Program strategies translate ideas into action. It is at this stage that logic must pass the first reality test.

Potential users of the program and program sponsors are very important to the program development process at this stage. It is they who can best judge if the program strategy is realistic. They are the experts on what strategies are likely to work in the program environment because they *are* the program environment. Many conceptually sound program strategies have gone down the tubes because naive program developers did not test the degree of sensitivity and receptivity of potential program users and sponsors. Being right is not enough to guarantee success in the program development world!

At the completion of Stage III, the program developer will have a bridge between theory and practice, the end product being a program strategy. That strategy defines the "what" and "how" of the program.

Issues, Implications, and Other Assorted Practical Tips

- In strategy design, never lose sight of your long-term vision, but be sure to build in short-term, tangible results for both program participants and sponsors.
- Use a conceptual model as a guide for both overall strategy design and that all important component—evaluation design. A good example of such a model is Crites' model of career maturity (Crites, 1973).
- Codesign with those who will pass judgment on the program. The program developer cannot afford to be the Lone Ranger. Even he had Tonto!
- If you want success, the benefits had better outweigh the costs, and the resources outweigh the obstacles.
- Start small with a pilot that has strong support and a high probability of success. First efforts form lasting impressions.
- Build in a follow-up for each program activity to reinforce results and assess whether those results were utilized in the "real" world.

STAGE IV: IMPLEMENTATION

Description

The primary learning objective of Stage IV is to answer the question, "What steps need to be taken?" Previous stages defined what was desirable, what was possible, and what was realistic. Those stages are considered by most program developers as the exciting "fun" stages of program development. Stage IV involves the unglamorous—but very important—logistical nuts and bolts of bringing a program into reality. The program development activity involved in this stage is logistical action planning. There needs to be a concrete, detailed game plan that spells out "who needs to do what, by when" to ensure that the program content and strategy will be implemented in an effective and efficient manner.

The major tasks involved in this stage, which should be incorporated into the logistical game plan, are as follows:

- publicizing and "marketing" the program activities;
- involving key players;
- collecting and publicizing endorsements from credible supporters and sponsors;
- identifying and negotiating environmental politics and sensitivities;
- dentifying and negotiating potential obstacles and impediments;
- identifying or developing necessary resources;
- budgeting and staffing;
- identifying and selecting participants;
- providing effective physical setting and facilities;
- scheduling;
- contingency planning;
- preparing evaluation tools;
- defining a step-by-step "who does what, by when"; and
- considering a million other things one does not think of until the last minute!

Kolb's *accommodative learning* style includes important behaviors utilized at this stage. According to Kolb (1984), accommodative learning requires a "doer" orientation. This type of learning requires a "doer" orientation, active experimentation, and concrete experience. The focus of both of these types of behaviors emphasizes action that will "get things done."

The activities of Stage IV can utilize the help of potential program users and sponsors as catalysts. It is they who are most knowledgeable of how to get things done in the program environment. There is no substitute for experience with and knowledge of the unique, idiocentric characteristics of program environments. Negotiating or getting around "the system" is no easy task. In this stage of program development, the old adage "it's who you know that counts" holds much truth.

The primary end product of this stage is a logistical action plan. This action plan is the cookbook for implementing the program activities and strategies. It is highly recommended that this cookbook be in written form, particularly if a sizable team of people are involved in program implementation.

Issues, Implications, and Other Assorted Practical Tips

- Ensure visible endorsement by those who have credibility and influence.
- Involve key players—particularly those who sit in judgment of the program.
- The activities of this stage can be frustrating, time-consuming, and boring. However, these activities have to be done. Much of the shoddiness in program development can be attributed to underemphasizing or taking for granted the tasks of Stage IV.
- "When in doubt, leave it out" does not apply to this stage.
- What works in one place will not necessarily work in another.

- You will need your sense of humor to meet the challenges and frustrations of Stage IV.

STAGE V: EVALUATION/REDESIGN

Description

The primary learning objective of Stage V is to find answers to the questions: "What needs to be changed?" and "What should be retained?" Implicit in these questions is the need to redesign the program to improve future efforts. However, redesign must be based on program outcomes as measured by a thorough analysis of the program's evaluation data. Program development, in the truest sense of the term, builds and improves upon what is accomplished. The program development activity that serves as the basis for developmental changes is program evaluation.

The reflective observation and the abstract conceptualization skills of Kolb's *assimilative learning* style will come in handy in the analysis and interpretation of evaluation data in Stage V. The results of these analyses will dictate what stages of the program development process need to be reexamined and modified. Ideally, the overall program development process should be recycled because the stages of the program development model are not mutually exclusive. A change in meeting the objectives of one stage may very well affect the other stages.

The program is not an end in itself. It must provide results for both program users and sponsors. Both users and sponsors serve as important sources of feedback in the program evaluation. Perhaps one of the most important uses of evaluation data is as stimuli for discussion with program users and sponsors. They play a crucial role in determining whether the outcomes of the program are significant in meeting their needs. The program developer must identify the outcomes of greatest interest to all key players. What is important to program users may not be most important to program sponsors. Also, outcomes that may intrigue the program developer may get the dreaded "So what?" response from program users and sponsors. Sound program evaluation should be considered from the beginning. Potential measures and outcomes should be clearly tied to the objectives and activities of the program that were established in earlier stages.

The end result of Stage V should be ideas for improving the program. Consequently, program evaluation is both an ending and a beginning of a learning process for the program developer. The program developer who ceases to learn has stopped practicing the craft of program development.

Issues, Implications, and Other Assorted Practical Tips

- Evaluation design involves definition of "*who* needs *what* kind of data by *when*?"
- Use multiple program strategies and multiple evaluation methods. It is better to overkill than to strike out.
- Recycle the wheel. Do not remake it.

- Give evaluation feedback to those who need it—whether they ask for it or not!
- Celebrate/publicize accomplishments.
- There is no such thing as too much follow-up.
- Evolutions are easier than revolutions. Did your program try to take small steps or giant leaps?
- Never take personal credit for program successes. Give the credit to those who helped you.
- Failures are opportunities to learn, not license for self-abuse.

THE IMPACT OF PROGRAM DEVELOPERS' INDIVIDUAL LEARNING STYLES ON THE PROGRAM DEVELOPMENT PROCESS

KOLB'S EXPERIENTIAL LEARNING THEORY

Kolb and Plovnick (1977; Kolb, 1984) conceived of learning as a four-stage cycle. Experience is the basis for reflective thought. Reflections are organized into hypotheses, theories, and concepts. These hypotheses are then tested in reality, the end result being a new set of experiences from which to recycle the learning process. Implicit in this cycle are four types of learning behaviors:

Concrete experience (CE): The ability to involve oneself without bias in new experiences.

Reflective observation (RO): The ability to observe and reflect upon experiences from multiple perspectives.

Abstract conceptualization (AC): The ability to integrate observations into logical theories.

Active experimentation (AE): The ability to use theories to make decisions and solve problems.

Kolb contends the learning cycle is made up of two polar dimensions: concrete experience versus abstract conceptualization, and reflective observation versus active experimentation (see diagonals of Figure 1). Although all four sets of behaviors are viewed as necessary to learning, one cannot easily experience (CE) and conceptualize (AC) simultaneously, nor can one act (AE) and reflect (RO) at the same time. One gets in the way of the other.

Kolb further contends that, due to hereditary and environmental influences, people tend to develop learning styles that emphasize some learning behaviors over others. His research has identified four statistically prevalent learning styles: divergent, assimilative, convergent, and accommodative. Figure 1 illustrates the relationship between learning styles and learning behaviors. Each style tends to emphasize two of the four types of learning behaviors. Diagonal styles tend to emphasize very different learning behaviors, whereas adjacent styles hold one type of learning behavior in common.

Figure 1
Correspondence of Learning Behaviors and Learning Styles.

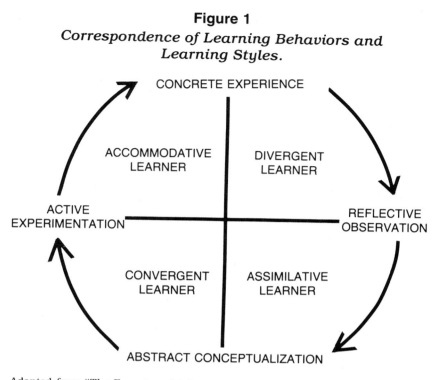

Adapted from "The Experimental Learning Theory of Career Development" (pp 65–87) by D.A. Kolb and M.S. Plovnick. In J. Van Maanen (Ed.), *Organizations Careers: Some New Perspectives*, 1977, New York: Wiley. Copyright 1977 by Joh Wiley & Sons. Adapted by permission.

IMPLICATIONS FOR PROGRAM DEVELOPMENT

It is the thesis of this chapter that program development is a learning process, and that, to be effective, the program developer must utilize learning abilities. The first four stages of the program development process outlined in this chapter roughly correspond to Kolb's Experiential Learning Model (see Figure 2). Data-gathering (Stage I) relies on the experiential and observational abilities of divergent learning. The visioning and model building of Stage II rely on the conceptual abilities of assimilative learning. The development of a program strategy that is central to Stage III of the program development process relies heavily on the ability to apply theoretical ideas (an ability which is characteristic of convergent learning). The implementation requirements of Stage IV rely on the "how to do" abilities of accommodative learning. Stage V utilizes the analytical abilities of assimilative learning in the evaluation phase of that stage, but subsequent redesign of the program recycles both the program development and learning process. In sum, different stages of the program development process utilize different abilities at different times.

Figure 2
Correspondence of Program Development Stages and Learning Styles

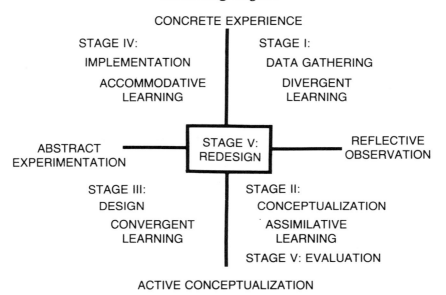

Kolb contends that different people tend to prefer and emphasize different learning styles. Few, if any, are strong in all of the learning styles. Consequently, every program developer brings a unique set of strengths and weaknesses to the program development process. Unfortunately, the tendency is to overemphasize the learning style with which we are most comfortable and "force fit" it on all of the program development stages. Any learning style applied at an inappropriate time can be a liability. For example, the pragmatic, reality-based emphasis of the convergent and accommodative learning styles can be too conservative and restrictive for the creative objectives of Stage I and Stage II. On the other hand, the idealism and creativity of the divergent learning style and the highly rational orientation of the assimilative style can be impractical when confronting the political realities of Stages III and IV.

IMPLICATIONS FOR PRACTICE

Now for a rude awakening. In the wonderful world of program development, one must accept the fact that the job is bigger than the person. We all have our deficiencies! Consequently, here are some "words to the wise":

- Program Developer, know thyself.
- Program Developer, monitor your behavior. Does your behavior reflect what is needed or what you like to do?

- Do what you do best. Use others to do those things you cannot do.
- Force yourself to develop adequate skills in all program development areas. Become excellent in areas that are your strengths.
- Ideally, program development is a team effort and should encompass a team of people with differing but complementary skills.
- Move on or step aside when someone else can better serve the program. Beware of ownership.
- When you move, be prepared to grieve. Letting go is not always easy.

SUMMARY

This chapter has described a five-stage model for the development of adult career programs based on an experiential learning theory. The stages focus on learning the answers to five basic program development questions:

- What needs to be done?
- What is possible?
- What is realistic?
- What steps need to be taken?
- What needs to be retained, and what needs to be changed?

Program development is a dynamic process. The questions are permanent; the answers are temporary. The need to learn never ceases.

REFERENCES

Crites, J.L. (1973). *Theory and research handbook: Career maturity inventory*. Monterey, CA: McGraw-Hill.

Dalton, G.W., Thompson, P.H., & Price, R. (1977, Summer). Career stages: A model of professional careers in organizations. *Organization Dynamics*. pp. 19–42.

Deal, T.E., & Kennedy, A.A. (1982). *Corporate cultures*. Reading, MA: Addison-Wesley.

Holland, J.L. (1973). *Making vocational choices: A theory of careers*. Englewood Cliffs, NJ: Prentice-Hall.

Kolb, D.A. (1984). *Experiential learning*. Englewood Cliffs, NJ: Prentice-Hall.

Kolb, D.A., & Plovnick, M.S. (1977). The experiential learning theory of career development. In J. VanMaanen (Ed.), *Organizational careers: Some new perspectives* (pp. 65–87). New York: Wiley.

Leibowitz, Z.B., Farren, C., & Kay, B. (1985, April). The twelve-fold path to CD enlightenment. *Training and Development Journal*. pp. 29–32.

Levinson, D.J., Darrow, C.N., Klein, E.G., Levinson, M.H., & McKee, B. (1978). *The seasons of a man's life*. New York: Knopf.

McCaskey, M.B. (1977). Goals and direction in personal planning. *Academy of Management Review, 2*, 454–462.

Super, D.E., Crites, J.O., Humme, R.C., Moser, H.P., Overstreet, P.L., & Warnath, C.F. (1957). *Vocational development: A framework for research*. New York: Teachers College, Columbia University.

CHAPTER 5

Appraising Adults' Career Capabilities: Ability, Interest, and Personality

John O. Crites
Crites Career Centers
Boulder, Colorado

In his Model of Career Maturity, Crites (1978, p. 4) made the distinction between career choice *content* and career choice *process* in decision making:

> The former encompasses the Consistency of Career Choices and Realism of Career Choices factors in the model (Figure 1). To operationally define these dimensions it is necessary to elicit a career choice from an individual. A question like, "Which occupation do you intend to enter when you have completed your schooling or training" (Crites, 1969, p. 139) is asked, and, if the individual has made a choice, an occupational title, e.g., machinist, copywriter, or dancer, is given in response. This is career choice *content*. In contrast, career choice *process* refers to the variables involved in arriving at a declaration of career choice content. These variables include the group factors of Career Choice Competencies and Career Choice Attitudes in the model of career maturity.

A recent chapter on "Instruments for Assessing Career Development" (Crites, 1984), in the third NVGA commemorative volume *Designing Careers* (Gysbers, 1984), reviewed contemporary measures of career choice process such as Crites' (1978) *Career Maturity Inventory* and the Career Pattern Study's (Thompson, Lindeman, Super, Jordaan, & Myers, 1981, 1982) *Career Development Inventory*. This chapter describes and discusses some of the tests and inventories available to appraise adults capabilities (both intellective and nonintellective) for career choice content.

With the increased focus on *adult* career development during the past decade, well exemplified by this book devoted entirely to the topic, more and more career counselors and career development specialists, particularly in business and community organizations, find themselves confronted with the task of assisting adults in appraising their career capabilities—their abilities, interests, and personality characteristics.

Figure 1
A Model of Career Maturity in Adolescence and Adulthood

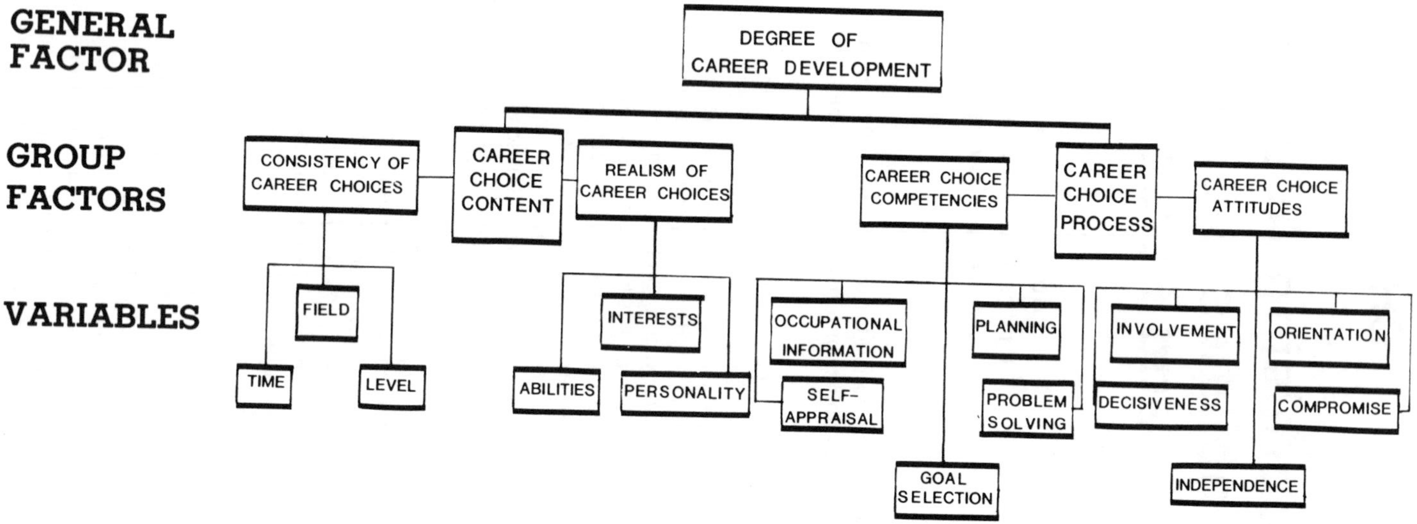

GENERAL FACTOR

GROUP FACTORS

VARIABLES

DEGREE OF CAREER DEVELOPMENT

CAREER CHOICE CONTENT

CAREER CHOICE PROCESS

CONSISTENCY OF CAREER CHOICES

REALISM OF CAREER CHOICES

CAREER CHOICE COMPETENCIES

CAREER CHOICE ATTITUDES

TIME

FIELD

LEVEL

ABILITIES

INTERESTS

PERSONALITY

OCCUPATIONAL INFORMATION

SELF-APPRAISAL

GOAL SELECTION

PLANNING

PROBLEM SOLVING

INVOLVEMENT

DECISIVENESS

ORIENTATION

COMPROMISE

INDEPENDENCE

70

Yet many of these professionals are either unaware of existing standardized measures for adult career appraisal and use none, or they construct homemade surveys and questionnaires (e.g., self-reported skills) that have unknown or uncertain reliability and validity. The need for a review of appropriate tests and inventories for career counseling and group work with adults seems apparent. To identify these assessment instruments, a search was first made for all the measures listed in *TESTS* (Sweetland & Keyser, 1983) that were applicable to adults. Then, for each instrument, the number of references cited in Buros' (1978) *Eighth Mental Measurement Yearbook* (MMYB) was calculated. The most extensively researched instruments were selected for review, the assumption being that they would have sufficiently documented psychometric characteristics to be useful in career counseling and career development programs.

In addition to these well-established tests and inventories, other less studied but promising instruments are mentioned so that users can assess their usefulness for particular situations (see Sweetland & Keyser, 1983). Certain judgmental constraints have been imposed on the selection of the adult appraisal instruments included in this review, in terms of the pragmatics of career counseling practice (Crites, 1981). Experience indicates that some are better than others. This review and critical analysis is, therefore, a *synthesis* of scientific findings on appraisal instruments for adult career capabilities (career choice content) *and* informed experience with them. Ability tests, including measures of general intelligence, achievement, and aptitudes (multifactor), are presented first and are followed by a discussion of vocational interest inventories, with a final section on personality measures. The chapter concludes with presentation of a microcomputer systems approach for appraising adult career capabilities. It has been used extensively in organizational "in-house" career development programs, Private Industry Council (PIC) programs for the unemployed, and outplacement career counseling for released workers.

ABILITY TESTS

There are certain desiderata that ability tests, including general intelligence, achievement, reading, and aptitude, should have for the appraisal of adult career capabilities. Foremost among these is that the test be a *power* measure, that is, *untimed*, because adults beyond ages 25–30 have a decrement in performance under hurried conditions (Super & Crites, 1962). In addition, all tests, but particularly those for intelligence and aptitude, should have evidenced vocational validity—that is, be predictive of occupational level or occupational aptitude patterns (OAPs). Two other, different parameters are whether both (a) verbal and nonverbal and (b) group and individual tests are available. Given these specifications, only a few ability tests can be recommended for the appraisal of adult career capabilities. These are classified in Table 1 and are reviewed in the following discussion.

Table 1

Classification of Recommended Adult Ability Measures by Desiderata

	General Intelligence	Achievement	Reading	Specific Aptitudes
Power	OSPE Wonderlic Beta II	ABLE		
Speeded	Wonderlic Wesman	TABE WRAT	Iowa Nelson-Denny	GATB EAS
Paper-and-Pencil	OSPE		Iowa Nelson-Denny	GATB EAS
Individually Administered Verbal	WAIS-R OSPE Wonderlic Wesman		Iowa Nelson-Denny	Performance GATB EAS
Nonverbal	Beta II WAIS-R Performance			GATB Performance

Intelligence Tests

No one test of general intelligence has all the characteristics desired in such measures for appraising the intellectual functioning of adults. If there is sufficient administration time and a qualified examiner available, then the Wechsler Adult Intelligence Scales—Revised (WAIS-R) has much to recommend it, particularly its extensive age norms, which allow the comparison of an adult's score with those of peers (Matarazzo, 1972). It has only modest vocational validity (Super & Crites, 1962), but can yield a good estimate of an adult's probable level of occupational attainment, which corresponds generally to the levels axis in Roe's occupational classification system (Roe, 1956), as well as to the DOT ratings of general ability given in Holland's *Dictionary* (Gottfriedson, Holland, & Ogawa, 1984). Another possible test of "g" is the Wonderlic Personnel Test, which is a group paper-and-pencil instrument that can be given under either timed (12 minutes) or untimed conditions. It has had extensive use and validation in employee selection situations, as has the Wesman Personnel Selection Test, a timed (28 minutes) paper-and-pencil measure of the verbal and numerical components in general intelligence. The Ohio State Psychological Examination can also be used with adults, under untimed directions, but appropriate norms for older (than college age) individuals are lacking. Finally, for an excellent untimed, nonverbal assessment of intelligence, the Revised Army Beta Examination (Beta-II) is the choice, having been restandardized for adults in 1978.

Achievement Tests

Although achievement tests are usually associated with school assessment programs, their use with adults has increased in recent years with the introduction of career development workshops in business/industrial organizations and the establishment of Private Industry Council programs for the unemployed. There is often a need to assess level of educational development, particularly with the latter group, to determine whether remedial basic education is indicated before proceeding with job search. *TESTS* and Buros' *MMYB* cite three measures of adult achievement: Adult Basic Learning Examination (ABLE), Tests of Adult Basic Education (TABE), and the Wide Range Achievement Test (WRAT). Of these ABLE (revised edition, 1986) has the best-established psychometric properties. It appraises vocabulary, reading comprehension, spelling, arithmetic computation, and problem-solving skills at three different levels: grades 1 to 6, grades 3 to 9, and grades 9 to 12. A short screening test, called SelectAble (sic), is used to determine which level of testing is appropriate. Tests at Levels I and II take 2 hours, whereas Level III requires 3 hours and 25 minutes to administer. Norms expressed as percentile ranks and stanines are reported for all levels. The TABE also includes tests of vocabulary, mathematics, and language at different levels. It is simply an edited version of the 1970 California Achievement Tests (CAT), which were developed for the elementary and secondary school population, but new norms for adults are now available. The WRAT offers the advantage of measuring many of the same variables as the

TABE, but expresses scores in age- rather than grade-equivalents, which is obviously much more appropriate for adults (cf., WAIS-R).

Reading Tests

If, in addition to the reading subsets of achievement batteries, a more comprehensive appraisal is needed, probably the best available reading test for adults, of which there are few, is the Iowa Silent Reading Tests (ISRT). The Buros' (1978, p. 1197) review by Filby concludes that the 1973 edition is "the product of a careful, long-term developmental effort. It contains interesting subtests, with a variety of scoring options. It is well-packaged and presented. The Guide for Interpretation and Use is a model of thoroughness and clarity." The subtests measure vocabulary, comprehension, directed reading (work-study skills), and reading efficiency (rate with comprehension), although directed reading is not included for Level III, which is appropriate for adults. Contrary to the recommended uses of the subtests, Hakstian (Buros, 1978, p. 1199) concludes from a review of subtest intercorrelations that the ISRT is *not* multifactorial: "Quite clearly, one and only one common factor accounts for the [above] correlations. For this reason, it is difficult to envision the ISRT—or its competitors—as having much *diagnostic* utility" (italics in original). This conclusion must be qualified for several reasons, as far as adults are concerned: First, the data were on seventh graders; second, most factor analytic methods yield only *one* principal factor; and, third, for adults as compared with seventh graders, developmental age may make the subtests more independent statistically. Certainly, with an individual client, given *reliable* difference scores among subtests, they *may* have diagnostic significance. The only other alternative is the Nelson-Denny Reading Test, which has had a hallowed history, with its comprehension, vocabulary, and reading rate subtests, but again the question is raised: How *independent* are they? Both the ISRT and the Nelson-Denny are timed, which may be an exogenous variable accounting for the well-established high correlations between rate and comprehension. Perhaps someone will construct a reading test for adults that is untimed—why is *time* per se so important? It is the time one puts into reading, not reading time (rate), that seems to make the difference in learning.

Aptitude Tests

Clearly, the best documented and most widely applicable aptitude tests for adults are in the General Aptitude Test Battery (GATB). Not only were they developed on and for adults (Super & Crites, 1962), but they have an extensive "Occupational Aptitude Pattern" (OAP) database, which Hunter (1983) extended to 12,000 occupations, using the new techniques of validity generalization. There are now 66 OAPs that encompass most of the distinct occupations in the world of work (Droege & Padgett, 1979), and Crites (1984) [see below] has designed a microcomputer system that prints out in less than 1 minute on a programmed interpretative form (the Career Decision Maker) all the OAPs a person is qualified for—no more visual or graphic profile comparisons necessary by the career coun-

74

selor. A major drawback with the GATB, however, is that it is tightly controlled by local employment services, and can be administered only by them or certificated examiners. As a result, this highly developed instrument is also highly restricted in its availability. Fortunately, there is an equally useful alternate, although it does not include performance tests as the GATB does. The Employee Aptitude Survey (EAS) is a battery of 10 short but reliable and valid tests of such variables as verbal reasoning, numerical ability, spatial visualization, and visual speed and accuracy. The occupational norms are broadly based, but not to the extent of the GATB. In developing the Career Decision Maker, however, which also includes a ranking of expressed interests, Crites (1984) equated the EAS to GATB, with the exception of the latter's performance measures, so that the OAP database can be used with both batteries. Thus, the EAS, supplemented as needed with performance tests such as the Purdue Pegboard and the Purdue Mechanical Adaptability Test, gives the career specialist a viable option to the GATB.

VOCATIONAL INTERESTS

In the discussion that follows, the focus is on vocational interests, both expressed and inventoried, but measures of work needs and job satisfaction are also reviewed. For a comprehensive appraisal of adult career capabilities, it is often useful to assess needs that are satisfied in the work environment, as well as vocational interests.

Expressed Interests

For many years simply asking people questions about their interests, such as "Which occupation(s) do you plan to enter when you have completed your education or training" (Crites, 1969), was considered unreliable and, therefore, invalid for predicting their eventual occupation (e.g., Berdie, 1950; Darley & Hagenah, 1955; Super & Crites, 1962). Since the late 1960s, however, when Holland and Lutz (1968) compared expressed interests with the Vocational Preference Inventory (VPI), regard for the predictive validity of expressed interests has increased greatly. The Holland and Lutz study indicated a much higher "hit rate" for expressed interests than the VPI against a common criterion of career choice 8 months later. With an interval of 3 years, Borgen and Seling (1978) essentially replicated this finding using the Strong Vocational Interest Blank (SVIB). And, in a review of relevant research on the comparative predictive validity of expressed and inventoried interests, Dolliver (1969, pp. 103–104) concluded:

> The predictive validity of expressed interests is at least as great as the predictive validity of SVIB. In no study where direct comparison was made (Dyer, 1939; Enright & Pinneau, 1955; McArthur & Stevens, 1955) was the SVIB as accurate as the expressed interests in predicting occupation engaged in. . . . There is no evidence to show that the SVIB is superior to expressed interests.

The implication of these results and conclusions certainly is that expressed interests should be elicited in any thorough appraisal of adult career capabilities and that they should be given at least as much weight as inventoried interests.

Inventoried Interests

The question that immediately arises then, is why administer interest inventories, given that expressed interests are more predictive? There are at least two answers to this question: First, some individuals want to take an interest inventory to confirm (or reality test) their expressed interests. When inventoried and expressed interests are the same, their combined predictive efficiency is considerably greater than that of either separately, but when they differ, expressed interests are, of course, the better predictor in most cases (Borgen & Seling, 1978). Second, about 20–25% of adults in the career decision-making process are undecided and therefore have no expressed interests. For these individuals, interest inventories serve the very worthwhile purpose of stimulating them to explore areas of interest similarity.

At the professional, semiprofessional, and managerial/white collar occupational levels, the most widely used interest inventory is the Strong Interest Inventory (SII), but the Kuder Occupational Interest Survey (KOIS) is also highly recommended. Interpretation of the SII is sometimes complicated by the percentages of Like, Indifferent, and Dislike responses, particularly if the latter is high, because the General Occupational Theme and Basic Interest Scales are scored $+1$ for Likes and -1 for Dislikes. A strong Dislike response tendency produces, therefore, low scores on these scales, but high scores on some occupational scales such as Mathematician that are keyed to a high percentage of Dislikes (the so-called "doubting" attitude of the scientist). The SII also poses problems in the interpretation of cognate male/female scales when an individual scores higher on the opposite sex scale (Crites, 1978). The KOIS, on the other hand, avoids this difficulty because of its different construction (occupation vs. occupation as compared with occupation vs. in-general groups), but it is often awkward to explain Lambda scores to clients without a lengthy discussion that interferes with the test interpretation process (Crites, 1982).

At the nonprofessional occupational levels, the best available measure is the Career Assessment Inventory (CAI), which is formatted after the SII but with occupations largely within the semiskilled range, although this has been extended upward in the new Enhanced Version. Some of the same problems in interpretation occur with it as with the SII, particularly if response percentages are extreme. At the lower levels in the occupational hierarchy, there is no inventory directly applicable to unskilled and some semiskilled jobs. As Strong (1943) pointed out many years ago and Darley and Hagenah (1955) reiterated, *vocational* interests at these levels are largely undifferentiable. Rather, it is preference for different work environments or job conditions that is important to individuals. Crites (in process) is currently constructing an inventory of these preferences that assesses such dimensions as indoor-outdoor, clean-dirty, and noisy-quiet. This type of interest inventory has particular potential usefulness with unskilled and unemployed adults.

Work Needs

The extensive and long-term research of the Work Adjustment Project at the University of Minnesota, under the leadership of Dawis & Lofquist (1984), has produced several instruments to measure the variables in their "Theory of Work Adjustment." Not the least of these is the Minnesota Importance Questionnaire. It measures 20 needs, which are grouped into six general categories of work values: Achievement, Comfort, Status, Altruism, Safety, Autonomy. Also listed with each need are the corresponding "Work-Related Reinforcers" that satisfy them on-the-job. The rationale for the MIQ is that individuals gain greater job satisfaction, and ultimately accrue greater tenure, if their needs are fulfilled by the appropriate occupational reinforcer patterns (ORPs). The MIQ profile indicates high and low needs that are interpreted according to these patterns. Reliability and validity data on the MIQ are limited but encouraging. The MIQ's careful development and theoretical significance certainly justify its widespread use in appraising the career capabilities of adults.

Job Satisfaction

There are two major measures of job satisfaction: the Hoppock Job Satisfaction Blank (JSB) Form 5, and the Job Descriptive Index (JDI). The first of these, the JSB, provides a *global* assessment of job satisfaction based upon the individual's overall "hedonic tone" toward work (Crites, 1969). Four 7-point scale items ask workers how much they like their jobs, whether they want to change their work, and so forth. The total score is an expression of job satisfaction in relation to dissatisfaction. In contrast, the JDI uses the *summative* method to elicit satisfaction with five different facets of the work situation: (1) work on present job, (2) present pay, (3) opportunities for promotion, (4) supervision on present job, and (5) people on your present job. The assumption is that a worker can be differentially satisfied with these various components of the work environment, but provision is also made with the JDI for summing the part-scores to obtain a total job satisfaction score, which correlates highly with the JSB.

PERSONALITY INVENTORIES

Unlike ability tests and vocational interest measures whose items directly sample the context of the world of work, personality inventories come from a different tradition. There is no available inventory of *work* personality. Rather, there are several instruments, constructed for other purposes, that have been applied to the assessment of personality in the work environment. Their validity for the appraisal of the adult work personality, therefore, is indirect at best. But, some of them have demonstrated usefulness for career counseling and career workshops with adults, and they are reviewed and critically evaluated here. Four personality inventories have been sufficiently researched for career purposes to include in this discussion: (1) the California Psychological Inventory; (2) the Edwards Personal Preference Schedule; (3) the Myers-Briggs Type Indicator; and (4) the Sixteen Personality Factor Inventory (16PF).

California Personality Inventory (CPI)

Of the personality measures available for assessing adult personality, the CPI is probably the most appropriate and the most extensively researched. In a recent revision (Gough, 1987), 18 items from the original 480 were dropped (12 of which were repeated items), and 29 other items were changed in wording to update them, leaving a total of 462 items in the current edition. The CPI was originally standardized and validated to measure "folk concepts" of personality, such as dominance (Do) and good impression (Gi). Factor analysis indicates that these are the principal dimensions of the normal personality (Crites, Bechtoldt, Goodstein, & Heilbrun, 1961). They focus on how individuals deal with interpersonal relations, a behavioral domain that is critical to adult career adjustment. The findings of many studies (Crites, 1969; 1982) establish that more employees lose their jobs because of problems in interpersonal relations than for any other reason. In other words, coping with others on the job (superiors, subordinates, co-workers) is more important in career success than competence for job performance, at least above a minimal level. The CPI offers an objective measurement of interpersonal areas that might directly impinge upon job adjustment. Low scores on CPI scales in both "Class I. Measures of Poise, Ascendancy, Self-Assurance, and Interpersonal Adequacy" and "Class II. Measures of Socialization, Responsibility, Intrapersonal Values, and Character" are often diagnostic of potential difficulties in human relations at the workplace. Two-scale analyses of these measures have also been related to discriminating self-descriptive adjectives, and means and standard deviations for various occupational groups are given in the *Manual* (1975). To augment and extend the interpretation of the CPI, the revised edition presents a conceptual schema based on factor analytically derived "Vectors." It has also added two scales— Empathy and Independence—to the previous 18 scales.

Edwards Personal Preference Schedule (EPPS)

In contrast to the CPI, the EPPS was constructed to measure variables from an explicit personality theory—Murray's (1938) system of needs. The 15 need scales of the EPPS (e.g., Autonomy, Dominance, Order, etc.) are not organized, however, into a readily interpretable conceptual schema. To provide such a framework, Crites (1981) arranged the needs into a circumplex that defines Horney's (1945) major orientations in interpersonal relations: (a) moving toward people, (b) moving against people, and (c) moving away from people. Used with these constructs, the EPPS gains increased diagnostic significance for identifying possible human relations problems of adult workers. There is growing evidence, for example, that employees more frequently lose their jobs because they are nonassertive than because they are aggressive. In the circumplex (Figure 2), the EPPS Abasement and Deference scales define a self-effacing personality that may experience interpersonal problems on-the-job because of nonassertiveness and an indiscriminate tendency to move toward people. Other configurations of scores identify orientations that are likely to create different job adjustment problems. In interpreting these patterns, it is important to remember that the EPPS is ipsative, in other words, has a "forced-choice" response format, and consequently only high and low scores *within* the individual should be reported. Normative interpretations are not appropriate.

Figure 2
EPPS Circumplex for Appraisal of Work-Related Interpersonal Orientations.

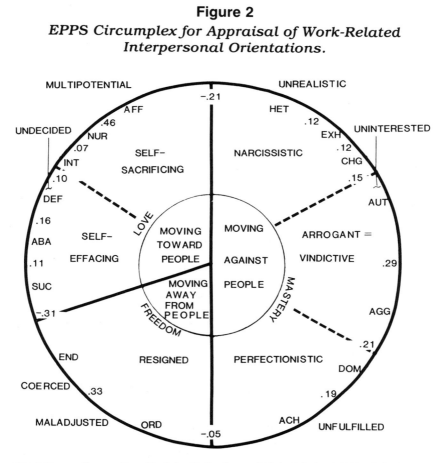

From *Career Counseling: Models, Methods, and Materials* (p. 100) by J.O. Crites, 1981, New York: McGraw-Hill. Copyright 1981 by McGraw-Hill, Inc. Reprinted by permission.

Myers-Briggs Type Indicator (MBTI)

During the past decade, after a 20-year hiatus, interest in the MBTI, concurrent with a revival of Jungian psychology, has increased, and there is accruing research on it, as well as new applications in business and industry (Hirsch, 1984). The MBTI was originally designed to operationally define the major constructs in Jung's theory of personality. It yields scores on four bipolar dimensions representing these variables: (1) Extraversion-Introversion; (2) Thinking-Feeling; (3) Intuition-Sensing; and (4) Judgment-Perception. From combinations of scores on these basic personality orientations, types are derived that indicate the individual's dominant modes of interacting with the world. These obviously are relevant to the work environment and suggest how an adult worker might best fit into a compatible occupational role (Hirsch, 1984). To use the MBTI for the appraisal of adult career capabilities, however, it is essential to have a thorough understanding of the Jungian concepts it measures. Its usefulness is largely "clinical," although there are studies of it for different occupational groups. The Center for Applications of Psychological Type in Gainesville, Florida, offers the relevant training for professionals through a variety of seminars and workshops and also holds an annual national conference.

Sixteen Personality Factor Questionnaire (16PF)

This instrument is included here because it is widely known and has norms for over 50 occupational groups, as well as regression equations for predicting job performance criteria. The 16PF nevertheless has some serious shortcomings (Buros, 1978). First, despite its factorial construction and its name, there is considerable disagreement from one study to another on exactly how many factors there are in the 16PF—some results indicate fewer, others more. Second, the factors measured by presumably equivalent forms have average intercorrelations of cognate scales only in the .50s—hardly support for equivalence. Third, the internal consistencies of the factor scores are also low, again averaging in the .50s. And, fourth, although there are numerous validity studies of the 16PF, there is no consistent pattern of results that supports either its convergent or divergent validity. In conclusion, then, if the 16PF is used with adults, for whom extensive norms are available, caution should be exercised in making other than descriptive statements (i.e., this individual is high, average, or low on the several scales).

A MICROCOMPUTER SYSTEM FOR APPRAISING ADULTS' CAREER CAPABILITIES

With the advent of the microcomputer in recent years and its widespread availability to measurement and counseling professionals, unlimited possibilities have opened up for formulating a systems approach to educational and vocational assessment, both intellective and nonintellective. In the past, career counselors and personnel managers have had to rely on largely subjective procedures for comparing an individual's test scores with profiles of traits required by occupations. With over 12,000 different occupations in the world of work, the best that could be done was to make general judgments about occupational "fitness." Usually, a visual comparison of the client's or employee's test scores with rationally derived occupational profiles, such as the Revised Minnesota Occupational Rating Scales and Worker Trait Requirements for 4,000 Jobs, was made. Seldom was it possible to derive quantitative indices of similarity between person and position.

However, the microcomputer has made possible such quantitative comparisons, and it is far from having realized its full potential. One problem has been that most computerized test interpretations are printed out in lengthy, and often discursive, narratives. One interpretive printout for the Strong-Campbell Interest Inventory actually runs 29 fanfold pages. Not only is it difficult to read, often being loaded with psychometric jargon, but it inhibits the test interpretation process, particularly in career counseling. Obviously, what is needed is a test report form that can be printed from the microcomputer and easily interpreted, in either individual or group career counseling sessions. Another problem, even more critical for the efficacy of the interpretative process, is the passive-receptive mode of the narrative printouts. Much more desirable would be an active-participative interaction between the individual and the test report. Such a mode should be based on a programmed instructional design that involves the client in the test interpretation.

In response to what seems to be a clear need for a microcomputer system that interprets test results in a meaningful and interactive way, a model was formulated that not only addresses these problems but also relates the testing process to assessment and career development theory. Figure 3 graphically depicts a career-counseling system designed to meet these specifications. It represents two parallel levels of discourse—"Theory" and "Testing"—both of which are further delineated into "Career Choice Process" and "Career Choice Content." Although the former is not discussed in this chapter (see Crites, 1984, cited earlier), it is included here to give a comprehensive overview of the entire theory and testing model.

On the Theory level, career choice process has been conceptualized as involving certain Attitudes and Competencies that must be sufficiently mature for an individual to make a realistic career choice (content). The attitudes of involvement, independence, orientation, compromise, and decisiveness are more connative or dispositional in nature, whereas the competencies of self-appraisal, occupational information, goal selection, planning, and problem solving are cognitive capabilities (Crites, 1978). On the Testing level, these career choice process variables have been measured by the Career Readiness Inventory (CRI), which is a wide-range measure (grades 9 to 12, adult) of attitudes and competencies derived from 25 years of research on the Career Maturity Inventory (CMI) (Crites, 1978, 1984). The CRI can be either hand- or machine-scored, and profiled and interpreted with a self-administered booklet called the *Career Developer*, which is based on programmed instructional principles. If scores are high enough (above statistically established cut-offs), the individual

Figure 3
A Systems Approach to Career Counseling

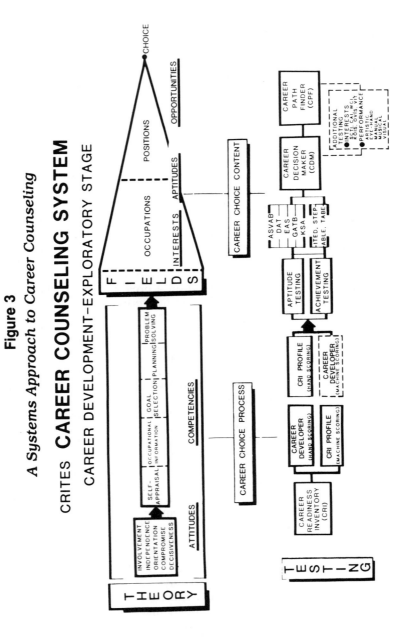

CRITES **CAREER COUNSELING SYSTEM**

CAREER DEVELOPMENT–EXPLORATORY STAGE

is presumably mature enough in career choice process to proceed to career choice content. If not, then further intervention (individual or group career guidance) is indicated.

On the Theory level, arriving at career choice content involves what has been termed the "exclusion process." Choices are progressively made from broad Fields through Occupations to Positions by eliminating career options that the individual dislikes. These negative decisions are based on an appraisal of interests, aptitudes, opportunities, and a variety of other personal and environmental factors. On the Testing level, the individual takes achievement tests, multifactor aptitude batteries, interest inventories, and other measures to assess manual dexterity and special talent (artistic and musical), if needed, to supplement the overall educational and vocational assessment procedure.

Protocols from these tests and measures are then processed on the microcomputer system, which consists of an NCS Sentry 3000 Scanner, an IBM PC-XT, and a compatible printer. Answer sheets are scanned by the Sentry 3000 and item responses fed into the IBM PC-XT for scoring. For the multifactor aptitude batteries, scores are compared with the extensive General Aptitude Test Battery database for Occupational Aptitude Patterns (OAPs), and those for which the individual is qualified are printed out on the Career Decision Maker (CDM). The CDM (Figure 4) is a programmed test interpretation form that takes the individual, step by step, through a survey of expressed-ranked interests, using Holland's RIASEC taxonomy; aptitude score presentation in relation to Level of Educational Development; and a synthesis of choices, interests, general intelligence, and special aptitudes (OAPs) on the "Career Choice Chart."

The chart is cross-referenced to the *Guide for Occupational Exploration* (GOE), published by the United States Employment Service, and to the *Career Path Finder* (CPF), the last component in the system. The CPF lists occupations indexed in the GOE, classified by RIASEC category. The CPF also provides charts for planning education or training over a five-year period for the individual's two most preferred career choices, taking into consideration interests, intelligence, special aptitudes, and other personal/social characteristics. Both the CDM and CPF have been used in individual and group career counseling with highly positive results. They are applicable to adults in organizational career development programs, outplacement workshops for dislocated workers, and employment services. Because of the systems approach used, implemented with the scanner-microcomputer-printer in-line processing, and the programmed instructional forms designed for active involvement and personal understanding, the delivery base for this career counseling model is extensive and comprehensive.

CONCLUSION

This chapter has presented a review of ability, interest, and personality appraisal instruments that may be used in the career counseling of adults. The instruments presented represent both an objective review of scientific findings and the subjective experience of the author with the instruments. The instruments discussed are those which the author

Figure 4
Career Decision Maker

CAREER
DECISION
MAKER

STEPS IN CHOICE

Step **1** Rank your INTERESTS

Step **2** Know your APTITUDES

Step **3** Make your CHOICE

INTRODUCTION

CAREER DECISION MAKING is a 3 step process (⟶) based upon your APTITUDES, INTERESTS, and CHOICES. From the tests you recently took, this form gives you information about your GENERAL APTITUDE, as well as your SPECIAL APTITUDES in relation to many occupations. It also surveys your INTERESTS and CHOICES and relates them to your APTITUDES as a basis for making career decisions.

It emphasizes making career decisions based upon ALL your capabilities and characteristics. Consider your hobbies, work experience, recreational activities, and other resources. Also explore training programs and further education, necessary to qualify for the careers you choose. Consider not only possible careers for the present but also the future. NOW, turn this page over and rank your INTERESTS (⟶) first.

84

1 INTERESTS

The 1ST STEP in making a career choice is to inventory your interests in different career fields. Your interests, in contrast to your aptitudes, are what you LIKE to do. Six broad areas of interests are defined to the right (→). They describe the major focus of the work in each field, the characteristics of people who work in each field, and the nature of the work in each field and where it is usually performed. Read each description and decide how closely you would fit into that career field. Would you enjoy the work, are you similar to the workers, and do the working conditions appeal to you? The more your interests match those of a career field, the greater your chances of staying in it and being satisfied with it. After reading the descriptions of the career fields, rank them according to your preferences, following the directions below (↓) where it says INTEREST RANKINGS.

INTEREST RANKINGS

Rank your interests in the different career fields from high to low. Write a "1" on the opposite line (→) for the field you like most, a "2" for the one you like next, and so on to a "6" for the field you like least.

R EALISTIC occupations deal mostly with things. The activities in them are practical and concrete. They involve using tools, machines, and raw materials. They are often technical, and many of them are outdoors. People in these occupations are described as frank, honest, persistent, modest, stable, practical, and thrifty. The working conditions are bodily active, outdoors, and sometimes noisy and hazardous. Limited social interaction.

I NVESTIGATIVE occupations solve problems in a systematic, often scientific way. They focus on ideas and creating new products and services. Sometimes laboratory equipment is used, and usually written reports are made. People in these occupations are described as analytical, critical, curious, intellectual, methodical, precise, rational and reserved. The working conditions are typically clean, indoors, and sedentary. Some social interaction.

A RTISTIC occupations usually require a special talent in graphic art, music, writing, performing, or photography. Artistic expression is highly individual and creative. It is original and may be unconventional. People in these occupations are described as expressive, imaginative, impulsive, intuitive, original, idealistic, and nonconforming. The working conditions are usually clean, both indoors and outdoors, quiet, and non-hazardous. Minimal social interaction.

S OCIAL occupations assist people to solve their problems, to provide them services, or to teach them. They assist people as individuals or in groups to make decisions, to stay well, to participate in recreational activities, and to generally live better. People in these occupations are described as cooperative, friendly, helpful, kind, sociable, and understanding. The working conditions are typically clean, both indoors and outdoors, non-hazardous, quiet and sedentary. Considerable social interaction.

E NTERPRISING occupations sell products and offer services. They may involve administration and management or professional politics, buying, marketing, and advertising. Key activities are directing and planning. People in these occupations are described as ambitious, energetic, optimistic, self-confident, popular, sociable, and sometimes adventurous. The working conditions are usually clean, social, and varied. They are both indoor and outdoor, sometimes involving travel.

C ONVENTIONAL occupations are mostly routine and repetitive. They are highly structured. Record-keeping, accounting, calculating, filing and typing, and date processing are central duties and tasks. Accuracy in detail is expected. People in these occupations are described as dependable, careful, conservative, orderly, persistent, practical and efficient. The working conditions are clean, indoors, non-hazardous, quiet, and sedentary. Some social interaction.

Adapted from Holland J. L. (1979) The Self Directed Search, Professional Manual 1979 Ed. Palo Alto CA Consulting Psychologists Press

R	I	O	A	S	E	C

Mark your Interest Rankings in the above boxes. ● Press firmly to make a copy on the following page.

Now, go on to the next page and read about your APTITUDES

2 APTITUDES

The 2ND STEP in making a career choice is assessing your aptitudes for further education, specific vocational preparation, and different occupations. Your aptitudes give you an estimate of what you CAN do. Reported below are combinations of your test scores called composites, which can give you an idea of (1) what you might

expect your Level of Educational Development to be, and (2) which Occupational Aptitudes you may have. Your actual score is reported where it says "T-Score". Since scores are not perfect, however, the range your score falls in most of the time is indicated by the band of XXXXX's.

NAME _____

I.D. _____

AGE _____

EDUCATION YRS _____

JOB _____

EXPERIENCE YRS _____

LEVEL OF EDUCATIONAL DEVELOPMENT

How far you go in school is called your Level of Educational Development (LED). There are four levels, which are defined below. DECIDE how far you can go with your GENERAL APTITUDE, as well as study habits, motivation, financial support, etc.

GENERAL APTITUDE

T-SCORE	70	80	90	100	110	120	130
LED LEVELS	1		2	3		4	

4 — College or University (4 years or more)
Use logic and abstract concepts in thinking.
Study advanced mathematics or statistics.
Read literature or scientific journals.
Write books and use theory.

3 — College (2 to 4 years)
Use logical principles or scientific method.
Apply algebra or statistics in problem solving.
Read literature or scientific journals.
Learn persuasive communication in educated speech.

2 — Business – Technical School (1 to 2 years)
Apply principles of bookkeeping, navigation, wiring, etc.
Use geometry, algebra, or shop mathematics.
Learn drawing or mechanical drafting.
Study applied physics (for example, mechanics).

1 — High School (4 years or less)
Follow written or oral instructions.
Use common sense understanding.
Read manuals, rules, or instructions.
Make computations and calculations.

The higher your GENERAL APTITUDE score, the better your chances for completing education. At LED level 4, you probably do not need specific vocational preparation, except in certain occupations, as indicated by their Occupational Aptitude level 3. At LED level 3, some of you will need some college or terminal degree programs and possibilities. At LED level 2, business and technical schools offer as well as a full four-year major. At LED level 2, business and technical schools offer

OCCUPATIONAL APTITUDE FACTORS

Occupations differ in the aptitudes they require for success in them. Special aptitudes that are important in most occupations are defined below. Note which of your FACTOR SCORES are high and low as they relate them to your GENERAL APTITUDE and LEVEL OF EDUCATIONAL DEVELOPMENT (LED) (Note that you may have fewer scores reported than there are Factors because of the number of tests in the battery you took).

VERBAL — The ability to comprehend language, to recognize relationships between words and to understand sentences

T-SCORE	70	80	90	100	110	120	130

NUMERICAL — The ability to perform arithmetic operations quickly and accurately

T-SCORE	70	80	90	100	110	120	130

SPATIAL — The ability to visualize figures and shapes in two- and three-dimensional space

T-SCORE	70	80	90	100	110	120	130

CLERICAL — The ability to see details in words and numbers quickly and accurately

T-SCORE	70	80	90	100	110	120	130

FORM PERCEPTION — The ability to see slight differences in shapes and shadings of figures and widths and lengths of lines

T-SCORE	70	80	90	100	110	120	130

MOTOR COORDINATION — The ability to coordinate eyes and hands rapidly and accurately in making motor movements

T-SCORE	70	80	90	100	110	120	130

FINGER DEXTERITY — The ability to move the fingers and manipulate small objects with the fingers rapidly and accurately

T-SCORE	70	80	90	100	110	120	130

MANUAL DEXTERITY — The ability to move the hands easily and skillfully and to work with the hands in placing and turning motions

T-SCORE	70	80	90	100	110	120	130

Many specialized training programs over shorter periods of time. At LED level 1, apprenticeship training and on-the-job training (OJT) are options the higher your FACTOR SCORES, the greater your chances for success in occupations using those special aptitudes. Often occupations require more than one special aptitude—what is called an OCCUPATIONAL APTITUDE PATTERN. Your pattern of FACTOR SCORES has been compared with those of many different occupations. See your CAREER CHOICE CHART (next page) for those career fields and levels you are most similar to in your OCCUPATIONAL APTITUDES. ➤

3 CHOICE

YOUR CAREER CHOICES

IF YOU HAVE ONE OR MORE CAREER CHOICES—OCCUPATIONS YOU MIGHT ENTER WITH OR WITHOUT FURTHER TRAINING—LIST THEM BELOW:

_____

_____

_____

_____

After you finish charting your career choice on this page, compare the career choices you just listed with the occupations suggested by your chart. Sometimes they are the same, sometimes different. If they are different, you may want to change them to agree more with your aptitudes and interests.

LED	CAREER LEVELS
4 College or University (4 years or more)	At this level, you need GENERAL APTITUDE at 110 or above in most Career Fields. Some OC-CUPATIONAL APTITUDES with a minimum from 105 to 110 are also essential in certain fields. For the other fields at this level, a college degree and often professional graduate training are necessary
3 College (2 to 4 years)	At this level, you need GENERAL APTITUDE at or above 100 for a college education. You also need special OCCUPATIONAL APTITUDES in many of the Career Fields. Look for the squares with occupational titles and code numbers in them. Your aptitude patterns are most similar to those required by these occupational groups.
2 Business Technical Schools (1-2 years)	At this level, you need GENERAL APTITUDE in the 90 to 100 range for most business colleges and technical institutes. In addition, special OCCUPA-TIONAL APTITUDES are often essential. Your's are most similar to those required by the occupational groups identified by the names and code numbers printed in the squares.
1 High School (4 years or less)	At this level, you need GENERAL APTITUDE sufficient to finish high school or the equivalent. Special OC-CUPATIONAL APTITUDES are needed in some fields. If you have them, the names and code numbers for the occupational groups you most resemble are printed in the squares. Most occupations at this level, however, are learned on-the-job (OJT) or in short courses given by employers.

The 3RD STEP in making a career choice is to relate your AP-TITUDES to your INTERESTS. Consider FIRST the range of your GENERAL APTITUDE, plotted on the boxes below the different career CAREER LEVELS You are qualified for all occupations within this range which require no special aptitudes. If you also qualify for occupations at this Level which require special OCCUPATIONAL APTITUDES, their names and code numbers from the Guide for Occupational Exploration (see below) are printed in the squares. Your chances for career SUCCESS are best at this LEVEL, in

These occupations NEXT note your INTEREST RANKINGS (1 to 6) from the previous page in the boxes below the different career fields (R, I, A, S, E, C). Your interest fields are where you are most likely to find career SATISFACTION NOW. With a pen or red pencil outline the squares where your three highest (1, 2, & 3) ranked interest FIELDS intersect your CAREER LEVELS and complete CHARTING your CAREER CHOICE, following the directions at the bottom of the page

CAREER CHOICE CHART

CAREER FIELDS Career fields are broad groupings of occupations which have common interests. The more your interests are similar to those of others in a career field, the better your chances for satisfaction in it. Combinations of them, such as Selling and Engineering might lead to a career as a Sales Engineer. And some occupations, for example Manager, which is classified as Conventional, are found in several different career fields. View your interests as signposts that give you direction. If you are unsure what your interests are, explore them further with an interest inventory. Also consider your personal characteristics, values, and previous experience.

GEN. APT.	REALISTIC	INVESTIGATIVE	ARTISTIC	SOCIAL	ENTERPRISING	CONVENTIONAL
120-30						
110						
100						
90						
70-80						
Interest rankings	R	I	A	S	E	C
GOE	03, 04, 05, 06	02 (11)	01 (12)	09, 10, 11	08 (11)	07

The numerical codes shown above refer to occupational groups in the Guide for Occupational Exploration (GOE), which is explained below. They have been classified according to the RIASEC categories for easy cross-reference. If names and code numbers are printed in the squares of your CAREER CHOICE CHART, they refer to more specific occupational groupings which are also in the GOE.

To CHART your CAREER CHOICE look for the occupational groups where your Career Fields and Levels agree most. These are the squares you outlined in pen or red pencil. NOTE also if you have Occupational Aptitudes in these squares. Where they are all in the same square and correspond to your CAREER CHOICES, your chances for SATISFACTION and SUCCESS are greatest. When they are in different squares, or when you are undecided, explore occupations which agree most with FIRST your General and Occupational Aptitudes and SECOND your in-

terest Fields. To learn about additional occupations that are options for you, use the Guide for Occupational Exploration published by the United States Employment Service (USES). Find the occupational codes in it that correspond most closely to your APTITUDES and INTERESTS. They will lead to the best Career Choices for you agree most with your Aptitudes and INTERESTS They will lead to the greatest SUCCESS and SATISFACTION in your CAREER considers the most pragmatic for career counseling practice. Readers are encouraged to continue the ongoing critical search for the most useful and scientifically sound tools for their professional practice.

REFERENCES

Berdie, R.F. (1950). Scores on the SVIB and the Kuder Preference Record in relation to self-ratings. *Journal of Applied Psychology, 34*, 42–49.

Borgen, F.H., & Seling, M.J. (1978). Expressed and inventoried interests revisited: Perspicacity in the person. *Journal of Counseling Psychology, 25*(6), 536–543.

Buros, O.K. (1978). *The eighth mental measurements yearbook.* Highland Park, NJ: Gryphon Press.

Crites, J.O. (1969). *Vocational psychology.* New York: McGraw-Hill.

Crites, J.O. (1978). *Theory and research handbook for the career maturity inventory.* (2nd ed.). Monterey, CA: CTB/McGraw-Hill.

Crites, J.O. (1981). *Career counseling: Models, methods, and materials.* New York: McGraw-Hill.

Crites, J.O. (1982). Testing for career adjustment and development. *Training and Development Journal, 36*, 20–24.

Crites, J.O. (1984). Instruments for assessing career development. In N.C. Gysbers & Associates, *Designing careers* (pp. 248–274). San Francisco: Jossey-Bass.

Crites, J.O., Bechtoldt, H.P., Goodstein, L.D., & Heilbrun, A.B., Jr. (1961). A factor analysis of the California Psychological Inventory. *Journal of Applied Psychology, 45*, 408–414.

Darley, J.G., & Hagenah, T. (1955). *Vocational interest measurement.* Minneapolis: University of Minnesota Press.

Dawis, R.V., & Lofquist, L.H. (1984). *A psychological theory of work adjustment.* Minneapolis: University of Minnesota Press.

Dolliver, R.H. (1969). Strong Vocational Interest Blank versus expressed vocational interests: A review. *Psychological Bulletin, 72*(2), 95–107.

Droege, R.C., & Padgett, A. (1979). Development of an interest-oriented occupational classification system. *Vocational Guidance Quarterly, 27*, 302–310.

Dyer, D.T. (1939). The relation between vocational interests of men in college and their subsequent histories for ten years. *Journal of Applied Psychology, 23*, 280–288.

Enright, J.B., & Pinneau, S.R. (1955). Predictive value of subjective choice of occupation and of the Strong Vocational Interest Blank over fifteen years. *American Psychologist, 10*, 424–425. (Abstract).

Gottfriedson, G.D., Holland, J.L., & Ogawa, D.K. (1984). *Dictionary of Holland occupational codes.* Palo Alto, CA: Consulting Psychologists Press.

Gough, H.G. (1987). *CPI Administrator's Guide.* Palo Alto, CA: Consulting Psychologists Press.

Gysbers, N.C., & Associates (1984). *Designing career.* San Francisco: Jossey-Bass.

Hirsch, S. (1984). *MBTI training guide*. Palo Alto, CA: Consulting Psychologists Press.

Holland, J.L., & Lutz, S.W. (1968). The predictive value of a student's choice of vocation. *Personnel and Guidance Journal, 46*, 428–436.

Horney, K. (1945). *Our inner conflicts*. New York: Norton.

Hunter, J.E. (1983). *Overview of validity generalization for the U.S. Employment Service*. Washington, DC: Division of Counseling and Test Development, Employment and Training Administration, U.S. Department of Labor.

Matarazzo, J.D. (1972). *Wechsler's measurement and appraisal of adult intelligence* (5th ed.). Baltimore: Williams & Wilkins.

McArthur, C., & Stevens, L.B. (1955). The validation of expressed interests as compared with inventoried interests: A fourteen-year follow-up. *Journal of Applied Psychology, 39*, 184–189.

Murray, H.A. (1938). *Explorations in personality*. New York: Oxford University Press.

Roe, A. (1956). *Psychology of occupations*. New York: Wiley.

Strong, E.K., Jr. (1943). *Vocational interests of men and women*. Palo Alto, CA: Stanford University Press.

Super, D.E., & Crites, J.O. (1962). *Appraising vocational fitness* (rev. ed.). New York: Harper & Row.

Sweetland, R.C., & Keyser, D.J. (1983). *Tests*. Kansas City, MO: Test Corporation of America.

Thompson, A.S., Lindeman, R.H., Super, D.E., Jordaan, J.P., & Myers, R.A. (1981). *Career development inventory: Vol. 1. User's manual*. Palo Alto, CA: Consulting Psychologists Press.

Thompson, A.S., Lindeman, R.H., Super, D.E., Jordaan, J.P., & Myers, R.A. (1982). *Career development inventory, supplement to user's manual*. Palo Alto, CA: Counseling Psychologists Press.

CHAPTER 6

Counseling Adults for Career Change

Lawrence Brammer
Department of Educational Psychology
University of Washington
Seattle, Washington

Philip Abrego
Independent Practice
Seattle, Washington

The purpose of this chapter is to explore counseling approaches for assisting adults in managing their career changes or transitions. First, a general model of the helping process will be presented. Second, developing and utilizing coping skills will be discussed. Finally, career development skills for negotiating career transitions will be delineated.

Counseling goals and approaches for career changers will vary depending on the individual and whether the client is preparing for an anticipated career change or reacting to a career transition which has already occurred. Preventive approaches will help clients prepare for career transitions by increasing their awareness of potential consequences and developing strategies for preventing or coping with such consequences. Clients who are currently experiencing or responding to past career transitions may need a counseling approach which focuses on developing skills to respond to external situational demands and manage their feelings related to the transitions.

The purpose of counseling is to help clients conceptualize and effectively pursue personally valued outcomes to their career transitions. This process involves increasing client self-efficacy expectations over potentially controllable goals and attainable outcomes while helping the client to emotionally disengage from losses over which little control is possible.

THE HELPING PROCESS

To discuss strategies for teaching coping skills to career changers, it is useful to review a general model of the helping process. Our model of career counseling places an emphasis on both establishing a therapeutic relationship with the client as well as on developing effective action strategies and interventions to facilitate change. This model is useful in many different counseling formats. The stages described are typical of the process, but they do not always occur in this exact sequence.

Building a Relationship

Initially, the goal of the counseling process is to form a positive relationship with the person seeking help. Because it is often difficult for adults to seek help, it is important to respect the courage and trust involved in asking for help. A counselor can encourage mutual trust and respect by being warm, empathetic, and genuine. Respect is also conveyed by careful listening, eye contact, speaking in the same language style as the other person, and allowing the expression of a wide range of affect and beliefs. Respect for the person is given when the counselor identifies, supports, and validates the efforts a client has made to solve his or her problems.

Identifying the Problem

The second stage of counseling involves identifying and clarifying the problem that the person is experiencing. In this stage, the counselor explores the presenting problem and seeks to learn the personalized meaning of the problem to the client. It is often useful to begin with a general question such as, "What brings you to counseling at this time?" If the person responds vaguely, it is helpful to ask whether there was a particular event that made the person decide to call to make a counseling appointment. Such events provide concrete experiences of frustration that can help clarify the present problem.

It is also helpful to learn about other aspects of the person's life. Learning about satisfactions and dissatisfactions in other life roles and about styles of coping with previous transitions can help the counselor and client explore the strengths and weaknesses in coping skills. Brammer, Shostrom, and Abrego (1989) have described in further detail a comprehensive career assessment that integrates information from the clients presenting problems, unique personal history, interpersonal style, and larger systemic context.

Gender-role conflicts are also an important area of problem assessment in career counseling. These culturally regarded expectations and behavior prescriptions for male and female roles can discourage men and women from developing and implementing certain abilities, interests, and personality characteristics. Gender-role expectations can create conflict between various life roles, impact the decision-making process, and limit the range of career choices perceived by women and men. For example, many women are socialized to expect that all women should engage in child rearing and that child rearing is either antithetical to or should take precedence over career development.

This information is useful in making a mutual assessment about whether this transition is primarily a career transition or reflects other developmental conflicts. The person and the counselor can then discuss the appropriate counseling interventions and formats to be utilized, as well as the client's expectations for counseling.

Facilitating Change

The third stage of counseling involves facilitating change. In this stage the person can identify, develop, and utilize new types of coping skills. Some people benefit by learning general transition skills, whereas others need mostly career-related skills. These coping strategies are presented later in this chapter.

Evaluation and Termination of Counseling

The last stage of counseling involves evaluation of the outcomes of counseling, and then termination. Accomplishments are summarized and future plans are formulated. The termination process can be phased out by less frequent meetings, and clients can be encouraged to make greater use of their own support systems. Groups often schedule follow-up meetings and may structure a "buddy system" of mutual support for a specified period of time.

DEVELOPING AND UTILIZING COPING SKILLS

The process of coping successfully with career transitions is facilitated by broad, flexible coping skills for managing life transitions. We believe that the greater the diversity of options in a person's behavioral repertoire, the less habitual their performance, and the more diverse are the future developmental trajectories available to that person (Ford & Ford, 1987). In this section various coping skills and strategies for assessing and teaching them will be described. It is important to match coping skills to the client's needs.

Basic Coping Skills for Managing Transitions

Although it is impossible to describe all forms of effective coping methods, some broad coping skills have been proposed that seem useful across a variety of transitions (Brammer & Abrego, 1981). The taxonomy listed in Table 1 can be useful in formulating therapeutic interventions and in designing groups for people in transition. Certainly other types of useful coping skills have been mentioned; however, those listed in Table 1 are emphasized as particularly useful to people in career transitions.

Category 1: Skills in perceiving and responding to transitions. The first group of skills relates to a person's perceptions and responses to transitions. Perceptions toward change have an important relationship to how people interpret events. Two important perceptions are (a) the acceptance of problematic situations as a normal part of living, and (b) a belief that each person has a variety of strengths that help him or her to cope with most of these situations effectively. When these beliefs are held, the individual gains an increased sense of self-control and self-esteem. Threats are no longer perceived as overwhelming.

These beliefs can be explored by discussing the person's reactions to previous life transitions. In this discussion, the counselor can validate

Table 1
Level 1 Basic Coping Skills for Managing Transitions

1. **Skills in perceiving and responding to transitions.**
   1.1 The person mobilizes a personal style of responding to change. He or she—
      1.11 Accepts the proposition that problematic situations consitute a normal part of life and that it is possible to cope with most of these situations effectively. (Perceived control over one's life)
      1.12 Recognizes the importance of describing problematic situations accurately. (Problem definition)
      1.13 Recognizes the values and limitations of feelings as cues to evaluate a change event. (Feelings description)
      1.14 Inhibits the tendency either to act impulsively or to do nothing when confronted with a problematic situation. (Self-control)
   1.2 The person identifies his or her current coping style. (Style of responding to change)

2. **Skills for assessing, developing, and utilizing external support systems.**
   2.1 The person can assess an external support system. He or she can—
      2.11 Identify his or her emotional needs during times of transition.
      2.12 Identify people in his or her life who provide for personal needs.
      2.13 Describe a personal support network in terms of physical and emotional proximity.
   2.2 The person can develop a personal network. He or she can—
      2.21 Seek sources (groups, organizations, locales) of potential support persons.
      2.22 Apply social skills to cultivate persons to meet identified needs.
   2.3 The person can utilize an established support network. He or she can—
      2.31 Develop strategies for spending time with persons considered most helpful.
      2.32 Apply skills for utilizing persons in his or her network when a transition is anticipated or arrives.

Table 1 (Continued)

3. **Skills for assessing, developing, and utilizing internal support systems.**
   3.1 The person can assess the nature and strength of positive and negative self-regarding attitudes. He or she can—
      3.11 Identify personal strengths.
      3.12 Identify negative self-descriptive statements as well as the assumptions and contextual cues which arouse such statements.
   3.2 The person can develop positive self-regard attitudes. He or she can—
      3.21 Affirm personal strengths.
      3.22 Convert negative self-descriptions into positive descriptive statements when the data and criteria so warrant.
   3.3 The person can utilize his or her internal support system in a transition. He or she can—
      3.31 Construe life transitions as personal growth opportunities.
      3.32 Identify tendencies to attribute personal deficiencies as causative factors in distressful transitions.

4. **Skills for reducing emotional and physiological distress. He or she is able to—**
   4.1 Practice self-relaxation responses.
   4.2 Apply strategies to control over-stimulation/under-stimulation.
   4.3 Express verbally feelings associated with his or her experience of transition.

5. **Skills for planning and implementing change.**
   5.1 The person can analyze discrepancies between existing and desired conditions.
   5.2 The person exercises positive planning for new options. To the best of his or her abilities, the person—
      5.21 Thoroughly canvasses a wide range of alternative courses of action.
      5.22 Surveys the full range of objectives to be fulfilled and the values implied by the choice.
      5.23 Carefully weighs whatever he or she knows about the cost and risk of negative consequences that could flow from each alternative.
      5.24 Searches intensely for information relevant to further evaluation of the alternatives.
      5.25 Utilizes feedback to reassess his or her preferred course of action.
      5.26 Reexamines the positive and negative consequences of all known alternatives.
      5.27 Makes detailed provisions for implementing or executing the chosen course of action including contingency plans.
   5.3 The person is able to implement successfully his or her plans. He or she can—

5.31 Identify stressful situations related to implementing goals.

5.32 Identify negative self-statements which interfere with implementing plans.

5.33 Utilize self-relaxation routines while anticipating the stressful implementation of plans.

5.34 Utilize self-rewards in goal attainment.

5.35 Identify additional skills needed to implement goals (e.g., anxiety management, training in assertiveness, overcoming shyness).

the individual's strengths and coping skills. This is particularly important in situations where the career change is involuntary and people doubt their ability to cope with and survive the situation. They might also be asked to write an autobiography describing their life course with special emphasis on the coping skills that were helpful to them in the past. Sometimes information about developmental transitions as a normal part of life can also be useful. Readings such as *Seasons of a Man's Life* (Levinson, Darrow, Klein, Levinson, & McKee, 1978), *Passages* (Sheehy, 1976), or *Transformations* (Gould, 1978) might be suggested and discussed.

Several other important skills are included in this first category. These skills relate to one's initial response to threat. They include describing threats accurately, recognizing the role of feelings in appraising a situation, and inhibiting both impulsiveness and passivity. These skills in responding to transitions allow individuals to gain awareness of how they think, feel, and behave when confronted with problematic situations. People's reactions are important clues about transitions that signal a need to heed other data from the environment. Inhibiting impulsiveness or passivity allows one time to appraise a problem situation accurately and to construct a proactive and reasoned coping response (Kahara & Kahara, 1976).

Sometimes a person considering career change will complain vaguely about his or her job. It is useful to help such a person describe the situation, using specific behavioral language such as: "When my supervisor criticizes me, he calls me 'slow' in front of my coworkers and I feel humiliated." It is often helpful for the person to keep a journal describing the emotional high and low situations on the job. This can be used to clarify complaints about one's job as well as to discover elements that might be desirable in a new job. Some people may have difficulty understanding their feelings and thus are unable to use their feelings as cues. Self-monitoring of feelings could be assigned during different times of the day and a list of feeling words provided as an aid to identifying possible feelings.

People can create metaphors to describe their complaints. For example, one woman stated that she was a "kaleidoscopic thinker in a telescopic job." She explained that she usually thinks about all the different facets of a problem but that her job requires her to focus her attentions on only one facet at a time. Inhibiting the tendency to act impulsively or passively is important. Sometimes people cope with developmental challenges by running away from them through changing careers. For instance, one man said that he found himself changing jobs whenever he was on the verge of becoming successful. He was afraid to face his fear of failure, and he knew that if he were given a challenging responsibility he might fail. Consequently, by changing jobs he failed to resolve his fear of failure and was left with a nagging ambivalence about success. Other people can become immobilized by transitions and become overly passive. A woman who was terminated became so anxious about seeking another job that she could not leave her house.

By discussing previous transitions, it is possible for a person to become aware of her or his general coping style. It is often useful to have people write autobiographies of their current career transitions, describing each transition in detail from the moment they became aware of it to their current situation, and then finishing the description with several possible endings. This can help them recognize coping skills that have been useful to them and may instill a greater sense of having some choice about the eventual outcome. For example, a woman who considered leaving her job wrote one ending of a description in which she had a long discussion with her supervisor. The result was a restructuring of her work roles. In a second ending, she "networked" with professional colleagues and found a more suitable job with another organization. Her third ending involved changing her personal investment in her job. She imagined mentally letting go of some of the responsibilities that weighed her down with worry and then focusing on enjoyment that came from several key aspects of her job.

Category 2: Skills for assessing, building, and utilizing external support systems. Individuals in transition often need extra sources of emotional support during times of change. Skills for developing and utilizing an external social support network involve identifying one's emotional needs and then seeking specific people to serve in one's support network. This search results in intentionally planning to spend time with people who provide support or increasing the supportive quality of present relationships.

People often expect all of their support to come from a few people—typically a spouse or close friend of the family. Clients need to be urged to expand their social networks to include a variety of people, including some of Hopson's types (Hopson & Adams, 1977): (a) on whom we can depend in a crisis, (b) with whom to discuss concerns, (c) to whom we can feel close, (d) who can make us feel competent and valued, (e) who can give us important information, (f) who will challenge our stereotyped thinking, and (g) with whom we can share good news and feelings.

Counselors can help clients assess their support needs by asking them to list people in various categories, or to pictorially represent them, using a method described by Walters and Goodman (1981). Sometimes key support people such as family members can be included in the counseling. Individuals may be able to change the quality of support by rene-gotiating expectations.

People in career transitions who lack a support network, such as those who have made geographic moves and have left friendships in another community, may need to participate in formalized support groups generally consisting of individuals also involved in career transitions. Other groups, organized around various interests, provide support as a secondary benefit. These include groups where members share common interests in the outdoors, dancing, religious faith, or a variety of avocations.

Category 3: Skills for assessing, developing, and utilizing internal support systems. Internal support refers to "self-messages"—messages people give themselves about how they experience a transition. This internal self-talk provides critical or supportive messages during a transition. These internal thoughts and mental images allow people to remember and use past experiences in their current decisions and plans. However, their thoughts could function as "self-defeating instructions" also. This principle of self-instruction is true particularly for career changers who may unduly hamper themselves by fears of failure, low self-esteem, or inability to cope with frustrations.

Counselors can assist career changers in becoming more internally supportive in various ways. One method uses visualization to help them picture themselves as they would ideally like to be. As people relax, they are asked to picture themselves *in detail* feeling confident and happy, satisfied in their relationships with others, healthy, and spiritually at peace. They are asked to picture themselves in a variety of life roles, especially career roles, as they imagine feeling effective and well in each of these areas. As they visualize themselves behaving in the future, they are asked to notice as many details about themselves as they can. These include facial expressions, mannerisms, movements, voice tone, dress, eating habits, and interpersonal style, so that they can remember specific behavior whenever they want to remember the picture. Because this image represents an unattained ideal of themselves, they are asked to choose one or two details of this image to begin to implement in their lives. This might involve exercising daily, choosing healthful foods, or walking with greater confidence. People are introduced to the process of becoming the positive people they have imagined themselves to be.

A second useful strategy to help career changers develop internal support is to teach them about cognitive distortions that lead them to feel discouraged, depressed, and frustrated. Burns (1980) described 10 typical cognitive distortions of career changers. For example, they may catastrophize their job circumstance, disqualify their positive attributes, or think in ways that increase their fears and limit their positive responses to career transitions. People can learn to recognize these distortions in their own thinking and substitute a natural alternative for these thoughts.

Category 4: Skills for managing emotional and physiological distress. Selye (1974) stated that stress is a normal condition of meeting changes and threats with adaptive responses. Stress involves physiological changes (general adaptation syndrome) that may be experienced as either anxiousness (distress), or as pleasure (eustress). The task for each person is to find the optimum amount of stressful stimulation that is exhilarating and energizing, and yet that maintains a feeling of relation and flow. Each person must also seek a balance between alternating periods of stress and quietness. Skills in this fourth group of coping skills are intended to manage the stress effects often associated with transition.

Counselors can help career changers assess their responses to stress by discussing physiological, cognitive, emotional, and behavioral signs of distress. It is useful to elicit the methods the person has used previously to manage stress. He or she may have some useful methods of managing stress that are not being used at this time but that could be reactivated. Numerous strategies exist for managing stress. Muscle relaxation exercises, meditational breathing, cognitive restructuring, stress inoculation, and setting priorities are representative of these strategies.

It is important to note that not all approaches to stress management necessarily involve reducing stress. Some individuals lack sufficient stimulation to feel comfortable. Employees who are distressed because of occupational boredom, for example, may need to increase their activity level to manage stress.

Category 5: Skills for planning and implementing change. Personal transitions are usually accompanied by a desire to reassess one's current life style and to plan strategies for responding to the change constructively. Because of the importance of making effective decisions during transitions, some of the decision-making and implementing skills required have been specified.

Transitional decisions differ from routine life decisions because they involve the risk of suffering further loss. As a result of perceiving the potential risks, many people feel overwhelmed and experience acute choice conflict. This conflict is characterized by feelings of anxiety, hesitation, vacillation, and uncertainty. These feelings also may be accompanied by self-blame or a desire to escape from the situation (Lazarus, 1977).

Although there are various styles of decision making, skills in rational decision making are emphasized. According to Janis and Mann (1977), people who cope well under stressful conditions tend to utilize rational decision-making skills. The decisions of these people are more likely to lead to satisfactory outcomes than are those of people who use other methods. In contrast, poor decision making often leads to regrettable outcomes, feelings of helplessness or disappointment, and increased expectations of vulnerability.

The ability to identify and set life goals is key to clients involved in career decisions. Ford and Nichols (1987) have developed a useful taxonomy of personal goals according to desired consequences within the person and goals that refer to desired consequences for the relationship between the person and the environment. Examples of intrapersonal goals include affective goals (e.g., happiness, physiological well being), cognitive goals (e.g., understanding), and "subjective organization" goals (e.g., unity, transcendence). Person-environment goals, in contrast, reflect desired relationships between the individual and other people in the environment. Examples are social relationship goals (e.g., self assertion, integration, and belonging), and task goals (e.g., mastery, material gain). Interview procedures based on this taxonomy can be used in identifying a client's "core goals."

Counselors can also help career changers assess their decision-making skills by exploring previous decisions they felt were made effectively. From past experiences, people can clarify their typical decision-making styles, beliefs about risk taking, and abilities to implement plans.

Decision-making skills can be learned through various methods. Workbooks, such as those of Loughary and Ripley (1976), provide structures for applying rational decision-making skills to career decisions. Computer programs such as SIGI, DISCOVER and Careerpoint can be useful in clarifying trade-offs in contrasting career choices. Visualization can be used to imagine oneself implementing divergent career choices. Self-management skills such as using self-rewards for attaining goals can be practiced as one takes action to explore career alternatives.

Career Development Coping Skills

In addition to general transition coping skills, career changers often need specific career development coping skills. These skills can be grouped as skills in self-assessment, gaining occupational and work environment information, and conducting a job search.

Category 1: Self-assessment skills. Self-assessment skills involve the ability to identify one's goals, values, and abilities related to work. Career goals are generally based on analysis of skills and values. One's career skills and values are usually assessed by reviewing previous accomplishments, present interests, and future dreams. Many writers have described approaches to identifying values and skills. Bolles (1985, 1988), Haldane, (Germann & Arnold, 1980), Crystal and Bolles (1974), and Brammer and Humberger (1984) systematically reviewed life accomplishments, describing each accomplishment and then clustering skills that clients enjoyed using. Loughary and Ripley (1976) provided workbook exercises for identifying values and abilities. Interest tests such as the Strong Campbell Interest Inventory can provide another perspective on work interests.

Career skills are usually divided into three categories: self-management skills, transferable skills, and specific knowledge skills. *Self-management* skills refer to personal attributes or traits describing a person's style of responding to problems and demands. These skills can be of great importance to success in various occupations. They include being dynamic, versatile, responsible, perceptive, concerned, compassionate, candid, sensitive, reliable, warm, open-minded, and outgoing. Self-management skills can be identified from checklists based on autobiographies, interpersonal feedback, and certain psychological tests.

Transferable "functional" skills can be utilized across a variety of occupations. These skills include communicating, managing, reporting, planning, organizing, coordinating, leading, delegating, and instructing.

They can be clustered in various ways, such as data/people/things, or into Holland's categories. Transferable skills can be analyzed using materials developed by Bolles (1985), Crystal and Bolles (1974), and Haldane (Germann & Arnold, 1980).

Specific knowledge skills are the least transferable. They include specific knowledge or procedures that are useful in one field of work but are not always transferable to other occupations. A nurse's knowledge of anatomical terms, for example, would be a specific knowledge skill with limited transferability to other career fields. Specific knowledge skills are most often learned through formal education.

Category 2: Skills in learning about occupations, employers, and work environments. Once career changers have identified their category 1 career skills, they then need to gather information about occupations, employers, and work environments. The *Occupational Outlook Handbook*, the *Dictionary of Occupational Titles*, and professional or trade journals can provide useful occupational information. Additional occupational information about specific employers or work environments can be learned by networking and establishing personal contacts in organizations of interest. These personal contacts can then be interviewed for career information. A Department of Labor study reported that 54% of jobs are found through friends and relatives and another 31% are found through direct contacts. Only 5% were found through ads and 9% were found through a combination of school placement, state employment services, and private placement agencies (U.S. Department of Labor, 1981). Networking strategies have been described by Bolles (1979a), Germann and Arnold (1980), and Brammer and Humberger (1984).

Category 3: Skills in job search, career enhancement, and life-style change. When a career changer has targeted an occupational role, potential employer, and work environment in which to utilize her or his skills, the next step involves the career change. At this stage, it is often important to develop job search or career enhancement skills. Interviewing and writing resumes are particularly important. For career changers who remain in the same organization, other skills may be useful for career transfer or advancement. One man, for example, took an advanced management course to develop skills to enhance his chances of obtaining a promotion. Skills for interviewing and writing resumes have been described by Bolles (1988) and Brammer and Humberger (1984). Counselors can assist career changers by role playing interviews and reviewing resumes.

CONCLUSIONS

As mentioned at the beginning of this chapter, career changers will vary in their needs to develop new coping skills. The needs of voluntary changers will be different from involuntary career changers. Some people will benefit most from general coping skills and others will need primarily career-specific coping skills. It is hoped that the information presented in this chapter will help counselors working with adults with a variety of career concerns.

REFERENCES

Bolles, R. (1985). *The new quick job hunting map.* Berkeley: Ten Speed Press.

Bolles, R. (1988). *What color is your parachute?* Berkeley: Ten Speed Press.

Brammer, L., & Abrego, P. (1981). Intervention strategies for coping with transitions. *The Counseling Psychologist, 9*(2), 19–36..

Brammer, L., & Humberger, D. (1984). *Inplacement and outplacement counseling.* Englewood Cliffs, NJ: Prentice-Hill.

Brammer, L., Shostrom, E., & Abrego, P. (1989). *Therapeutic psychology: Fundamentals of counseling and psychotherapy.* Englewood Cliffs, NJ: Prentice Hall.

Burns, D. (1980). *Feeling good.* New York: Morrow.

Crystal, J., & Bolles, R. (1974). *Where do I go from here with my life?* Berkeley: Ten Speed Press.

Ford, M.E. & Nichols, C.W. (1987). A taxonomy of human goals and some possible applications. In Ford, D.M. & Ford, M.E. (Eds.) Humans as self constructing living systems: An overview (pp. 289–311). Hillsdale, NJ: Lawrence Erlbaum Associates.

Germann, R., & Arnold, P. (1980). *Bernard Haldane Associates' job and career building.* Berkeley: Ten Speed Press.

Gould, R. (1978). *Transformation: Growth and change in adult life.* New York: Simon & Schuster.

Hopson, B., & Adams, J. (1977). Toward an understanding of transition. In J. Adams & B. Hopson (Eds.), *Transition: Understanding and managing personal change* (pp. 3–25). Montclair, NJ: Allenhald and Osmund.

Janis, I., & Mann, L. (1977). *Decision making: A psychological analysis of conflict, choice and commitment.* New York: Free Press.

Lazarus, R.S. (1977). Cognitive processes in emotion and stress. In A. Monat & R. Lazarus (Eds.), *Stress and coping: An anthology* (pp. 145–158). New York: Columbia University Press.

Levinson, D.J., Darrow, C.N., Klein, E.B., Levinson, M.H., & McKee, B. (1978). *The seasons of a man's life.* New York: Knopf.

Loughary, J. & Ripley, T. (1976). *Career and life planning guide.* Chicago: Follett.

Selye, H. (1974). *Stress without distress.* Philadelphia: Lippincott.

Sheehy, G. (1976). *Passages: Predictable crises of adult life.* New York: Dutton.

U.S. Department of Labor, Manpower Administration. (1981). *Career thresholds.* (A training package of how people find jobs.) Monograph 16. Washington, DC: Superintendent of Documents.

Waters, E., & Goodman, J. (1981). I get by with a little help from my friends: The importance of support systems. *Vocational Guidance Quarterly, 29*(4), 362–369.

CHAPTER 7

Systematic Career Guidance and Computer-Based Systems

JoAnn Harris-Bowlsbey
Educational Technology Center
American College Testing
Hunt Valley, Maryland

Career development professionals need to make a distinction between computer-based career *information* systems and computer-based career *guidance* systems and how each can contribute toward the delivery of a systematic career guidance program. Once a conceptual base is defined for the utility and applicability of systems, the task of identifying needed counselor roles and understandings as well as strategies for incorporating computers into the program delivery process becomes less difficult. This chapter has three major purposes: (a) to suggest some assumptions and a generic model for the content of a career guidance program; (b) to draw distinctions between computer-based career *information* and career *guidance* systems; and (c) to relate these two types of systems to the generic model proposed for the specific purpose of defining areas that need counselor support and intervention.

BASIC ASSUMPTIONS OF A DEVELOPMENTAL CAREER GUIDANCE PROGRAM

In proposing a model for any activity, the model-maker must be working from a set of theoretical assumptions. Obviously, lack of acceptance of the assumptions may result in lack of acceptance of the model. For that reason the following clear statement of assumptions is set forth:

Assumption 1: Career guidance is a process, not a single or multiple choice-point event. A related assumption is that a career guidance program is also a process that can be systematic, rather than a single one-shot treatment or a series of same. Super (Super, 1953; Super, Starishevsky, Matlin, & Jordaan, 1963; Super & Thompson, 1979; Super, 1981) has elaborated on the maxistages and developmental tasks and behaviors of this process whereas Tiedeman (Tiedeman & O'Hara, 1963; Tiedeman & Peatling, 1977) has defined and described the ministages and decisions inherent in them. Career development, then, is a normal developmental process that will ideally result in appropriate vocational maturity (i.e., knowing how to cope with the career development tasks of each life stage) and in satisfying vocational choices.

One natural inference from this assumption is that mastering the process of meeting and making career choices is at least as important as the choice itself. In other words, our career guidance programs should be designed in such a way that a process of choice making is learned. Having mastered this process, the student/client/decider is outfitted for reinitiating the process throughout life whenever new choice making is required or desirable. A further inference is that evaluation of programs should not rest with comparing an occupational selection at point A with a job placement at point B to see if guidance effected a "good" decision, but rather with finding out if a process was learned at point A that could be applied again and again at Points B–Z.

Assumption 2: Good choice making (decision making) can only take place when the student/client/decider is in a state of readiness for doing so. The three predominant career choice and development theorists—Holland, Super, and Tiedeman—describe this "readiness" differently, but each is confident about its existence. Holland (1973) described it in terms of consistency (having interests and competencies that are correlationally related to each other on his hexagon) and differentiation (having some areas of interest and competency significantly higher than others). Super (1974, 1981) described it in terms of vocational maturity, that is, in terms of having high vocational maturity scores at least on attitudinal scales of the Career Development Inventory, specifically "Awareness of Need to Plan" and "Knowledge and Use of Resources." Tiedeman (Tiedeman & O'Hara, 1963; Tiedeman & Peatling, 1977) described it in terms of having gone through the anticipation stage of the decision-making process, that is, exploration, crystallization, tentative choice, and clarification.

An inference from these theorists is that attempting to move students and clients ahead to choice and implementation before a state of readiness has been achieved may be a waste of time and money. For Holland, a state of consistency and differentiation of interests and competencies must be achieved before "good" choices can be made. For Super, a higher-than-average degree of vocational maturity as measured by the attitudinal scales in his Career Development Inventory (Super & Bowlsbey, 1981) needs to be achieved before moving on to cognitive content from which choice emerges. For Tiedeman, the implementation stage of decision-making cannot be achieved without adequately going through the steps involved in the anticipation stage. For career guidance programs it means that elements must be built into programs to help accomplish these preliminary tasks to create the needed readiness for choice.

Assumption 3: Clear, realistic knowledge of self—especially preferred interests, strong competencies, and values—is a necessary prerequisite to vocational choices. Again, each of the major theorists addresses this topic in his own words. For Holland (1973) the choice of an occupation should be the congruent implementation of a consistent, well-differentiated code as measured on his Self-Directed Search (SDS) or Vocational Preference Inventory (VPI). The code is a simple statement of an individual's interests, competencies, and desired rewards. For Super (Super, Starishevsky, Matlin, & Jordaan, 1963; Super, 1980; 1981), the choice of an occupation should be the implementation of a self-concept. For Tiedeman, (Tiedeman & O'Hara, 1963; Tiedeman & Peatling, 1977) it should be a statement of self-identity.

Ideally, all individuals would have the luxury of such self-actualization through work. In the reality of vocational choice and compromise, many individuals may not be able to actualize self ideally through work alone due to the economy, shifts in work force caused by rapid technological change, and high unemployment. For many, this ideal self-actualization may have to take place in life roles—such as parent, spouse, homemaker, citizen, leisurite (Super, 1980)—other than worker or at least partially so. Nonetheless, focused self-knowledge is essential and prerequisite to utilization of interests, abilities, and values in any combination of life roles.

Assumption 4: Career and world of work information is likewise a necessary prerequisite to satisfying vocational choice. Parsons (1909) said it at the beginning of the vocational guidance movement, and none of the theorists would minimize it today. Holland (1973) said that individuals have to know which occupations are congruent with their personal codes. Super (1974) said that one has to process career information, world of work information, and specific occupational information to be vocationally mature. In Super's terms, career information refers to general information about the roles that make up career and the types of career patterns that one may design or fall subject to. World of work information refers to knowledge of the structure and interrelationships of occupations. Occupational information refers to knowledge of facts about job tasks, training, employment outlook, salary, and the like for specific occupations. Though it's as old as Parsons, it bears repeating that students/clients must acquire cognitive knowledge of a structure for organizing occupations, of general career development principles, and of basic facts about occupations that bear exploration.

Assumption 5: The catalyst that puts this all together as a workable system within an individual is decision-making skill. The need to make decisions is triggered by the awareness addressed in Assumption 2. The knowledge of self and of the outside world is the grist in the mill of decision making. The power for the mill is an internalized process of decision making that gives the individual control over the decisions and their outcomes as well as over the compromises that will inevitably have to be made. The decision-making process provides the structure for choice and the linkages needed between self-information and world of work/ occupational/career information. From these linkages flow a list of alternatives for further exploration, including reality testing.

Assumption 6: Implementation is not an activity unto itself, but should be a late step in the guidance process. Implementation behavior, such as applying for financial aid, college entrance, entry into the military or apprenticeships, or job seeking should flow from the previous steps of the process described here.

A GENERIC MODEL FOR SYSTEMATIC CAREER GUIDANCE

Although models must usually be presented in such a way that one step logically follows another (and this model will be presented that way, too) the linear sequence of these steps is not that clear-cut, and some activities (such as acquiring self-information and world of work information) may be going on simultaneously. Based on the six assumptions stated previously, it seems that a developmental, systematic career guidance program has the following components:

Component 1: Development of readiness for career planning, information, and decision making. This may be the most difficult component of those described here. There has been very little recognition in the guidance field of the need for this component and even less research about how to develop it. Extensive research and development have been done (Super & Overstreet, 1960; Crites, 1971; Westbrook & Clary, 1967), however, to measure the level of existence of readiness, and this construct has been identified as a significant factor of vocational maturity. One possible outcome of such assessment is the design of differential career guidance programs for individuals of differing levels of readiness. A second possible outcome is the assignment of individuals with different levels of readiness to these differential treatments. Further, a third use of such assessment is for the measuring of the differing effects of different methods of career guidance treatment.

How can systematic, developmental career guidance programs foster readiness, or stated in another way, create awareness of the need to plan ahead? Some things seem clear, based on research in Charles County, Maryland (Super & Bowlsbey, 1981). First, the development of this awareness should be begun in the middle school years and is probably much more important than many of the activities currently included in career education. Second, parents have a large role in the development of these attitudes, and therefore the counselor should find ways to support the parent in this task. Third, time perspective or awareness of present-future relationships is a concept that grows with maturity; hence, the activities that are planned to foster it must be appropriate to the age level of the learners.

Creative work, not now existent, needs to be done to design appropriate activities for the development of readiness. These activities not only need to focus on awareness of need to plan and time perspective, but also on autonomy, internal locus of control, strength of self-concept, positive role models, exploration, information-seeking, and decision-making skill (Super & Bowlsbey, 1981).

Component 2: Acquisition of relevant self-data. Given the assumption that good vocational choice provides an outlet for self-variables such as interests, abilities, values, and personality traits, assisting the decision maker to become aware of these aspects of self in an organized way is critical. There are at least three modes in which such self-infor-

105

mation can be acquired by the decider. First, a knowledgeable theory-based counselor can ferret out these aspects of self and provide students/clients with structure through one-to-one interviews. Second, a variety of measurement instruments—inventories of interests and values and batteries of aptitude tests—can be administered. Through them an individual is compared to a theory-based schema, to norm groups of others of similar age, or to adults already in specific occupations. Third, a computer can be programmed to perform the same functions as the measurement instruments by providing on-line test administration, scoring, and interpretation. In each of the three modes of delivery, the key variable is that linkages be made between the individual's profile on these variables and the titles of occupations that relate to the individual's profile, as described in Component 3.

Component 3: Translation of self-data into information. Tiedeman (1970) made a distinction between "data" and "information." *Data* are a collection of facts, in this case, about the self. *Information* is data that have been personalized so that they inform the self about potential choice and paths of behavior. Starishevsky & Matlin (1963) referred to the same phenomenon as "translating *psychtalk* to *occtalk*," where "psychtalk" means a collection of fragments about the self and "occtalk" means occupational titles. I Corinthians may have stated the same principle as "Though I know all there is to know about self but cannot relate this knowledge to occupational choice, I am woefully destitute in relation to career planning."

The message is that any systematic career guidance program or material must assist the decider to make the linkage between relevant self-variables (interests, skills/aptitudes, values, goals) and occupational alternatives. Being able to do so implies an abundance of research to validate the linkages.

Component 4: Acquisition of relevant information about identified occupations. Information is absolutely central to the career guidance and decision-making process. Both the National Career Development Association (NCDA) [formerly the National Vocational Guidance Association (NVGA)] and the Association of Computer-Based Systems for Career Information (ACSCI) have written guidelines in regard to the content, accuracy, and recentness of occupational information. Well-developed information may be made available to deciders on paper, on microfiche, through computers, or by interviewing workers in the community. Obtaining comparable, complete, and timely information about all occupational alternatives under consideration is clearly needed as a basis for decision making.

Not only is occupational information needed, but likewise career and world of work information. Career information refers to knowledge of life stages, the tasks related to each, the composite of life roles that make up career in the broad sense and the career patterns that one might follow. This knowledge is important in assisting the individual with the lifelong process of career development and change and in helping with the understanding of the worker role in relation to all others. World of work information refers to knowledge about the organization of occupations, characteristics on which they vary, and their interrelationships. This information can help individuals understand the potential for career change with or without retraining and the concept of transferability of skills.

Component 5: Acquisition and development of decision-making skills. This component has been consistently identified by researchers as an ingredient of vocational maturity. It seems to include cognitive knowledge about decision-making styles and steps and the development of skills to follow the steps of a planned decision-making process. Such content and skills can be taught through didactic instruction by humans or computers or by guiding a person through the process without direct didactic instruction until the individual internalizes the process. The goal, of course, of such instruction/simulation is to assist the individual in learning a process that can be used repeatedly in all life roles, work-related as well as others. Practice of the decision-making process allows the decider to gather appropriate information about identified alternatives, weigh the potential risks and rewards of each, judge which alternatives offer the best combinations of satisfaction and likely success, make tentative choices accordingly, and prepare for reality testing and implementation.

Component 6: Reality-testing of favored alternatives. The purpose of this component is to assist deciders to experience as realistically as possible the favored alternatives. Such testing may be done through simulations, course work, work-study programs, jobs, internships, or practical laboratory experience. The closer these experiences are to reality the more helpful they will be to the decision-making process. It is important for both the student and the counselor to remember that finding out that a given alternative is not a viable one is as important as finding out that an alternative is viable. The counselor should assume the role of "engineer of experience" for the decider and should assist in the process of identifying or creating useful reality-testing experiences.

Out of reality testing, further collection of detailed information and clarification should come choice. Choice consists of the selection of one alternative from among the several that may exist. This alternative should be the one that seems to have the highest probability of assisting the decider to find self-actualization in work and reach desired goals.

Component 7: Implementation of choice. The choice of an occupation always implies some next steps. These next steps may include preparing to enter a college or technical school, applying for financial aid, entering an apprenticeship or the military, or seeking and finding a job. Traditionally counselors have provided a great deal of assistance with some of these implementation steps without adequate attention to the preceding components of career development and choice. Assistance with implementation should lead to specific action steps and involvement in and commitment to a set of behaviors.

Presentation of this model in seven defined components can erroneously lead the reader to believe that after Component 7 the task is finished. Such is not the case. Career development is a series of completions of this process, each leading the decider, it is hoped, to a higher level of vocational maturity and healthy growth. Skills, once learned, can be applied again and again to this process as personal desire and external circumstances demand.

INFORMATION SYSTEMS AND GUIDANCE SYSTEMS

Several modes of delivery of services can be utilized to assist deciders with the components or steps of the career guidance process. They include one-to-one counseling, workshops, group guidance, curriculum, telephone service, self-help materials, and the computer. In this chapter we focus our attention on the computer as a mode of delivery although it may be enhanced by one or a combination of the other modes.

The several computer-based systems that are available for lease or purchase in schools, agencies, and other settings can be viewed as plot points on a continuum with two poles. One pole is computer-based *information* systems, and the other is computer-based *guidance* systems. As development continues to grow in this field it becomes increasingly difficult to allocate systems to this continuum. This is true because the systems that once represented the information end of the continuum are making some movement toward adding elements of the guidance process. Similarly, the systems that once represented the guidance process end of the continuum are making movement toward improved methods of information development and addition of local data. Professionals who are reviewing and evaluating systems should consider the continuum and attempt to assign a relative position to each system under consideration as well as to assign a position to the "ideal" system desired to meet local needs.

Some functions are common to both information-emphasis and guidance-process-emphasis systems. These functions are (a) the storing of large files of data; (b) the accessing of these files by a successive combination of variables; and (c) the provision of detailed information about options in the files as requested by the user. These files may contain information about occupations, colleges, technical schools, graduate schools, apprenticeships, military programs, financial aids, or employers. Access variables may be internal or external to the user. For example, internal variables may be interest or aptitude scores. External variables may be job characteristics, physical requirements, or related programs of study. Detailed information may be short summaries, responses to interactive questions, or lengthy printouts.

There are at least four characteristics on which information-emphasis and guidance-process-emphasis systems typically vary. These are (1) the assessment of self-variables on-line (at the computer); (2) the development of local occupational information; (3) the teaching of career development concepts; and (4) the storage of a user record.

Typically, information-emphasis systems do not administer any assessment instruments (that is, interest inventories, ability rating scales, values inventories, and the like) at the computer. Some may, however, utilize scores of such assessment instruments that have been taken on paper. Guidance-process-emphasis systems, on the other hand, do typically provide self-assessment instruments or simulations at the computer because, by definition, they are considered to be at the heart of the guidance process.

Relating to the second distinction, information-emphasis systems specialize in the development of local labor market information. Although guidance-process-emphasis systems are highly concerned about accurate and timely occupational information, they do not typically engage in the development of state labor market supply-and-demand information. Rather they utilize general occupational information (work tasks, training, general employment outlook, salary ranges, etc.) of a national scope garnered from a variety of national sources.

Third, information-emphasis systems do not typically use the computer to teach career development concepts such as clarification of values, organization of the world of work, the decision-making process, job-seeking skills, or life/career stages. On the other hand, career guidance-emphasis systems do because these topics and others are central to the career-development-process approach described in the beginning of this chapter.

Finally, information-emphasis systems do not typically store individual records of use in computer files. There is no need to do so because no personalized user data are being generated and no long-term process is being monitored. Guidance-emphasis systems, alternatively, do create individual computer-stored records to "save" the results of self-assessment instruments for systematic use, remind the user of parts of the system used or not used, and generally monitor the user's progress through the prescribed process.

The boxed information entitled "Information and Guidance Systems Continuum" summarizes the information-guidance process continuum proposed here and the four specific elements that characterize this distinction.

Information and Guidance Systems Continuum

←--→

Information-Emphasis Systems	Guidance-Process-Emphasis Systems
1. *Do not* assess self-variables on-line.	1. *Do* assess self-variables on-line.
2. *Do* develop localized labor market information.	2. *Do not* develop localized labor market information.
3. *Do not* teach career development concepts on-line.	3. *Do* teach career development concepts on-line.
4. *Do not* store user records.	4. *Do* store user records.

COMPUTER-BASED SYSTEMS AND THE MODEL

At the outset of consideration of the role of the computer in relation to a systematic model of career guidance, it is important to state that none of the computer-based systems were designed to replace counselors or to be "stand-alone" systems. Research (Garis, 1982; Penn, 1981) has indicated that the best career guidance treatment for students is the combination of the computer and the counselor. If, however, there is inadequate staff to provide this combined treatment, the use of the computer alone produces positive and desirable effects far in excess of no treatment at all.

The real questions, then, relate to how much of the career guidance process to assign to the computer, how much to other modes of delivery, and how these roles can be shared. Table 1 summarizes the career guidance model that has been presented and provides an indication of the roles of computer-based information and guidance systems, counselors, and other modes of delivery in relation to the model. A review of Table 1 shows possible combinations of modes of delivery of the suggested components and indicates that guidance-process systems provide relatively more support to the guidance process than information systems. This does not necessarily translate to the need for fewer counselors or a lighter load for counselors because available research (Myers, Thompson, Lindeman, Super, Patrick, & Friel, 1972) on this topic indicates that individuals go to counselors more, not less, due to the use of computer-based systems. The topics that they discuss with counselors, however, are well beyond the information-giving level, thus providing the individual with an increased amount of help and the counselor with much more professional job duties.

Note that neither information systems nor guidance systems currently attempt to develop the readiness of their users for career information, decision making, and planning. This is currently a task left to counselors and to planned experiences in the classroom, home, and the community.

The second component—acquisition of relevant self-data—is peculiar to the guidance systems, with a sharing of this role by counselors. Typical computer-delivered activities offered in this regard are the on-line administration and interpretation of inventories of work-related values or interests and the self-ratings of abilities or skills. The prominent career guidance systems assess interests, abilities or skills, and values. This organization of self-data is used to provide a list of occupational titles for exploration. Further, the computer may be used to show the user the overlap or inconsistency between or among interests, values, and abilities. Doubtless future guidance systems will provide abilities testing in an adaptive mode so that data better than self-ratings can be acquired with a minimum of computer and user time. The computer is an excellent medium for this kind of self-assessment because it provides the maximum in objectivity and is capable of providing a variety of personalized interpretations dependent upon the user's specific profile. Such interpretations, though personalized for a variety of specific combinations, can be delivered in a standard, objective way to each individual and with

Table 1

Steps of the Career Guidance Model in Relation to Information and Guidance Model

Steps of the Career Guidance Model	Other (curriculum, parents, work experience, etc.)	Computer-based Information Systems	Computer-based Guidance Systems	Counselor (one to one and/or group)
1. Development of readiness for career planning, information, and decision making.	XX	—	—	XX
2. Acquisition of relevant self-data.	—	—	XX	XX
3. Translation of self-data into occupational alternatives.	—	X	XX	XX
4. Acquisition of relevant information about identified occupations and related educational programs.	—	XX	XX	—
5. Acquisition and/or development of decision-making skills.	XX	—	XX	XX
6. Reality-testing of favored alternatives.	XX	—	—	X
7. Implementation of choice.	—	XX	XX	X

XX = Primary responsibility.
X = Secondary responsibility.

the advantage of the most expert knowledge behind both the assessment instruments and the interpretation.

The linkage of self-data to occupations is performed by career guidance systems and by some information systems that utilize scores of assessment instruments taken on paper. The counselor also shares this role.

Both types of computer-based systems can potentially do an excellent job of providing information about occupations targeted for exploration as well as providing cognitive knowledge of career and world of work information. Both the National Career Development Association (NCDA) and the Association of Computer-Based Systems for Career Information (ACSCI) have provided guidelines in regard to the content, accuracy, timeliness, and scope of vocational information. Given that system developers adhere to these guidelines, the computer is an excellent mode of delivery for such information, which can be presented in an interactive question and answer format or in lengthy descriptions.

The computer has several significant advantages in the delivery of occupational information. First, it has high motivational appeal. At least one study (McKinlay & Adams, 1971) has indicated that poor readers can read text broken into segments and displayed on a screen considerably better than they can read the same text in printed form. In addition to its appeal in computer-delivered form, occupational information can be presented in a totally objective, nonbiased way (assuming the text is written that way) without the subtle nonverbal messages that we humans sometimes transmit. Finally, computer-stored occupational information can be updated much more dynamically (assuming the availability of new data) than printed information because of the capability for constant on-line maintenance.

It has already been stated that Component 5—the acquisition and development of decision-making skills—is a hallmark of the guidance systems. There is insufficient knowledge about how decision-making skill is acquired or can be taught. Nonetheless guidance systems are attempting to make a contribution in this area both by didactic teaching (utilizing computer-assisted instruction methods) of the steps of the decision-making process and by utilizing the monitoring function of the computer to shepherd users through a planned process (hoping that they may internalize it) whether they are cognitively aware of it or not.

Neither information nor guidance systems are currently doing an adequate job with Component 6—assisting individuals with the reality-testing of favored occupational alternatives. By definition, reality-testing is a trial run in the real world, a putting of self into the real situation to experience the resulting satisfaction or dissatisfaction. For this reason computers will never do the whole job; simulation will never be enough. This is a component with which the community, the employer, and the school can provide substantial help. Guidance and information systems may approach this goal by the use of the videodisk or compact disk with full sound and motion. With this new medium under computer control, the user will be able to see and hear work settings and work tasks, and this will be closer to reality than reading alone.

Both guidance and information systems are providing significant assistance in the implementation of choice. This component involves assisting people with the next steps after choice of an occupation. These next steps involve selecting a major, a college, graduate school, technical school, job, military program, or acquiring financial aid. The different guidance and information systems vary considerably in terms of the number of these files provided and the extent of the data in each file. Potentially computers can provide assistance with this component well beyond that which the counselor can provide because the best capabilities of the computer are utilized.

SUMMARY

This chapter has stated some basic assumptions of a developmental career guidance program. From these assumptions, seven components deemed essential to a career guidance program were derived and described. Following that, two types of computer-based programs—information-emphasis and guidance-process-emphasis—were described and defined. Finally, these types of systems and other modes of delivery were reviewed in light of the seven components. Observations were made about the contributions of each type of system to the proposed generic model.

REFERENCES

Crites, J.O. (1971). *The maturity of vocational attitudes in adolescence.* (Inquiry Services, No. 2). Washington, DC: American Personnel and Guidance Association.

Garis, J.W. (1982). The interpretation of a computer-based guidance system in a college counseling center: A comparison of the effects of DISCOVER and individual counseling upon career planning. *Dissertation Abstracts International, 43,* 2236A. (University Microfilms No. DA8228889)

Holland, J.L. (1973). *Making vocational choices.* Englewood Cliffs, NJ: Prentice-Hall.

McKinlay, B., & Adams, D. (1971). *Evaluation of the occupational information access system as used at Churchill High School: A project report.* Eugene, OR: University of Oregon.

Myers, R.A., Thompson, A.S., Lindeman, R.N., Super, D.E., Patrick, T.A., & Friel, T.W. (1972). *Educational and career exploration systems: Report of a two-year field trial.* New York: Teachers College.

Parsons, F. (1909). *Choosing a vocation.* Boston: Houghton-Mifflin.

Penn, P.O. (1981). Differential effects on vocationally-related behavior of a computer-based career guidance system in conjunction with innovative career exploration strategies. *Dissertation Abstracts International, 42,* 5070–5071A. (University Microfilms No. DA8206408)

Starishevsky, R., & Matlin, N. (1963). A model for the translation of self-concepts into vocational terms. In D.E. Super (Ed.), *Career development: Self-concept theory* (pp. 33–41). New York: College Entrance Examination Board.

Super, D.E. (1953). A theory of vocational development. *American Psychologist, 8,* 185–190.

Super, D.E. (1974). Vocational maturity theory: Toward implementing a psychology of careers in career education and guidance. In D.E. Super (Ed.), *Measuring vocational maturity for counseling and education* (pp. 9–24). Washington, DC: National Vocational Guidance Association.

Super, D.E. (1980). A life-span, life-space approach to career development. *Journal of Vocational Behavior, 16,* 282–298.

Super, D.E. (1981). Assessment in career guidance: Toward truly developmental counseling. *Personnel and Guidance Journal, 61,* 555–562.

Super, D.E., & Bowlsbey, J.H. (1981). *Career education in the upper grades: A project in Charles County, Md.* Unpublished report.

Super, D.E., & Overstreet, P.L. (1960). *The vocational maturity of ninth-grade boys.* New York: Teachers College Press.

Super, D.E., Starishevsky, R., Matlin, N., & Jordaan, J.P. (1963). *Career development: Self-concept theory.* New York: College Entrance Examination Board.

Super, D.E., & Thompson, S.S. (1979). A six-scale, two-factor test of vocational maturity. *Vocational Guidance Quarterly, 28,* 6–15.

Tiedeman, D.V., Davis, R.G., Durstine, R.M., Ellis, A.B., Fletcher, W.J., Landy, E., & O'Hara, R.P. (1970). *An information system for vocational decisions, final report.* Cambridge, MA: Harvard Graduate School of Education.

Tiedeman, D.V., & O'Hara, R.P. (1963). *Career development: Choice and adjustment.* New York: College Entrance Examination Board.

Tiedeman, D.V., & Peatling, J.H. (1977). *Career development: Designing self.* Muncie, IN: Accelerated Development.

Westbrook, B.W., & Clary, J.R. (1967). *The construction and validation of a measure of vocational maturity.* Raleigh, NC: Center for Occupational Education, North Carolina State University.

CHAPTER 8

A Multi-Strategy Approach to Career Planning

Carol A. Blimline
Independent Practice
Rockville, Maryland

David R. Schwandt
George Washington University
Washington, D.C.

Adult career development requires collaboration. For optimal career counseling of working adults, it is necessary to consider the contributions and resources that can be provided by three players: the professionally trained career counselor, the individual employee or potential employee, and the employer or potential employer. Each has a role in the career planning process.

The career planning and counseling process is only as good as the data upon which it is based. The career counselor may identify needs and facilitate the career planning process. The work place can provide guidance relevant to environmental expectations and needs, but the final steps—weighing information, selecting goals, and taking action—can be accomplished only by the individual.

Because different players make different contributions to the career planning process, a variety of counseling interventions should be used to optimize the potential contributions of each of these three players whenever possible. Three major categories of counseling interventions are discussed in this chapter: professionally assisted counseling, self-paced counseling, and managerial counseling.

COUNSELOR-ASSISTED CAREER PLANNING

Although theoretical approaches differ, most professional career counselors attempt to follow these general guidelines:

- appreciate, understand, and attend to the unique life planning history and future needs of each client;
- explore the dynamic history of each client and understand that career planning must go hand in hand with overall life planning and adult development issues;

115

- instruct the career planner in a decision-making model that can have ongoing significance as it is applied to other life decisions and that can be used without a counselor;
- give general career information when it is available, but, more important, teach the adult career planner how to find information specific to his or her needs; and
- help the adult career planner use the resources of the work environment by developing network mentor relationships and managerial appraisal and coaching contacts.

Another particularly valuable counseling tool for working with adults is the career planning workshop. In addition to being more cost-effective than individual counseling, it may, for a number of reasons, be more effective in facilitating the career planning process (Bowen & Hall, 1977). Group members help each other both practically and emotionally. First, the leader and other participants can provide information on job possibilities and alternative solutions to career problems that might not be available without group input. Second, group participants find that they share many concerns, worries, and aspirations with others. This realization reduces both their sense of isolation and fear of being alone in their confusion and struggle.

The group is instrumental in developing social skills that can generalize to such career planning skills as interviewing, dealing assertively with a boss, and selling one's ideas. In addition, the workshop leader and other participants can serve as role models for the risk taking required in career decision making. Furthermore, a group can serve as a motivational force and stimulant to independent action. Reporting back to the group on progress made over time works as effectively in career planning as it has for so many others in groups such as Alcoholics Anonymous and Weight Watchers.

An effective career development workshop for the adult learner can easily mirror the overall career-planning process used in self-paced or individual career-counseling efforts. The core of such programs would consist of segments devoted to understanding self, understanding the environment, and eventually taking action. An additional life-management component could effectively address those specific adult transition issues that often make career planning more complex in adult years. Those adult issues may include family and parenting responsibilities, financial management, and divorce and separation difficulties.

SELF-PACED CAREER INTERVENTIONS

In the real world of adult career planning, the career counselor has limited resources and energy to reach the many clients who could benefit from career counseling. In the place of, and sometimes alongside of, one-to-one counseling and group interventions are self-paced career explorations and the use of appropriate adult models and coaches in the career development process. As Holland (1974) suggested, ". . . the provision of information about self and careers in comprehensive, accessible and inexpensive ways may do for vocational counseling what penicillin has done

116

for medicine." However, a self-paced approach requires a capacity for self-direction and motivation that many adult career planners lack, particularly because most have not been instructed in such methods.

Self-paced career resource centers can give structure to this approach by providing self-administered career assessment tools, organized and classified occupational information, and computer-assisted vocational exploration. These systems are particularly well suited for adult career planners who have initiative and readiness to learn. Such career resource centers currently operate in many colleges and universities, community-based counseling centers, and employment settings.

For example, the career resource center at the U.S. General Accounting Office is based on a model developed at Goddard Space Flight Center. The center serves a dual purpose. It is designed to help individual employees in their career development while also serving as a tool to help managers and supervisors promote and facilitate their staffs' career development. The center includes four work stations, each corresponding to one of the major phases of the career/life planning process.

Station A—*Understanding Self:* Provides self-scored instruments and materials to help the individual clarify personal values, goals, needs, interests, and skills.

Station B—*Understanding Environment:* Provides information on career path patterns and skill requirements for various occupations both within and outside the Federal Government. Station B is designed to help individuals analyze realistic educational options and employment opportunities.

Station C—*Taking Action:* Provides a decision-making strategy that integrates information about self with information about the environment to construct a realistic action plan. Guides to implementation, such as interviewing techniques, assertiveness skills, and resume preparation, are included.

Station D—*Life Management:* Involves self-assessment checklists, pamphlets, resource books, and referral sources on a wide range of adult development concerns. These include marriage, family, parenting, self-understanding, intimacy, midlife transition, retirement, financial management, health, stress, and grief.

Skills learned through use of a career resource center may be applied to any life or career transition. Both the individual and the organization gain from self-paced career resource programs, particularly when organizational systems exist to support such programs.

EMPLOYER-ASSISTED CAREER PLANNING

The third category of the career planning interventions is centered on the assistance of the employers in the work place. To support a truly integrative process, career planning should be a cooperative effort among the employee, the professional counselor, and the manager. Each of these parties has a distinct role, but each is dependent on the other. The manager's role is critical. Leibowitz and Schlossberg (1981, p. 73) listed nine roles the supervisor/manager may play:

- communicator: One who promotes a two-way exchange between himself or herself and the employee;
- counselor: One who helps the employee clarify goals and identify steps necessary to reach these goals, whether or not they relate to the present organization;
- appraiser: One who evaluates an employee's performance and helps to work out a development plan so the employee can achieve objectives specific to the current job;
- coach: One who gives instruction or skill training to enable an employee to do his or her job more effectively;
- mentor: One who serves as a sponsor to facilitate an employee's career growth;
- advisor: One who gives information about career opportunities both within and outside the organization;
- broker: One who serves as an agent (go-between) for the employee and recommends him or her to other resources such as people or institutions;
- referral agent: One who identifies resources to help an employee with specific problems; and
- advocate: One who intervenes on behalf of an employee for benefits, promotions, and elimination of obstacles.

The manager's success in each of these roles is dependent on effective communication and an understanding of how career development activities fit into the manager's job. Changing social values, different career patterns, and varying employee aspirations present today's manager with problems that the typical Master of Business Administration program does not address. One of the roles of the professional counselor is to help the manager acquire and perfect the career coaching skills needed in the work place.

The concept of the manager as career coach has not been accepted with open arms by most managers. Many see it as taking away from time they traditionally devote to work production. Adding to this concern is the fear of not having the ability to handle these activities adequately.

In some organizations professional counselors in the work place have begun implementing educational and support activities to help the managers develop career coaching skills. Their primary objective is to provide the manager with:

- an understanding of the career planning process;
- an understanding of the organization's obligations and the individual's responsibilities; and
- an opportunity to learn and practice interpersonal and career coaching skills.

Government and business organizations are replete with illustrations of these efforts. Some efforts, such as the General Electric Company program (Jones, Kaye, & Taylor, 1981), stress the expansion of the manager's knowledge of career development, whereas others, such as those at IBM and the U.S. General Accounting Office, offer workshops that emphasize interpersonal and counseling skill building. Common to all of these programs is the effort to bring counseling techniques to the work place and to emphasize the connection between individual career planning and development and organizational needs. If such programs are to be beneficial for both the individual and the organization, an effective working relationship must be established between supervisor and employee, as Edgar Schein (1977) emphasized: "If the organization can open up the communications channel between employees, their bosses, and whoever is managing the human resource system, the groundwork is laid for realistic individual development planning."

Managers must focus on one-to-one career coaching with their employees. They must structure sessions to discuss topics such as:

- employees' goals and aspirations, both long- and short-range;
- employees' expectations of themselves and the organization;
- the organization's plans and objectives, and how they relate to the work within the unit;
- real and possible opportunities for employees;
- other alternatives such as training, job rotation, and career transitions;
- employees' strengths and weaknesses as they pertain to present assignments and possible future assignments; and
- ways to develop individual development plans or to seek additional data or counseling.

For career coaching to work, information must be available to the manager and employee. Information about employees can emanate from personal assessments, counselor interaction, career resource materials, or in some instances, formal assessment centers. The assessment center is becoming a major counseling tool for both managers and employees. Assessment of styles and competencies, coupled with career counseling and individual development planning, gives employees the opportunity to explore their potential fully and evaluate their goals and the expectations of the organization realistically. Although information obtained from the assessment centers has in the past focused on handling various production aspects of the job, centers now examine the individual's unique development potential. The manager and employee can then look at this information as it relates to career planning. For instance, in many assessment programs, such as IBM-United Kingdom (Landon & Bray, undated), participants are required to write out their career and life goals, information that is used later during the counseling sessions.

A major area of confusion for the manager is the relationship between career counseling and performance appraisal. Many authors have discussed this topic (Schnier & Carroll, 1982) from varying perspectives. One of the recurring principles is that the performance appraisal session must be separate from the counseling session that deals with potential performance and career progression. This is especially true if the manager must determine salary based on the employee's performance appraisal.

Often, the employee-manager relationship becomes strained because of misunderstandings about future assignments, promotions, and other expectations. These misunderstandings then lead to distrust and deeper organizational and personal problems. The career planning process provides the opportunity to discuss freely the employee's expectations as they relate to the job. If realistic goals are set and agreed to by the manager and the employee, future discussions will be easier for both parties.

Counselors can use the career planning process as a means of impressing upon management the need for counseling services in the work place. By working with managers in career planning, professional counselors increase their ability to identify other counseling needs such as emotional problems that manifest themselves on the job. This could lead to a more systematic approach to life and career planning.

A relatively recent approach to managerial coaching is mentor programs. Several corporations are employing the mentor concept in the development of future managers and employees. Both private corporations, such as Federal Express, and public organizations, such as the U.S. Government Senior Executive Service, have enjoyed high success with this approach to career guidance. The mentor-mentee counseling relationship connotes a longer and more intimate relationship than that of manager-employee or employee-counselor and therefore must be treated somewhat differently. The mentor relationship, as seen by Lundberg (1984), has two functions: the career function, which includes sponsorship, exposure and visibility, coaching, protection, and challenge, and the psychosocial function, which includes role modeling, acceptance and confirmation, counseling, and friendship.

Following are the major characteristics of the mentor-mentee relationship:

1. Mentors must possess interpersonal skills that promote openness and candor, and a willingness to share concern and provide constructive feedback.
2. The mentor-mentee relationship should be voluntary and the mentor should not be the immediate supervisor. In fact, the mentor should be from another unit within the organization.
3. The mentor should have multifunctional experience at the top of the organization and should have enough power to assist in supporting the mentee's developmental needs.
4. The mentor-mentee relationship should be a "no-fault" one so that if it doesn't work, neither party is harmed.

The mentor concept can be important to career planning because it provides an added dimension that is missing in counselor-assisted or self-paced programs—knowledge of informal organizational realities based on the mentor's considerable experience.

SUMMARY

Professional counselors, employers, and the individual all have a mutual goal—to promote career decisions and actions that lead to productive and satisfying employment. Professionally assisted counseling, self-paced counseling, and managerial coaching should accomplish entry in a mutually supportive relationship to maximize the probability of success for both organizations and their employees.

REFERENCES

Bowen, D.D., & Hall, D.T. (1977, Winter). Career planning for employee development. *California Management Review.* pp. 23–25.

Holland, J.C. (1974). Career counseling: Then, now, and what's next? *The Counseling Psychologist,* 4(3), 24–26.

Jones, P.R., Kaye, B., & Taylor, H.R. (1981). You want me to do what? *Training and Development Journal,* 35(7), 56–62.

Landon, M., & Bray, D.W. (undated). An assessment center to study career motivation. *The Career Center Bulletin.* Special Report from Columbia University.

Leibowitz, Z.B., & Schlossberg, N.K. (1981). Training managers for their role in a career development system. *Training and Development Journal,* 35(7), 72–79.

Lundberg, C. (1984, February 21). Comments from presentation at University of Southern California Seminar for Senior Personnel Executives. Los Angeles, CA.

Schein, E.H. (1977, Fall). Increasing organization effectiveness through better human resource planning and development. *Sloan Management Review,* pp. 1–20.

Schnier, C.E., & Carroll, S. (1982). *Performance appraisal and review systems.* Glenview, IL: Scott, Foresman.

SECTION III:

TARGET POPULATIONS

FOR A VARIETY OF PEOPLE . . .

CHAPTER 9

Women's Career Development: Theory and Practice From a Feminist Perspective

Louise F. Fitzgerald
Lauren M. Weitzman
University of Illinois
at Champaign

Although the study of vocational behavior is fast approaching its centennial, interest in women's career development is a much more recent phenomenon, dating only from the mid-1960s. Since the first articles began to appear, stimulated by the return of women to the labor force that characterized that decade, the study of the vocational psychology of women has become the fastest growing area of the discipline. In the last two decades, fueled by the growth of a resurgent women's movement, women's work behavior has undergone a virtual revolution, and researchers and scholars have produced an enormous body of literature attempting to understand and explain it.

The present chapter is an attempt to synthesize major portions of that literature, with particular focus on variables that inhibit or facilitate women's career behavior. It is based on several assumptions concerning women, work, and the relationship between them. First, we agree with Betz (in press) that meaningful work is central to women's lives, that it serves as a buffer against psychological distress, and is a critical source of life satisfaction. Although such sentiments have always been assumed with reference to men, we are still not used to thinking about women's lives in this way. Even today, when most women work and much research demonstrates the many positive effects of employment (see, for example, Bart, 1971; Ilfeld, 1977; Warr & Parry, 1983; Wampler, 1982; Repetti, Matthews, & Waldron, 1989), it is not considered remarkable for adult women (but not men) to choose to be nonemployed. We suggest that such a position is both sexist [for example, few appear to believe that such a choice is a healthy one for men (Robertson & Fitzgerald, 1990)], and an unfortunate remnant of the time when it was believed that "a woman's place is in the home," a cultural lag that will become increasingly dysfunctional over the next few decades.

Related to this belief in the important role of work in women's lives is the assumption that the fulfillment of one's individual potential is critically important for a satisfying life. To push out one's boundaries, to set challenges and meet them, to develop an ever richer and more complex psychological existence (Csikszentmihalyi, 1990)—in short, to seek to actualize one's possibilities—has long been considered the *sine qua non* of psychological adjustment—for men. Such self actualization, however, has not always been considered necessary or even desirable for women, who have generally been thought to satisfy their achievement strivings through others. One result of this belief has been the assumption that marriage and motherhood are the most desirable life roles for women, and that the most appropriate occupational activities are those that parallel these helping, nurturing, familial activities.

Although we agree that the marital and maternal roles are centrally important sources of satisfaction for many if not most women at this time, it seems to us that the notion that these activities are somehow definitive of women's nature and *should* be reflected in their occupational lives has been very damaging. Such beliefs, which even now are surprisingly common, have reinforced a narrow set of fairly traditional vocational choices with little consideration given to each woman's unique capabilities and even less encouragement offered for her achievement strivings. In addition, such beliefs continue to place important limitations on women's vocational adjustment (i.e., success and satisfaction) throughout their working lives.

This important interface, both perceived and actual, between women's family and work lives is the basis of our third assumption—that, as argued by Fitzgerald and Crites (1980), the career development of women, although not fundamentally different from that of men, is demonstrably more complex due to a socialization process that has emphasized the dichotomy of work and family life since at least the Industrial Revolution of the 19th century. Despite the enormous social change of the last few decades, this argument still seems to us to be a valid one. Although more women than ever before are working outside the home, and although the great majority of young women expect to combine work and family activities, the understanding of women's work lives still requires attention to variables only rarely salient to the work behavior of men. For example, the presence and number of children is still an extremely powerful predictor of the level and nature of women's work force participation, whereas it is essentially unrelated to that of men. And, although many of the traditional indicators (e.g., family vs. career orientation) have lost their power as the "new cultural imperative" (Rand & Miller, 1974) of combining work and family has become a reality, others have taken their place (e.g., role conflict, role overload, coping strategies for multiple roles, barrier variables such as sex discrimination and sexual harassment). Therefore, we assume that at the present time and for the foreseeable future women's career development will remain more complex than that of men, and those who work with women clients will require knowledge of factors that have specific importance for women's lives.

Finally, if we assume that it is important to recognize the ways that women's lives differ from those of men, we emphasize that it is equally important to recognize that individual women also differ from one another. As suggested elsewhere (Fitzgerald & Betz, 1983; Betz & Fitzgerald, 1987), women are not a homogeneous group, and statements about *women's* vocational interests, *women's* work values, the vocational satisfaction of *women*, and so forth, are necessarily incorrect and misleading. Such formulations are currently fashionable in other areas of psychology (e.g., Gilligan, 1982; Chodorow, 1978; Belenky et al., 1986) and, although representing an important corrective to previous work that either assumed that women behaved like men or ignored them altogether, are overly simplistic, represent an undesirable reification of group characteristics, and obscure the importance of attending to individual differences in behavior.

Gilligan (1982), for example, argues that women as a group emphasize the welfare of others over abstract notions of justice and right and wrong, whereas Chodorow (1978) suggests that women do not develop the same sense of separateness as do men, and that they retain a world view that emphasizes their connectedness and relationship to others throughout their lives. Such theories have proven difficult to test, and there is little research (at present) that either supports or refutes them; still, they have attained considerable popularity, especially among some schools of feminist counselors who wish to celebrate what they see as women's special gifts.

The implications of such a view for women's career development are, to our minds, unfortunate, because they provide one more rationale for viewing women as somehow fundamentally *different*. This difference once again suggests the unique fitness of women for the supporting, nurturing roles to which they have so long been consigned; this time the basis is their own psychological needs and uniquely female value systems. We emphasize here the critical importance of treating each woman as a unique individual who—as the famous dictum would have it—is in some ways like *all* other women, in some ways like *some* other women, and in some ways like *no* other woman. This commitment to appreciating and fostering the individuality of all persons has long been a fundamental tenet of applied differential psychology (Tyler, 1978).

PLAN OF THE CHAPTER

Our chapter is loosely organized to parallel the developmental continuum of women's lives, with sections devoted to the sequential developmental tasks of vocational choice, job entry, and career adjustment. We begin our work by considering the two major theoretical frameworks that have been proposed to describe, predict, and explain the ways in which individuals choose their life's work. We will see that each of these frameworks offers important ways of thinking about women's vocational choices, but that each fails in important respects to adequately account for those choices. Following this, we move to a discussion of the process of vocational adjustment, beginning with a discussion of the barriers women face in selection, promotion, and compensation, and outlining the particularly difficult issues raised by the widespread harassment of women in the workplace. We then review the literature on the interface of women's work and family lives, present a critique of current conceptualizations of what is generally called multiple role conflict, and examine what is known about the ways in which women attempt to resolve such conflicts. Finally, we conclude with a discussion of the implications of these issues for career counseling with women. Throughout the chapter, we emphasize the important role played by cultural and social influences in shaping women's lives, and return again and again to the critical need for structural change.

WOMEN'S CAREER CHOICES: CONTENT AND PROCESS

The original and most durable model of career choice content, and the one which to some degree underlies all others, is known as trait-and-factor theory. Formulated originally by Parsons (1909), this model rests on three basic tenets:

1. Individuals differ in their interests, abilities, and personal characteristics (traits and factors).
2. Occupations differ in their requirements for various skills, the opportunities they provide to fulfill various interests, and so forth.
3. The quality of a vocational choice (and, thus, the degree of success and satisfaction) is a function of the degree of agreement between the characteristics of the person and the requirements of the job.

The most recent and complete statement of this type is that of Holland (1985). He suggests that individuals have unique patterns of interests and abilities, whereas occupations have characteristic environments, both of which can be described in terms of the degree to which they conform to some configuration of six basic types:

Realistic: practical, down-to-earth, thing-oriented; prefers the outdoors and concrete activities where mechanical dexterity and similar abilities are required.

Investigative: Scientific, analytical, idea-oriented; independent; prefers to work alone.

Artistic: Creative, expressive; prefers to express ideas and feelings in many forms of artistic media; dramatic, artistic, and sensitive.

Social: Outgoing, friendly, people-oriented; prefers to solve problems by arranging and rearranging relationships.

Enterprising: Outgoing, persuasive, and energetic; adept at selling and verbal persuasion.

Conventional: Prefers structured activities in a well-oriented hierarchy; careful, orderly.

According to this model, a successful and satisfying vocational choice is one that results in **congruence**, or fit, between the person and environment. Thus, this model is often referred to as a person-environment interaction theory.

From its inception as the somewhat simplistic "matching men (sic) and jobs" approach, through trait-and-factor theory, to the more comprehensive Holland categories of contemporary person-environment interaction theory, matching models have proved a durable and useful way of thinking about and predicting the content of career choices. Heuristic

127

as these concepts have been, however, it has become increasingly clear that they are of limited usefulness for describing or explaining the career decisions of large numbers of women. For example, despite consistent evidence that the distribution of intelligence, or general ability, is essentially identical in the sexes, women are largely concentrated at the lower and middle levels of the occupational distribution. Similarly, with respect to interests, the Investigative and (particularly) Realistic fields have very small proportions of women workers, relative to their number in the population. Finally, the concept of *choice realism* itself is to some degree problematic when applied to women. This section of the paper will review evidence bearing on these criticisms and an expanded notion of realism will be proposed.

Abilities

Although contrary stereotypes abound, research has consistently demonstrated no differences between men and women with respect to intelligence or general ability, widely accepted as the most important predictor of occupational performance (Gottfredson, 1986). Further, although small, consistent gender differences have been demonstrated in the special areas of verbal and (some) visual-spatial abilities; such differences are so small as to be of little practical importance, accounting as they do for less than 1% of the variance in scores (Hyde, 1985; Betz, in press). Given this general equivalence in occupationally relevant abilities, a trait-and-factor model of vocational choice would predict that women should aspire to and be found in the same range and distribution of occupations as men; obviously, this is not the case.

Interestingly enough, the literature suggests that girls actually outperform boys at all educational levels (Carnegie Commission on Higher Education, 1973; Hyde, 1985), that their school progress is superior to that of boys, and that they achieve better college grades, even in the sciences, engineering, and mathematics. Unfortunately, these abilities and performance are *not* reflected in women's occupational choices and attainments. For example, Terman and Oden (1959) found that half their sample of gifted women (IQ > 135) did not work outside the home, a finding essentially replicated in followups of the Project Talent students (Flanagan, 1971) and in studies of contemporary samples of highly gifted women (Kerr, 1988). Kerr found that the occupational distribution of contemporary gifted women who worked outside the home was essentially identical to that in the Terman sample over 40 years before; that is, nearly half were either secretaries or school teachers. Similar patterns of ability underutilization are apparent in the Project Talent data (Card, Steel, & Abeles, 1980) where, despite higher test scores and grades, the women achieved less education than the men and earned significantly less money. This effect was most apparent for those women who were the most gifted students.

In addition to such studies of the gifted and talented, each succeeding summary of labor market statistics demonstrates that among the general population women are extensively over-represented in the lower level, lower paying traditionally "female" occupations, e.g., clerical, service, etc. Although much of this is attributable to external factors [what Astin (1984) has labeled the "structure of opportunity"] it is also clear that women "select" themselves out of a large number of higher level occupations, particularly those requiring mathematical or technical background. The literature suggests that enormous numbers of young women are selecting and training for occupations that are inappropriately low level with respect to their measured skills and abilities, a problem in choice realism that Crites (1981) has termed "unfulfilled."

Interests

Not only are women disproportionately concentrated at the lower *levels* of the occupational spectrum, but they are also heavily clustered into relatively few *fields*, primarily clerical and service. There is currently no research to suggest that such women are actually mismatched with respect to their interests, as they quite clearly often are with respect to their abilities. However, it is also clear that girls are consistently socialized to develop such interests; that families, teachers, and often counselors strongly reinforce this socialization; and that young women are encouraged to pursue patterns of education and training that effectively close off other options at a very early age. [See, for example, Sells (1973, 1982) for a discussion of the repercussions of early high school decisions not to take a full mathematics curriculum.] Thus, it does not appear reasonable to explain the narrow range of women's occupations solely or even primarily in terms of women's interests and choices, since we have no way of knowing what such choices would be if they were not prematurely constrained.

Historically, the major issue with respect to women's vocational interests had to do with whether or not a woman planned to work at all, at least after marriage (which was assumed to be a universal role). Early studies that addressed this issue (e.g., Hoyt & Kennedy, 1958) did so in terms of *homemaking* versus *career* orientation, which were conceptualized more or less as categorical and mutually exclusive (Zytowski, 1969) or at least, sequential (Super, 1957). The notion of women actually *combining* career and family roles as men generally do was considered, at the least, highly unusual. From the vantage point of the early 1990's, when most women plan to pursue occupations and careers, and Super's (1957) *double track* career pattern is the norm rather than the exception, such research and theorizing seems quaintly dated. However, as we noted above, the assumed primacy of the family role in women's lives has resulted in a powerful set of influences, both social and psychological, that combine to produce a distinct over-representation of women in occupations that parallel this role. Although trait-and-factor models can to some degree describe this situation, they offer little to explain it. This lack of explanatory power suggests that some of the core constructs of these models require revision if they are to account for the behavior of women. One such construct is choice realism.

Choice Realism

As outlined by Crites (1969, 1981), the concept of realism encompasses three distinct types of problems: the *unrealistic* individual, whose measured ability is less than that required by the chosen occupation; the *unfulfilled*, whose ability is considerably *higher* than that required; and the *coerced*, whose ability lies within the appropriate range but whose *interest* pattern is incongruent with that typical of the occupation selected. Each of these individuals is said to have made an *unrealistic* choice. As outlined above, it is abundantly clear that these problems characterize a large segment of the female population. Yet there are several problems with this conceptualization.

First, such a formulation considers *vocational* realism to be the only relevant issue; that is, it considers occupational decisions in isolation from those concerning other important life areas, particularly family roles. Such a separation is congruent with Western social structures since the Industrial Revolution of the 19th century, and accurately describes the life experiences of men, at least until very recently. This conceptualization, however, ignores a basic reality of women's lives—that heterosexual women generally do not enjoy the same degrees of freedom in making career decisions that men do unless they decide not to marry or form permanent partnerships. In particular, independently of sexual preference, women bear and are responsible for raising children, which makes some kinds of careers difficult if not impossible, at least without considerable stress, enormous effort, and a great deal of luck.

A hypothetical example may be informative here. Consider a woman with a high level of ability and strong interests in human biology or medical science who compromises her original goals of research biologist or physician in favor of a BS in nursing. She makes this decision because the social and organizational supports are simply not available that would allow her to engage in these very demanding pursuits while at the same time assuming family responsibilities. The option of sequencing her family and career activities, or "stopping out" until childrearing duties are completed is similarly unavailable due to the nature of scientific career paths. Thus, her decision may be extremely realistic, given the different factors she is weighing, but it would be classified as *unfulfilled*, *coerced*, or possibly even *maladjusted* (a mismatch of both interests and abilities) in the usual systems.

These descriptions seem to us to be inappropriate ways of thinking about complicated, multiattribute decisions and, furthermore, like all descriptive diagnostic constructions, appear to locate the source of the problem within the individual. What is needed here is a more dynamic motivational analysis, one that takes into account *why* any particular woman makes the choices she does. The general rationale for this analysis can be found in Crites' (1981) call for a comprehensive approach to career choice diagnosis; he argues convincingly that to understand any choice problem requires not only a reliable method of categorization (differential diagnosis), but also a dynamic understanding of the motivational roots of the problem (dynamic diagnosis), as well as some understanding of the process the individual has gone through in arriving at the choice (decisional diagnosis). Although Crites emphasizes the key role that choice anxiety may play in motivational conflicts, it is not necessary to limit the analysis to this variable.

Betz (in press) has recently suggested that trait-and-factor models may be most useful for explaining the behavior of highly motivated, nontraditional women whose career behavior closely parallels that of traditional males, whereas other women may be better described by a *deficit* model of vocational choice. We agree with this formulation and would expand it further. To the classical and deficit models she describes, we would propose to add two concepts: *satisficing* and *optimization*. The concept of satisficing, first proposed by Simon (1957), characterizes an individual (in this case a woman) who makes choices that meet minimal requirements (i.e., are "good enough") without evaluating alternative situations, usually because such alternatives are uncertain or unknown. The optimizing individual, on the other hand, is one who is highly committed to both career and family, is cognizant of the tradeoffs that may be necessary, and has proactively sought to maximize her outcomes in both areas. Although from the usual perspective her vocational choice may seem unrealistic (in the sense of being at a somewhat lower level than indicated by her abilities, or possibly in a field that is more tangentially related to her inventoried interests), such a description does not appear accurate. Rather, such an individual would likely be characterized by strong goal selection, planning, and problem-solving competencies (Crites, 1978), as well as a willingness to accept the necessity of compromise.

Readers familiar with career maturity theory will recognize these attributes as characteristic of the vocationally mature individual. Career theorists have long puzzled over the fact that girls traditionally receive higher career maturity scores than boys, yet often select occupations that are unrealistic in the traditional sense. Such results are anomalous as vocational theory predicts a strong positive relationship between career maturity and choice realism. We submit that this anomaly results from an inappropriately narrow view of the concept of realism, at least with respect to women and at the present time.

Thus, from our perspective, the question of whether any particular choice is "realistic" or wise, requires attention not only to occupationally relevant characteristics, but also to the degree of commitment to various life roles (e.g., worker, spouse/homemaker, parent) and, in particular, the environmental supports and constraints available to support the favored options.

Summary and Implications

For many years, trait-and-factor theory has proven the most powerful and robust method of describing and explaining career choice. Generations of counselors have used its precepts to guide their work and frame their interventions. There is little question that such individual differences formulations are the core foundation of vocational psychology and career counseling.

As women have drastically expanded their roles, however, and men slowly begin to follow suit, the traditional dichotimization of work and family responsibilities that was a critical if unspoken underpinning of these theories is rapidly crumbling. It is apparent that if these conceptualizations are to retain their viability, they must be expanded to take into account variables that have traditionally been irrelevant and their outcome criteria (particularly choice realism) must be re-evaluated. To do otherwise is to perpetuate androcentric theoretical formulations that are increasingly irrelevant for understanding women's behavior.

It should be emphasized here that we are not suggesting that the realities of women's lives should be considered reason not to encourage women to explore beyond the traditional occupational boundaries—quite the contrary. We agree with Kerr (1988) that women's failure to realize their potential is most often the result of a "lifelong history of small compromises and adjustments" (p. 262) and that "a gifted woman's excellent adjustment to lower societal expectations . . . may be her greatest handicap" (pp. 262–263), a statement that applies as well to the majority of the general female population. Indeed, it is critical to continue efforts to expand women's opportunities and to support and encourage their participation in nontraditional areas, especially those such as math and science from which they have historically been discouraged.

Nor are we suggesting that it is appropriate to accept current patterns of women's family and maternal responsibilities as rationale for consigning them to alternative career paths, e.g., the so-called "Mommy Track" (Schwartz, 1988), in the name of an expanded notion of realism or optimization. We believe such suggestions are regressive and would perpetuate and reify present social arrangements, rather than facilitate change.

However, we do suggest that it is critical for theorists and practitioners alike to pay attention to variables that are important in women's lives and to expand their theories and practice to take them into account, or else theory and practice alike will suffer. Brooks (1988) argues convincingly that the reason interventions designed to expand women's career options have so often failed is because they are conceptually flawed; her proposed expectancy-value model is an excellent example of how theoretical formulations can be expanded to include motivational variables important to women. The work of Betz and Fitzgerald (1987) as expanded by Fassinger (1985; in press; Fitzgerald, Fassinger, & Betz, 1989) offers an expanded individual differences model in the trait and factor tradition that emphasizes the importance of the variables we have discussed here. These formulations are examples of the types of theory-building that are necessary if individual differences theories are to have relevance for women's lives.

Developmental Self-Concept Theory

In contrast to the differential model described above that portrays career choice as a point-in-time occurrence, the developmental model conceptualizes choice as a process that spans many years, proceeding in predictable stages from early adolescence through adulthood, and culminating finally in retirement. Originally outlined by Ginzberg, Ginsburg, Axelrad, and Herma (1951) and more full elaborated by Super (1953), this original version of developmental career theory accepted the importance of person-environment congruence, but chose to highlight the process the individual goes through in arriving at the clear specification of a choice and the attendant developmental tasks that must be mastered to successfully negotiate each stage. Figure 1 is based on the early theoretical formulations of both Ginzberg and Super. It depicts these stages, highlights the exclusionary nature of the choice process, and shows the increasing reality base of choice across time. Note that the matching and developmental models are actually complementary ways of thinking about career choice, as the latter incorporates the former and casts it into a developmental framework.

According to this framework, during the exploration stage individuals base career preferences first on their interests, then abilities, and finally,

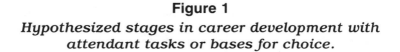

Figure 1

Hypothesized stages in career development with attendant tasks or bases for choice.

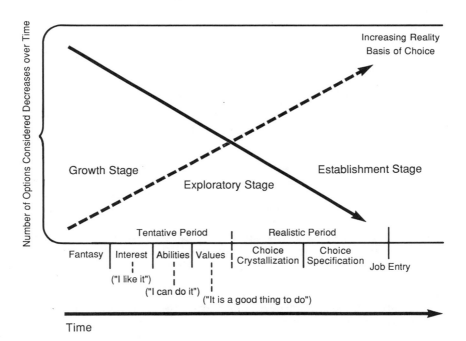

Time

133

According to this framework, during the exploration stage individuals base career preferences first on their interests, then abilities, and finally, values. There is an ever-increasing reality base to this process as people first consider work based only on what they like to do, then consider what they are able to do (e.g., special skills and talents, weaknesses and handicaps), and finally incorporate their values. Through exploration of self and the world, the individual eventually crystallizes a vocational preference, and finally specifies an actual choice. This process is thought to occupy the years of junior high, high school, and postsecondary or college training, and concludes with the implementation of the choice through occupational entry, which is the empirical boundary between the exploration and establishment stages. Contemporary statements of developmental theory (e.g., Super, 1984) underscore the probability that people may "recycle" through these stages one or more times as they change jobs, fields, or careers during the course of their lives. The often cyclical nature of career development across the life span should be kept in mind, although for the sake of simplicity the process is described here in linear terms.

Counseling approaches based on developmental theory thus include assessment of the client's stage of development, as well as the traditional assessment of interests, abilities, needs, and values. For those who are developmentally delayed (i.e., career immature), counseling focuses first on orientation to the choice process, and then on exploration, reality testing, and decision making. As Super and Overstreet (1960) have noted, counseling with the immature client is counseling to develop readiness for choice (to assist the client in understanding the choice process) rather than counseling concerning specific choices. In describing developmental career counseling, Crites (1981) has written

> In sum, the overall process of career development progresses from orientation and readiness for career choice to decision making and reality testing, and the developmental career counselor initiates counseling at that point in the process which the client has reached. (p. 125)

Development theory has proven relatively robust to the revolution in vocational behavior produced by the return of women to the workforce that began in the 1960's, in large part due to its process orientation and focus on developmental tasks that are more or less universal. Still, its description of career stages was often problematic for predicting women's work behavior, particularly to the degree that they were seen as nonrecursive or tied to a particular age or life stage. Osipow (1983) noted that many traditional women did not actually progress through a stage of exploration, nor successfully crystallize and specify a choice. Rather, female exploration was often actually "pseudoexploration," pending marriage plans; true vocational development occurred later when childrearing duties were largely completed.

More recently, Super (1980) has expanded his theory to include an additional dimension, one that he terms **latitudinal**, and which seeks to take into account the "life space" or various life roles the individual may choose or be called upon to play: child, student, leisurite, citizen, worker, and homemaker. Cast against the traditional longitudinal stages of growth, exploration, establishment, maintenance, and disengagement or decline, this model offers a more comprehensive formulation than was possible before, and one that is explicitly able to take into account the multiple roles that characterize most women's lives.

Figure 2 portrays a woman who, like most individuals, occupied only the role of child until entering school. As she got older, she added additional roles, entering the worker role part time during her teen years and full time at 21. Concurrently, she added the role of homemaker and temporarily abandoned her role as student. Note the return to this role a short time later as she enters graduate school, with a concurrent reduction in the worker role. Participation in the homemaking role continues unabated as schooling ends, full time work resumes, and the woman enters a stable dual-tract career pattern, continuing until later maturity signals disengagement from the work role and a concomitant increase in leisure, citizen, and (once again) student roles.

The life span-life space formulations offer useful and heuristic ways of thinking about women's lives, particularly when combined with an expanded trait-and-factor approach. Such a theory has great usefulness for predicting and describing the complex patterns of behavior engendered by the multiple roles that most women play, and can prove particularly useful for guiding career counseling interventions. As with individual differences theories, however, the motivational component of the model has not yet been sufficiently articulated. What motivates any individual woman to make the particular choices and follow the particular pattern that she does? Super (1981, 1984) suggests the critical role of the self concept—i.e., one's dynamic constructions of self-in-the-world—a concept richer than but compatible with the traditional matching notions. In addition, his recent writings have emphasized the crucial role of work importance in determining life choices, as well as the meaning attached to them. In support of this proposition he has offered data (Super & Nevill, 1984) indicating that the relative importance of work as a major life role is a more significant influence on vocational maturity than either gender or social class.

Contemporary formulations of developmental self concept theory may thus offer the most complete description available of women's vocational behavior. With the incorporation of both personal construct and role theory, this work captures the essential core of the classic matching theories, acknowledges the multidimensional nature of women's (and men's) lives, and casts these into a lifespan developmental perspective.

We suggest, however, that it is important to realize that these roles do not always fit together as neatly as the Life Career Rainbow (see Figure 2) would suggest. Super himself suggests as much when he writes, "These various roles, it has been shown (Super, 1940) can be supportive, supplementary, complementary, or conflicting. They can enrich life or overburden it" (Super, 1984, p. 204). Sadly, for women, both of these are often true.

Traditional socialization processes do not prepare women for the complex nature of the choices they will make or the life roles they will face. Society still assumes that however much the work role has expanded,

Figure 2

The career-life rainbow: A hypothetical example.

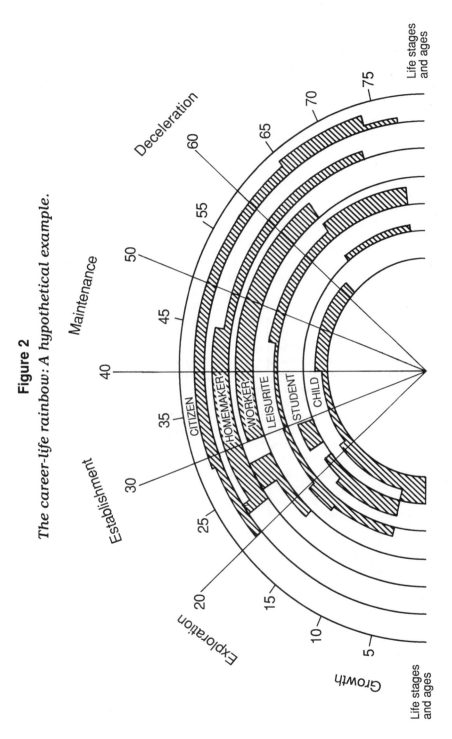

homemaker and (particularly) maternal responsibilities command the same degree of temporal and affective commitment as always. The social realities arising from these assumptions are easily identified; the United States continues to be the only country in the developed world without a national childcare policy. And the President recently vetoed a fairly conservative family leave policy that would have guaranteed the security of women's (and men's) jobs when they had to take time off for family responsibilities.

Thus, women are now expected to "do it all" but are given almost no support or assistance in doing so; men, on the other hand, are only required to do half of it, although they are allowed to **have** it all, as their family roles generally do not intrude on their work lives. Research indicates that young women, although generally committed to a dual-role pattern, have very little notion of what such a life choice actually entails or how to implement it. Yet, when constructing their career patterns, most women are faced with important barriers, both social and psychological, that are linked to their gender and to the meanings that gender has in American society. It is to these barriers that we now turn.

CAREER ADJUSTMENT: FRUSTRATION, CONFLICT, AND COPING

Vocational theory has traditionally made a distinction between the processes of career choice and career adjustment (Crites, 1969; Betz & Fitzgerald, 1987), with the adjustment process concerning itself with the individual's success and satisfaction after entering the work force. Although the most generally influential theory of this sort (Dawis & Lofquist, 1984) is a congruence model that explains vocational adjustment in terms of person-environment fit, it is Crites' (1976) process model that has proven particularly useful for thinking about women's success and satisfaction in the workplace (Fitzgerald & Betz, 1983; Betz & Fitzgerald, 1987).

Based on early work in the psychology of adjustment (Shaffer & Shoben, 1956), Crites (1976) has proposed that workers are motivated to achieve certain goals in the work environment (usually, success and satisfaction, although more general or particular goals can also be postulated). According to this model, when

a motivated worker encounters some thwarting condition, either frustration (external) or conflict (internal), [it] necessitates adjustive responses in order to fulfill needs or reduce drives. If the worker copes effectively with the adjustment problem, a tension or anxiety reducing response is made and career satisfaction and success are achieved. To the extent that the problem is not integratively resolved, the worker is less well career adjusted. The dynamics of this process are the same at all points on the continuum of career development, but the content changes from one stage to another because workers mature and tasks change. (p. 109)

From this model can be extrapolated, then, three major variables of interest to the present discussion: barriers, which can be divided into external *frustrations* (e.g., discrimination in selection or pay), internal *conflicts* (e.g., home-career conflict), and *coping* (the responses that the worker makes to either eliminate the barrier and/or to reduce the feelings of tension and anxiety that arise from the frustration or conflict). The next section of the chapter will discuss some of the important barriers to women's career adjustment that have been identified in the literature and the ways that women respond to and cope with such barriers. It will conclude with a brief consideration of the ways in which minority group membership may be expected to influence this process.

External Barriers: Discrimination, Differential Treatment and Harassment

Selection. Although formal discrimination in selection and treatment has been illegal in the United States since the passage of the Civil Rights Act of 1964, informal discrimination, i.e., the differential treatment of women workers as compared to men, persists as a serious barrier to women's career adjustment. With respect to selection, informal discrimination involves favoring a male candidate over an equally or better qualified female candidate. For example, Arvey (1979) concluded that when only one position is available the male candidate tends to be evaluated more favorably. More importantly, the sex-type of the job under consideration has been found to interact with applicant gender such that individuals pursuing gender-incongruent positions are likely to experience greater discrimination. In addition, irrelevant applicant characteristics, e.g., physical attractiveness, have also been shown to affect hiring and treatment decisions. For example, a woman's perceived physical attractiveness may have different implications depending on the position being sought. Heilman and Saruwatari (1979) have shown that although physical attractiveness may be an advantage in traditionally female occupations (e.g., secretary, flight attendant), attractive female candidates may be at a disadvantage when applying for upper-level managerial positions.

Such factors reflect stereotypic notions about the validity of women's participation in the work world, and highlight some of the difficulties women encounter when applying for work. Favoring a male applicant over an equally-qualified female applicant may be based on the belief that he has a greater need to work than she does, a belief that is not only irrelevant, but usually mistaken. Similarly, emphasizing physical attractiveness (or its lack) introduces a criterion for selection that generally has nothing to do with job skills and qualifications. Rather, it subtly reinforces the idea that for women, beauty is incompatible with ability.

Promotion. Blau and Ferber (1987) suggest that "vertical separation" (i.e., differences in the distributions of men and women in the specific positions that make up a given occupation) exists in addition to the occupational segregation of women into traditionally female fields. The documented differences in the numbers of women employed in the lower levels of an occupation when compared to higher level or management positions, suggest that women face additional difficulties in their efforts to become upwardly mobile. For example, within the teaching profession women are overrepresented at the elementary school level (86% of teachers), but underrepresented as administrators (only 26%). In the university setting, 52% of non-tenured lecturers and instructors are women, compared to only 10% of tenured full professors (Betz & Fitzgerald, 1987; Blau & Ferber, 1987).

Dipboye (1987) identifies specific barriers that may limit career advancement for women. Such barriers include biases in job assignments and promotions, biases in the perception and evaluation of performance in supervisory roles, lack of a sponsor or mentor, and exclusion from informal relationships with male peers.

With respect to the first of these, it has long been acknowledged that career success, particularly in the business world, is often dependent upon the types of job assignments one receives as well as promotions to positions of increased status and responsibility. In a review of the research related to job assignments and promotions, Dipboye (1987) reports empirical evidence for discrimination against female managers. For example, both male managers and college students were less likely to assign women subordinates to challenging tasks when compared to men (see Mai-Dalton & Sullivan, 1981). Women are less likely than men to obtain the progressive increases in responsibility and authority that are usually associated with promotion (Stewart & Gudykunst, 1982), including control over hiring, firing, and salary decisions (Wolf & Fligstein, 1979). Finally, women have been shown to receive less feedback on their work from their superiors (Harlan & Weiss, 1982).

When a woman is evaluated for promotion, she may risk different perceptions of her behavior than would be the case for a man exhibiting identical behavior. For example, the existence of appropriate leadership behaviors, such as assertion, may be evaluated in a woman as "aggressive" whereas the same behavior may be viewed more positively for men (Harlan & Weiss, 1982).

Women often have difficulties in finding a sponsor or mentor to aid their organizational progress and in developing effective relationships with their male colleagues. In a study of managers, Fernandez (1981) found that nearly half of the managers surveyed (44%) believed that it is more difficult for women to find a mentor than it is for men. More than half of the male managers surveyed indicated that they felt female managers tended to be excluded from informal networks by men. This form of discrimination reflects what Bernard (1976) has labeled the "stag effect," whereby such practices as male-only clubs and professional activities (e.g., the infamous businessman's golf game) create an "old-boy network" that is difficult for women to penetrate.

The difficulties and biases many women face in their career advancement may result in the perception that different career tracks for women, especially working mothers, are necessary (see, for example, Schwartz, 1989). It is true that women who retain primary responsibility for young children have been shown to be at a disadvantage when offered promotions; many such women are reluctant to take offers requiring relocation (see, for example, Breen, 1983) or unwilling to put in the amount of hours traditionally expected of upper-level managers. However, relegating all such women to a working mothers' "ghetto" perpetuates vertical segregation and compounds the difficulties women currently have in gaining appropriate amounts of responsibility and status. It also perpetuates the androcentric culture of the workplace, implying that women must find ways to adapt to current patterns rather than the other way round. Until career advancement on the "fast-track" is no longer defined by traditional standards that make it nearly impossible for women with families to compete with male colleagues who have wives, barriers to promotion and advancement will remain a reality for upwardly mobile women.

Compensation. When the economic compensation of women workers is discussed, it is inevitably in terms of the "wage gap." The wage gap is a major deterrent to women's success and satisfaction on the job, as is the inadequacy of the provisions for maternal leave and childcare to which it is related.

"Fifty-nine cents to the dollar" is a familiar slogan highlighting the discrepancies in women's pay relative to that of men. The wage gap is a documented reality of women's working life in the United States. In 1984, the median annual salary of full-time women workers was 63.7% that of men's, a figure that is almost identical to that found in 1955 (63.9%; Blau & Ferber, 1987). This wage gap, which was indeed 59% in 1977, has barely changed in fifty years. It stands in stark contrast to the recent narrowing of the wage gap between men and women in other industrial nations such as Britain, Italy, West Germany, and Denmark (Hewlett, 1986).

An examination of the annual salaries for men and women in several occupations illustrates the dramatic effects of the wage gap. Male lawyers aged 25 to 34 earned $27,563 compared to the $20,573 earned by female lawyers in the same age bracket. Male busdrivers earned $15,611; female busdrivers only $9,903. Male retail sales clerks earned $13,002, with female sales clerks earning $7,479 (Hewlett, 1986). In 1983, the salaries of women in executive, administrative, and managerial occupations were 60% of those earned by their male colleagues (Dipboye, 1987). These figures suggest that the wage gap exists across a wide range of occupational categories.

The implications of the wage gap for women are profound. With 60% of working women earning less than $10,000 a year, the term "feminization of poverty" accurately reflects the economic condition of many women today (Betz & Fitzgerald, 1987). Increasingly large numbers of families are maintained solely by women, and the majority of these families (57%) are poor (Hewlett, 1986).

Although level of education moderates women's earning potential, it is also true that women must complete many additional years of schooling before their salaries approximate that of men's. For example, the average female college graduate earns as much as the average male high school drop-out, and a man who failed to complete grade school earns more on the average than a woman with a high school education (Betz & Fitzgerald, 1987; Blau & Ferber, 1987).

As was the case with discrimination in selection and promotion, the passage of the Equal Pay Act (1963) and Title VII of the Civil Rights Act (1964) made overt discrimination (e.g., paying a woman less than a man for the same job) illegal. However, the documented wage gap suggests that there are other factors operating to create a disparity between women's and men's earnings. The explanations that have been offered for the wage gap generally focus on either occupational segregation or the greater tendency for women to stop working for some time during their careers (see, for example, Blau & Ferber, 1987; Dipboye, 1987; Hewlett, 1986).

As discussed above, occupational segregation results in many women workers being employed in "pink collar" jobs, that are characterized by overcrowding, low pay, and low status. Because the majority of women workers are in such occupations their median salaries remain lower than men's, who in comparison do not experience this restriction to lower status occupations. Although more women are entering traditionally male-dominated fields, even greater numbers are seeking employment in the clerical and service sectors. And, as previously noted, wage gaps exist even for women in male-dominated occupations and for women with college educations.

Comparable worth procedures (the practice of paying equally for jobs of similar skill and difficulty even though their actual content may differ), has been suggested as a possible solution to reduce the proportion of the wage gap created by occupational segregation. Assessing comparable worth would entail a systematic evaluation of the levels of knowledge, skill, and ability that are required for particular jobs, cutting across occupational field (Fitzgerald & Betz, 1983). Although procedures are available for implementing comparable worth evaluations and there has been some legal precedent set for their use, this solution to the wage gap has met with considerable resistance (Hewlett, 1986) and its future remains unclear.

The second explanation for the wage gap is closely linked to the interaction between traditional notions of women's childbearing responsibilities and the lack of adequate provisions for maternity leave and childcare. Three times as many women as men are likely to interrupt their careers for a substantial period of time (usually after the birth of a child), and the typical woman drops out of the labor force for nine years (Hewlett, 1986). Such interruptions influence a woman's ability to maintain seniority on the job, and contribute to the risk of being unable to compete with younger colleagues who remain at work and maintain their job-related skills.

Maternity leave benefits in the United States are seriously inadequate, thus hindering the progress of the increasingly large portion of working mothers currently in the labor force. The only federal provision for maternity leave falls under the 1978 Pregnancy Disability Amendment to Title VII of the Civil Rights Act, which makes it illegal to fire a worker solely because she is pregnant. The mandatory provision of temporary disability insurance for a pregnant worker is determined by individual states, with only *five* states currently providing such compensation (Hewlett, 1986)!

Aside from this small provision for maternity leave, there exists no federal maternal or parental leave policy in the United States, which is thus the *only* industrial nation without statutory maternal leave. In sharp contrast, 117 other countries provide leave from employment for childbirth; job protection while on leave; and the provision of a cash benefit that replaces all or most of a woman's earnings (Hewlett, 1986). Clearly, the current perception in the U.S. that childrearing is a "private" matter works to the strong disadvantage of the majority of American women who both work and raise families, and perpetuates the stereotype that a woman's "place" is at home, not in the workforce.

Such social policies take a tremendous economic toll on individual women, as well as on the children and families that depend on them. Women without parental leave benefits lost 607 million dollars over a three-year period when compared to women with such benefits, as estimated by the cost of the loss of seniority, increased unemployment, and the return to lower paying jobs (National Report on Work and Family, 1988). In addition, Census Bureau data has documented that women with maternal leave are likely to return to work sooner than women without maternal leave; during 1981 to 1984, 71% of women receiving such leave returned to work within six months compared to only 43% without maternal leave (National Report on Work and Family, 1989).

The lack of adequate childcare provisions also creates serious problems for women workers and their families. Not only are individual women left with the responsibility of finding and paying for childcare, but many women are simply not able to work when such services are not available. Bloom and Steen (1990) provide evidence suggesting that an increased supply of childcare would bring many more women workers into the labor force (especially those with lower levels of education), would allow women already working to work more hours, and would increase the skill level and economic benefits of women employees. Again, when compared to other nations, the childcare policies of the United States are inadequate and do not reflect the current realities of working mothers (see, for example, Kamerman, 1980). Further, given the link between the lack of adequate childcare and women's decisions to drop out of the work force, this lack is clearly implicated in the lower salaries earned by women workers.

The many forms of discrimination outlined in this section represent barriers for most women workers. Discrimination in selection, promotion, and compensation is rooted in the stereotypical notion that women's place is in the home and not at work. Sexual harassment, an equally serious external barrier, poses a different sort of dilemma for women employees, and we now turn to this topic.

Sexual harassment. Of all the barriers to women's career development, none is more dramatic and at the same time more insidious than sexual harassment. As Goodman (1981) has pointed out, the harassment of women workers has been a problem since women first worked outside the home; however, only recently have data become available to document the reality of the phenomenon. Over the last 10 years a large body of research has accumulated that examines the issue, addressing such questions as how widespread is the problem and what types of harassment are experienced most frequently.

In what is clearly the largest and probably the most well known study conducted to date, the United States Merit Systems Protection Board

142

(USMSPB, 1981) investigated harassment in the federal workplace and reported that 42% of all female employees reported being sexually harassed. Merit Systems noted that many incidents occurred repeatedly, were of long duration, and had a sizeable practical impact, costing the government an estimated minimum of $189 million over the two year period of the study. With respect to particular types of harassment, 33% of the women reported being the target of unwanted sexual remarks, 28% reported suggestive looks, and 26% reported being deliberately touched. These behaviors were classified as less severe forms of harassment. When more severe incidents were examined, 15% of the women reported experiencing pressure for dates, 9% reported being directly pressured for sexual favors, and 9% had received unwanted letters and telephone calls. One percent of the sample (which consisted of approximately 10,000 women) had experienced actual or attempted rape or assault. Merit Systems repeated their study in 1987 and reported essentially identical results. Studies of the civilian workplace (e.g., Gutek, 1985) report comparable findings.

In addition to prevalence studies, several investigations have documented the impact of harassment on women's lives and wellbeing. With respect to work-related outcomes, Merit Systems (1981) reported that nearly one in 10 women who were harassed reported changing jobs as a result. Their more recent study (USMSPB, 1987) reported that over 36,000 federal employees left their jobs due to harassment in the two-year period covered by the study, including women who quit, were fired from their jobs, or were transferred or reassigned because of unwanted sexual attention. The most dramatic results were reported by Coles (1986), who noted that fully *half* of those women who filed a formal sexual harassment complaint were fired; an additional 25% resigned due to psychological stress associated with either the harassment or the complaint. In addition to outright job loss, many women report other negative work-related outcomes, including decreased morale and absenteeism (USMSPB, 1981), changes in work quantity and quality, and deleterious effects on interpersonal relationships at work [See Koss (1990) for a review].

In the short time that harassment has been formally studied, it has become clear that it takes a tremendous toll on women's lives. In addition to the damage done to women's careers, the psychological costs are enormous and many individuals suffer serious psychophysiological reactions as well. Koss (1990) reports that harassment victims describe feeling fearful, angry, anxious, and depressed. Silverman (1976–77) documented similar results much earlier, noting reports of feeling anger, upset, fear, helplessness, guilt, and alienation. More recently, Crull (1982) and Gutek (1981) have documented the sometimes severe physical consequences as well, including anxiety attacks, headaches, sleep disturbance, disordered eating, gastrointestinal disorders, nausea, weight loss (or gain), and crying spells.

Space does not permit a discussion of the several theories that have been advanced to explain the widespread harassment of working women; interested readers are referred to Fitzgerald and Ormerod (in press) for a review. It is important to note, however, that the majority of these proposals highlight the salience of women's sex and gender-role, as well

143

as the perceived incompatibility of these characteristics with the role of worker. Although explanations at the individual level of analysis have been proposed (e.g., the woman elicited the harassment by her dress or behavior, the harasser was psychologically deviant in some way or, conversely, did not mean to be offensive), such explanations are clearly unable to account for the sheer overwhelming numbers of women who are harassed every day or for the serious consequences of harassment for women as a group. Rather, it seems more reasonable to propose that, although exceptions certainly exist, the majority of harassment stems from the continued androcentric nature of the workplace itself. Women are often perceived as tokens (Kanter, 1977), and thus interlopers. Particularly in the nontraditional blue-collar trades, where women are few, hostility toward them is often quite fierce. Such women report higher rates of harassment than any other group (Baker, 1989, and others). Conversely, in the traditional "pink collar" occupations, almost totally dominated by women, where the duties tend to parallel the activities traditionally associated with the female role, women are harassed in different, more clearly sexual ways (see Gutek's 1985 discussion of the sex-role spillover hypothesis).

Baker (1989) has pointed out that "Increasingly, researchers and theorists . . . are recognizing that no one factor or variable can account for or explain all of the aspects of how, why and when sexual harassment occurs. Simple assertions that harassment is an expression of male power which serves to keep women in subordinate positions are being replaced with efforts to determine the relative impact of various factors and types of factors (i.e., situational, societal or individual) on the occurrence and effects of sexual harassment" (p. 38). Whatever these explanations ultimately turn out to be, it is clear that sexual harassment is an everyday reality of working women's lives, and one that has extremely serious consequences both for their vocational adjustment and their psychological wellbeing.

Internal Barriers

In addition to frustrations such as the external barriers described above, the model of vocational adjustment highlights the important role played by internal, or psychological barriers, particularly the conflict generated by commitment to goals that are incompatible with one another. For women, the most obvious of these conflicts is that between work and family roles, and we now turn to these considerations.

The Conflict of Multiple Roles. Given the salience of both work and family in women's lives, the quality of the interface between them is critically important to their career adjustment. As previously discussed, employed women generally retain primary responsibility for parenting and homecare (see, for example, Baruch & Barnett, 1986; Hirsch & Rapkin, 1986; Hochschild, 1989; Weingarten, 1978), even when working full time. Such arrangements can place severe limitations on the potential for career success and satisfaction, particularly in combination with the external barriers described above. The following section will attempt to unravel some of the many issues and concerns associated with multiple role participation.

It has become commonplace in the vocational psychology literature to assert that the major difficulty in women's career development is that of participating simultaneously in two activity systems whose claims are, both practically and philosophically, incompatible (Coser & Rokoff, 1971; Fitzgerald & Betz, 1983; and others). Discussions of role conflict and role overload are common in the literature, and in particular the presumed conflict between working and mothering has received considerable attention.

Recently, the traditional assumptions underlying the research on multiple role participation have begun to be questioned. Some writers have criticized the construct of multiple role conflict on the grounds that it may be used to justify excluding women from the paid labor force (Fowlkes, 1987); others warn that emphasizing the difficulties working mothers face when combining multiple roles may mask misogynist objections to women's entrance into the work force and serve to restrict their potential for multiple successes (Epstein, 1987). Most agree, however, that there is no clearcut answer to the question of whether the experience of participation in multiple roles is exclusively positive or negative, and that current research and practice should focus on ways to improve the quality of women's multiple role participation so that the benefits associated with such involvement can be maximized.

Before considering the research on multiple role participation, some relevant distinctions are in order. The term *role conflict* generally refers to "the simultaneous occurrence of two or more role expectations such that compliance with one would make compliance with the other more difficult" (Katz & Kahn, 1978). *Role overload*, on the other hand, is the inability to satisfy all of one's role expectations in the time that is available to do so, even though each of the demands is perceived as valid (O'Leary, 1977).

Factors leading to interrole conflict are psychological in nature and may involve lack of support for participation in the work role, the perceived incompatibility of career success with components of the traditional female role, and the conflict and guilt associated with combining the roles of worker and mother (Fitzgerald & Betz, 1983). As we will show, these factors influence whether or not the combination of multiple roles results in positive or negative outcomes for women. In addition, because they represent attitudes and beliefs rather than external realities, change in the influence of such factors is often possible. In contrast, role overload relates to practical concerns reflecting the lack of sufficient time to satisfy multiple role demands. Taken together, these two factors can be seen to create *role strain* for multiple role women (Barnett & Baruch, 1985), role strain being a general term referring to the negative psychological and physiological effects of conflict and overload.

The issue of whether multiple role participation results in negative or positive outcomes is reflected in the evolution of the research in this area. Originally, research on such participation reflected the influence of the "scarcity hypothesis" (Coser, 1974; Goode, 1960; Slater, 1963). This perspective emphasized the negative aspects of role overload, viewing the amount of time and energy individuals have at their disposal as limited, and the demands of organizations (for men) and families (for women) as "greedy," i.e., as demanding all of a person's allegiance. Thus, role strain was viewed as the normal consequence of not having enough energy to fulfill one's many role obligations. The more roles an individual engaged in, the more his or her resources would be exhausted, resulting in increased amounts of role strain and psychological distress. The predictions resulting from this hypothesis, however, do not appear to accurately reflect women's experience; rather, as the number of roles increases, in many cases so does the woman's well-being (see, for example, Thoits, 1983). Role conflict and role overload have been found to be related to anxiety only in unemployed women, refuting the assumption that it is employed women who will experience greater amounts of role strain (Barnett & Baruch, 1985).

In contrast, the "expansion hypothesis" (Marks, 1977; Sieber, 1974) has received greater empirical support and provides a more optimistic framework for viewing the multiple role participation of women. Here, the focus is on the net positive gains that result from involvement in multiple roles. A fundamental assumption of this hypothesis is that multiple roles create a network of supports, benefits, and privileges (e.g., self esteem, recognition, economic reward) that an individual woman may draw on. Thus, an enriched self-structure is the result of accumulated role rewards (both monetary and otherwise) that provide an opportunity for increased autonomy (Hirsch & Rapkin, 1986). Empirical support for this position includes the existence of superior physical health for multiple role women (Verbrugge, 1983); enhanced well-being associated with multiple role involvement (Gove & Tudor, 1973); lower levels of depression for married working mothers when compared to nonworking mothers (Kandell et al., 1985); and evidence that involvement in family roles creates a buffer against symptoms of strain (Cooke & Rosseau, 1984).

Although the expansion hypothesis has enjoyed considerable empirical support, the answer to whether multiple role participation is a negative or positive experience for women is not straightforward. In her review of relevant studies, Thoits (1987) concludes that there is no evidence for either a purely harmful or purely beneficial effect. Instead, she suggests that the lack of clearcut results suggests the existence of variables that moderate the amount of psychological and physical strain or wellbeing any individual woman experiences. Such moderating variables include the quality of the roles engaged in, the existence of social and emotional support for working, the nature of the marital relationship, and, importantly, participation in the maternal role.

With respect to work role quality, important variables include the degree of job satisfaction a woman experiences and the type of work schedule she must contend with (irregular versus consistent). The quality of the family role, on the other hand, involves such factors as satisfaction with her spouse's participation in domestic and childcare tasks, and the amount of guilt associated with delegating such tasks. Baruch and Barnett (1987) provide evidence for the contention that it is not the number of roles a woman occupies, but the quality of her experience in those roles that moderates well-being. For example, social role quality was found to be a major independent predictor of role overload, role conflict, and anxiety in a study of middle-aged women, with increased quality of the maternal role inversely related to anxiety (Barnett & Baruch, 1985). Hirsch and Rapkin (1986) found that different profiles of marital and occupational satisfaction were associated with differences in the amount of psychological symptomatology, overall life satisfaction, and social network support and rejection in married female nurses (e.g., high levels of both marital and occupational satisfaction were associated with greater life satisfaction and less symptomatology; low levels resulted in the opposite pattern).

Independently of role quality, strong evidence exists for the positive effects of employment for women. In a review of the literature on the psychological and physical adjustment of working mothers, Nye (1974) concluded nearly 20 years ago that employed mothers were physically healthier and enjoyed a more positive self-image when compared to housewives. Working women have been found to have greater power in the marital relationship and a larger degree of influence in fertility and childrearing decisions (Bahr, 1974). In addition, the worker role may serve as a buffer against the stress experienced in other roles (Barnett & Baruch, 1985). Given this evidence, the perspective that it is women's employment that is the source of interrole conflict is misleading and ignores the many benefits associated with involvement in the work role.

When the maternal role is examined, however, the data suggest that this particular role is more often associated with greater amounts of stress for women. For example, Gove and Zeiss (1987) found nonmothers to be happier than mothers, although attitudes toward working moderated well-being (i.e., employed mothers were less happy if they did not want to work). Cooke and Rosseau (1984) review evidence suggesting that the presence of children, especially those under six years old, is associated with symptoms of psychological strain. They highlight characteristics of motherhood (e.g., greater demands on one's time and resources, less personal freedom, and more loneliness and depression) that are likely to contribute to such strain. They also state that these disadvantages can be offset by employment (Brown & Harris, 1978), especially when the work role is viewed as a career, not as a job (Holahan & Gilbert, 1979).

Steil and Turetsky (1987) conclude that motherhood is a liability for women, both with respect to the power differential within a marriage and in its influence on marital satisfaction; mothers in their sample enjoyed less equality in their marriages, with greater responsibility for childcare associated with increased dysphoria and somatic stress. Finally, Barnett and Baruch (1985) suggest that motherhood, not paid employment, may be the most important source of stress in women's lives. In their study of middle-aged women, mothers across all levels of education, age, income, and employment status experienced greater levels of role conflict than nonmothers.

Given the evidence described above, we agree with those who suggest a need to move beyond the simple question of whether multiple role participation has positive or negative effects for women. Rather, the conditions under which the benefits of multiple roles outweigh the costs must be identified; that is, it is important to understand ways to maximize women's experiences as they participate in multiple roles. This is particularly true given that this lifestyle has become the normative reality for most women at this time.

One approach to this problem is to examine how the structural and normative constraints on women's lives influence role conflict and role strain. Thoits (1987) believes that greater amounts of such conflict are associated with external constraints on interpersonal bargaining and thereby on the relative social power between marriage partners. Constraints such as the unavailability of childcare and the belief that men's involvement in parental and domestic tasks is inappropriate decrease women's bargaining power. Thoits suggests that bargaining power, essential to a more positive experience of multiple role participation, can be facilitated by greater access to monetary rewards, education, and social networks. This viewpoint suggests that women's lives would be greatly enhanced by structural changes such as access to quality childcare, adequate parental leave policies, and flexible work schedules (Voydanoff, 1988), as well as by normative changes in attitudes and beliefs that reflect egalitarian divisions of work and household labor.

Thus, we emphasize the importance of understanding the critical role played by structural and normative constraints, i.e., the external barriers discussed previously, in the generation and maintenance of "internal" barriers such as multiple role conflict. As with the notion of vocational realism, it is important to recognize the realities involved in most women's experience of multiple role involvement. Viewing role conflict as an intrapsychic issue having solely to do with the woman's own psychological dynamics miscasts the issue and inappropriately locates the problem within the woman herself (e.g., her inability to handle both work and family) rather than within the reality constraints of current social arrangements. Although it is true that many women experience considerable psychological conflict and strain when attempting to integrate the different aspects of their lives, such negative outcomes appear to be a direct result of these constraints, the most important of which are traditional notions of the relative appropriateness of women's involvement in work and mothering, and the lack of access to "real world" support resources.

Paradoxically, it appears that a trade-off exists between the greater psychological well-being associated with multiple role participation on the one hand, and the deleterious effects of such involvement on vocational success and career development on the other. Participation in multiple roles appears to yield a higher quality of life for many women, with the positive effects of employment providing a buffer for the negative effects of the maternal role. The effects of family responsibilities, however, continue to set boundaries on the occupational attainment and advancement of most women. Until the structural changes necessary to enhance the career adjustment of women are introduced, it is important to examine ways to maximize the benefits of multiple role participation, while at the same time attempting to reduce the associated stresses and costs. Thus, issues related to the ways in which women cope with their complicated lives become an important factor which will be discussed in the next section.

Coping With Complex Lives

The assumption that combining work and family is a somewhat "risky business" that can lead to negative outcomes for both the woman herself and for her family as well, appears to influence the types of coping strategies that women consider. Thoits (1987), for example, suggests that such strategies would entail abandoning one or more roles, segregating roles in time and space, and assigning priority to roles. None of these options are compatible with the view that participating simultaneously in multiple roles is a positive experience for women, and some such strategies have actually been found to be negatively related to satisfaction (see discussion below; Gray, 1980).

Alternatively, a constructionist perspective views a woman as an active force in her environment. She is able to manipulate her multiple role involvement to enhance her well-being, thus increasing the personal benefits she accrues from such participation (Thoits, 1987). In describing the different frameworks from which coping strategies may be viewed, we will emphasize those strategies that result in a greater sense of empowerment for women.

Hall's Coping Strategies. One well-known framework that has been important in understanding multiple role coping strategies is that delineated by Hall (1972a). He identifies three types of coping methods: *structural role redefinition* (actively changing or re-negotiating the role expectations that are imposed by other people such as one's partner or boss); *personal role redefinition* (changing one's individual role expectations without making external changes in the environment); and *reactive role behavior* (trying to meet all of one's role demands without any attempts to negotiate changes). These strategies are known in the literature as Types I, II, and III coping, respectively.

Hall (1972b) found that a positive correlation existed between Type I coping and satisfaction, with a negative relationship existing between Type III coping and satisfaction. In a study that re-evaluated Hall's categories, Gray (1980) reported that the strategies of overlapping roles, keeping roles totally separate, attempting to meet all expectations, eliminating entire roles, and the absence of a conscious strategy for dealing with role conflict were negatively related to satisfaction.

Of the strategies described by Hall, none appears entirely effective. Type I coping seems the most integrative of solutions, but is difficult to implement as it requires the agreement of role senders (e.g., supervisors and family members) that may be impossible to obtain. Personal role redefinition (Type II in the Hall typology) is an attractive alternative, and is congruent with the constructionist perspective described above. However, it is unrealistic to expect that all women will be able to implement this strategy, as it requires considerable assertiveness and clarity about the importance of one's own needs. Unfortunately, many women are apt to engage in the reactive role behavior that characterizes Type III coping, currently popularized as the "superwoman" stereotype who is capable of "doing it all." Beutell and Greenhaus (1983) found that women with traditional attitudes were most likely to utilize such strategies. The prevalence of Type III coping suggests the widespread belief that the responsibility for managing all of one's role demands lies within the individual woman, and fails to recognize the importance of structural changes.

The Challenges of Special Group Membership

In the spirit of recognizing individual differences and the wealth of diversity that exists among women, this section will briefly discuss concerns related to women of color and lesbian women. Although a comprehensive overview is not possible here, we hope that his section will stimulate readers to seek further information concerning the unique needs of women from diverse backgrounds.

Women of color. Current estimates show that 20% of women in the labor force are women of color (Malveaux & Wallace, 1987). As is true of psychology in general, the vocational behavior literature has tended to overlook issues related to the career development of minority women, although the experiences of African American women have been studied to a somewhat greater degree than those of other minority groups. In this section of the chapter, we will first examine characteristics of the labor force participation of women of color, and then provide examples of how racial-ethnic status influences career development.

In contrast to white women, African American women have traditionally expected to work all of their adult lives (Betz, in press), an expectation reflected in their labor force participation rates which are generally higher than those of white women. Although the labor force participation of Hispanic women has shown the greatest increase in recent years, the participation of women in this group is still lower than that of African American and white women (Malveaux & Wallace, 1987). When unemployment is examined, both African American and Hispanic women are found to have higher rates than white women.

Not surprisingly, the earnings of women of color are lower than those of white women. African American women earn 92% of the salaries reported by their white counterparts; the corresponding figure for Latina women is only 85%. As is the case for women in general, the largest proportion of women in all racial-ethnic groups work in clerical occupations. African American women are also highly concentrated in retail sales, operative occupations, and private household jobs, whereas Latina, Asian, and Native American women are likely to be found in operative occupations (Malveaux & Wallace, 1987). Thus, occupational segregation places even more severe constraints on the occupational attainment of women of color, a condition exacerbated by the lower wages minority women tend to receive. One exception to this pattern is that there are more minority women than white women in blue collar occupations (Malveaux & Wallace, 1987).

The increased discrimination and occupational segregation that women of color experience has been described as a state of "double jeopardy" (Beale, 1970), suggesting that such women are discriminated against twice: once for being female and once for being non-White. In addition, Malveaux and Wallace (1987) have suggested that African American women often suffer from a third disadvantage—that is, they are more likely to be single heads of households (over 42% of such families) due to a variety of factors including a decrease in Black male employment rates, a decrease in the gender ratio among African Americans, and higher rates of divorce or family disruption (Betz, in press). These households with single heads are also much more likely to exist at the poverty level.

This doubling or tripling of factors related to discrimination can result in extremely limited opportunities for women of color. Women from lower socioeconomic groups are less likely to have access to education, thus limiting their career choice options. The traditional conceptualization of the process of career development (that assumes access to a range of vocational choices) may not accurately describe the experiences of women whose primary motivation for work is economic survival for themselves and their families.

External barriers to career adjustment are likely to be exacerbated for women of color. Even within clerical occupations, women of color receive less economic compensation for their work, and those in management have fewer opportunities for promotion than their White colleagues. Women of color in the trades and blue collar occupations may be even more vulnerable to sexual harassment due to their racial-ethnic background (which results in a "double token" status) and their more extreme economic disadvantage.

The issue of multiple role conflict described earlier appears to manifest itself differently for women of color. Especially for African American women, the roles of career and family may not be viewed as conflicting, given their general expectation for employment during the adult years. Rather, different types of coping strategies may be utilized to ease work and family participation, such as a "kin help exchange" childcare arrangement, whereby relatives in one's extended family share childcare responsibilities (McAdoo, 1981). On the other hand, however, women from cultures that adhere to more traditional sex-role norms (e.g., Latina women) may experience even greater amounts of role strain and multiple role conflict.

Thus, the career development of women of color is likely to differ in important ways from that of White women. It would be erroneous to assume, however, that women within any broad racial-ethnic group (e.g., Hispanic women or Afro-American) will have identical experiences. In addition, it is important to consider factors that interact with race (such a socioeconomic status) to best understand any individual woman's experience. The dictum that an individual woman is in some ways like *all* other women, in some ways like *some* other women, and in some ways like *no* other woman is particularly true for the consideration of the career development of women of color.

Lesbian women. Lesbian women are rarely mentioned in discussions of women's vocational behavior. They are thus even more invisible than women of color, due both to heterosexist cultural assumptions and the prevalence of homophobic attitudes that insure that most such women must conceal their lifestyle. Federal statistics on the labor force participation of lesbians do not exist, and only recently have the special concerns related to the career development of lesbians been examined.

The choice of a lesbian lifestyle is one with important implications for an individual woman's career development, however. When compared to heterosexual women, lesbian women are likely to have a stronger commitment to work and career as well as a greater recognition of the need to support themselves financially. In choosing not to have a male partner, lesbian women are unable to rely on a source of economic security that has traditionally been available to married, heterosexual women (Hetherington & Orzek, 1989).

Hetherington and Orzek (1989) provide an excellent summary of issues relevant to the career counseling of lesbian women, emphasizing the importance of examining the ways in which stages of lesbian identity development interact with those of career development. For example, women in early stages of identity formation may be less likely to disclose their identity in their work environment, whereas women in the later stages may make a conscious choice to be involved in a career field that actively supports a lesbian lifestyle.

The existence of homophobic attitudes in the workplace can severely inhibit the job satisfaction of lesbian women. Such attitudes generally make it necessary to conceal one's lesbian identity, a process that can be stressful as well as damaging to self esteem. Thus, lesbian women are faced with decisions about the degree to which they feel comfortable being "out" at their job, and with considerations of how pertinent their sexual identity is to their occupational choice, issues that for heterosexual women are simply not relevant.

Hetherington and Orzek (1989) discuss several issues relevant to the career adjustment of lesbian women. They suggest the importance of determining organizational policy on nondiscrimination with respect to sexual preference, and of gauging the sensitivity to a gay and lesbian lifestyle that exists in individual work settings. Dual-career issues can be problematic as well, with concerns arising as to if and how to introduce one's partner or to acknowledge one's relationship.

Finally, multiple role issues may play themselves out in a different fashion for lesbian women. Employers generally assume that all women are oriented toward marriage and a family, an assumption that reinforces prevailing heterosexist biases. However, it is also inaccurate to assume that lesbian women are not family-oriented as many lesbians are mothers who live with their children, thus sharing the increased responsibilities and stresses inherent in single parent families. For women with partners, relationships are often characterized by greater role flexibility and a more egalitarian sharing of tasks than are traditional heterosexual marriages, and so may facilitate the balancing of multiple role responsibilities.

As the foregoing discussion makes clear, lesbian women bring particular strengths and vulnerabilities to the developmental tasks of career choice and adjustment. Despite the stress inherent in membership in a mostly invisible and often highly stigmatized group, such women exemplify many of the factors known to facilitate women's career development (e.g., nonmarried, nontraditional sex role attitudes, and greater work commitment). Thus, as was the case for women of color, it is critical for research as well as practice to begin to attend to the unique influences that lesbian identity exerts on women's vocational behavior.

Implications for Counseling Interventions

Over the course of the last decade, a number of recommendations for counseling practice have appeared (Betz, 1982; Betz & Fitzgerald, 1987; Fitzgerald & Crites, 1979, 1980; Fitzgerald, 1986). Although differing in their specifics, these guidelines share three basic assumptions concerning the appropriate role of career counselors who work with women clients.

First, it is critical that counselors be knowledgeable in the area of women's career development. For example, Fitzgerald and Crites (1979, 1980) emphasize the necessity of familiarity with the applications and limitations of theories of career development, including the research on vocational maturity and achievement motivation; classical test theory and psychometrics, with emphasis on vocational interest and aptitude measurement, and sex bias in instrumentation; and accurate information concerning the place of women in the labor market, discrimination, myths about working women, and so forth. Similarly, Betz (1982; Betz & Fitzgerald, 1987) notes that counselors must be familiar with the research on the factors that influence women's career development, and be aware of counselor and test biases that perpetuate sterotyped roles and limited options for women. The implication of these guidelines is that counselors must first be familiar with the general literature on research and practice in career psychology and in addition be knowledgeable concerning the ways in which this literature does and does not apply to women. Betz and Fitzgerald (1987) provide a thorough presentation of this material, and updated reviews (such as Betz, in press, and the present chapter) appear frequently.

Second, there is general agreement that such knowledge, although necessary, is not sufficient. To facilitate women's career development requires an active stance and the willingness to encourage women to expand their options and choices, while simultaneously weighing the various reality factors that are important in their lives. For example, Betz (1982) suggests that counselors should actively encourage the development of nontraditional interests and competencies, particularly continuation in mathematics so that options are not unnecessarily restricted. Further, she suggests that counselors should proactively confront internalized socialized stereotypes and beliefs that serve to restrict the client's options, and should assist women in dealing with reality based issues and fears. Although this active stance contrasts with the more typically nondirective approach generally espoused in counselor training programs, we believe that a rigid adherence to the humanistic ideal of individual self determination actually represents unwitting collusion with the limitations that society places on women. As Betz and Fitzgerald (1987) have pointed out, "psychology needs to confront the fact that leaving a woman to 'do what she thinks best' actually results in abandoning her to fight societal sex stereotypes alone—society is only too ready to influence her in stereotypic directions" (p. 252). A similar argument has been made by Brooks (1988).

Finally, counseling guidelines suggest, and we agree, that a stance of actively encouraging women's career development must be accompanied by a commitment to working for social change. It is not reasonable to encourage women to expand their horizons and at the same time accept a social structure that penalizes them economically, discriminates against them occupationally, harasses them extensively, and still assumes they do all the housework and childcare! It is critical that counselors participate in attempts to restructure present social arrangements, else their work with individual women will ultimately prove futile. As Vetter (1973) has
written,

> "Counselors must not continue to perpetuate such a situation. . . . It seems time for counseling psychology to pick up the challenge, rather hesitantly offered by Samler (1964) to become involved in social action; to make it a definite part of our professional task to set out to affect the status quo" (p. 64).

REFERENCES

Arvey, R.D. (1979). *Fairness in selecting employees.* Reading, MA: Addison-Wesley.

Astin, H.S. (1984). The meaning of work in women's lives: A sociopsychological model of career choice and work behavior. *The Counseling Psychologist, 12,* 117–126.

Bahr, S.J. (1974). Effects on power and division of labor in the family. In L.W. Hoffman & F.I. Nye (Eds.), *Working mothers.* San Francisco: Jossey-Bass.

Baker, N.L. (1989). *Sexual harassment and job satisfaction in traditional and nontraditional industrial occupations.* Unpublished doctoral dissertation, California School of Professional Psychology, Los Angeles, CA.

Barnett, R.C., & Baruch, G.K. (1985). Women's involvement in multiple roles and psychological distress. *Journal of Personality and Social Psychology, 49,* 135–145.

Barnett, R.C., Biener, L., & Baruch, G.K., Eds. (1987). *Gender and stress.* New York: Free Press.

Bart, P. (1971). Depression in middle-aged women. In V. Gornick and B.K. Moran (Eds.), *Woman in sexist society* (pp. 163–186). New York: Basic Books.

Baruch, G.K., & Barnett, R.C. (1986). Consequences of fathers' participation in family work: Parents' role strain and well-being. *Journal of Personality and Social Psychology, 51,* 983–992.

Baruch, G.K., & Barnett, R.C. (1987). Role quality and psychological well-being. In F. Crosby (Ed.), *Spouse, parent, worker: On gender and multiple roles* (pp. 91–108). New Haven: Yale University Press.

Beale, F. (1970). Double jeopardy: To be black and female. In T. Cade (Ed.), *The black woman: An anthology* (pp. 90–100). New York: New American Library.

Belenky, M.F., Clinchy, B.M., Goldberger, N.R., & Tarule, J.M. (1986). *Women's ways of knowing: The development of self, voice and mind.* New York: Basic Books.

Bernard, J. (1976). Where are we now? Some thoughts on the current scene. *Psychology of Women Quarterly, 6,* 55–71.

Betz, N.E. (1982). *Guidelines for career counseling women.* Unpublished paper, Department of Psychology, The Ohio State University. Cited in Betz, N.E., & Fitzgerald, L.F. (1987). *The career psychology of women.* New York: Academic Press.

Betz, N.E. (in press). Women's career development. In M. Paludi and F. Denmark (Eds.), *Handbook of the psychology of women.* Westport, CT: Greenwood Press.

Betz, N.E., & Fitzgerald, L.F. (1987). *The career psychology of women.* New York: Academic Press.

Blau, F.D., & Ferber, M.A. (1987). Occupations and earnings of women workers. In K.S. Koziara, M.H. Moskow, & L.D. Tanner (Eds.), *Working women: Past, Present and future* (pp. 37–68). Washington, D.C.: Industrial Relations Research Association.

Bloom, D.E., & Steen, T.P. (1990). The labor force implications of expanding the child care industry. *Population Research and Policy Review, 9,* 25–44.

Breen, G.E. (1983). *Middle management morale in the '80s.* New York: American Management Association.

Brooks, L. (1988). Encouraging women's motivation for nontraditional career and lifestyle options: A model for assessment and intervention. *Journal of Career Development, 14,* 223–241.

Brown, G.W., & Harris, T. (1978). *Social origins of depression: A study of psychiatric disorders in women.* New York: Free Press.

Beutell, N.J., & Greenhaus, J.H. (1983). Integration of home and non-home roles: Women's conflict and coping behavior. *Journal of Applied Psychology, 68,* 43–48.

Card, J.J., Steel, L., & Abeles, R.P. (1980). Sex differences in realization of individual potential for achievement. *Journal of Vocational Behavior, 17,* 1–21.

Carnegie Commission on Higher Education (1973). *Opportunities for women in higher education.* New York: McGraw-Hill.

Chodorow, N. (1978). *The reproduction of mothering.* Berkeley, CA: University of California Press.

Coles, F.S. (1986). Forced to quit: Sexual harassment complaints and agency response. *Sex Roles, 14,* 81–95.

Cooke, R.A., & Rosseau, D.M. (1984). Stress and strain from family roles and work-role expectations. *Journal of Applied Psychology, 69,* 252–260.

Coser, L. (1974). *Greedy institutions.* New York: Free Press.

Crites, J.O. (1969). *Vocational psychology.* New York: McGraw-Hill.

Crites, J.O. (1978). *Theory and research handbook for the CMI* (2nd ed.). Monterey, CA: CTB/McGraw-Hill.

Crites, J.O. (1976). A comprehensive model of career development in early adulthood. *Journal of Vocational Behavior, 9*, 105–118.

Crites, J.O. (1981). *Career counseling: Models, methods and materials.* New York: McGraw-Hill.

Crull, P. (1982). Stress effects of sexual harassment on the job: Implications for counseling. *American Journal of Orthopsychiatry, 52,* 539–544.

Csikszentmihalyi, M. (1990). *Flow: the psychology of optimal experience.* New York: Harper & Row.

Dawis, R.V., & Lofquist, L.H. (1984). *A psychological theory of work adjustment.* Minneapolis: University of Minnesota Press.

Dipboye, R.L. (1987). Problems and progress of women in management. In K.S. Koziara, M.H. Moskow, & L.D. Tanner (Eds.), *Working women: Past, present and future* (pp. 118–153). Washington, D.C.: Industrial Relations Research Association.

Epstein, C.F. (1987). Multiple demands and multiple roles: The conditions of successful management. In F.J. Crosby (Ed.). *Spouse, parent, worker: On gender and multiple roles* (pp. 23–38). New Haven: Yale University Press.

Fassinger, R.E. (1985). A causal model of career choice in college women. *Journal of Vocational Behavior, 27,* 123–153.

Fassinger, R.E. (1990). Testing of a model of career choice in two populations of college women. *Journal of Vocational Behavior,* in press.

Fernandez, J.P. (1981). *Racism and sexism in corporate life.* Lexington, MA: Lexington Books.

Fitzgerald, L.F. (1985). Career counseling women: Principles, procedures and problems. In Z. Leibowitz and D. Lea (Eds.). *Adult career development: Concepts issues and practices.* Alexandria, VA: AACD.

Fitzgerald, L.F., & Betz, N.E. (1983). Issues in the vocational psychology of women. In W.B. Walsh & S.H. Osipow (Eds.), *Handbook of vocational psychology,* Vol. I. Hillsdale, NJ: Erlbaum.

Fitzgerald, L.F., & Crites, J.O. (1979). Career counseling: Standards for counselors. *The Counseling Psychologist, 9,* 33–34.

Fitzgerald, L.F., & Crites, J.O. (1980). Toward a career psychology of women: What do we know? What do we need to know? *Journal of Counseling Psychology, 27,* 44–62.

Fitzgerald, L.F., Fassinger, R.E., & Betz, N.E. (1989). *An individual differences model of vocational choice in college women.* Paper presented at the annual meeting of the American Psychological Association, New Orleans, LA.

Fitzgerald, L.F., & Ormerod, A.J. (in press). Breaking silence: The sexual harassment of women in academia and the workplace. In M. Paludi and F. Denmark (Eds.), *Handbook of the psychology of women.* Westport, CT: Greenwood Press.

Flanagan, J.C. (1971). *Project TALENT: Five years after high school and appendix II: Final Report.* Pittsburgh: University of Pittsburgh, American Institute for Research.

Fowlkes, M.R. (1987). Role combinations and role conflict: Introductory perspective. In F. Crosby (Ed.), *Spouse, parent, worker: On gender and multiple roles,* (pp. 3–10). New Haven: Yale University Press.

Gilligan, C. (1982). *In a different voice.* Cambridge, MA: Harvard University Press.

Ginzberg, E., Ginsburg, S.W., Axelrad, S., & Herma, J.L. (1951). *Occupational choice.* New York: Columbia University Press.

Goode, W.J. (1960). A theory of strain. *American Sociological Review, 46,* 443–452.

Goodman, J.L. (1981). Sexual harassment: Some observations on the distance traveled and the distance yet to go. *Capital University Law Review, 10,* 445–469.

Gottfredson, L.S. (1986). The *g* factor in employment. *Journal of Vocational Behavior, 29,* Whole No. 3.

Gove, W.R., & Tudor, J. (1973). Adult sex roles and mental illness. *American Journal of Sociology, 78,* 812–835.

Gove, W.R., & Zeiss, C. (1987). Multiple roles and happiness. In F. Crosby (Ed.), *Spouse, parent, worker: On gender and multiple roles* (pp. 125–137). New Haven: Yale University Press.

Gray, J.D. (1980). Role conflicts and coping strategies in married professional women. *Dissertation Abstracts International, 40,* 3781-A.

Gutek, B. (1981). *Experiences of sexual harassment: Results from a representative survey.* Paper presented to the annual meeting of the American Psychological Association, Los Angeles.

Gutek, B. (1985). *Sex and the workplace.* San Francisco, CA: Jossey-Bass.

Hall, D.T. (1972a). A model of coping with role conflict: The role behavior of college educated women. *Administrative Science Quarterly, 17,* 471–489.

Hall, D.T. (1972b). Role identity processes in the lives of married women. Unpublished paper. Quoted in O'Leary, V.E. (1977). *Toward understanding women.* Monterey, CA: Brooks/Cole.

Harlan, A., & Weiss, C.L. (1982). Sex differences in factors affecting managerial advancement. In P.A. Wallace (Ed.), *Women in the workplace* (pp. 59–100). Boston: Auburn House.

Heilman, M.E., & Saruwatari, L.R. (1979). When beauty is beastly: the effects of appearance and sex on evaluations of job applicants for managerial and nonmanagerial jobs. *Organizational Behavior and Human Performance, 23,* 360–372.

Hetherington, C., & Orzek, A. (1989). Career counseling and life planning with lesbian women. *Journal of Counseling and Development, 68,* 52–55.

Hewlett, S.A. (1986). *A lesser life: The myth of women's liberation in America.* New York: Warner Books.

Hirsch, B.J., & Rapkin, B.D. (1986). Multiple roles, social networks, and women's well-being. *Journal of Personality and Social Psychology, 51,* 1237–1247.

Hochschild, A. (1989). *The second shift: Working parents and the revolution at home.* New York: Viking.

Holland, J.L. (1985). *Making vocational choices* (2nd ed.). New York: Prentice-Hall.

Holohan, C.K., & Gilbert, L.A. (1979). Inter-role conflict for working women: Career versus job. *Journal of Applied Psychology, 64,* 86–90.

Hoyt, D.P., & Kennedy, C.E. (1958). Interest and personality correlates of career-motivated and homemaking-motivated college women. *Journal of Counseling Psychology, 5,* 44–49.

Hyde, J.S. (1985). *Half the human experience: The psychology of women* (3rd ed.). Lexington, MA: Heath.

Ilfeld, F., Jr. (1977). *Sex differences in psychiatric symptomatology.* Paper presented at the meeting of the American Psychological Association, San Francisco.

Kamerman, S.B. (1980). Child care and family benefits: Policies of six industrialized countries. *Monthly Labor Review,* Nov, 23–28.

Kandel, D.B., Davies, M., & Raveis, V.H. (1985). The stressfulness of daily social roles for women. *Journal of Health and Social Behavior, 26,* 64–78.

Kanter, R.M. (1977). *Men and women of the corporation.* New York: Basic Books.

Katz, D., & Kahn, R.L. *The social psychology of organizations* (2nd ed). New York: John Wiley.

Kerr, B.A. (1988). Career counseling for gifted girls and women. *Journal of Career Development, 14,* 259–268.

Koss, M.P. (1990). Changed lives: The psychological impact of sexual harassment. In M. Paludi (Ed.), *Ivory power: Sex and gender harassment in the academy.* New York: SUNY Press.

Mai-Dalton, R.R., & Sullivan, J.J. (1981). The effects of managers' sex on the assignment to a challenging or dull task and reasons for the choice. *Academy of Management Journal, 24,* 603–612.

Malveaux, J., & Wallace, P. (1987). Minority women in the workplace. In K.S. Koziara, M.H. Moskow, & L.D. Tanner (Eds.), *Working women: Past, present, future.* Washington, D.C.: Bureau of National Affairs.

Marks, S.R. (1977). Multiple roles and role strain: Some notes on human energy, time and commitment. *American Sociological Review, 41,* 921–936.

McAdoo, H.P. (1981). Stress and support networks of working single black mothers. In *Black working women: Debunking the myths, a multidisciplinary approach* (pp. 169–196). Berkeley, CA: University of California Women's Center.

National Report on Work & Family (1988). Parental leave would save women $607 million a year (p. 6). Washington, DC: Burasf Publications.

National Report on Work & Family (1989). Women with maternity leave likely to resume work sooner (Sept, p. 4). Washington, DC: Burasf Publications.

Nye, F.I. (1974). Emerging and declining family roles. *Journal of Marriage and the Family, 36,* 238–245.

O'Leary, V.E. (1977). *Toward understanding women.* Monterey, CA: Brooks/Cole.

Osipow, S.H. (1983). *Theories of career development* (3rd ed.). New York: Prentice-Hall.

Parsons, F. (1909). *Choosing a vocation.* Boston: Houghton Mifflin.

Rand, L.M., & Miller, A.L. (1972). A developmental cross-sectioning of women's career and marriage attitudes and life plans. *Journal of Vocational Behavior, 2,* 317–331.

Repetti, R.L., Matthews, K.A., & Waldron, I. (1989). Effects of paid employment on women's mental and physical health. *American Psychologist, 44,* 1394–

Robertson, J.R., & Fitzgerald, L.F. (1990). (Mis)treatment of the nontraditional man: The effects of client gender-role and life-style on diagnosis and attribution of pathology. *Journal of Counseling Psychology, 37,* 3–9.

Samler, J. (1964). *The vocational counselor and social action.* Washington, DC: National Vocational Guidance Association.

Schwartz, F.N. (1989). Management women and the new facts of life. *Harvard Business Review,* January-February, 65–76.

Sells, L. (1973). High school mathematics as the critical filter in the job market. In *Developing opportunities for minorities in graduate education.* Proceedings of the Conference on Minority Graduate Education, University of California, Berkeley.

Sells, L. (1982). Leverage for equal opportunity through mastery of mathematics. In S.M. Humphreys (Ed.), *Women and minorities in science* (pp. 7–26). Boulder, CO: Westview Press.

Shaffer, L.F., & Shoben, E.J., Jr. (1956). *The psychology of adjustment* (2nd ed.) Boston: Houghton Mifflin.

Sieber, S.D. (1974). Toward a theory of role accumulation. *American Sociological Review, 39,* 567–578.

Silverman, D. (1976–77). Sexual harassment: Working women's dilemma. *Quest: A Feminist Quarterly, 3,* 15–24.

Simon, H.A. (1957). *Models of man.* New York: Wiley.

Slater, P. (1963). On social regression. *American Sociological Review, 28,* 339–364.

Steil, J.M., & Turetsky, B.A. (1987). Marital influence levels and symptomatology among wives. In F. Crosby (Ed.), *Spouse, parent, worker: On gender and multiple roles* (pp. 74–90). New Haven: Yale University Press.

Stewart, L.P., & Gudykunst, W.B. (1982). Differential factors influencing the hierarchical level and number of promotions of males and females within an organization. *Academy of Management Journal, 25,* 586–597.

Super, D.E. (1940). *Avocational interest patterns: A study in the psychology of avocations.* Stanford, CA: Stanford University Press, 1940.

Super, D.E. (1953). A theory of vocational development. *American Psychologist, 8,* 185–190.

Super, D.E. (1957). *The psychology of careers.* New York: Harper & Row.

Super, D.E. (1980). A life-span, life-space approach to career development. *Journal of Vocational Behavior, 16,* 282–298.

Super, D.E. (1981). A developmental theory: Implementing a self concept. In D.H. Montross & C.J. Shinkman (Eds.), *Career development in the 1980s: Theory and practice.* Springfield, IL: Charles C. Thomas.

Super, D.E. (1984). Career and life development. In D. Brown & L. Brooks (Eds.), *Career choice and development,* San Francisco: Jossey-Bass.

Super, D.E., & Nevill, D.D. (1984). Work role salience as a determinant of career maturity in high school students. *Journal of Vocational Behavior, 25,* 30–44.

Super, D.E., & Overstreet, P.L. (1960). *The vocational maturity of ninth-grade boys.* New York: Teachers College Press.

Terman, L.M., & Oden, M.H. (1959). *Genetic studies of genius: V. The gifted group at midlife.* Stanford, CA: Stanford University Press.

Tyler, L.E. (1978). *Individuality.* San Francisco: Jossey-Bass.

Thoits, P.A. (1983). Multiple identities and psychological well-being. A reformulation and test of the social isolation hypothesis. *American Sociological Review, 48,* 174–187.

Thoits, P.A. (1987). Negotiating roles. In F. Crosby (Ed.), *Spouse, parent, worker: On gender and multiple roles* (pp. 11–22). New Haven: Yale University Press.

U.S. Merit Systems Protection Board (1981). *Sexual harassment of federal workers: Is it a problem?* Washington, DC: United States Government Printing Office.

U.S. Merit Systems Protection Board (1987). *Sexual harassment of federal workers: An update.* Washington, DC: United States Government Printing Office.

Verbugge, L.M. (1983). Multiple roles and physical health of women and men. *Journal of Health and Social Behavior, 24,* 16–30.

Vetter, L. (1973). Career counseling for women. *The Counseling Psychologist, 4,* 54–66.

Voydanoff, P. (1988). Work and family: A review and expanded conceptualization. *Journal of Social Behavior and Personality, 3,* 1–22.

Wampler, K.S. (1982). Counseling implications of the housewife role. *Counseling and Values, 26,* 125–132.

Warr, P., & Parry, G. (1982). Paid employment and women's psychological well-being. *Psychological Bulletin, 91,* 498–516.

Weingarten, K. (1978). The employment pattern of professional couples and their distribution of involvement in the family. *Psychology of Women Quarterly, 3,* 43–52.

Wolf, W.C., & Fligstein, N.D. (1979). Sex and authority in the workplace: The causes of sexual inequality. *American Sociological Review, 44,* 235–252.

Zytowski, D.G. (1969). Toward a theory of career development of women. *Personnel and Guidance Journal, 47,* 660–664.

CHAPTER 10

Adult Men's Career Transitions and Gender-Role Themes

James M. O'Neil
School of Family Studies
University of Connecticut
Storrs, Connecticut

Diane M. Fishman
Counseling Psychology Program
School of Education
University of Connecticut
Storrs, Connecticut

A man's view of career and gender roles is central to his personal identity, self-esteem, and developmental change. Many men experience career transitions that prompt redefinition of their gender roles and masculine values. Some men strive to demonstrate their success. Others try to avoid seeming feminine, but harbor fears about their femininity. Many men have difficulty recognizing the transitional nature of their gender and career roles. Some resist change, fearing losses of power and status. Men often experience difficulty with transitions and need special assistance maneuvering life's unpredictable events.

This chapter investigates the interaction of men's gender roles and career transitions. Hansen (1984) recommended an analysis of how gender and career processes interact. No collective analysis of men's gender role themes and career transitions has emerged in career psychology. Empirical research on career and gender role transitions is limited because few concepts explain what transitions mean to men. Career development theory can expand its framework by examining how masculinity and femininity are driving forces in people's lives. Currently, few concepts describe how adult, career, and gender role development run parallel courses over the life span. The purpose of this chapter is to define, describe, and delineate men's career transitions and gender role themes.

The essence of this chapter can be summarized in the following way. Men: (a) redefine their career and gender role identities over the life cycle; (b) experience numerous career transitions; (c) struggle with gender role themes during career transitions; (d) experience gender role conflict during career transitions from career socialization and fears of femininity; (e) experience gender role devaluation, restriction, and violation during career transitions. Many of these assumptions are applicable to women but our focus is exclusively on men.

The chapter makes numerous assumptions about how gender and career interact in men's lives (Hansen, 1984). Foremost, we suggest that knowledge of gender socialization over the life cycle is essential for counseling men in career transition. It is important for counselors to be familiar with how men learn their masculine values over the life span. This includes recognizing how men may be threatened by their femininity and fear ridicule if they deviate from masculine norms and standards. Second, we assume that by identifying men's career transitions, greater understanding of men's gender role conflicts and strains can be gained. Third, we propose that men's career transitions are best understood by identifying gender role themes that can negatively affect the transitions. Fourth, we posit that men can experience gender role change during their career transitions. Therefore, knowledge of gender role themes is essential for helping men redefine their career goals and personal self-concepts. As men change over the life cycle, they may ask significant questions about the meaning of their masculinity and femininity (Levinson, Darrow, Klein, Levinson, & McKee, 1978). These questions emerge from early gender role socialization as well as from a man's beliefs about what is appropriate masculinity. Fifth, we assume that men experience emotional feelings of devaluation, restriction, and violation during career transitions and as they redefine gender role themes over the life span. Finally, we assume that career transitions and gender role themes can be assessed during career counseling and psychotherapy.

This chapter has numerous sections that expand on the above assumptions. The first three sections define transition, briefly review adult and career development theory, and enumerate 21 career transitions in men's lives. These transitions provide practitioners with a comprehensive list of critical events that can change the meaning of a man's career and self-concept. Sections 4—9 define gender role conflict and discuss men's career socialization as interacting with 15 gender role themes. Furthermore, these themes and conflicts are described as having specific emotional effects on men. Finally, an illustrative case study of Mr. Throck Morton's career transitions is provided to elucidate the chapter's concepts. Implications of the case study and chapter themes for practitioners are made.

ADULT DEVELOPMENT AND TRANSITIONS: FOUNDATIONS FOR UNDERSTANDING CHANGING MEN

Counseling adult men requires background in adult development theory and life transitions. There are substantial bodies of knowledge and conceptual frameworks to intervene with men in transitions. Although theory has grown faster than empirical data, there is a rich theoretical base in adult development to understand life cycle changes.

A complete analysis of adult development themes is beyond the scope of this chapter, yet certain themes provide a foundation for our analysis.

First, adult development is continuous and results from multiple influences of biological, psychological, and environmental determinants (Danish, 1981). Second, changes are rarely smooth, are ongoing, and are related. There can be varying degrees of stress and strain throughout adulthood (Hopson, 1981; Schlossberg, 1984; Gould, 1978; Brammer & Abrego, 1981; Offer & Sabshin, 1984; Lowenthal, Thurnher, & Chiriboga, 1975). Third, responding to life cycle events requires personal adaptation and flexibility. New self-assumptions and behavioral repertories are often needed to meet the demands of new situations (Schlossberg, 1984; Brammer & Abrego, 1981; Gould, 1978; Troll, 1981; Parkes, 1971; Brim, 1976; Brim & Ryff, 1980; Moos & Tsu, 1976; Hopson & Adams, 1977). Fourth, career and gender role changes in adulthood are continuous and require self introspection, assertiveness, and coping skills (Brammer & Abrego, 1981; Levinson et al., 1978; Super, 1957; Vaillant, 1977).

Transition, as a theoretical construct, has become a dominant theme in life-span psychology and adult development literature (Brammer & Abrego, 1981; Brim, 1976; Hopson & Adams, 1977; Levinson et al., 1978; Lowenthal et al., 1975; Schlossberg, 1981, 1984; Vaillant, 1977). Schlossberg (1981, 1984) has developed a thorough conceptualization of adults in transition. She defines a transition as "an event or nonevent that results in a change in assumption about oneself and the world and thus requires a corresponding change in one's behavior and relationships" (Schlossberg, 1981, p. 5). Transitions are part of human development and include changes in values, world views, and personal appearance. Few individuals escape these transitions and many experience them as painful life adjustments. There are gains and losses in stamina, life structures, and personal dreams. Two transitional areas identified for adults are career development and gender role development. Each will be defined and discussed in subsequent sections of the chapter.

ADULT CAREER DEVELOPMENT THEORY AND GENDER ROLES

The theory, research, and practice in career psychology has been primarily focused on adolescents rather than older adults (Campbell & Heffernan, 1983; Harmon & Farmer, 1983; Srebalus, Marinelli, & Messing, 1982). Theories of adult development over the life span have yet to be fully integrated with career development concepts. Harmon and Farmer indicated that the ". . . adult stages and transitions have some rather obvious applications to vocational behavior, but most of them are not even well established, let alone integrated in the theories of vocational behavior" (p. 49). Efforts to describe the stages of career development have been evident in the literature (Ginzberg, Ginsburg, Axelrad, & Herma, 1951; Miller & Form, 1951; Super, 1957). Adult career development has been most notably defined by Super's (1957) developmental theory. Super proposed stages of growth, exploration, establishment, maintenance, and decline. Other concepts in Super's theory described the processes of choosing, implementing, and terminating careers (Super, 1980, 1984). More recently, there has been increased literature on adult career development (Brown, 1984; Campbell & Cellini, 1981; Herr & Cramer, 1979;

Osipow, 1983). Campbell and Heffernan (1983) have written the most substantive synthesis of adult vocational behavior by reviewing Erikson, Havighurst, Levinson et al., Miller and Form, Super, and Schein. Their synthesis produced four major phases of the career development cycle including: (1) preparation for an occupation and obtaining a job; (2) demonstration of competence in and adjustment to a new work environment; (3) maintenance or advancement of one's position in an established occupation; and (4) decline in involvement with the work place. These stages were named preparation, establishment, maintenance, and retirement, and are consistent with Super and Hall's (1978) synthesis. The utility of these career development stages lies in their capacity to describe career movement as a continuous, ongoing process. What has not been systematically identified are the specific transitions that collectively fall in the stages described by Super (1957), Super and Hall (1978), and Campbell and Heffernan (1983). These transitions will be described in later sections of the chapter.

Gender roles were discussed in nearly every sector of society in the 1970s. Most of the discussion emerged from the feminist and women's movements and focused on the limitations of current theories and on how gender role stereotypes prohibited women's entry into a wide variety of careers. During the 1970s there was a published text on women's career development (Osipow, 1975), and numerous authors theorized that gender roles affected women's career-decision making (Farmer, 1976; Harmon, 1977; O'Neil, Meeker, & Borgers, 1978; Vetter, 1973). Fitzgerald and Crites (1980) have summarized much of the literature on career psychology of women, and Fitzgerald and Betz (1983) and Betz and Fitzgerald (1987) have completed the most extensive review of women's gender and career roles. Other authors have provided theoretical insights (Farmer, 1985; Gottfredson, 1981; Hansen, 1984), and practical suggestions have been made for career counseling with women (Fitzgerald & Crites, 1979; Hotchkiss & Borow, 1984; Richardson, 1979).

Overall, the current literature on gender roles and career development has been focused on women, whereas men's gender roles have been a neglected area of research. Morgan, Skovholt, and Orr (1979) indicated that "career counseling theories, being by necessity general explanations of career behavior, have nothing specific to say about the special problems of men" (p. 263). There is a need for more comprehensive frameworks to view men's career and gender role transitions over the life cycle. These frameworks need to be based on what is known about career transitions.

MEN'S CAREER TRANSITIONS IDENTIFIED

Given the many changes in a man's career, there is a need to identify and define the transitions that affect a man's career identity. Career transitions are defined as events or nonevents in the career development process causing changes in the meaning of the career, one's self-assumptions, and one's view of the world (O'Neil, Fishman, Kinsella-Shaw, 1987). The transition process may be initiated by events or nonevents resulting in changed assumptions about oneself and the world, and thus requiring a corresponding change in one's career behavior and relationships (Schlossberg, 1981; 1984). Career transitions can emanate from external events as well as internal or personal dynamics. They usually result in some change in the man's status, roles, and responsibilities. These changes offer opportunities for renewal and growth, but loss, stagnation, and failure can also occur. Most career transitions are "high stake" experiences because they affect economic, familial, and psychological dimensions of the person.

An analysis of career transitions by Super (1957) still remains the most complete treatise on career transitions available. Extending Super's work, Table 1 lists and defines 21 career transitions of adult men. The tran-

Table 1
Summary of Career Transitions of Adult Men

Career Transitions	Definitions
(1) Initial Career Choice	First decision about career area to pursue
(2) Obtaining Skill Development/Training	Obtaining expertise in career or job area
(3) First Job	Initial work pursued after training or education
(4) Career Advancement (new job)	Promotion in career choice with new responsibilities
(5) Career Change	Decision to pursue a different career
(6) Loss of Interest or Meaning in Career	Career and work loses its intrinsic value and status
(7) Serious Conflicts with Supervisor, Colleagues, or Work Setting	Continuous and severe difficulties with co-workers, supervisor, or setting resulting in stress and strain
(8) Being Fired or Unemployed	Losing your job
(9) Rapid Success	Back-to-back accomplishments over short period of time
(10) Rapid Failure	Back-to-back diminishments or defeats
(11) Rapid Income Loss	Quick loss in money earned
(12) Demotion	Being reduced to a lower grade or rank
(13) Leveling off—Job Peaking	Not being promoted to the next highest level or achieving the highest level possible

(14) Working with Women	Interaction with women as subordinates, supervisors, or peers
(15) Burnout	Fatigue and loss of interest in work because of overwork, role overload, and unhappiness
(16) Loss of Mentor	Relationship change with person who has sponsored and supported your career
(17) Becoming a Mentor	Taking on role of resource, sponsor, and transitional figure for another person entering a career
(18) Lost Career Dream or Goal	Recognition that ultimate career aspiration is not attainable
(19) Aging, Loss of Stamina and Endurance	Decreasing energy to perform in career role
(20) Preretirement	Period of time when plans for retirement are made
(21) Retirement	Period of time when formal work-career ends

sitions are listed on the left and each is operationally defined on the right. The transitions extend over the stages of career development, but are not completely exhaustive.

Reviewing these 21 career transitions, it is evident that they span Super and Hall's (1978) and Campbell and Heffernan's (1983) career stages of preparation, establishment, maintenance, and retirement. Many of these transitions could be experienced in more than one of Super's stages. Therefore, the transitions cannot be assigned to any age or stage contingent on any career, gender, or adult development theory. Career transitions do not necessarily occur in a smooth continuous pattern, but rather are experienced differently by each man. Additionally, a man's experience of these transitions depends on his personal perception of the change and his coping resources.

Numerous transitions found in Table 1 (1, 3, 19, 20, 21) result from the age and physical characteristics of the man. Some have the potential for increasing men's career satisfaction (4, 5, 9, 17) whereas others are clearly threatening or adverse (8, 10, 11, 12, 13, 15). Many transitions (2, 6, 7, 14, 16, 17, 18) have more moderate psychological implications that parallel normal developmental changes. A number of transitions (7, 8, 12, 14, 16, 17) affect work or family relationships in significant ways. In some cases, the absence of a transition occurring may indicate a problem area for the man (1, 2, 4, 5, 9, 17).

These 21 career transitions may signal areas in a client's life where career stresses and strains predictably occur. As such, these career transitions are viewed as normative career events that may shift a client into a state of disequilibrium. The extent to which these career transitions are perceived as positive or negative relates to the individual's capacity to make new career and personal adjustments. Almost all transitions place demands on men that result in stresses and strains. Each situation calls for varying degrees of adaptation and different coping mechanisms. All the transitions can result in men's redefining themselves and their worlds.

The transitions in Table 1 provide counseling practitioners with some typical male career transitions. Many of these transitions have direct relevance for women across the life cycle. Practitioners can use the list to assess a client's transitional situations. By discussing the series of career transitions with a client, emphasis can be placed on discovering the unique meaning of each transition. The Career Transitions Checklist (CTC) (O'Neil & Fishman, 1985b) is a simple means of helping clients and adults assess their past, present, and future transitions. Although this instrument needs empirical research and development, it operationalizes the concepts in Table 1.

GENDER ROLES AND GENDER ROLE CONFLICT

The career transitions specified above are not usually experienced separately from a man's gender role identity. Gender roles are behaviors, expectations, and role sets defined by society as masculine or feminine that are embodied in the behavior of the individual man or woman and culturally regarded as appropriate to men or women (O'Neil, 1981a, 1981b, 1982). These roles are learned through gender role socialization and change with the demands of adulthood and aging (Moreland, 1979, 1980). Gender role conflict is a psychological state where gender roles have negative consequences or impact on the person or others. (O'Neil, Helms, Gable, David, & Wrightsman, 1986). The ultimate outcome of this conflict is the restriction of the person's human potential or the restriction of someone else's potential. Gender role conflict occurs when rigid, sexist, or restrictive gender roles, learned during socialization, result in the personal restriction or devaluation of others or self (O'Neil, 1981a, 1981b, 1982). One outcome of gender role conflict is gender role strain. This occurs when mental or physical tension is experienced as a result of the expectations and norms of masculinity, femininity, and androgyny. Garnets and Pleck (1979) operationally define sex-role strain "as a discrepancy between the real self and that part of the ideal self-concept that is culturally associated with gender" (p. 278). They believe that sex-role strain is an intrapsychic process that can lead to poor psychological adjustment, particularly low self-esteem. It is hypothesized that inflexible sex-role norms set standards that do not allow people to freely express themselves (Komarovsky, 1976).

There are four ways to conceptualize gender role conflict that provide categories for assessment (O'Neil et al., 1986). First, gender role conflict can be experienced as a cognition—how we think about gender roles and aspects of our masculinity, femininity, and androgyny. Second, gender role conflict can be experienced as affect—how we feel about gender roles and conflicts within ourselves and those of others. Third, gender role conflict can be experienced as behavior—how we act, respond, and relate to ourselves. Fourth, gender role conflict can be experienced as an unconscious and intrapsychic phenomenon. This implies that some gender role conflicts are repressed and beyond our conscious awareness. How we think, feel, and behave because of gender roles are useful parameters to assess gender role conflict in adulthood.

There has been no comprehensive analysis of men's gender role conflicts during career transitions. Much of a man's perception of his masculine identity is governed by the development of his career. For counselors to understand men's gender role conflict, it is necessary to recognize the values of the "masculine mystique" that men internalize during career socialization. From this knowledge, the gender role themes can be identified and used with men experiencing career and gender role changes.

MEN'S GENDER ROLE SOCIALIZATION: THE MASCULINE MYSTIQUE AND FEARS OF FEMININITY

Masculine Mystique and Value System

Gender role socialization and notions of masculinity and femininity directly affect men's career and gender role transitions. A comprehensive analysis of how men are socialized and the effects of family, environment, and biology are beyond the scope of this chapter and are found elsewhere (Basow, 1986; Weitz, 1977). Of greatest importance is the notion that there are expected male norms and values that typify American manhood. We call the complex set of values and beliefs that define appropriate masculinity in our society the masculine mystique and value system. These values are based on rigid stereotypes and beliefs about men, masculinity, and femininity. A complete delineation of these values and assumptions has been published elsewhere (Farrell, 1974; O'Neil, 1981, 1981b, 1982).

Overall, the masculine mystique and value system implies that: (a) men are superior to women and masculinity is superior to femininity; (b) power, control, and dominance are essential to prove one's masculinity; (c) emotions, feelings, vulnerability, and intimacy are to be avoided because they are feminine; (d) career and economic success are measures of one's masculinity. These masculine values are part of men's socialization and have negative consequences for men, women, and children. These values violate women because they devalue women's feminine attitudes, values, and behaviors. They violate children because they create rigid expectations that can limit the free expression of a child's personality and potential. These values violate men by denying them the opportunity to express their feminine aspects, therefore restricting their range of emotional and behavioral expression. Failure to accept these values or live them out can produce self-devaluation or punishment from others; Mayer (1978) suggested that these values may contribute to men's self-destruction at midlife. In varying degrees, the masculine mystique and value system devalues femininity, overvalues masculinity (acts of hypermasculinity), and produces fears about a man's femininity.

Fears of Femininity

One unifying theme that results from the masculine mystique and value system is the fear of femininity (Farrell, 1974; O'Neil, 1981b, 1982; O'Neil, David, & Wrightsman, 1985; O'Neil, Helms, Gable, David, & Wrightsman, 1986). The fear of femininity is defined as a strong negative emotion associated with feminine values, attitudes, and behaviors. These emotional reactions are learned primarily in early childhood when gender identity is being formed by parents, peers, and social values. Men's fears of their feminine aspects and of women have been noted in the theoretical literature for many years (Hays, 1964; Horney, 1967; Jung, 1953, 1954; Lederer, 1968; Menninger, 1970). Most of these analyses rely upon a psychodynamic foundation. Jung's archetype in men, the anima, is a well-known concept that is relevant to men's difficulty in integrating their feminine aspects. More recently, Levinson et al. (1978), in their case study of 40 men, found that these men not only neglected or repressed their feminine aspects of self, but also regarded their feminine aspects as dangerous.

When a man fears his feminine aspects, he really fears that others will see him as stereotypically and negatively feminine (weak, dependent, submissive) rather than positively masculine. Being considered "a wimp" by others is the worse fear possible. This is not an unreasonable fear because femininity is subordinated, depreciated, and maligned in our hypermasculine society. Men who express their feminine aspects fear they will be restricted, devalued, and violated by others. The cost of showing stereotypic feminine qualities can be disrespect, failure, and emasculation. These are high costs for a man who wants to fulfill the masculine mystique over the life cycle.

MEN'S CAREER AND GENDER ROLE SOCIALIZATION

Hansen (1984) provided the most cogent analysis of how gender and career interact. Her analysis indicates that gender continuously affects men and women over the life span. She indicates that "at the heart of issues of gender and career is the sex-role system, which is the network of attitudes, feelings, and behaviors that result from the pervasiveness of sex-role stereotyping in the culture" (p. 218). The masculine mystique and value system and fear of femininity described earlier are central to the sex-role system that Hansen describes. For the most part, specific information on the male sex-role system has not been described in career psychology but has emanated from the men's literature. A more focused analysis of the masculine career and gender role socialization has been discussed elsewhere (O'Neil, 1981a, 1982). Below is a summary of assumptions made about men's gender-career socialization synthesized from the men's literature. These assumptions are not absolute truths or ways to categorize all men. Clearly, there are individual, class, race, ethnic, and socioeconomic differences affecting the validity of these assumptions for each man.

Men are socialized to work by families, peers, and schools (Bucher, 1976; Fasteau, 1974; Goldberg, 1977; Olson, 1978) and to be competitive, achievement-oriented, and competent (Bucher, 1976; Crites & Fitzgerald, 1978; Olson, 1978). Due to gender role stereotypes, many men incorrectly interpret male and female sex differences as dictating different career options for each sex. Men also learn that measures of their masculinity are calculated by success, achievement, and ascendancy up the career ladder (Bucher, 1976; David & Brannon, 1976; Nichols, 1975; Pleck & Sawyer, 1974). In other words, men learn that manhood and masculinity are contingent on career success (Fasteau, 1974; Goldberg, 1977; Tolson, 1977). Many men look to work as the primary way to define personal and self worth (Bucher, 1976; Morgan et al., 1970; Pleck & Sawyer, 1974; Skovholt, 1978). Furthermore, men learn that being masculine and achieving career success involves becoming competitive, powerful, and in control of self and the environment (Nichols, 1975). Men are concerned that others will critically evaluate their masculinity based on their career success, achievement, power and control (David & Brannon, 1976). When some men marry they may expect exclusive rights to the breadwinner or career role unless it is economically necessary for their wives to work (Goldberg, 1977). Many men are socialized to believe that they will earn security and happiness by hard work, success, and achievement (David & Brannon, 1976; Nichols, 1975). Sometimes they seek personal rewards and goals that cannot be met in their work (Mayer, 1978). Many times when these rewards do not emerge, men work harder, believing that this will yield the desired outcomes of status, security, and success. Faced with stiff competition, unmet goals, and uncooperative work situations, men may experience fear of failure, low self-esteem, and emotional crises. Unresolved career issues related to achievement, power, success, and competition may be part of unresolved masculinity issues, or vice versa. Fearing emasculation, some men work so hard to demonstrate success that they neglect important relationships with spouses, friends, and children (Goldberg, 1977). All these stresses can culminate in overwork, fatigue, and marital discord, posing serious threats to the man's physical and psychological health (Goldberg, 1977; Mayer, 1978; O'Neil, 1981b).

GENDER AND CAREER DEVELOPMENT: AN INTERACTIVE AND DEFINITIONAL PROCESS

The above analysis of men's career and gender socialization highlights a central reality—that men's career and gender role development is rarely smooth, is often quite demanding, and ultimately can produce stress and strain. Moreover, gender role development and career development run parallel courses over the life cycle. The development of a career and gender identity is a process of negotiation and renegotiation within self and with others. A man's perception of his gender identity and his career identity is difficult to separate. Both identities operate simultaneously to determine choices, changes, and transitions. Additionally, career and gender role changes have interactive qualities. Changes in a person's view of their gender roles affect their view of their career possibilities, and vice versa. Each man develops adaptive or nonadaptive coping mechanisms to respond to the changes over the life cycle.

For most men, career and gender role values change with age and experience. In other words, men experience their career and gender role change as a definitional process. For some men, as the limitations of the masculine mystique become apparent, masculinity and femininity become redefined. For other men, the limitations of the masculine mystique are not readily apparent, and they struggle with unidentified feelings of discontent as years progress. When masculinity does not become redefined, men may cling to traditional male values. Gender role and career change may be precipitated by new adult roles including those of husband, parent, or mentor. Redefinition may also occur during personal crises, losses, or prolonged illnesses. Those men who are not flexible in their gender role behaviors may fail to cope effectively with changing life events.

Many times the redefinition process is experienced on a vague, existential level before there is any attitudinal or behavioral change. Gender role redefinition is not readily discernible to most clients or counselors. When the artificiality of masculine stereotypes can be recognized, the limitations of sex-typed behavior can be explored. For many men, there is a yearning for more in-depth meaning than the narrow masculine world can provide. Usually, there is a need to redefine one's masculinity at home and at work.

This redefinition process is done with varying degrees of success, stress, and strain. Men who alter their masculine views of self and their worlds confront established values that have stabilized their lives for years. It is difficult to change values that have guided one's existence, even when the values no longer provide a sense of meaning or vitality. Additionally, gender role and career reevaluations are undertaken in a capitalist world that continues to employ stereotypes of masculinity to reward men and keep the system operating. The external career world persists in rewarding men for being masculine. Yet, internal processes within the man may provoke serious reevaluation of gender role themes and life options.

GENDER ROLE TRANSITIONS AND THEMES

Gender role transitions are events or nonevents in a person's gender role development process stimulating changes in gender values and self-assumptions (O'Neil, Fishman, & Kinsella-Shaw, 1987). These transitions occur when there are demonstrations, reevaluations, and integrations of masculinity and femininity over the life span. The *demonstration* of masculinity is central to the formation of a functional gender identity. For men, demonstrating one's masculinity is accomplished by striving for power, control, achievement, and success. Later in adulthood, *reevaluation* of masculine and feminine values may occur. This reevaluation may inspire questions about the limit of one's masculinity, and feminine values may seem more acceptable. The reevaluation of gender role values includes an assessment and redefinition of the man's feelings, thoughts, and behaviors about masculinity and femininity. *Integration* of both masculine and feminine values can occur if the man is able to reconcile previous socialization with new definitions of gender. These integrations may be in conjunction with developmental growth and the acceptance of new roles and responsibilities. The demonstration, reevaluation, and integration of masculine and feminine values may occur during crisis, critical points, or during the normal maturation process. Role transitions may produce confusion, anxiety, and despair. Yet these transitions can also open up internal aspects of the man, expanding his self-definition and promoting personal exploration and growth.

Personal changes and modifications in gender role values are not completed in a vacuum. They are experienced in the context of certain gender role transition themes. A gender role transition theme is defined as a developmental and human issue involving the demonstration, reevaluation, or integration of masculinity or femininity. What are the themes that men struggle with during career and gender role transitions? What themes need to be demonstrated, reevaluated, and finally integrated? What themes produce gender role conflict and strain?

Table 2 lists and defines 15 gender role transition themes that relate to men's career transitions. Each of these themes can involve the demonstration of the values of the masculine mystique or the reevaluation/integration of masculinity and femininity. Any of the gender role transition themes can affect the 21 career transitions found in Table 1. Consequently, the gender role themes have the potential to alter a man's view of himself, his career, and his world.

Several of the gender role transition themes from Table 2 may be reevaluated. Themes 1–3 (success, achievement, and competence) may be redefined as men enter the career maintenance stage. The limits of gender role themes 4–7 (control, power, competition, and strength) may become more apparent as men struggle to validate their masculine values from the limited domain of economic and career success. Changes in work situations whereby men feel restricted or constrained can affect men's sense of personal worth (theme 8) and produce worries about their capacity to fulfill the provider role (theme 9). Themes 10 and 11 (personal communication and women's work role) may become problematic if men are unable to recognize the artificiality of rigid masculine norms and values. Changes in roles such as themes 12 and 13 (fatherhood or mentoring) may demand new skills and greater interpersonal sensitivity. Finally, changes in body functions and aging (theme 14) may mean less energy and stamina, and health care issues (theme 15) may become dominant during the later years as retirement approaches.

Each man will struggle with different themes depending on his situation, coping styles, and gender role values. Most men will modify to some degree their self-concepts and work values. Changes in meaning are rarely sudden and usually emerge slowly over the years. Many times the redefinition of these themes and the integration of new notions of masculinity/femininity occur through the internal questions men struggle to answer. Some examples of the personal inquiries and themes men examine are:

1. What is success and is it worth all the strain?
2. Is power and control really that important to me?
3. If I redefine power, control, and competition, will I be able to be an effective man?

Table 2

Gender Role Transition Themes Affecting Men's Career Development

Gender Role Transition Themes	Definitions
1. Success	1. Attaining wealth, favor, or eminence
2. Achievement	2. Successful completion and accomplishment brought about by resolve, persistence, or endeavor
3. Competence	3. Having adequate ability, qualities, and capacity to function in a particular way
4. Control	4. Regulating, restraining, and having people or situations under one's command
5. Power	5. Obtaining authority, influence, or ascendancy over others and one's environment
6. Competition	6. Striving against others to gain something and establishing one's superiority or skill
7. Strength	7. Having capacity for endurance physically, emotionally, intellectually, and spiritually
8. Personal Worth	8. Being valued by others and valuing self
9. Provider Role	9. Assuming economic responsibility for family
10. Personal Communication	10. Verbal and nonverbal ways of interpersonal exchange
11. Women's and Men's Work Roles	11. Perceptions of appropriate work roles for each sex
12. Fatherhood	12. Parental role with sons and daughters
13. Mentor Role	13. Resource, sponsor, and transitional figure for another person
14. Aging	14. Showing the effects or characteristics of getting older
15. Health Care	15. Recognition of factors that maintain a healthy life

Copyright, 1986, James M. O'Neil, University of Connecticut, Storrs, and The Center for Social and Gender Role Change, Box 1019, South Windsor, CT 06074.

4. If I change, will I be able to deal with the masculine system that uses power, control, and competition in sometimes oppressive ways?
5. If I give up my preoccupation with work and career success, will there be other ways for me to validate myself and my human worth? Will I respect myself and will others respect me as I broaden my human interests outside of work? Will I find these new human interests as satisfying as work?
6. If I express more of my emotional self, how will I be viewed by others? Will there be positive or negative consequences? Exactly what is my emotional self and how can I use it effectively in my career and life?
7. Overall, if I change, how will I handle the devaluations that I will experience from others?
8. How can I handle working with women as equals when I do not really understand them and their perspectives? How does one treat women as equals? What does it mean to cooperate and compete with women?
9. How can I better coexist with all parts of myself: masculine/feminine; strength/vulnerability; thought/emotion?
10. If I change my masculine values, does that mean that I am feminine, less of a man, homosexual, or weak?

These questions and others may be important issues to explore in counseling and psychotherapy. Gender role change is often associated with career transitions, although it may not be apparent to many men. The gender role transition themes defined in Table 2 may be vehicles for exploring men's other emotional experiences related to gender and adult change.

EMOTIONAL EXPERIENCES OF GENDER ROLE CONFLICT DURING GENDER AND CAREER TRANSITIONS

One of the central points of this chapter has been to investigate the interrelation between gender role transitions and career transitions. It was proposed that gender role conflict can have negative psychological consequences during career transitions. Additionally, gender role conflict was described as occurring when rigid, sexist, or restrictive gender roles learned during socialization result in personal restriction, devaluation, or violation of self or others.

What has not been described are the personal experiences of gender role conflict. What happens to men as they experience the career transitions in Table 1 or redefine the gender role transition themes in Table 2? What are the personal and private experiences of transitional change and what emotions surface for men as they negotiate life cycle events?

The personal experience of gender role conflict that emerges during career and gender role transitions can be conceptualized in four categories: (1) discrepancy and incongruity, (2) devaluation, (3) restriction, and (4) violation. These categories provide a common vocabulary for clients and counselors to discuss gender role conflicts that emanate from the transitional process. These categories help clarify men's private pain as they demonstrate, redefine, and integrate notions of masculinity and femininity over the life span. Each are defined and briefly discussed below.

Discrepancy and Incongruity

This category of gender role conflict is experienced when men recognize a difference between their real and ideal self-concept based on the stereotypic values of the masculine mystique (Garnets & Pleck, 1979). When men do not live up to the masculine expectancies of society, they will feel discrepant and incongruent with their masculine ideals. The internal experience of these incongruencies is manifest in feelings of inadequacy, depression, anger, and sometimes self-hatred. Many men feel that their personal success and achievement are on public display. When they are unable to demonstrate their masculine values, they become defensive and overcompensate to hide the discrepancies.

Devaluation

Men feel devaluated when they negatively criticize themselves for not meeting their masculine norms, goals, and expectations. Gender role devaluation produces a lessening of personal status, stature, and self-esteem. Men blame themselves for being inadequate and not being able to effectively integrate failures or losses. Many times fear and anger are turned inward, resulting in self-criticism, loss of self-confidence, and depression. Devaluation can also come from others including spouses, family members, and competitors.

Restriction

Gender role restrictions occur when masculine norms limit flexibility in work and family roles. The man with gender role restrictions has limited options and may not be able to respond to the wide variety of demands of adult life both at work and at home. As men confine themselves to certain roles, they may demand that women restrict themselves to traditionally feminine roles. This kind of restriction can mean the violation of personal freedom and human rights. Rigid masculine norms may be so enforced at home that emotional expression and close relationships are impossible. Men may be so driven by their work that they restrict themselves from family roles and responsibilities. The gender restricted man is inflexible and not able to unleash his capacity for growth. This usually results in anger, stress, and interpersonal conflict.

Violation

Men feel violated when they experience harm demonstrating and redefining gender role themes of masculinity. To be violated is to be abused and victimized in one's career and gender role. Violations occur when rights are taken away or freedom of experience is denied. Men feel particularly violated when they are demeaned for deviating from the values of the masculine mystique. When men do not conform to the masculine standards of success, achievement, competition, and power, they can punish and may become alienated. Men can be violated by employers, fellow workers, or by the rigid masculine norms of the organizational system. Additionally, men can feel violated by family members and in interpersonal relationships where rigid adherence to the male role is demanded.

MR. THROCK MORTON: CASE STUDY OF CAREER AND GENDER ROLE TRANSITIONS

This case study is an illustration of how the career transitions and gender role themes can "come to life" for one man. The previous concepts are now integrated in a case study format of a man named Throck Morton. This case highlights the interactive qualities of career and gender role socialization and how family dynamics can affect one man's transitional processes. Using recognized career stages (Super & Hall, 1978; Campbell & Heffernan, 1983), four vignettes are used to describe Throck Morton's transitions in the preparation, establishment, maintenance, and retirement stages. The career transitions and gender role themes (see Tables 1 and 2) will be identified and summarized in Table 3 for each of Throck Morton's stages of career development.

Background and Family History

Throck Morton was born in 1948 and was socialized in the 1950s and 60s, a product of the post-World War II baby boom. He was the second oldest of four children in a close, Irish-Catholic family living in a suburban town outside of Albany, New York. The Mortons enjoyed an upper middle class status. They were able to afford college for the children, summer vacations, two cars, and a comfortable home in a respectable neighborhood. In fact, the Mortons lived in three progressively larger homes during Throck's adolescence, reflecting his father's ambition to be upwardly mobile.

The Morton's family dynamics would be categorized as traditional, meaning that mother and father had distinct and separate roles. Throck's father worked as a real estate broker while his mother had responsibility for homemaking. Throck's father was a hard worker and traveled widely to meet high expectations for sales quotas. He was usually tired, under stress, and as Throck remembers, "His weary face was usually glued to the TV." Throck's father found some emotional release and escape by taking minor acting roles in local theatrical productions.

After the youngest child entered school, Mrs. Morton obtained employment as a bank teller, and after three years she became administrative assistant to the bank president. Although this raised her self-esteem, she felt guilty about neglecting household duties. Mr. Morton refused to help with domestic tasks and fulfill parental responsibilities. There were continual tensions between Throck's parents regarding work, family, and leisure pursuits.

Throck's father experienced a career transition (crisis) when he was forced to retire early to make way for a younger and more energetic man. This event brought a tailspin of self-destructive behavior, apathy, and depression. Throck's mother mobilized the family's resourcefulness and convinced Throck's father to start a small consulting business, thus keeping him occupied and feeling useful.

Young Throck was socialized according to the values of the masculine mystique and traditional norms of American manhood. He learned from his father that manly worth was obtained through success, achievement, power, and competence at work. The more wealth and power one obtained, the more masculine one would be perceived. In the community, Throck's father was a respected man because of his success. Throck desperately wanted to imitate his father's qualities.

Throck learned from his father and mother that emotionality and vulnerability were inappropriate for men. He also recognized his father's drinking problem as a symptom of career stress and pressure. Concurrently, he observed his father's retreat to television and interest in the theatre as outlets for his unexpressed emotions. The theater provided Throck's father with outlets for expressive, artistic, and emotional release without making him seem feminine. On the other hand, he perceived his father as being powerful, strong, successful, and competent when it came to business matters. In many ways, Throck was confused by his father's striving for masculinity and his "closet" feminine interests in acting. Overall, Throck received strong messages from his parents—"Work hard, succeed, forget your emotions, be a man in the world." Unable to reconcile all of these messages, Throck began his own career exploration.

Career Preparation Stage

Throck's interest in business occupations was shaped by his family, school experience, and his parents' career success. These factors formed a primary value—"Hard work, perseverance, and drive pay off." In high school he enrolled in college preparatory courses and played varsity sports. He secretly wished to enter law school and enjoyed political science, journalism, and English. He rarely dated, considered himself a late bloomer in relationships, and "hung out" with the boys playing sports, driving cars, and drinking beer.

During college, he coasted through coursework, delayed thinking about careers, and panicked in his senior year about what to do with his life. He was afraid to commit himself to a career, job, or professional training. He lacked self-awareness, was naive about the world of work, and indecisive about law school, missing the application deadline. He had not achieved good grades in college (GPA = 2.2) and feared rejection from law schools. Additionally, questions about his competency and self-worth produced a vacuum of inertia and inaction.

Following college graduation, his parents disapproved of his lack of academic achievement and delayed decision making. His father called him lazy, which was unfair and inaccurate. Throck felt devalued by his father, feared failure, and felt he was disappointing his parents. Avoiding all of this, he opted for a year off on the West Coast to "get his head together." He wanted to do some self-reflection and career exploration. Instead, he was plagued by greater self-doubts about success and concerned about parental approval. Throck's father added "insult to injury" by describing Throck's year off as "cowardly escape to the West Coast." The message was that the sooner he started making money, the sooner he could be somebody. "Somebody" meant a man who succeeds and gets things done. Throck felt further devaluation and worried about his inadequacy as a man. Furthermore, he felt restricted by his own limited self-knowledge and indecisiveness.

Career Establishment Stage

Returning from the West Coast, Throck had a series of sales-related jobs. To his surprise, he did quite well and moved from selling vacuum cleaners, sports equipment, and computer software to selling business machines. After a few years with each company he became restless, yearning for more challenges. Financially, he could afford a new car and a down payment on a small starter home. He dated casually and at age 28 met an attractive business colleague. They married two years later and had their first child, a son, the following year.

Throck continued his sales job, worked long hours, and traveled extensively. He felt much pressure to be the family protector and to fulfill the provider role through large salary increases. He felt pulled between his professional and familial priorities, and his excessive drinking became more problematic. Throck became increasingly dissatisfied with his job. He began to feel apathetic about going to work in the morning because he derived little pleasure from selling. His wife sensed that a sales career was a real compromise to Throck's career dream of being a trial lawyer. She urged him to begin career counseling. Throck resisted, wanting to avoid fears of incompetence, and retreated into alcohol. He had felt out of control since high school and his relationship with his parents had continued to be distant and strained. His sales career did not make him feel like a successful man and the work had no inherent meaning. His sales quotas dropped drastically, as did his income. He was reprimanded by his district manager for failing to meet six consecutive months of sales quotas.

The lowest point Throck can remember was on his 35th birthday when he was fired from the company. To Throck, being fired and unemployed was the worst kind of failure, personal embarrassment, and loss of control. Hitting the bottom in an ironic way left him debilitated on one hand, and desperate to prove himself as a persevering man on the other. There was a sense of relief, freedom to start over, and a possibility for a career change. During this crisis, he began career counseling and decided to enter law school. Even though this meant severe income loss for three years, his wife was supportive. He was the oldest student in his law classes, but he felt a renewed sense of commitment and achievement. He began to feel like an effective man, the one his parents wanted him to become. Throck had established himself as an effective trial lawyer by age 43. His success was rapid. He was recognized as someone who had achieved legal competence and he gained power quickly. The courtroom was a dramatic environment for displaying his showmanship and flair for public speaking. With this secure career, he hoped to settle down and enjoy life. He hoped the career change would bring status, success, and worth as well as acceptance from his parents.

Career Maintenance Stage

During this stage Throck could not relax and enjoy life, but rather was preoccupied about maintaining his success. He had lost status and position before as a salesman and it could happen again. Throck's rapid success and courtroom style were admired by many younger attorneys. Two female attorneys sought Throck as their mentor, which added to his feelings of worth and credibility. Mentoring women was a new experience for Throck, and he was unaccustomed to their assertiveness. After closer inspection of Throck's personality, the female attorneys viewed Throck as paternalistic, sexist, and controlling. At issue for Throck was how to effectively guide the women's careers without losing his own power, control, and masculine status. The women were offended by Throck's condescension and subtle sexism. The mentoring relationships did not last and the women sought more secure and nonsexist mentors.

Throck's stereotypic view of women continued to cause conflict at work. One incident turned into an embarrassing public situation when he was accused of sexual harassment as a result of some crude jokes he had told at a conference meeting. He was surprised to find out that his "good old boy network" did not support his sexist and distasteful remarks. Nonetheless, he was not about to take abuse from a woman and decided to confront the situation directly. He wasn't sure how to deal with the accusation or with the women, but he sheepishly apologized for the sexist jokes. He was ridiculed by other colleagues for apologizing to a woman and the whole ordeal lowered his masculine image. He had restored his relationship with the female colleague, but he had been emasculated and embarrassed. Throck was able to maintain his status as a lawyer but he was passed over when judges were appointed. In Throck's early 50s, he realized that his career was leveling off. He had reached the last rung on his career ladder, and it was sooner and lower than he had wished.

Retirement Stage

At 60, Throck considered early retirement to ease out of the work force gracefully. He had observed his father's abrupt retirement and the pain associated with disengaging from the work force. Moreover, he was physically and mentally exhausted when cases went to court. He got more enjoyment out of quiet afternoons doing legal paperwork. The pace of his career made retirement a welcomed event.

In the last 10 years of his career, he had reached his peak. Promotions, visibility, and responsibilities had leveled off. He was never appointed a judge, which left one dream unmet. He rationalized his disappointment about not becoming a judge by recognizing that it might have been too much stress and pressure. In his 60s he realized he could no longer handle the increasing competition from younger attorneys in the courtroom setting. His wife labeled him burned out when he really needed to retire early. He feared that early retirement would be seen as a weakness. Many men work well past 65, yet he just didn't have the stamina anymore.

After retirement, Throck became a recluse at home and severed most social relationships with colleagues. As his career faded, Throck felt his masculinity had also been diminished. Fearing his retirement would be perceived as a lack of strength, he confined himself to his home. Throck acknowledged that he was not the venerable wise man he had hoped to be in old age. He searched for ways to occupy his time including daily exercise, reading, and church functions. With his wife and son preoccupied, Throck felt lonely. He spoke with his parish priest about not wanting to die without feeling at peace with himself. He couldn't understand his discontentment because his professional career entitled him to be labeled a successful man. There was still something missing at age 70. At age 72, while tending his garden, Throck Morton died of a massive heart attack.

ANALYSES OF THROCK MORTON'S CAREER TRANSITIONS AND GENDER ROLE THEMES

Table 3 shows a summary of Throck Morton's career and gender role themes according to specified career stages (Campbell & Heffernan, 1983; Super & Hall, 1978). Each of these stages will be summarized below.

Preparation Stage

Throck avoided serious career planning in college and failed to apply his academic skills toward possible careers or advanced training. These factors as well as parental pressure made Throck confused about an initial career. His father's pressure to succeed was immobilizing and caused Throck's indecisiveness. In Throck's private moments, he questioned his personal worth, competence, and potential for success. Throck's father questioned his manhood because he was hesitant about making a career commitment and lazy about pursuing economic achievement. Taking a year off was the ultimate "cop-out" according to Throck's father. Throck's gender role conflict was focused on identifying what career would allow him to be a successful man like his father. Instead of facing the competition issues with his father, he opted for no career choice, advanced training, or first job. Not meeting his father's masculine ideals represented to Throck a discrepancy/incongruence that created career inertia. Throck's father devalued his son for not pursuing a financially lucrative career or applying to law school. The outcome was that Throck devalued himself and experienced gender role conflict.

Establishment Stage

During this stage, Throck's life changed dramatically. He experienced eight career transitions: first job, loss of meaning in career, rapid failure, unemployment, advanced training, rapid income loss, career change, and rapid success. Many career conflict issues emerged during these career transitions. There were worries about success, failure, role adoption, role conflict, and loss. These conflicts and transitions substantially altered Throck's perception of himself and his world view. Concurrently, many gender role transition themes were reevaluated. The responsibility of a family forced him to reexamine his role as provider. He worried about integrating the new family roles with a demanding sales job. An unpredictable income created continual worries about money and personal worth. Questions about competence and ability to compete with other men were prominent. When his career was in flux, so too was his identity as a man. He questioned his masculinity when he was unemployed, yet this process allowed him to make a career change that would augment his status and personal worth. Emotionally, Throck still felt incongruent with the masculine norms that he had learned from his parents. He had also been devalued by his coworkers for losing control of his career and being fired from his job. These gender/career stressors were painful, but Throck forged ahead with a new career in law. Law school training forced Throck back into the preparation stage of career development where he was able to find a match between his interests and abilities. He was able to demonstrate competence and achievement, gained power rapidly, and was recognized as a successful lawyer in his early 40s.

Maintenance Stage

This stage included four career transitions: becoming a mentor, working with women, serious conflict with a colleague, and leveling off and job peaking. All of these transitions affected gender role themes and created gender role conflict. Throck's rapid career advancement as a lawyer was not enough to fulfill him. He thought career achievement would bring wealth, satisfaction, security, eminence, and manhood. This was not the case, and there was an uneasy emptiness about the success and competence. He continually worried about losing his status and position to younger and more aggressive trial lawyers. Many aspects of Throck's role as a trial lawyer restricted his personality. He had to be tough, combative, and unrelenting in the courtroom. Masculine values and power were essential during trials. He was unable to provide effective mentoring for women because of stereotypic views of gender roles. He also acted in a sexist manner toward women and his harassment charge became a longstanding joke in legal circles. Often he could not make the transition from work to home, and his wife complained of his bossiness, moodiness, and alcohol abuse. He felt guilty and unsupported at work and misunderstood at home. He found himself particularly critical of his son, when he so wanted to be tender and nurturing. Socialized by the values of the masculine mystique and fearing femininity, he felt more comfortable demonstrating power, control, and strength rather than tenderness, self expression, and vulnerability. His manliness was questioned when he resolved a conflict with a female colleague, thereby losing respect of other men. He struggled with the demands of work and family commitments, and felt inadequate as a father. He was finally successful in the provider role, but the stresses and strains made it difficult to be a loving husband and father.

Table 3

Summary of Throck Morton's Career Transitions and Gender Role Transition Themes

Stage	Career Transitions	Gender Role Transition Themes
Preparation	Initial career choice	Personal worth
	Obtaining skill development/training	Success
	First job	Achievement
		Competence
		Competition
Establishment	First job	Success
	Loss of interest and meaning in career	Provider role
	Rapid failure	Fatherhood
	Being fired—unemployment	Personal worth
	Obtaining training	Competence
	Rapid income loss	Control
	Career change	Achievement
	Rapid success	Power

Maintenance	Becoming a mentor	Achievement
	Working with women	Success
	Serious problem with colleague	Competence
	Leveling off—Job peaking	Personal worth
		Control
		Power
		Women's and men's work roles
		Mentor role
		Personal communication
		Fatherhood
Retirement	Aging	Success
	Preretirement	Achievement
	Retirement	Personal worth
	Loss of stamina and endurance	Strength
	Lost career dream or goal	Aging
	Burnout	Competition
		Health care

Throck's career transitions stimulated redefinition of certain gender transition themes. He was worried about proving his worth as a man and maintaining his career success. The customary use of power and competition seemed ineffective and inappropriate when working with women. He was unprepared to manage conflict with women and communicated ineffectively with them. At the same time he lost status in the "old boy network." In his mentoring attempts, he was unable to alter his competitiveness without feeling a loss of control. He lacked flexibility in maintaining mentoring relationships. He was so concerned about maintaining his power and image that he was unable to empower others. He really did not enjoy his work. Preserving his achievements and successes seemed more taxing than earning them.

The personal experience of these gender/career transitions left Throck feeling violated and restricted by his career. The ideals of success and achievement did not yield the happiness he had expected. The demands of his career were so great that he felt restricted from developing leisure interests. He was, much to his dismay, a marginal spouse and father, just like his own father.

Retirement Stage

The career transitions Throck experienced in this stage included preretirement; aging; loss of stamina and endurance; retirement issues; loss of career dream; and burnout. Preretirement consisted of reviewing his career and assessing his achievements, successes, and failures. He had decreased his work output because of limited energy and stamina. Now in his early 60s, he was concerned about whether he was a real man. He mourned the loss of his lifelong dream of becoming a judge. The competition was keen and the younger attorneys appeared to be more competent for these demanding judicial positions. The transition from work to retirement did not provide the closure Throck desired. There was no gold watch or retirement party. It was a challenge to find leisure activities that made Throck feel useful. As age advanced, minor health problems summoned questions on death and dying. Throck spent much of these later years thinking about his career and personal accomplishments. Gender role transition themes emerged as he philosophized about his life. Had he proven his competence, success, personal worth, and strength to his family, friends, colleagues? Were his efforts appreciated? Had he made a significant contribution? Was he a valued man and person? The personal experience of the retirement stage left Throck with many unresolved discrepancies/incongruencies. Had he succeeded at the career/family game? Had he achieved what was expected of him? He wished there were a finite answer.

IMPLICATIONS FOR PRACTITIONERS

The case study analysis illustrates how career transitions and gender role themes can be applied to one man's life. The adult career and gender role concepts enumerated in this chapter provide practitioners with new vocabulary to assess men's transitions. These concepts have implications for women, and their career and gender role transitions need to be described in the future analyses and case studies. For now, the definitions of career transitions and gender role themes in Tables 1 and 2 provide practitioners with an initial diagnostic classification of transition issues to be assessed in career counseling.

The question remains how to help men in career transitions as they demonstrate, redefine, and integrate gender role themes. It is probably premature to suggest specific counseling approaches for men experiencing career transitions or gender role conflict. The present analysis has deliberately avoided suggesting treatment modes for men based on specific age, stage, transition, symptom, or crisis. Overall, men's career transitions are best explored by helping men understand their own gender role socialization. Men can learn much about themselves by examining their gender role and career socialization processes. Exploring the meaning of a career transition or gender role theme will require trust, support, and confrontation from counselors sensitive to gender role. Men can learn by labeling how they have been hurt and helped by gender role dynamics in their lives. Cognitive constructs like incongruence, devaluation, restriction, and violation can be useful for men as they express emotional pain and conflict. Recently, a diagnostic schema using these constructs as contexts for men's gender role conflict has been developed for counselors working with men (O'Neil, 1990). Moreover, counselors can legitimize career and gender role change as part of the normal maturation process. As counselors advocate more effective career and gender role transitions, gender growth will be better accepted as part of the adult learning process.

Numerous publications provide background on approaches to counseling men (Collison, 1981; Dosser, 1982; Goldfried & Friedman, 1982; Kahn & Greenberg, 1980; O'Neil, 1981a, 1981b, 1982; Scher, 1979, 1981; Scher, Stevens, Good, & Eichenfield, 1987; Skovholt, Gormally, Schauble, & Davis, 1980; Solomon & Levy, 1982; Stein, 1982). These sources are recommended reading for practioners working with men. Most of these publications do not give prescriptions for counseling, but provide valuable ideas and conceptual information for intervening with men's problems. In many ways, counselors working with men's career and gender role transitions are on their own. Until research documents specify treatment for specific gender role and career problems, our established approaches to counseling and psychotherapy provide the best foundation.

On a behavioral level, counselors can teach men problem-solving skills and help them develop emotional expressiveness and understanding. Goldfried and Friedman (1982) provide an excellent review of behavior therapy techniques to use with men. Dosser (1982) discusses training procedures to enhance male expressiveness. Kahn and Greenberg (1980) recommend expanding sex role definition through journal writing, focusing, imagery and fantasy, internal dialogue, and differentiated reconstruction. Collison (1981) has specified a five-step process for counseling men including: (1) identifying gender–role issues; (2) determining consequences of gender–role issues; (3) examining probabilities and consequences of alternatives; (4) deciding on alternatives and identifying resources needed to implement decisions; and (5) planning for evaluation and review.

On a more emotional and psychodynamic level, men will need to learn to express painful emotions that may touch early childhood learning as well as present conflicts. Many norms of appropriate masculine behavior are established in primary families and remain unchallenged through adulthood. Men able to reexperience repressed emotions of early adolescence can gain understanding of their current pain and conflicts. For example, the internationalization of parental attitudes and gender related conflicts about success, failure, and achievement can plague a man throughout his life. Fathers and mothers who expressed pain and conflict about their own career transitions can communicate these to their sons. Many men experience their fathers as "wounded" (Pleck, 1984), and therefore carry these wounds into their own adulthood. Sometimes these wounds are reexperienced as conflicts in the son's life, representing intergenerational transmission of gender role conflict. Father–son relationships are fertile areas for counseling men with gender–career conflicts.

Furthermore, the conceptualizations in this manuscript and others (Levinson et al., 1978; Moreland, 1979, 1980; Pleck, 1981) need a greater empirical base. Case studies and empirical research on the dynamics of gender role conflict in career and gender role transitions are needed for both men and women. For example, a recent empirical study (Good, Dell, & Mintz, 1989) found that patterns of gender role conflict do affect men's help-seeking behavior. Earlier attempts to assess gender role conflict in college students (Komarovsky, 1976; O'Neil et al., 1986) need extension to older adults across different socioeconomic, class, and race parameters. Additionally, the information in Tables 1, 2, and 3 needs to be extended to more comprehensive and focused analyses of women's career and gender role transitions. Likewise, the personal symptoms of gender conflict (incongruence/discrepancy, devaluation, restriction, violation) need both greater elaboration and empirical validation.

If anything, men need to recognize that their career transitions and gender role conflicts are not just personal failures but result from complex biological, societal, and socialization influences. Career and gender role transitions are inevitable across the life cycle, and men need to continually reassess how they define healthy masculinity and a healthy career life. Counselors can help men gain perspective on normal life cycle changes. Men who blame themselves for not living up to stereotypic masculine norms are candidates for self-devaluation, anger, depression, and alienation. These men need to be exposed to more flexible ways of solving the problems of everyday living.

Men can generate ways to validate themselves other than through economic success, achievement, and power. This can and has been done by men over the life cycle. Young boys and men need to recognize that masculinity can mean more than strength, career success, and economic status. They need to know that there are limits to this narrow conception of power and masculinity. Men need to develop other interpersonal or spiritual "power bases" to enrich their lives and negotiate changing life events. Counselors and psychologists can be advocates for socializing men to be effectively human as well as appropriately masculine. Functional criteria that transcend sex and gender, are needed to validate humankind if the sexes are to survive and negotiate gender and career transitions effectively.

Acknowledgments

The authors appreciate the clerical assistance of Anny Boisvert, Theresa Gamble, Kathy Mann, Lisa McPherson, Louise Patros, Carol Roberts, and Gail Rowland in the preparation of the manuscript. Danny Lea and Zandy Leibowitz's critiques of earlier drafts were very helpful in the chapter's development. Our spouses (Lisa McCann and Jim Fishman) were supportive of our efforts and accepting of the time demands required to write this analysis.

The authors appreciate Tom Magoon's creation of Throck Morton at the University of Maryland. The fictitious Morton was used there to describe a typical client needing counseling from a professional counselor.

REFERENCES

Basow, S.A. (1986). *Gender stereotypes: Traditions and alternatives.* Monterey, CA: Brooks/Cole.

Betz, N.E. & Fitzgerald, L.F. (1987). *The career psychology of women.* New York: Academic Press.

Brammer, L.M., & Abrego, P.J. (1981). Intervention strategies for coping with transitions. *The Counseling Psychologist, 9* (2), 19–36.

Brim, O.G. (1976). Theories of the male mid-life crisis. *The Counseling Psychologist, 6* (1), 2–9.

Brim, O.G. & Ryff, C. (1980). On the properties of life events. In P. Baltes & O. Brim (Eds.), *Life-span development and behavior.* Vol. 3 (pp. 368–388). New York: Academic Press.

Brown, D. (1984). Mid-life career change. In D. Brown & L. Brooks (Eds.), *Career choice and development* (pp. 369–387). San Francisco: Jossey-Bass.

Bucher, G.R. (1976). *Straight, white, male.* Philadelphia, PA: Fortress Press.

Campbell, R.E. & Cellini, J.V. (1981). A diagnostic taxonomy of adult career problems. *Journal of Vocational Behavior, 19,* 179–198.

Campbell, R.E., & Heffernan, J.M. (1983). Adult vocational behavior. In W.B. Walsh & S.H. Osipow (Eds.), *Handbook of vocational psychology: Vol. 1. Foundations* (pp. 223–260). Hillsdale, NJ: Lawrence Erlbaum Associates.

Collison, B.B. (1981). Counseling adult males. *Personnel and Guidance Journal, 60,* 219–222.

Crites, J.O., & Fitzgerald, L.F. (1978). The competent male. *The Counseling Psychologist, 7,* 10–14.

Danish, S.J. (1981). Life-span human development and intervention: A necessary link. *The Counseling Psychologist, 9* (2), 40–43.

David, S., & Brannon, R. (1976). *The forty-nine percent majority: The male sex role.* Reading, MA: Addison-Wesley, pp. 545–579.

Dosser, D.A. (1982). Male impressiveness: Behavioral intervention. In K. Solomon & N.B. Levy (Eds.), *Men in transition: Theory and therapy* (pp. 343–432). New York: Plenum Press.

Farmer, H.S. (1976). What inhibits achievement and career motivations in women? *The Counseling Psychologist, 6*, 12–14.

Farmer, H.S. (1985). Model of career and achievement motivation for women and men. *Journal of Counseling Psychology, 32*, 363–390.

Farrell, W. (1974). *The liberated man*. New York: Bantam Books.

Fasteau, M.F. (1974). *The male machine*. New York: McGraw-Hill.

Fitzgerald, L.F., & Betz, N. (1983). Issues in the vocational psychology of women. In W.B. Walsh & S.H. Osipow (Eds.), *Handbook of vocational psychology: Vol. 1. Foundations* (pp. 83–159). Hillsdale, NJ: Lawrence Erlbaum Associates.

Fitzgerald, L.F., & Crites, J.O. (1979). Career counseling for women. *The Counseling Psychologist, 8*, 33–35.

Fitzgerald, L.F., & Crites, J.O. (1980). Toward a career psychology of women: What do we know? What do we need to know? *Journal of Counseling Psychology, 27*, 44–62.

Garnets, L., & Pleck, J.H. (1979). Sex role identity, androgyny, and sex role transcendence: A sex role strain analysis. *Psychology of Women Quarterly, 3*, 270–283.

Ginzberg, E., Ginsburg, S.W., Axelrad, S., & Herma, J.L. (1951). *Occupational choice: An approach to a general theory*. New York: Columbia University Press.

Goldberg, H. (1977). *The hazards of being male*. New York: New American Library.

Goldfried, M.R., & Friedman, J.M. (1982). Clinical behavior therapy and the male sex role. In K. Solomon & N. Levy (Eds.), *Men in transition: Theory and therapy* (pp. 309–336). New York: Plenum Press.

Good, G., Dell, D.M. & Mintz, L.B. (1989). Male roles and gender role conflict: Relationship to help-seeking in men. *Journal of Counseling Psychology, 3*, 295–300.

Gottfredson, L. (1981). Circumscription and compromise: A developmental theory of occupational aspirations. *Journal of Counseling Psychology, 28*, 545–579.

Gould, R.L. (1978). *Transformations: Growth and change in adult life*. New York: Simon & Schuster.

Hansen, L.S. (1984). Interrelationship of gender and career. In N. Gysbers (Ed.), *Designing careers* (pp. 216–247). San Francisco: Jossey-Bass.

Harmon, L.W. (1977). Career counseling for women. In E. Rawlings & D. Carter (Eds.), *Psychotherapy for women* (pp. 197–206). Springfield, IL: Charles C. Thomas.

Harmon, L.W., & Farmer, H.S. (1983). Current theoretical issues in vocational psychology. In W.B. Walsh & S.H. Osipow (Eds.), *Handbook of vocational psychology: Vol. 1. Foundations* (pp. 39–77). Hillsdale, NJ: Lawrence Erlbaum Associates.

Hays, H.R. (1964). *The dangerous sex: The myth of feminine evil*. New York: Pocket Books.

Herr, E.L., & Cramer, S.H. (1979). *Career guidance through the life span: Systematic approaches*. Boston, MA: Little, Brown.

Hopson, B. (1981). Response to the papers by Schlossberg. Brammer, and Abrego. *The Counseling Psychologist, 9* (2) 36–39.

Hopson, B., & Adams, J. (1977). Toward an understanding of transition: Defining some boundaries of transition. In J. Adams, J. Hayes, & B. Hopson (Eds.), *Transition: Understanding and managing person change* (pp. 3–25). Montclair, NJ: Allanheld & Osmun.

Horney, K. (1967). *Feminine psychology.* New York: Norton.

Hotchkiss, L., & Borow, H. (1984). Sociological perspectives and career choice and attainment. In D. Brown & L. Brooks (Eds.), *Career choice and development* (pp. 137–168). San Francisco: Jossey-Bass.

Jung, C.G. (1953). Animus and anima. *Collected works. Vol. 7* New York: Pantheon.

Jung, C.G. (1954). Concerning the archetypes, with special reference to the anima concept. *Collected works: Vol. 9 Part 1.* New York: Pantheon.

Kahn, S.E., & Greenberg, L.S. (1980). Expanding sex-role definitions by self-discovery. *Personnel and Guidance Journal, 59,* 220–225.

Komarovsky, M. (1976). *Dilemmas of masculinity: A study of college youth.* New York: Norton.

Lederer, W. (1968). *The fear of women.* New York: Harcourt Brace Jovanovich.

Levinson, D.J., Darrow, C.H., Klein, E.B., Levinson, M.H., & McKee, B. (1978). *The seasons of a man's life.* New York: Ballantine Books.

Lowenthal, M.F., Thurnher, M., & Chiriboga, D. (1975). *Four stages of life: A comparative study of women and men facing transitions.* San Francisco: Jossey-Bass.

Mayer, N. (1978). *The male mid-life crises: Fresh start after 40.* New York: New American Library.

Menninger, K. (1970). *Love against hate.* New York: Harcourt Brace Jovanovich.

Miller, D.C., & Form, W.H. (1951). *Industrial sociology: An introduction to the sociology of work reactions.* New York: Harper & Row.

Money, J. (1980). *Love and love sickness: The science of sex, gender differences, and pair bonding.* Baltimore, MD: Johns Hopkins University Press.

Moos, R.H., & Tsu, V. (1976). Human competence and coping: An overview. In R.H. Moos (Ed.), *Human adaptation: Coping with life crises* (pp. 3–16). Lexington, MA: Heath.

Moreland, J.R. (1979). Some implications of life-span development for counseling psychology. *Personal and Guidance Journal, 57* 299–303.

Moreland, J.R. (1980). Age and change in the adult male sex role. *Sex Roles, 6,* 807–818.

Morgan, J.I., Skovholt, T.M., & Orr, J.M. (1979). Career counseling with men: The shifting focus. In S.G. Weinrach (Ed.), *Career counseling: Theoretical and practical perspectives* (pp. 260–266). New York: McGraw-Hill.

Nichols, J. (1975). *Men's liberation: A new definition of masculinity.* New York: Penguin Books.

Offer, D., & Sabshin, M. (1984). *Normality and life cycle: A critical integration.* New York: Basic Books.

Olson, K. (1978). *Hey man! Open up and live.* New York: Fawcett Gold Medal.

O'Neil, J.M. (1981a). Male sex-role conflicts, sexism, and masculinity: Psychological implications for men, women and the counseling psychologist. *The Counseling Psychologist, 9,* 61–80.

O'Neil J.M. (1981b). Patterns of gender role conflict and strain: The fear of femininity in men's lives. *Personnel and Guidance Journal, 60,* 203–210.

O'Neil, J.M. (1982). Gender and sex role conflict and strain in men's lives: Implications for psychiatrists, psychologists, and other human service providers. In K. Solomon & N. Levy (Eds.), *Men in transition: Theory and therapy* (pp. 5–44). New York: Plenum Press.

O'Neil, J.M. (1990). Assessing men's gender role conflict. In D. Moore & F. Leafgren (Eds.), *Problem solving strategies and interventions for men in conflict* (pp. 23–38) Alexandria, VA: AACD Press.

O'Neil, J.M., David, L., & Wrightsman, L. (1985). *Fear of femininity scale (FOFS): Men's gender role conflict.* Storrs, CT: University of Connecticut, Department of Educational Psychology. (ERIC Document Reproduction Service No. ED 24780).

O'Neil, J.M., Fishman, D.M., & Kinsella-Shaw, M. (1987). Dual-career couples' career transitions and normative dilemmas: A preliminary assessment model. *The Counseling Psychologist, 15* (1), 50–96.

O'Neil, J.M., & Fishman, D.M. (1985b). *Career transition checklist.* Storrs, CT: Counseling Psychology Program, University of Connecticut.

O'Neil, J.M., Helms, B., Gable, R., David, L., & Wrightsman, L. (1986). Gender role conflict scale: College men's fear of femininity. *Sex roles, 14,* 335–350.

O'Neil, J.M., Meeker, C., & Borgers, S. (1978). A developmental, preventive, and consultative model to reduce sexism in the career planning of women. *JSAS Catalog of Selected Documents in Psychology, 8*(39), (Ms. 1984).

Osipow, S.H. (1983). *Theories of career development* (3rd ed.). Englewood Cliffs, NJ: Prentice-Hall.

Osipow, S.H. (Ed.). (1975). *Emerging woman: Career analysis and outlooks.* Columbus, OH: Charles E. Merrill.

Parkes, C.M. (1971). Psycho-social transitions: A field of study. *Social science and medicine: Vol. 5.* London: Pergamon Press.

Parsons, J.E. (1980). *The psychobiology of sex differences and sex roles.* New York: McGraw-Hill.

Pleck, J.H. (1981). *The myth of masculinity.* Cambridge, MA: The MITT Press.

Pleck, J.H. (1984, July). *Healing the wounded father.* Workshop presented at the 9th National Conference on Men and Masculinity, Washington, D.C.

Pleck, J.H., & Sawyer, J. (1974). *Men and masculinity.* Englewood Cliffs, NJ: Prentice-Hall.

Richardson, M.S. (1979). Toward an expanded view of careers. *The Counseling Psychologist, 8,* 34–35.

Schaffer, K. (1981). *Sex roles and human behavior.* Cambridge, MA: Winthrop.

Scher, M. (1979). The little boy in the adult male client. *Personnel and Guidance Journal, 60*(4), 198–264.

Scher, M. (Ed.). (1981). Counseling men (Special issue). *Personnel and Guidance Journal, 60*(4).

Scher, M., Stevens, M., Good, G., & Eichenfield, G.A. (1987). *Handbook of counseling and psychotherapy with men.* Newbury Park, CA: Sage Publications.

Schlossberg, N.K. (1981). A model for analyzing human adaptation to transition. *The Counseling Psychologist, 9,* 2–18.

Schlossberg, N.K. (1984). *Counseling adults in transition.* New York: Springer.

Skovholt, T. (1978). Feminism and men's lives. *Counseling Psychologist, 7,* 3–10.

Skovholt, T., Gormally, A., Schauble, P., & Davis, R. (1980). *Counseling men.* Monterey, CA: Brooks/Cole.

Solomon, K., & Levy, N. (1982). *Men in transition: Theory and therapy.* New York: Plenum Press.

Srebalus, D.J., Marinelli, R.P., & Messing, J.K. (1982). *Career development: Concepts and procedures.* Monterey, CA: Brooks/Cole.

Stein, T.S. (1982). Men's groups. In K. Solomon & N. Levy (Eds.), *Men in transition: Theory and therapy* (pp. 275–307). New York: Plenum Press.

Super, D.E. (1957). *The psychology of careers.* New York: Harper.

Super, D.E. (1980). A life-span, life space approach to career development. *Journal of Vocational Behavior, 16,* 282–298.

Super, D.E. (1984). Perspectives on the meaning and value of work. In N.C. Gysbers (Ed.), *Designing careers* (pp. 27–53). San Francisco: Jossey-Bass.

Super, D.E., & Hall, D.T. (1978). Career development: Exploration and planning. *Annual Review of Psychology, 29,* 333–372.

Tavris, C., & Offir, C. (1977). *The longest war: Sex differences in perspective.* New York: Harcourt Brace Jovanovich.

Tolson, A. (1977). *The limits of masculinity: Male identity and women's liberation.* New York: Harper & Row.

Troll, L.E. (1981). Comments. *The Counseling Psychologist, 9.* 46–48.

Vaillant, G.E. (1977). *Adaption to life.* Boston, MA: Little, Brown.

Vetter, L. (1973). Career counseling for women. *Counseling Psychologist, 4,* 54–67.

Weitz, S. (1977). *Sex roles: Biological, psychological, and social foundations.* New York: Oxford University Press.

CHAPTER 11

A Culturally Relevant Perspective for Understanding the Career Paths of Visible Racial/Ethnic Group People

Robert T. Carter
Teachers College
Columbia University
New York, New York

Donelda A. Cook
University of Maryland
College Park, Maryland

Recent reviews of the career development literature pertaining to visible racial/ethnic group people (this term refers to black, native, Latino, and Asian-Americans and is offered as a substitute for minority; see Cook & Helms, 1988) have convincingly pointed out the shortcomings of career development theories and research where racial/ethnic group people are concerned. Smith states that

> life stage development as typically described by career theorists may have limited generalizability to racial minorities. External constraints, limited economic resources, and racial discrimination make the concept of life-stage career development for racial minorities more of a dream than a reality for all but the most persistent, the most fortunate, and the group or mixture of individuals perceived as most socially desirable within a given racial group. (p. 186)

Furthermore, "social desirability" connotes "acculturation"; that is, within a given racial group, the most socially desirable individuals, as perceived by employers, are those most acculturated to mainstream white American standards.

In addition, career theorists have been criticized because (a) they developed their theories based on research with white middle class males; (b) theoretical models are based on Euro-American cultural assumptions or world views (see Carter & Swanson, 1990); (c) they ignore the socio-political and psychological realities that visible racial/ethnic group people experience; (d) they ignore the economic and social circumstances which impact most visible racial/ethnic group members irrespective of their social status; and (e) they ignore the cultural institutions (e.g., churches, social organizations, tribal communities) that serve as "social equalizers" for visible racial/ethnic group members in that they promote expressions of vocational talents which may not be realized or recognized in the dominant cultural arena.

These omissions also exist in books and texts devoted to career development. For the most part, writers may devote a chapter to all visible racial/ethnic group members and other underrepresented groups (e.g., Brown & Brooks, 1990; Zunker, 1981; Walsh & Osipow, 1983) and point to general trends in their experiences, like employment and educational achievement, but seldom do authors incorporate the educational and occupational experiences of visible racial/ethnic group members into their theory building or other discussions of career development issues.

In essence, these criticisms suggest that the external environmental factors which impinge and in part shape the life course of many visible racial/ethnic group members is all too often missing from the work of career theorists and writers. Moreover, we believe that the cultural perspectives and experiences as well as within-group variation of visible racial/ethnic group members also tend to be overlooked. Visible racial/ethnic group members are usually discussed as if they were monolithic and vary only with regard to socioeconomic status. The monolithic view suggests that visible racial/ethnic group personalities and racial/cultural group perspectives are identical within a particular group.

Brooks (1990) has noted that while many criticisms have been offered about the shortcomings of the career literature, no research has been conducted in the area and no theoretical framework has been offered. At best it has been assumed that the only way to understand visible racial/ethnic group members is to compare them to whites.

In this chapter we would like to offer a culturally relevant perspective for understanding the career paths of visible racial/ethnic group members. Our perspective is intended to begin to address the particular experiences and challenges which visible racial/ethnic group members encounter.

CAREER PATHS FOR VISIBLE RACIAL/ETHNIC GROUP MEMBERS

To understand the varied forces and influences that interact with one another and together impact visible racial/ethnic group members' career choices, it is essential that we conceptualize these influences in terms of a systems model. Therefore, systems theory will be described as a way to represent the various influences which affect visible racial/ethnic group members' career paths.

Systems Theory

Systems theory suggests that human systems can be thought of as organized structures and operations with interacting components constrained by or dependent on other components. These organized structures are seen as being "composed of mutually dependent parts and processes standing in mutual interaction" (von Bertalanffy, cited in Okun, 1984, p. 31). The organizing systems are also believed to be self-regulating, active, and rule governed. The system operates to maintain its own survival. In this manner we conceptualize the elements and components associated with career paths for visible racial/ethnic group members as a system. Thus, the sociocultural system which influences visible racial/ethnic group members' career paths is seen as having interdependent, interconnected, and interactive elements or units. In addition, participants in the system have a history together and relate to one another in relatively stable and consistent ways.

Some of the primary principles associated with systems theory, particularly as applied to families, can be summarized in the following way (Minuchin, 1974): A system is an organized whole and each element within the system is interdependent on the other elements. For our purposes the whole system is American society and is characterized by its dominant cultural patterns (Stewart, 1972; Carter, 1990). In addition, each visible racial/ethnic group member's culture also contains separate subsystems within the larger dominant culture. Therefore, in considering the career paths of visible racial/ethnic group members, one must take into account the total patterns of occupational and educational participation that have developed over time and that regulate the interactions of the visible racial/ethnic group member with members of the dominant culture. The career behavior of each visible racial/ethnic group member is therefore seen in the context of the whole system.

The career path patterns of visible racial/ethnic group members are a manifestation of the structure of the general society. According to systems theory, structure has three elements: boundaries, alignment, and power. Boundaries are the rules that regulate participation and roles (that is, what each person or group is allowed to do and how they are allowed to interact within the system). Boundaries are the manifestation of the system's rules and regulations; they define the context in which communications occur. They can be external and internal, rigid or permeable. Boundaries also regulate the interactions between two subsystems.

Communication refers to the process and manner by which the rules and regulations of a system are transmitted. Communication patterns can be understood by studying the human interactions within the system, the relationship of the members and the subsystems, and the rules that govern the members. Relationships can be studied by analyzing the communicational (verbal) and metacommunicational (nonverbal) aspects of interactions within the system. As we observe communicational styles and patterns within a system, it is important to remember that the metacommunicational message, the command aspect, defines the nature of the relationship and establishes the rules governing which behaviors are to be included or excluded in a relationship. Boundaries within the system may be communicated to racial/cultural groups in many forms. For instance, ideas and beliefs about racial/cultural groups may serve as one type of feedback (e.g., stereotypes). Institutional inclusion or exclusion may be another way the dominant society communicates to the racial/cultural group members the appropriate social and occupational boundaries. Socioeconomic resources distribution or labor force participation (or the lack of it) may also serve as a boundary. So, for instance, Native Americans communicate with the larger social system through the Bureau of Indian Affairs and are expected to adhere to this system boundary. Blacks, Hispanics, and many Asian groups are expected to live within specific geographic regions (typically, an urban or rural ghetto) and are usually subject to reprisals when they overstep these boundaries.

Another element of a system is alignment, which is a pattern of subsystem joining. If the various institutional subsystems in the dominant society function as separate subsystems that join or align with one another to achieve implicit sociocultural goals and uphold basic cultural values, educational and occupational systems can collude to restrict the success and participation of visible racial/ethnic group people. For example, state, city, and local governments align to allocate fewer resources to the often segregated communities where visible racial/ethnic group people live. The educational systems from elementary through post-secondary institutions align with the political bodies and each other in such a way that large numbers of visible racial/ethnic group people are subject to experiences that communicate to them that they do not belong (see Fine, 1990). The business community and the general occupational world set standards of employment that often conflict with the educational backgrounds and lifestyles of visible racial/ethnic group members.

The third element, power, refers to the ability of a person or a group in the system to change or determine boundaries or alignments. Occupationally, many visible racial/ethnic group people are regulated to low or marginal status, usually service or technical assistance occupations. When these boundaries are crossed, many subtle forms of communication are used to communicate to the individual that he or she is out of place. It is also important to note that systems seek to maintain their balance or homeostasis and stability even if these patterns are dysfunctional. "A system would rather retain its familiar pain than subject itself to the vulnerability of change, even when the outcome of that change is likely to alleviate pain" (Okun, 1984, p. 33). An example of the way balance may be maintained by a social system can be seen in the events of Reconstruction after the Civil War. Shortly after the Civil War, blacks began to participate more equally in the economic and social systems (Fredrickson, 1989), a situation which upset the historical, social, and economic racial balance. This led to the imposition of legal and social backlash in the form of Jim Crow laws and the creation of vigilante groups whose purpose was to re-establish a racial inequality which was (and some believe is) the norm in American society.

The systems perspective suggests a dynamic interaction of internal (physiological and psychological factors) and external or environmental variables such as social roles and sociocultural experiences (i.e., economic, social status, and living conditions). Okun observes that "the systems perspective also posits that individual career and family development (or paths) are interrelated and that one dimension of development is viewed as a multifaceted and interactional, and a continuous interplay of internal and external forces. . ." (p. 411).

Adult Career Development Theory

This conceptual perspective is adapted from Okun's (1984) conceptual model of adult career development. Okun proposes that adult career development be understood in terms of the interactions of individual, family, and career life cycles. The individual life cycle is characterized by biologically and socially determined needs, opportunities, and adjustments. "Each life stage comprises developmental tasks resulting from both biological forces and age-related social or cultural expectations" (Okun, 1984, p. 11). Individuals also have recently been seen as members of family systems and as influenced by those family systems. Family theorists have suggested that family systems are circular in that the experiences of one generation affect the progress and experiences of the next. Similarly, according to Okun (1984), "A career cycle is the life span of one's vocational development. Throughout its stages, the cycle may consist of various career, avocational, and leisure paths as well as specific jobs" (p. 12). These life cycles occur within the context of phases of adult development (i.e., early, middle, and late adulthood).

Okun (1984) begins her analysis of adult career development from the perspective of the individual life system. Thus she is able to describe various developmental, family, and career tasks which might impact on adult career development. However, for visible racial/ethnic group members it is necessary to begin with their history in the United States and an analysis of their sociopolitical circumstances.

Since Euro-Americans developed racial/cultural ideologies (see Thomas & Sillen, 1972) which have served to shape popular views of the respective contributions and characteristics of members of the various racial/cultural groups, these biased ideologies have operated to establish cultural norms for Euro-Americans which explicitly determined the roles and functions that visible racial/ethnic group members may have in the social system. These world views of Euro-Americans toward themselves and visible racial/ethnic group people form the context in which visible racial/ethnic group members are able to participate in the occupational and educational systems. According to this view, then, visible racial/ethnic group members' career options are influenced by access to occupational or career opportunities, and cultural, social, economic, and political circumstances.

Each visible racial/ethnic group member, as a consequence of Euro-Americans' world view regarding the group, has been subject to social, economic, political, and cultural limits and restrictions. These restrictions have influenced visible racial/ethnic group members' career, occupational, and educational options and choices. The circumstances resulting from systematic discrimination and segregation have impacted the family systems and in turn the developmental course of its members. In addition, each visible racial/ethnic group member is characterized by its own cultural traditions, language, lifestyles, norms, and cultural values. These cultural characteristics also interact with the social system influences to exert pressure on individuals' educational and occupational choices. The visible racial/ethnic group members' cultural traditions will affect the family system as well as influence the manner in which the individual and family will interact or react to society's views, and the manner of interacting with members of the particular group. Similar influences also operate at the individual level as well.

There exist tremendous group variations within and between visible racial/ethnic group members. While we use the terms black, Asian, Latino, and Native American, we also recognize that within each group there are considerable ethnic and cultural variations. For instance, there are black Americans, Haitian, Caribbean, African, Latino, and European-born Blacks. Among Asians, there are Chinese, Malaysians, Koreans, Japanese, Indochinese, Taiwanese, Vietnamese, etc. Among Latin people, there are Mexican, Cuban, Puerto Rican, Dominican, South American, Central American, etc. Native American ethnic groups consist of Navajo, Sioux, Shoshone, Hopi, Chippewa, Apache, etc. Each ethnic group will have its own sociopolitical history, language, culture, norms, and values. Moreover, individuals may vary with respect to the extent to which they identify with their respective racial/cultural groups (i.e., racial/cultural identity). Counselors and educators should be responsible for gathering and acquiring the particular information which is relevant for the group(s) with whom they are working.

Psychological and career development theorists began with the assumption that the focus of development is the individual devoid of social, cultural, and political context. Therefore, an individual's developmental process and structures are described in terms of how the individual copes with, responds to, and is influenced by various factors such as family, educational, and occupational systems. We, however, begin with the opposite assumption, that is, that visible racial/ethnic group peoples' career paths are shaped by sociocultural circumstances and their sociopolitical and historical-cultural backgrounds.

Historical-Cultural Perspective of Work

The concept of work has been ingrained in the cultural frame of reference of visible racial/ethnic group members dating back to the lifestyles of their original homelands and their beginnings on American soil. Work was viewed as an integral aspect of life, the foundation of developing and sustaining their cultural societies. Indeed, as the first settlers of North America, Native Americans provided the initial cultural base for career development in America. According to Axelson (1985), Native Americans migrated to North America more than 30,000 years ago, and developed the first cultural society in America, as hunters searching for food and furs for clothing. Initially, small family groups set out on hunting expeditions and eventually formed bands, tribes, and nations. "Native American tribal cultures have historically been identified by the way they gathered their food (hunting and farming) and the areas in which they pursued their livelihood" (Axelson, 1985, p. 29). Thus, Native Americans established the beginning of career identity paths in America.

Similarly, other visible racial/ethnic group members (i.e., blacks, Latinos, Asians) developed the cultural societies of their homelands through their labor as hunters, farmers, carpenters, and sustained their societies through their domestic, business, artistic, scientific, and health care skills. Therefore, career identity has historically been a central aspect of the cultural lifestyles of visible racial/ethnic group peoples. Tragically, however, the self-determined career identities of visible racial/ethnic group people were annihilated by the historical abduction, exploitation, suppression, and oppression by European immigrants conquering the New World and establishing their American homelands.

For instance, unlike the Native Americans who were "robbed of" their land in America, the majority of blacks were "robbed from" their land in West Africa to serve as slaves to European immigrants in America. The slavery system was designed to utilize the manual skills of blacks, while squelching their educational and critical thinking capabilities. Such "vocational retraining" was enforced to fit the work patterns for the most effective and profitable operation of plantations (Axelson, 1985). Labor capabilities were so much ascribed to the indentities of slaves that individual slaves were valued according to their physical stamina and specific work skills. In some cases, slaves were even given familial names based upon the work role which the mother served on the plantation. Although work-related activities were the benchmark of blacks' usefulness to American society, the slavery system undermined their free will in maintaining their natural career paths.

Interestingly, the history of black people in America also includes "free blacks" and blacks who migrated from the West Indies, both of whom experienced greater socioeconomic mobility than the blacks who were American slaves (Axelson, 1985). "Free blacks" included indentured servants who worked off their bondage and were economically self-sufficient and ". . .slaves who were owned by plantation employers or by other blacks, but were free to hire themselves out" (Axelson, 1985, p. 68).

While work was central to the lifestyles of free blacks, "stability of family life was based on moral and social values rather than on material possessions or income and occupational class distinctions" (Axelson, 1985, p. 70). This configuration of occupational identity relative to moral and social identity has been and continues to be a potent defense for visible racial/ethnic group members against extreme internalized oppression due to discriminatory practices in career opportunities. For example, the black church has historically served as a "social equalizer" in that, regardless of the status one holds with reference to career position in the dominant culture, within the black church one can maintain a position of great leadership and status. In many churches today, skilled and semi-skilled workers hold positions of trustee or deacon in their church; these are powerful positions which are involved in assisting the church pastor in making various financial and administrative decisions. Thus, the traditional notion of "career self-concept" has less meaning as visible racial/ethnic group members acknowledge that their career options may be limited due to institutionalized racism and discrimination. Therefore,

198

institutions within their own cultures provide viable outlets for expression of their self-concepts.

Similar to the black immigrants of the West Indies, various Latino and Asian ethnic groups entered the American labor force due to the limited economic conditions of their homeland and/or to escape political suppression. As immigrants and refugees, they were welcomed into this country to meet the cheap labor needs of American industries. For instance, ". . . much of the commerce and industry in the border cities and states developed by using Mexican labor. Today, many of the agricultural, business, and manufacturing enterprises in parts of the country are so dependent on Mexican labor that they would have difficulty continuing without it" (Axelson, 1985, p. 81). In fact, programs were enacted for the importation of immigrants (i.e., Mexican, Chinese, Japanese) into the United States for job exploitation; however, as the immigration numbers increased for specific visible racial/ethnic group members, laws were enacted which limited the numbers, patterns of settlement, and citizenship eligibility (Axelson, 1985). Given the historical sociopolitical perspective of the roles of visible racial/ethnic group peoples in the American labor force, the notion of "career choice" is relegated to "paths" within the confines of the oppressive restrictions imposed by the dominant culture. Furthermore, the "traditional" careers (e.g., education, social science) for visible racial/ethnic group members are based on the jobs which the dominant culture has "traditionally" allowed them to hold, rather than on the self-determined choices of visible racial/ethnic group people.

The historical, sociocultural, and political circumstances of visible racial/ethnic group members' career paths in this country have considerable implications for the career paths of visible racial/ethnic group members of today. From a cultural frame of reference, work is a functional aspect of life in that individuals contribute their skills and labor to their cultural societies and the maintenance of their families. Consequently, careers may represent a "collective" identity rather than an "individual" identity. Politically, visible racial/ethnic group members have traditionally and realistically expected that the "career" for which they are eligible will be a "job" which the dominant culture has relegated to a low status position. Thus, the high unemployment rate of visible racial/ethnic group members has scarring effects on their self-esteem in that they are unable to contribute to the good of the family or the culture. While underemployment is an unjust fact of life for visible racial/ethnic group members, the damaging consequences to the esteem are slightly minimized if an individual participates in aspects of the culture which promote a "social equalizing" effect (e.g., churches, social organizations, political groups, tribal activities).

The manner and types of work in which visible racial/ethnic group members historically engaged was, and continues to be, restricted. Richardson (1981), for instance, notes that "the life expectancy of Indians is 44 years . . . one county in Nebraska has 28% Indian, yet 98% of all arrests were of Indian people . . . . Between 40%-80% of the tribal members are unemployed . . . the average income is between $1200-$1500." For blacks, Jaynes and Williams (1989) remind us that "Five decades ago, most Black Americans could not work, live, shop, eat, seek entertainment or travel where they chose" (p. 3). The labor force and educational data suggest that the occupational paths which visible racial/ethnic group members must travel are strewn with innumerable obstacles. The majority of these barriers and obstacles exist in the sociocultural, environmental, and institutional structures of the society and, as such, function as boundaries which for many visible racial/ethnic group members are fairly impermeable. Many of these boundaries and the meta-messages which accompany them stem from historically rooted racist ideologies held by white Americans and internalized by some visible racial/ethnic group members (Jones, 1972).

For instance, the "promises" of equal employment opportunities brought about by the Civil Rights movement, have altered the psychological perspectives of work for many visible racial/ethnic group members. These promises have led to expressions of anger among the underemployed and subsequently unemployed visible racial/ethnic group members who are questioning why they do not have access to these available opportunities. In contrast, upwardly mobile visible racial/ethnic group people who have benefited from advanced educational opportunities believe that they can soar to the heights of their career aspirations; consequently, they are confused when they reach a "ceiling" to their career advancement which does not exist for members of the dominant culture. Such confusion is further exacerbated by the fact that in many instances upwardly mobile visible racial/ethnic group members have traded in their original cultural values, attitudes, behaviors, homes, friends, and family for the socially acceptable lifestyles required by their career advancement in the dominant culture.

The psychological trauma of the equal opportunity belief is maintained by the dominant culture which espouses that visible racial/ethnic group members are not succeeding occupationally because they are not capable, or they are not working hard enough toward achieving their goals. The victims of institutionalized discrimination, then, are blamed for their own plight. Subsequently, members of the dominant culture do not perceive that they must alter their role in impeding the career paths of visible racial/ethnic group members; visible racial/ethnic group members in turn are internalizing the message of self-blame which destroys their original cultural perspectives of contributing to the development, maintenance, and success of their families and cultural societies.

Hoyt (1989) reporting on the career status of visible racial/ethnic group members over a 20-year period noted that while some progress in occupational and educational attainment has been made by visible racial/ethnic group members, "one can conclude that minority persons in the labor force are worse off than they were in 1968" (p. 208). He also points out that "Both Blacks and Hispanics are overrepresented in the slow growing or declining occupations, but underrepresented in the fast growing occupations" (Kutcher, 1987, cited in Hoyt, p. 207). It is also true that the majority of visible racial/ethnic group people when they are employed are hired into low level service or semi-skilled occupations. When visible racial/ethnic group members do achieve higher level occupational status, this has historically occurred so they could provide professional services to members of their own segregated communities. When this is not the case, they more often than not become one of the few visible racial/ethnic group members in their professional or occupational setting. Being one of the few is associated with a number of social, psychological, and emotional consequences.

In summary, the economic and career consequences of racism are clearly seen in the life circumstances of visible racial/ethnic group people. They have fewer economic resources as seen in lower incomes in comparison to whites, they hold the least desirable jobs, and have higher unemployment rates. Even when visible racial/ethnic group members overcome the numerous obstacles, they still have difficulty capitalizing on their investments in education and training. The systemic and structural barriers and boundaries hinder the occupational paths of visible racial/ethnic group members. Nevertheless, these social forces have not hindered the development of distinct cultures among the visible racial/ethnic group.

WITHIN VISIBLE RACIAL/ETHNIC GROUP DIFFERENCES

Consideration of within group and intrapsychic diversity is a cornerstone of our perspective. What we offer is a systems framework of ways the different influences may apply to particular members of racial/cultural groups. It is also true that the influences may vary according to the unique circumstances and personalities of particular individuals.

Cultural and Family Systems Characteristics

The career paths of visible racial/ethnic group individuals are often influenced by the specific characteristics of their lifestyles. Some elements of lifestyles include family structure and cultural characteristics; marital status (e.g., single, married, divorced, separated, widowed); parental status (e.g., no children, number and ages of children); family responsibilities (e.g., dependent children, parents, relatives); and household financial responsibility (e.g., single income, degree of contributing income). Traditionally, family has been very important to the culture of visible racial/ethnic group members, and individuals have followed career paths based on the financial support of the nuclear and extended family. Therefore, lifestyle characteristics have varying effects on visible racial/ethnic group individuals' career decision-making.

One way to understand visible racial/ethnic group people's lifestyles and how these lifestyles influence their career paths is through an analysis of the groups' cultural values and the manner in which these values are transmitted through family socialization practices. Such an analysis provides a way to understand some of the cultural conflicts and transitional issues faced by visible racial/ethnic group members. Counselors are then able to understand their own cultural perspectives, the manner in which the cultural perspectives of visible racial/ethnic group members are similar and different, and the factors which account for variation within and among the various racial/cultural groups. The importance of this cultural contextual frame is seen in the ways groups define families. For example, the dominant American (White Anglo-Saxon Protestant) definition of family is the nuclear family consisting of parents and their offspring. Black families conceive of family as a wide network of kin and, in some cases, the larger community. Asian peoples include in their view of family all their ancestors and all their descendants (McGoldrick, Pearce, & Giordano, 1982). More importantly, the occupations that groups choose reflect their world views or cultural values. For instance, the overrepresentation of blacks in education may in part be a reflection of black's belief that education is an important mechanism for social mobility. Similarly, the choice of math and science by Asians may, in part, reflect their non-confrontational interpersonal styles.

Also there is tremendous variation among visible racial/ethnic group members in their physical appearance. As McGoldrick et al. (1982) points out,

> Race has been [and continues to be] a major factor in [visible racial/ethnic group members' family and cultural systems] since those whose skin color marked them as different always suffered more discrimination than others—they could not "pass" as other immigrants might try to do. This has left immigrants [and Natives] who are noticeably different physically from the dominant norm with no choice about their ethnic and racial identifications. (p. 14)

Racial/cultural inequality in American life, while contributing to visible racial/ethnic group members' inferior social status and their exclusion from educational and occupational sectors of American life, has also helped visible racial/ethnic group members foster and maintain distinct cultural patterns (Carter & Helms, 1990; Sue, 1981).

Kluckhohn and Strodtbeck (1961) have presented a theory of variation in value-orientations or cultural values which has been used (e.g., Papajohn & Spiegel, 1975) for understanding racial/cultural groups' value systems. Their model is intended to be universal in that Kluckhohn and Strodtbeck hold that all social and cultural groups must solve five common human problems, each of which has three possible solutions or alternatives (see Table 1). Posed in the form of questions, they are: (a) what is the character of human nature?; (b) what is the relationship of people to nature?; (c) what is the proper temporal focus?; (d) what is the proper mode of human expression/activity?; (e) what is the focus of social relations? A culture's distinctiveness is determined by the solutions it chooses to these problems. Researchers (e.g., Kluckhohn & Strodtbeck, 1961; Papajohn & Spiegel, 1975; Carter, 1990) have found the dominant white American cultural values to be characterized by preferences for Individual Social Relations, Doing Activity Orientation, Mastery-Over-Nature Person/Nature, and a Future Time Sense. These preferences or world view influence the way white middle class Americans' careers develop. For example, the future preference is expressed in the manner in which white Americans plan their families, educations, and occupations. The Doing preference is seen in how they compete for upward mobility in work and their emphasis on controlling feelings in work situations to gain recognition. White American children are taught from childhood to be independent, to express their own needs and desires.

Table 1

Kluckhohn and Strodtbeck Value-Orientations Model with Alternative Solutions

Orientation		Alternative	
Mode of Human Nature	*Evil:* People are born with evil inclinations.	*Mixed:* Humans are born both good and evil.	*Good:* Humans born basically good.
Mode of Person/Nature	*Subjugation-to-Nature:* Nature guides one's life.	*Harmony-with-Nature:* Nature is one's partner in life.	*Mastery-over-Nature:* Use Nature for one's own purposes.
Time Sense Mode	*Past:* Traditional customs are paramount.	*Present:* Here and Now events are most important.	*Future:* Planning for events which are to occur.
Activity Mode	*Being:* Activity is spontaneous self-expression.	*Being-in-Becoming:* Integration of the personality	*Doing:* Action oriented self-expression.
Social Relations Mode	*Lineal:* Lines of authority are clearly established based on kinship or hereditary.	*Collateral:* Group oriented.	*Individualism:* Individual goals are most important.

Note: With permission of the American Association for Counseling and Development (AACD). Reproduced from "Cultured Value Differences Between African Americans and White Americans," by R.T. Carter, 1990, *Journal of College Student Development, 31* No. 1. pp. 71–79. Copyright AACD.

The dominant American choices in each dimension fit together nicely. Thus, if the personal achievement implied by Doing is to be facilitated, then it is good to be able to plan for the Future, as an Individual not too constrained by family or group ties, with optimism supplied by the Mastery-Over-Nature orientation, and the pragmatic morality, with which such self-interest is justified, afforded by the Neutral view of the Basic Nature of Man. (Spiegel, 1982, p. 42)

Native American Families

American Indian and Alaska native families and cultures have been described as indicating preferences for a Present Time, Harmony-with-Nature, Collateral Social Relations, Being-in-Becoming Activity, and A Good Human Nature (Atteneave, 1982). Time for Native Americans is cyclical and rhythmic. The events which are important "are geared to personal and seasonal rhythms rather than ordered and organized by external and mechanical clocks or calendars" (Atteneave, 1982, p. 62).

Native Americans seek to understand and work with natural forces as a way to maintain their sense of harmony with nature. However, when this is not possible, generational and intrapsychic conflict surrounding career and work paths may become obstacles for Native Americans. The group value is expressed in the view that individuals subordinate their wishes and wills to the decisions and consensus of the group. Among families, children are taught that possessions and property are shared.

. . . emphasis on group collaterality and identity, including the shared possessions and rapid redistribution of excess is again a source of ambivalence and tension for the urbanized Indian. This problem becomes more marked when an urban Indian family establishes itself with employment or when a student receives a stipend or fellowship. . . . Other Indian relatives see it as something to be shared. They cannot be Indian and at the same time be self-centered. . . . This tradition hinders more promising careers than perhaps any other obstacle to adaptation into full participation in the life of contemporary urban American society. (Atteneave, 1982, p. 69)

Black Families

Black/African-American cultural values are characterized by beliefs in collateral group relations, sharing, spirituality, present Time, and Harmony-with-Nature (Carter & Helms, 1987). Black families' major strengths as described by Hines and Boyd-Franklin (1982) have been and continue to be their adaptability of roles. Hill (1972) suggests that while slavery and socioeconomic oppression attempted to destroy the existence of black families, they have survived because of their strong kinship bonds, flexibility of family roles, and high value placed on religion, education, and work. Black families, according to Hines and Boyd-Franklin (1982), are organized around extended kinship networks which may include blood and non-related persons. Family roles and responsibilities, jobs, and functions are often interchanged among family members. This sharing of roles and functions cuts across generations and gender roles.

It is important to include the extent and degree blacks participate in social equalizer roles and activities in the community or churches. These types of activities are used by many blacks and other visible racial/ethnic group members to reinforce their self-worth. Counselors should understand the extremely strong emphasis that black families place on work and education. As Pinderhughs (1982) points out, these efforts by black parents to instill the value of education and work are potentially undermined by the realities of a racist American society. Black parents expect their children to take advantage of opportunities and to strive for a better life than theirs. Children who are able to earn a living and maintain themselves are likely to receive as much parental approval as those who pursue professional careers. However, black families must often sacrifice for one child to go to school. In families with few resources, it is not uncommon for young adults to be faced with major decisions about work and educational goals at younger ages than may be true for those with more economic resources. The cultural values of blacks and their families may lead them to pursue career paths with a here-and-now focus (i.e., where is there access now?) that allow expression of their value for collateral social relations, or that meet economic needs (i.e., service or business occupations).

Asian Families

East Asian cultural systems have been guided since the beginning of their civilization by the philosophies of Confucius and Buddha.

> Those systems do not stress independence and autonomy of the individual but rather that the individual is superseded by the family. Furthermore, the family adheres to the confucianistic tradition of specific hierarchical roles established for all members. Rules of behavior and conduct are formalized in members' roles to a greater extent than in most other cultures. An individual response and adherence to this code of conduct becomes a reflection not of the individual but of the family and kinship network to which he or she belongs. (Shon & Ja, 1982, p. 209)

In East Asian cultures, the view of the family is that each individual is a product of his or her ancestry line from its beginning. This belief is reflected in "rituals and customs such as ancestor worship and family record books which trace family members back over many centuries" (p. 211). Socialization in Asian families is usually done through "the use of shame and loss of face to reinforce prescribed sets of obligations" (p. 213). The concept of obligation is central in Asian cultures and families. Obligation is incurred either through the relationship of ascribed roles or status, such as those of parents and children, and employer and employee. The strongest obligation is to one's parents. Family obligations are communicated indirectly and by way of non-confrontational strategies. One always seeks to maintain harmonious interpersonal relationships.

Many Asian families immigrate to the U.S. for economic security. Therefore, parents usually expend considerable energy to provide basic necessities. Limited English skills trap many working adults in employment with little vocational mobility. These sacrifices are tolerated for future benefits.

> For the purpose of long-term security, the most prevalent investment is to send the children to school in hopes that professional careers, engineer or doctor, would provide the means for successful achievement, not only for the child but for the parents who made the educational and professional achievement possible. (Shong & Ja, 1982, p. 218)

Latino Families

There is variability among Latino Americans with regard to ethnicity (such as Puerto Rican, Cuban, and Mexican), as well as class differences. The value system and career paths are greatly influenced by socioeconomic status, as some Latinos migrated to America with an economic status which influenced their entry into the United States. With such variability in mind, however, there are some similarities in the traditional value system of Latino groups.

Traditional cultural values of fatalism, dignity, respect, spirituality, and personalism are often reflected in Latino lifestyles (Dillard, 1983). From a career perspective, these values would be represented by a humanistic approach to interpersonal interactions, sensitivity to the feelings of others, and interdependence and cooperation preferred over confrontation and competition. Many of the family characteristics may be re-created in the workplace as individuals tend to learn their values regarding interpersonal interactions from the family structure. Thus, the extended family affiliations might be displayed in a high need for affiliation and collaboration in the work setting. Additionally, status and role definition in the family and community is characteristic of Latino culture. That is, each person is aware of his or her responsibility to others, others' expectations of him or her, and the expectations he or she has of others (Dillard, 1983). These are qualities of an interdependent, responsible worker who would function best in a cohesive work environment.

Implications

Counselors should be aware of the cultural values of their clients and recognize the impact that these values have on the characteristics of their career choices. In addition, many of the familial characteristics of visible racial/ethnic group members are antithetical to the familial characteristics of white Americans, the latter of which has become the predominant standard in the American labor force. Consequently, counselors must help visible racial/ethnic group clients to negotiate the bicultural lifestyles required for upward mobility in their career options.

Visible racial/ethnic group members have discovered that they must become bicultural to be successful in the mainstream American work

206

force. Problems may arise when visible racial/ethnic group members' experiences conflict with their indigenous cultures and the general American culture. Many successful visible racial/ethnic group members suffer from bicultural stress as they are forced to cope with and adjust to two different cultures (Dillard, 1983).

Some visible racial/ethnic group individuals attempt to provide balance in their cultural lives by working in the mainstream cultures, yet living in a community that maintains their traditional cultural values. Other visible racial/ethnic group individuals find the discrepancy between the two cultural lifestyles so overwhelming that they seek a residential community which is consistent with the dominant culture's value system. However, sometimes visible racial/ethnic group individuals who become upwardly mobile find few opportunities to exercise these options and those who do choose to establish cultural balance in their lives may experience negative consequences in their work environments.

Castaneda (1976) has described three basic types of communities in which visible racial/ethnic group members may choose to live, concluding that the community influences the cultural values of the family and individuals residing there. One type is traditional in that the values exhibited are most closely related to the indigenous cultural orientation. A second type is dualistic in that the community reflects some degree of acceptance of modern or dominant American cultural values, while retaining many traditional cultural values. Third, an "atraditional community" exhibits indigenous cultural values integrated with those of the dominant American society. These respective communities reflect increasing degrees of acculturation into the dominant American culture. This acculturation has direct implications for the adjustment between the values of the American mainstream workforce and their home communities. Counselors must attend to the ongoing stress that accompanies such adjustments for visible racial/ethnic group individuals.

Cultural Transitions: Acculturation

Role and generational conflict has increasingly become a problem for visible racial/ethnic group individuals as opportunities for upward mobility have increased. For instance, Carey (1990) has observed that although black women have modeled so well that work and family are both compatible and complementary, this does not preclude their experiencing

> . . . conflict, tension, confusion and sometimes guilt. Family life affects work behavior, including how [men and] women choose jobs and how they behave on the job. . . . The extent to which occupational and family roles conflict is determined, in large measure, by such factors as the nature of the [person's] involvement in each role, by family structure—its events, stages, and conditions—and by the occupational level and attendant responsibilities. (p. 16)

Similarly, black men have often had to turn down opportunities for career changes because the risk of losing a "stable paying job" for a "possible career advancement" was too great for the economic welfare of the family (Carter, 1989).

The balance of work and intimacy in both the occupational and familial role structure has been a lifestyle struggle for visible racial/ethnic group members. According to Carey (1990),

> . . . work is defined as a mobilization for the accomplishment of a task; intimacy is the way people interact or relate to one another. Individuals will differ in their emphasis on one or the other, depending on the role domain. Work and interpersonal satisfaction in the occupational domain are different from work and interpersonal satisfaction in the family domain. (p. 17)

As visible racial/ethnic group members have become more acculturated, many have opted for work and interpersonal satisfaction in the occupational domain over the family domain. Thus, many visible racial/ethnic group individuals have postponed marriage and children until their careers are firmly established, and some have opted for divorce to resolve work and familial role conflict. Similar issues occur between generations within visible racial/ethnic group members' family systems. Consequently, in counseling visible racial/ethnic group individuals in career issues, it is important to assess their current and anticipated lifestyle characteristics so that these factors can be fully weighed.

SOCIOECONOMIC STATUS AND EDUCATIONAL BACKGROUND

In American society, the path to occupational or career achievement is through education and training. But for many visible racial/ethnic group members, this is a less viable path. Visible racial/ethnic group members have and continue to receive substandard educations. According to Jaynes and Williams (1989), "Black and White Educational opportunities are not generally equal. Standards of academic performance for teachers and students are not equivalent in schools that serve predominantly Black students and those that serve predominantly White students" (p. 5). These circumstances are similar for Native Americans and Hispanics. While some would have us believe that Asian-Americans are the model "minority," cultural and racist beliefs also influence their career paths. Smith (1983) points out that "stereotypes of the abilities of Asian-Americans (good in science and math) and the cultural characteristics such as restraint of strong feelings and difficulty with language facility may function to limit exploration of a wide variety of career options, notably those in the social sciences" (p. 179).

One government report noted that

> even in minority groups, better educated individuals tend to occupy more desirable occupational positions than do the less educated. Yet the returns on an investment in education are much lower for Negroes [or other visible racial/ethnic group people] than for the general population. Indeed, for a Negro [or visible racial/ethnic group person] educational attainment may simply mean exposure to more severe and visible discrimination than is experienced by the dropout or the unschooled. . . . Thus, in addition to the handicap of being in a family with few economic or other resources, the average Negro [or visible

racial/ethnic group person] also appears to have less opportunity because of his [or her] race [or culture] alone. (U.S. Department HEW, 1969, p. 24)

For example, the unemployment rate for black high school graduates ages 18–19 was 40.6%, more than three times the 13.8% rate for whites (American Council on Education, 1988).

Career paths for visible racial/ethnic group members must take into consideration the socioeconomic level of the individual. As Axelson (1985) explains:

Access to education and employment opportunities is more difficult under poverty conditions. Developing a career can be expensive, and low-income people have fewer resources that might enable them to take advantage of available education, to commute to work, or to move to another geographical area where employment or occupational opportunities are more readily available. . . . Many [visible racial/ethnic group] members lack the education and skills that are essential for entry into certain occupations and necessary for occupational mobility and advancement. The quality and quantity of basic education that is received especially affects the range of occupational opportunity open to any individual. (p. 202)

Gender

Within each visible racial/ethnic group, there are traditional roles for males and females which involve active contributions to the family and culture. Traditionally, men held the dominant role in the household; however, the status of the woman has varied from the egalitarian role of African women to the subservient role of Asian women (Payton, 1985). However, as the various cultural groups were forced to adapt to the oppressive conditions in the United States, the structure of the traditional sex roles eroded (Payton, 1985). For instance, as Native Americans were forced to live on reservations, the "warrior-hunter-provider" role of men was diminished, necessitating that women negotiate with soldiers and government agents (Medicine, 1980). Additionally, women were forced to work outside the home to sustain their families (Whiteman, 1980). Similar circumstances existed for the other visible racial/ethnic group members.

Ironically, while the white culture is responsible for the distortion of the sex roles of visible racial/ethnic group people, they have also labeled the adaptive sex role patterns as deviant, pathological, and counterproductive to the success of the culture. Stereotypic images of visible racial/ethnic group men and women are pervasive, and have an impact on occupational stereotyping. Consider, for example, the Hispanic male "machismo" as characteristic of an economic provider, the protector who assumes responsibility for the family, and the main authority for family decisions (Ruiz, 1981). The differences in the stereotypic view and the culturally correct view of "machismo" represent the difference between a man who would be characterized occupationally as a potential liability and one who would be perceived as a great asset.

Similarly, Payton (1985) has described the distorted image of black women who

> . . .have been presented as strong, competent, domineering, and the least "feminine" of all females. First, we may ask whether this is a true reflection of Black women. Next, we may ask to what degree these traits are attributable to our West African heritage rather than the impact of slavery. . . . the West African woman was independent, managing the market system and retaining her earnings. She did not expect her husband to bear responsibility for her. The conditions she experienced in slavery reinforced this independent lifestyle since there was no one else upon whom she could depend. (pp. 75–76)

Although there were circumstances supporting the development of the African-American woman's strength and self-reliance, these character-istics have been distorted in such a way that she has been viewed as "the matriarch" of the family and "castrator" of the African-American man. Additionally, the symbolic roles of the African-American woman during slavery (i.e., mammy, concubine) are often projected upon career women of today, especially women who exhibit occupational sophistication and leadership potential, as it serves to negate their power and authority (Dumas, 1980). African-American and other visible racial/ethnic group women in positions of leadership

> often struggle between expectations and demands attached to their symbolic roles and those inherent in their professional status and responsibilities. Such dilemmas which reflect a real insensitivity to their needs for support and reassurance, can challenge their own identity and threaten their inner security. (Carey, 1990, p. 17)

These symbolic caveats hold true for African-American men also.

Gender roles in Native American culture have affected their career paths. Indian women were responsible for nurturing; therefore, they were able to make easier transitions into the non-Indian world of work. "The ability to nurture children made them useful in domestic service roles . . . and other service positions followed fairly easily . . ." (Atteneave, 1982, p. 79), while males were generally left with unskilled jobs which resulted in more unstable employment patterns.

When conducting career counseling with visible racial/ethnic group clients, it is important that they be prepared for the gender-related forms of prejudice and discrimination which they will experience in the work world. They must develop an eye for perceiving the stereotypic and sym-bolic images projected upon them and develop strategies for manipulating and coping with these perceptions. It is also important to help visible racial/ethnic group men and women avoid buying into the myths of their competitive status in the work force. Visible racial/ethnic group women are often viewed as having a "double advantage" in hiring practices be-cause employers get two minorities for the price of one. However, visible racial/ethnic group women may actually face a double burden as they experience sexism and racism (Fulbright, 1986). Often visible racial/ethnic group men hold higher status positions than women and earn higher salaries for comparable positions (Cook, 1989; Graves 1990). Visible racial/ethnic group men and women should be encouraged to collaborate and assist each other in succeeding in the United States labor force, as they are both victims of occupational prejudice and discrimination.

Racial and Cultural Identity

Racial/cultural group membership based on racial/cultural heritage *per se* may not be a sufficient criterion for psychological identification with one's cultural group. It is not appropriate to assume that all members of a racial/cultural group are the same, or because of their racial/cultural category share a psychological awareness of a common culture. It is possible for individuals to respond differently to their cultural history, sociopolitical environment, and particular socialization experiences.

Furthermore, the legacy of racial/cultural attitudes of visible racial/ethnic group people and whites, and their consequent behavior, have affected individual visible racial/ethnic group people's psychosocial and cultural development. While most members of visible racial/ethnic groups in America are subject to similar social conditions and racial/cultural stereotypes and attitudes on the part of whites, visible racial/ethnic group individuals might vary with respect to their psychological response to racial/cultural inequality. Therefore, to consider visible racial/ethnic group members as homogeneous is probably as erroneous as the application of most Anglo-Saxon paradigms to racial/cultural groups. Some of the most promising models for examining psychological differences within racial/cultural groups are the Racial/Cultural Identity Models (cf. Atkinson, Morten, & Sue, 1979; Cross, 1978; Helms, 1990; Sue, 1981; see Table 2 for more detailed descriptions of the models).

According to Table 2, racial/cultural identity seems to be an important psychological characteristic which influences visible racial/ethnic group members' career paths. Visible racial/ethnic group individuals who do not identify with their race or culture may be more likely to pursue career paths which do not reflect their view of themselves as racial/cultural beings, while those immersed in their cultures may have more difficulty negotiating educational and occupational requirements because of their anger and hostility for Euro-American institutions and people. A study by Carter, Fretz, and Mahalik (1986) found that racial and cultural identity attitudes for blacks and Asians, respectively, in conjunction with cultural values, were associated with their level of career maturity and work role salience. Other empirical research (see Helms, 1990) has found racial identity attitudes to be related to a number of psychological and sociocultural variables, suggesting that this construct is central for understanding psychological differences among visible racial/ethnic group members.

In addition to a visible racial/ethnic group person's psychological orientation toward their racial/cultural group, visible racial/ethnic group people also evolve unique personalities. Visible racial/ethnic group individuals' psychosocial development and the manner in which they move through the stages of adult development, as well as ways they negotiate their career paths, are related to the dynamic interaction of their history in the United States, their sociopolitical situations, their cultural values and family systems, their racial/cultural identities and their personal identities.

Individual visible racial/ethnic group members come to understand what occupational paths are open to them and among those, which paths will meet their economic and sociocultural needs. In some cases, they may be able to consider whether a particular path also meets their personal needs. For many visible racial/ethnic group people, personal needs and interests may be pursued through involvement in social equalizer activities. Therefore, one's work may be more a reflection of efforts to cope with issues of access and acceptance than expressing one's self-concept.

Our perspective proposes that counselors and educators involved in career counseling with visible racial/ethnic group members examine their basic assumptions about how visible racial/ethnic group individuals' skills, interests, and abilities are experienced, expressed, and valued. This is an approach that is in contrast to traditional career counseling approaches which tend to focus on the individual and perhaps the influence of his or her parents. For example, when using traditional approaches, the time frame considered is usually restricted to a short past and a longer view into the future. Counselors tend to emphasize future plans, goals, and objectives (see Figure 1). As depicted in Figure 1, the culturally relevant perspective includes the individual, as influenced by his or her culture communicated through the family system, and the sociocultural environment. The time frame extends further into the past (not necessarily the individual's) so that the counselor can integrate his or her knowledge of the visible racial/ethnic group's historical and sociopolitical background and circumstances. Future planning and goal setting may not extend quite as far into the future since many visible racial/ethnic group members may be uncertain about the future. For instance, rather than make specific plans to attend graduate school while in college, visible racial/ethnic group members may wait to see if they finish college first.

We have argued that counselors must first *know* and *understand* the complex, dynamic, interactive, and multifaceted historical, sociopolitical, sociocultural, family, and psychological systems and processes which together influence the career paths of visible racial/ethnic group members.

Some of you at this point must be asking, "But what do I do? How do I apply or use this perspective?" Remember, this question comes out of a doing-oriented cultural value perspective. The culturally relevant view requires that career counselors take a different view or at least recognize that to work effectively across-cultures involves adapting or understanding the world view of visible racial/ethnic group people. The first step in this process involves resisting the temptation (and culturally appropriate tendency) to act and focus one's energy on *understanding* the extreme complexity associated with developing cultural knowledge. Understanding the career paths of visible racial/ethnic group people requires that counselors comprehend the fluid, complex, and dynamic interplay of the many factors which influence these career paths. Each visible racial/

Table 2

Summary of Racial/Cultural Identity Attitudes with Implications for Visible Racial/Ethnic Group Members' Career Paths

Racial and Cultural* Identity Attitudes	Implications for Career Paths
Pre-Encounter and Conformity Depending on white society for definition and approval— Negative attitudes toward one's own racial/cultural group.	Would tend to have broader view and knowledge of occupational options. May not see any limits (i.e., discrimination) so his/her aspirations may be accepted and aided by members of the dominate culture.
Encounter and Dissonance Marked by feelings of confusion and conflict about the meaning and significance of one's race/culture.	May tend to flounder and vacillate about career path. Will tend to be unsure about capabilities and conflicted about whether sociocultural factors matter with regard to their career path. May express one view when with whites, and another with racial/cultural group. May disassociate knowledge of sociocultural factors from self.
Immersion-Emersion and Resistance Active rejection of white or the dominant culture and immersed and idealizes one's own racial/cultural group.	May have limited career options. Focuses on paths which will make it possible to serve and help members of one's own racial/cultural group. May feel ambivalent in a predominantly white institution.
Internalization/Introspection and Awareness Marked by a sense of self-fulfillment. Accepts white culture and has internalized a positive racial/cultural identity.	Will see more clearly how to negotiate hostile systems. May have broader sense of career paths with a realistic sense of personal/social limitations.

*Racial identity attitudes apply to Black/African-Americans and are derived from Cross (1978) and Helms (1990).
Cultural Identity Attitudes apply to Native Americans, Hispanics, and Asians, and are derived from Sue (1981) and Atkinson, Morton, and Sue (1979).

Figure 1

Traditional vs. Culturally Relevant Perspectives in Career Counseling

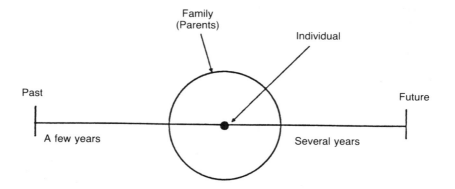

TRADITIONAL CAREER COUNSELING

Family
(Parents)

Individual

Past

Future

A few years

Several years

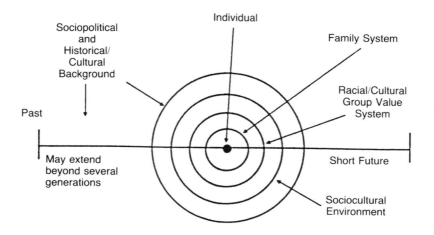

CULTURALLY RELEVANT PERSPECTIVE

Sociopolitical
and
Historical/
Cultural
Background

Individual

Family System

Racial/Cultural
Group Value
System

Past

May extend
beyond several
generations

Short Future

Sociocultural
Environment

ethnic group member should be seen as a new challenge for the career counselor or educator. Your task and goal in becoming a culturally relevant career counselor is to learn to understand how the many variables, systems, and processes described above influence the career path of your visible racial/ethnic group client, rather than applying our perspective to *all* visible racial/ethnic group members' cultures and families. We encourage you to work at understanding what it means to each individual and family to be native, Latino, African, or Asian Americans. In this way, counselors and educators will be able to engage in culturally relevant career and educational counseling with adult visible racial/ethic group members.

REFERENCES

American Council on Education. (1988). *Minorities in higher education.* Washington, DC: Author.

Atkinson, D.R., Morten, G., & Sue, D.W. (1979). *Counseling American minorities: A cross-cultural perspective.* Dubuque, IA: W.C. Brown.

Atteneave, C. (1982). American Indians and Alaska Native families: Emigrants in their own homelands. In M. McGoldrick, J.K. Pearce, & J. Giorandano (Eds.), *Ethnicity and family therapy* (pp. 55–83). New York: The Guilford press.

Axelson, J.A. (1985). *Counseling and development in a multicultural society.* Monterey, CA: Brooks, Cole.

Brown, D., & Brooks, L. (Eds.). (1990). *Career choice and development* (2nd ed.). San Francisco, CA: Jossey-Bass.

Brooks, L. (1990). Recent development in theory building. In D. Brown & L. Brooks (Eds.), *Career choice and development* (2nd ed.). San Francisco, CA: Jossey-Bass.

Carey, P.M. (1990). Beyond superwoman: On being a successful Black woman administrator. *Initiatives: Journal of the National Association for Women Deans, Administrators, and Counselors, 53,* 15–19.

Carter, R.T. (1989). *Quality of life for Black men.* Paper presented at the 97th annual Convention of the American Psychological Association, New Orleans, LA.

Carter, R.T., & Helms, J.E. (1990). White racial identity attitudes and cultural values. In J.E. Helms (Ed.), *Black and white racial identity: Theory, research, and practice* (pp. 105–118). Westport, CT: Greenwood Press.

Carter, R.T., & Swanson, J.L. (1990). The validity of the Strong Interest Inventory with Black Americans: A review of the literature. *Journal of Vocational Behavior, 36,* 195–209.

Carter, R.T., Fretz, B., & Mahalik, J. (1986). *An exploratory investigation into the relationships between career maturity, work role salience, value-orientation and racial identity attitudes.* Paper presented at the 94th annual Convention of the American Psychological Association, Washington, DC.

Carter, R.T., & Helms, J.E. (1987). The relationship of Black value orientations to racial identity attitudes. *Measurement and Evaluation in Counseling and Development, 19,* 185–195.

Carter, R.T. (1990). Cultural value differences between African-Americans and White Americans. *Journal of College Student Development, 31,* 71–79.

Casteneda, A. (1976). Cultural democracy and the educational needs of Mexican-American children. In R.L. Jones (Ed.), *Mainstreaming the minority child* (pp. 181–184). Reston, VA: Council for Exceptional Children.

Cook, D.A., & Helms, J.E. (1988). Visible racial/ethnic group supervisees' satisfaction with cross-cultural supervision as predicted by relationship characteristics. *Journal of Counseling Psychology, 33,* 268–274.

Cook, D.A. (1989). *Quality of life for Black women: Historical, present, and future perspectives.* Paper presented at 97th annual Convention of the American Psychological Association, New Orleans, LA.

Cross, W.E. (1978). The Thomas and Cross models of psychological nigrescence: A review. *Journal of Black Psychology, 5* (1), 13–31.

Dillard, J.M. (1983). *Multi-cultural counseling.* Chicago: Nelson Hall.

Dumas, R. (1980). Dilemmas of Black females in leadership. In R. Rose (Ed.), *The Black woman* (pp. 201–215). California: Sage Publications.

Fine, M. (1990). "The public" in public schools: The social construction/ constriction of moral communities. *Journal of Social Issues, 46,* 107–119.

Fredrickson, G.M. (1988). *The arrogance of race.* Connecticut: Wesleyan University Press.

Fullbright, K. (1986). The myth of the double-advantage: Black female managers. In M.C. Simms & J.M. Malveaux (Eds.), *Slipping through the cracks: The status of Black women* (pp. 33–46). New Brunswick: Transaction Books.

Graves, S.B. (1990). A case of double jeopardy? Black women in higher education. *Initiatives: Journal of the National Association for Women Deans, Administrators, and Counselors, 53,* 3–8.

Helms, J.E. (1990). *Black and white racial identity: Theory, research, and practice.* Westport, CT: Greenwood Press.

Hines, P.M., & Boyd-Franklin, N. (1982). Black families. In M. McGoldrick, J.K. Pearce, & J. Giordano (Eds.), *Ethnicity and family therapy.* New York: The Guilford Press.

Hill, R. (1972). *The strengths of Black families.* New York: Emerson Hall.

Hoyt, K.B. (1989). The career status of women and minorities persons: A 20 year retrospective. *The Career Development Quarterly, 37,* 202–212.

Jaynes, G.D., & Williams, R.M. (Eds.). (1989). *A common destiny: Blacks in American Society.* Washington, DC: National Academy Press.

Jones, J.M. (1972). *Prejudice and racism.* New York: Random House.

Kluckhohn, F.R., & Strodtbeck, F.L. (1961). *Variations in value-orientations.* Evanston, IL: Row, Peterson.

McGoldrick, M., Pearce, J.K., & Giordano, J. (Eds.). (1982). *Ethnicity and family therapy.* New York: The Guilford Press.

Medicine, B. (1980). The interaction of culture and sex roles in the schools. In *Conference on the Educational and Occupational Needs of American Indian Women*. Washington, DC: U.S. Department of Education, National Institute of Education.

Munuchin, S. (1974). *Families and family therapy*. Cambridge: Harvard University Press.

Okun, B.F. (1984). *Working with adults: Individual, family, and career development*. Pacific Grove, CA: Brooks Cole Publishers.

Papajohn, J., & Spiegel, J.P. (1975). *Transactions in families*. San Francisco: Jossey-Bass.

Payton, C.R. (1985). Addressing the special needs of minority women. In N.J. Evans (Ed.), *New directions for student services: Facilitating the development of women*. San Francisco: Jossey-Bass.

Pinderhughes, S. (1982). Afro-American families and the victim system. In M. McGoldrick, J.K. Pearce, & J. Giordano (Eds.), *Ethnicity and family therapy*. New York: The Guilford Press.

Richardson, E.H. (1981). Cultural and historical perspectives in counseling American Indians. In D.W. Sue (Ed.), *Counseling the culturally different: Theory and practice*. New York: John Wiley & Sons.

Ruiz, R.A. (1981). Cultural and historical perspective in counseling Hispanics. In D.W. Sue (Ed.), *Counseling the culturally different: Theory and practice*. New York: John Wiley & Sons.

Shon, S.P., & Ja, D.Y. (1982). Asian families. In M. McGoldrick, J.K. Pearce, & J. Giordano (Eds.), *Ethnicity and family therapy*. New York: The Guilford Press.

Smith, J.E. (1983). Issues in racial minorities' career behavior. In W.B. Walsh & S.H. Osipow (Eds.), *Handbook of vocational psychology, Vol. 1, Foundations*. Hillsdale, NJ: Erlbaum.

Spiegel, J. (1982). An ecological model of ethnic families. In M. McGoldrick, J.K. Pearce, & J. Giordano (Eds.), *Ethnicity and family therapy*. New York: The Guilford Press.

Stewart E.C. (1972). *American cultural patterns: A cross-cultural perspective*. Yarmouth, ME: Intercultural Press.

Sue, D.W. (1982). *Counseling the culturally different: Theory and practice*. New York: John Wiley & Sons.

Thomas, A., & Sillen, S. (1972). *Racism and psychiatry*. Secaucus, NJ: The Citadel Press.

U.S. Department of Health, Education, and Welfare. (1969). *Toward a social report*. Washington, DC: US Government Printing Office.

Whiteman, H. (1980). Insignificance of humanity: Man is tampering with the moon and the stars. In *Conference on the Educational and Occupational Needs of American Indian Women*. Washington, DC: U.S. Department of Education, National Institute of Education.

Zunker, V.G. (1981). *Career counseling*. Monterey, CA: Brooks Cole Publishers.

CHAPTER 12

Conjoint Career Counseling: Counseling Dual-Career Couples

Lynn Binder Hazard
Independent Practice
Rockville, Maryland

Diane Koslow
Independent Practice
Rockville, Maryland

Dual-career couples are a relatively recent phenomenon. This life style emerged primarily during the 1970s and is expected to be more prevalent in the future (Hall & Hall, 1979; Holmstrom, 1972; Hester & Dickerson, 1982). The rising aspirations of women coupled with greater educational and career opportunities and current economic conditions point to an ever-increasing number of dual-career couples.

For many years the "typical" American family was conceptualized to consist of a breadwinner father, a homemaker mother, and two school-aged children. By the 1980s only 7% of all married couples fit this description (U.S. Department of Commerce, 1981). Today, it is estimated that approximately 52% of all married women work, and they compose approximately 60% of the female work force. The majority of these women have dependent children. Dual-career couples with children have never been as well represented in the U.S. work force as they are currently. Many researchers (Berman, Sacks, & Lief, 1975; Gross, 1980; Rapoport & Rapoport, 1971a) have indicated that this "new" type of marriage with its emphasis on career achievement will be tomorrow's customary marriage. It is also predicted that women will evidence higher levels of work attachment than ever before by working full-time and continuously (Masnick & Bane, 1980).

Increasingly career counselors are being sought by individuals whose concerns and career dilemmas must be addressed within the context of their families and their relationships with their spouses. Dual-career couples share more of their family's responsibilities, and as a result they tend to be more interdependent than traditional couples. This interdependence dictates more role-sharing and interchangeability in task distribution and task completion. Career concerns rarely exist independently of these variables. The career counselor and his or her client cannot hope to address these concerns in isolation. A systems approach that allows for the interaction between and among the various factors is needed. For many career concerns, both spouses must become involved in the career counseling process if the issues that face the particular dual-career couple are to be addressed and solutions found. These solutions involve a balancing of roles and demands, the juggling of responsibilities and tasks, and the careful planning of career transitions and changes.

There is a need for more effective alternative approaches to career counseling that take into account the recent changes in the American family. Hence, we have developed an interactive conjoint career counseling model that takes into account a given couple's family and individual career stages. This model provides a conceptual framework for career counselors who work with dual-career couples.

The lives of dual-career couples operate in a delicate interdependent balance. The systems that support this life style are intricately interwoven. An analogy could be made between the dual-career family and a hanging mobile. If one part of a mobile hanging in space is removed, the other parts become unbalanced and tangled. Removing or adjusting one piece of the mobile requires that every other piece be adjusted accordingly. Many options exist as to which particular piece is lengthened and how much, but the point is that adjustments are required. The same is true of the dual-career family. If a promotion requires a move, an option to upgrade one's formal education presents itself, or a new child is born, each system will have to be adjusted accordingly. When one is working with a dual-career couple, the heads of household must plan together the necessary adjustments and accommodations. The dual-career life style is a complex one that demands a more complex career counseling approach. Career counseling cannot take only the individual into account. Instead, the career counseling of dual-career couples is often best done conjointly, so that all variables can be taken into account. These variables include each spouse's career values, aspirations, goals, and opportunities.

The dual-career life style has been identified as a stressful one. The evidence indicates higher divorce rates, conflicting demands, and time management concerns (Holmstrom, 1972; Weingarten, 1978). Career counselors can do much to help dual-career couples manage their careers and life styles more effectively. Thus, they maximize the possibility that these couples will experience more positive outcomes attributed to and associated with this life style. These positive benefits include higher general health (Feld, 1976; Burke & Weir, 1976), higher self-esteem (Feldman & Feldman, 1973), greater personal autonomy and power (Blood & Wolfe, 1960; Blood, 1976), greater marital communication (Burke & Weir, 1976) and the opportunity to pursue self-actualization and happiness.

This chapter will describe a conjoint career counseling approach for dual-career couples. First the history of dual-career couples and the issues they face will be presented. This will be followed by a discussion of family and career stages. Then these stages will be used as a context for a conjoint career counseling approach. Case studies will be used to demonstrate this approach.

DEVELOPMENTAL HISTORY OF DUAL-CAREER COUPLES

During the late 1960s and early 1970s the dual-career life style first emerged. Since then the concept has undergone a number of changes.

When the dual-career family first evolved there was continued debate for many years as to whether it was possible to adopt this life style without dire effects on the family. It was assumed that if a woman had a career, she would sacrifice her career for her husband's as a matter of course. She was also expected to reduce her work hours or work-related activities if they inconvenienced her family. The wife was the one who accommodated her work schedule to the needs of her family. The working wife in this type of family also assumed the traditionally female tasks related to household and child care in addition to assuming a work-related role. This phase was characterized by less work attachment for women (career salience). Employers were reluctant to promote or to train a woman because she might quit when family responsibilities conflicted with work-related responsibilities.

The second historical phase could be called the "superwoman" phase. This phase was different from the previous one in that women's career salience (work attachment) increased. During this phase women became more committed to their careers while still assuming primary responsibility for their children and home. They tried to do it all to avoid criticism for giving less attention to their socialized roles. Few women aspire to the superwoman role today largely because it is untenable. The superwoman role leads to exhaustion, an unbalanced life style, and a possible retreat to the home front.

The third phase is exemplified by the egalitarian dual-career marriage. Although individual couples may choose to be more traditional, increasingly the egalitarian model is being adopted. It seems to be the model of the future. The egalitarian marriage may not be a reality for the majority at present, but it seems to be on the horizon. Social and structural changes have made this model possible. Affirmative action opportunities, increased professional education, more visible female role models, and increasing acceptance by both men and women of less restrictive gender role behavior all encourage the dual-career life style. Increasingly, organizations are supporting the dual-career life style as evidenced by flexible hours, part-time professional jobs, paternity leave, and the increased availability of child care facilities.

In the egalitarian dual-career marriage there are two heads of household. Decisions are made in a democratic manner. The division of labor is based on interests, skills, and availability rather than gender roles. There is more sharing of roles and tasks as needs demand. The household and child care tasks are shared. Career development is a mutual concern. There is little change in career involvement and salience following childbirth. Accommodations are made by both spouses on an egalitarian basis. Both husband and wife simultaneously take on the demands of an employer, a spouse, and children. Of course what is described here is the optimum situation. There are lesser degradations of this model.

Career and family demands change as career and family stages change. The next two sections detail career and family stages.

Career Stages

The model of career stages presented here is adapted from Graves, Dalton, and Thompson (1980). It assumes that the necessary preparation, education, and preliminary socialization into an occupation have occurred prior to entering stage 1. The four stages are: Stage 1—apprenticeship; Stage 2—independence/specialization; Stage 3—interdependence/managerial; and Stage 4—director of organization. These stages are discussed below.

Stage 1: Apprenticeship. Stage 1 begins with one's first professional position. Although the apprenticeship is the first career stage, some people remain at this stage throughout their careers. The apprenticeship stage begins with training and indoctrination into the role of subordinate. Trust is built between the individual and the organization during this stage. The apprentice works under the guidance of a more senior worker or manager. At this stage one's work is collaborative, that is, the tasks are only a part of a larger project.

Beginning professionals have a strong need to test themselves in relation to their work. They want to apply the skills and competencies they have learned in formal training to challenging work tasks. Routine tasks seldom allow them to actually challenge themselves or demonstrate initiative and creativity. This can be a source of stress and strain. This stress can hold a beginning professional back or it can motivate and encourage the individual to move forward.

The apprentice is expected to accept supervision and criticism willingly. The giving and receiving of feedback requires accepting the dependent role of a subordinate. A delicate balance must be struck between this dependent role and demonstrating the initiative and skills to do independent work. If these skills and abilities are not demonstrated, it is unlikely that management will allow the individual to move into stage 2 and, thus, to work more independently.

The apprentice stage is characterized by less flexibility than the other stages. Deadlines are often strictly imposed because of the scope and deadlines of the larger project. This career stage demands much investment of time and effort to "prove" oneself and move into the next stage. One of the stresses of this stage is the lack of control over the timing of intensive work efforts. The apprentice may be expected to work long periods of overtime. This makes it difficult to plan for stable family or leisure activities and may cause tension among spouses and family members.

Stage 2: Independence/specialization. Earning the responsibility for an area or a project moves an individual into stage 2. In this stage the professional assumes full responsibility for a significant portion of a project or area and works in relative independence. The individual will

221

be expected to produce competently and establish credibility. The individual manages his or her own time during this stage and accepts responsibility for the outcome. The stage 2 professional is still a subordinate but one with increasing autonomy.

This transition can be a difficult one. It demands that the individual move from the security of depending on a supervisor to the independence of relying on his or her own judgment. Many professionals develop a specialty during this stage. If the focus is on one functional area, the credibility of doing solid professional work can be better established. Thus, visibility increases both inside and outside the organization. However, overspecialization at this stage could limit career mobility.

Most professionals remain in this stage throughout their careers. This is especially true for those who choose the career path of a specialist. Dalton, Thompson and Price (1977) found that people in this stage have more flexibility in terms of controlling their own hours. They are less directly supervised than in stage 1. However, long hours are frequently required in this stage to progress to stage 3.

Stage 3: Interdependence/managerial. In this stage the role changes to a higher level of responsibility. Responsibility for the work of others takes form as one coordinates, guides, directs, and supports the work efforts of subordinates.

At this stage effective skills for leading and maintaining the work group must be developed. The manager must attend to the maintenance needs of the group as well as production functions. If the maintenance (interpersonal) needs are ignored, the work team will have low morale, a low level of cohesion, and difficulty in working together to meet task demands. Learning the interpersonal skills necessary for ensuring maximum productivity is one of the challenges for the manager.

This career stage is described as interdependent because the manager's career development is intricately interwoven with that of subordinates. Managers are dependent on their subordinates because their success is evaluated on the quality, volume, and timeliness of work produced by their subordinates. Subordinates are dependent on their managers for protecting and maintaining the integrity of the work group, acquiring resources and benefits, and assisting with their career development. Effective managers must establish trust and come to terms with control and interdependence issues.

Another important task of a manager is to act as a mentor (developer of people). This requires patient teaching, coaching, and encouragement. It also involves encouraging the protégé(e) to move on to new career challenges. This can be painful, particularly if the mentor has much self-investment in the protégé(e).

The midlevel manager is often caught in the middle between the needs and desires of the work unit and the goals of top management. This can be a stressful position particularly if the organization is facing changes such as cutbacks and reorganizations. One of the challenges for the manager is coping with the stress of being the "buffer." Containing the stress and not transmitting it to subordinates is crucial. If this stress is transmitted to the work group, it is likely to cause insecurity and possible dissention. The manager must also play a dual role with peers. Although fellow managers are comrades and can form an important support network, there is also an element of competitiveness in these peer relationships. These two conflicting forces must be carefully balanced.

This career stage poses intellectual and interpersonal challenges. It offers opportunities for recognition from one's peers as well as the satisfaction of teaching and helping others' career progression. Managers at this stage have more flexibility and control over their work schedules than those at stages 1 and 2. There is also greater visibility.

Stage 4: Directing the path of the organization. In this stage the individual, as an upper-level manager, is able to exert significant influence on the future direction of the organization. The upper-level manager has the opportunity to make policy decisions that affect the organization and its employees. This tremendous responsibility can be both burdensome and challenging.

The upper-level manager represents the organization in many settings. His or her identity is often synonymous with that of the organization. This can be a comfortable situation if personal values and goals are congruent with organizational values and goals. If there is incongruence, it can produce stress. The upper-level manager must not allow his or her identity to become completely defined by an organizational role. This often requires making a conscious effort to separate personal and professional life. One must take care to permit time to pursue a personal life apart from the social and business obligations of one's job.

Because the upper-level manager is so visible, there are many opportunities to act as a sponsor or mentor. The upper-level manager can also interact with other upper-level managers both inside and outside the organization. These opportunities can provide the upper-level manager with a sense of camaraderie and a support network.

The upper-level manager has great latitude in terms of the many roles that may be assumed. More resources are available to the upper-level manager than to employees at other career stages. Yet the upper-level manager may find less flexibility in terms of personal leisure and socializing because much "business" is done in these settings. This may pose a problem for the spouse of the stage 4 employee. Spouses may view the social demands as excessive and as contributing little to their own career development.

Family Stages

Family stage development is diverse because of the complex interaction between the separate individuals composing the family unit, their personal development, the state of the marriage, and a number of outside factors such as the special needs of elderly parents and children. All exert stress on the family unit.

Sociological and developmental models exist that describe family stages with various levels of differentiation. The following model (Table 1) collapses family development into three major stages and highlights issues relevant to career stages. These issues center on family interactions and

Table 1

Model of Family Stages

Early-Stage Families
  Becoming a spouse
  Issues: the relationship
          finances
          how decisions are handled
          the setting of long-range goals for career and family

  Becoming parents
  Issues: child care arrangements—outside help
          additional costs for family
          contingency plans for emergencies
          rescheduling of time
          adjusting to losses and gains

  Raising preschoolers
  Issues: evaluating child's growth and development regarding past and future child care
          deciding the finite size of family
          accommodating to possible increase in family size
          evaluating resources: financial, psychological, physical

Middle-Stage Families
  Families of school-age children
  Issues: assuming additional task of interacting with school
          becoming responsible for raising responsible children—schoolwork, school concerns

(Table 1 continued)

deciding on level of extracurricular activity for children and possible extra duties of carpooling, participation, etc.

Maintaining the couple
Issues: not being overwhelmed by demands from work, children
maintaining separate and couple activities
socializing with other couples in areas other than child issues

Late-Stage Families
Weathering adolescent children
Issues: being able to maintain position at head of family hierarchy regarding limit setting
dealing with testing of limits, feelings of anger, frustration, and fear concerning the finished product
keeping lines of communication open
providing enough supervision
managing future plans for children
evaluating balance between work and home

Caring for aging parents
Issues: dealing with additional burdens, fears, guilt, anger, financial strains individual cases may present
managing time to care for own children at same time

Becoming a couple again
Issues: evaluating losses and gains as children depart
fine-tuning or overhauling relationship attending to more self development

Becoming grandparents
Issues: widowhood

decisions that are interactive with career issues and strains. Each affects the other in terms of time management, perceived support in the relationship, available resources and energies, and level of commitment.

Early-stage family (1). The major task of the early-stage family is the initiation of new roles and patterns of interaction. The distinct phases are: becoming a spouse, becoming parents, and raising preschoolers.

Becoming a spouse, even following a live-in relationship, requires an adjustment to the role proscriptions for husband and wife. Two lives must be meshed. Issues revolve around the basic functioning of a family. For example, relationships between spouses, in-laws, and friends; decision-making procedures; allocation and distribution of finances; and setting long-range career/family goals are generally major concerns.

Becoming parents requires an adjustment to the role proscriptions for mother and father. The couple is also introduced to the pressures of child care arrangements if both parents pursue continuous careers. Relationship issues center on adjusting to each other as parents, to their own parents as grandparents, and to friends. Adjustment entails both gains and losses. Financial concerns center on adjustment to additional costs. Time, a major stress factor at this stage, must be managed and negotiated. Raising preschoolers initiates new developmental tasks for the couple. They must take charge of the growth and development of offspring. Decisions involve determining the finite size of the family and evaluating the family's resources (financial, psychological, and physical). If additional children are planned and conceived, the family must accommodate to the increase in numbers.

Middle-stage family (2). The major task of the middle-stage family is maintenance. The distinct phases are raising school-age children and preserving the couple relationship.

Parents of school-age children have worked out their roles, and children have not yet reached the more tenuous age of adolescence. However, another potential stressor is the formalized school system. Parents decide how much responsibility to accept in raising responsible children who will complete school work and study for exams. The balance may change with each child and each set of teachers a new school year brings. Decisions must also be made as to the level of involvement children may develop in extracurricular activities. This is contingent on needs for financing, parental participation, and transportation requirements. Couples' issues center on the balance between their own commitments and those for their children.

Maintenance is very important in preserving the couple relationship. The concern here is that the couple does not become so overwhelmed by demands from work and children that they lose the male-female relationship. In other words, the parent, cohousekeeper, and taskmaster roles must not overtake the couple completely.

Late-stage family (3). Late-stage families in our model face two major tasks: conflict and integration. Specific phases include weathering adolescent children, caring for aging parents, becoming a couple again, becoming grandparents, and facing widowhood.

Conflict during this stage is cross-generational. The couple faces potential stress from their children and their own parents. As parents of adolescents, they must remain at the head of the hierarchy. They face the testing of limits. They must be able to set limits while keeping lines of communication open. They must deal with feelings of anger, frustration, and fear concerning the "finished products" their children will become. They must help decide upon and manage future plans for their children.

Individually, spouses are concerned with evaluating the balance between work and family roles. Each spouse may attend to more self development as family demands lessen.

During the late stage, the task of caring for aging parents frequently emerges. Additional burdens, fears, guilt, anger, time, and money strains may prevail. The amount of conflict varies with each case.

As children are launched, the parents enter the integrative phase of becoming a couple again. During this phase the couple adjusts to new losses and gains. They deal with fine-tuning their relationship as well as establishing adult relationships with their grown children.

The final phases of the late-family stage also include becoming grandparents and facing widowhood. Often, by this stage, couples are considering retirement or planning for a second career. Interestingly, many career-planning retirement seminars invite both spouses to participate. The rationale is that they will spend the rest of their years together and thus should plan for this conjointly. However, conjoint career counseling should be a viable approach for dual-career couples not only at this late-family stage but at any point in their career progression. This allows them to plan a mutual sharing of responsibilities throughout the years.

CONJOINT CAREER COUNSELING

The term "dual-career family" implies more than attention to two careers. The whole picture of dual decisions, responsibilities, accomplishments, transitions, and strains is greater than the sum of its parts. Three role stages are operant: the career-role stage of the husband, the career-role stage of the wife, and the family-role stage that the couple shares (Rapoport & Rapoport, 1971b, 1978).

In dual-career families, both adults live in two distinct worlds: work and family. In the past, men typically lived in both worlds, whereas women lived in the family world and vicariously shared in the male work world. The female role included the task of compensating the husband for the trials of a hard working life. Such a model is not appropriate for the dual-career family. The safe haven of a comfortable, well-run home with food and companionship waiting has been exchanged for a new life style. A house is vacated by day with couples off to work and children off to various forms of education and child care. Then a tired family group arrives, often simultaneously, to face the evening chores. Career is thus newly defined, incorporating the total life interactions of family members. As Derr (1980, p. 237) states, " . . . the new definition of a career . . . includes relevant nonwork aspects of the person's life that impact on the actual work history."

Because career and family life have cycles, each with stages differing in terms of tasks, expectations, and stressors, the effects of change are multiplied when both partners pursue careers. Career counseling becomes a relationship problem because the family unit no longer revolves around one career. When one person is struggling with a career issue, often all family members feel the impact in some way. Schein (1978, p. 53) stated, "The potential conflicts between work and family are likely to be more severe than the conflict between work and self-development, or self and family development, because work and family are likely to involve more extensive external commitments." Also interdependency of systems means that dysfunction in one area affects all other areas.

Family homeostasis is a term that refers to that balance in relationships toward which families work (Jackson, 1957). If homeostasis is threatened, members act overtly and covertly to maintain it. Usually some event occurs that precipitates symptoms or imbalance leading to the client's seeking counseling. Examples of such events are usually work or family changes (see Table 2). Integration of the change becomes necessary. Strain is put on family members and redefinition of the system affects homeostasis. In relating the concept of homeostasis to conjoint family therapy, Satir (1967, p. 6) stated, "The family homeostasis can be functional (or 'fitting') for members at some periods of family life and not at others, so events affect members differently at different times. But if one member is affected by an event, all are to some degree."

Conjoint career counseling follows the same principles. Dual-career involvement forces decisions on the couple about when to give and when to receive. This is a constantly changing scenario. They need to strike a balance in each situation of what each wants, does best, will perform, and in what manner. The outcome must be dual; yet each must perform individually and assertively without invading or overriding the other. Both need to be reality-oriented and set realistic goals.

Conjoint career counseling allows the counselor to observe the client in both work and family roles. The opportunity also exists to be an objective observer on occasion rather than the more typical interactive career counselor.

Conjoint career counseling can best be illustrated by cases taken from the author's files dealing with dual-career couples at various stages of career and family development. As with any counseling speciality, knowledge of the client population is essential. For conjoint career counseling, this knowledge incorporates life-span developmental psychology, specifically family stages and career stages, as discussed earlier.

Family and career stages have been incorporated into a notational system for identifying cases. The letters M and F indicate sex of each spouse and the notation following each indicates the career stage of each spouse. The number at the end in parentheses ( ) indicates the family stage the couple shares. A notation, M1F2(2) would refer to a family at middle stage (2), with the husband M at apprentice stage 1, and the wife F at the specialist/independent stage 2.

Table 2

Issues of Change for Dual-Career Couples

Work:	*Interpersonal*—change related to relationship with subordinate, supervisor, top management
	Monetary—increase or decrease in pay base for self, spouse, co-worker
	Power—increase or decrease in power status for self, spouse, or co-worker
	Work Assignment—change in work assignment or work location for self, spouse, or co-worker
Family:	*Biological*—developmental stage of self, spouse, or child such as puberty, adolescence, menopause, illness
	Educational—change for self, spouse, or child; further training or time commitment; departure of child for college
	Social—entrance or exit of family member from basic unit, temporary or permanent; increase or decrease in external activities; geographical move
	Interpersonal—change related to relationship with spouse, or other family member

Case 1 M3F2(3)

Bob and Anne are both 44, have been married 20 years, and have three children, ages 18, 15, and 14. He is a chemist in charge of a research division, and she is a high school history teacher.

Anne has tired of her teaching career. It suited her interests and needs when her children were younger. She recently attended a career development workshop at a local college. During the workshop she decided to return to school for a law degree.

Because Bob was skeptical about Anne's decision, Anne sought individual career counseling. It was apparent that Bob's input was very important to Anne and that her uncertainty was triggered by Bob's doubts. Bob was asked to attend the next sessions. Bob stated that he felt law was a very boring profession. It was an occupation with longer hours than teaching. Also he wasn't sure exactly why, but he felt Anne would really be better off remaining in her original field or seeking a less stressful new career. They had already had long hours of discussion, and Anne was upset by Bob's negative attitude.

Counseling revealed that Bob was at a point in both career and family stages where people were maturing, changing, and moving away from his guidance and control. At work, one of his junior level scientists had received a highly valued award and, in assuming independent research projects, had left a void in Bob's professional team. At home, Bob's eldest daughter had just entered an out-of-state college. Anne's desire to retrain had paralleled these themes and as a result Bob had resisted. He had not really been aware of contributing events and his underlying fears that Anne, too, would succeed and move away from him.

Anne also was able to share her feelings of loss from their oldest daughter's move. She expressed a need to embark on a new career to fill the perceived void left by children going off on their own. Also she felt increasing boredom with the same yearly curriculum in her present job.

She emphasized her deep commitment to Bob and her belief that their lives together had always held top priority for both of them. She sincerely wanted his approval before moving forward, but stated that she probably would persist in spite of disapproval. When Bob was able to recognize the losses he felt by changes in career and family members' roles and to separate this from his relationship with Anne, he was able to understand her career needs and put his support behind her appropriate second career choice. At the last session, he jokingly referred to himself as the "little man behind the woman" who was destined to be a great success because of his excellent experience in launching people effectively.

Case 2 M2F3(1)

John, age 50, and Ellen, age 38, have been married 8 years and have two children, ages 3 and 5. The children are enrolled in a nursery/daycare center.

John, an engineer, came for individual career counseling hoping to become "motivated," and didn't understand why he lacked drive. He was uneasy about his career progression, feeling he should be more interested in "getting ahead." He just seemed to have an apathetic attitude toward life.

Further sessions revealed that John adored spending time with his two sons and had several avocations that he actively pursued. John described Ellen as a "dynamo." She was an advertising executive who he said was somewhat annoyed at John's complacency toward his career. It was suggested that Ellen participate in the counseling. After overcoming some scheduling problems, they continued in conjoint career counseling until termination.

Through counseling, John recognized that he truly enjoyed a no-pressure work environment and that the press to change was not his, but one he had internalized from Ellen. John and Ellen began to recognize that he was in fact motivated in other areas of his life. It was not lack of drive, but a comfortable fit, that kept him at career stage 2. In fact, when asked to fantasize his ideal job, he closely described his own position. Both John and Ellen were surprised by this, having assumed that John's concerns about apathy were rooted in firm convictions. When they first met 10 years before, John had been very career-oriented.

John's case further illustrates an adult life transition where, at or around midlife, one seeks a balance between work, family, and personal needs based on a reevaluation of priorities. John was enjoying the challenges his young family and his hobbies brought. Ellen, on the other hand, enjoyed being immersed in a fast-paced, competitive work atmosphere, often spending long hours on projects, with less time to spend with the children, and no current interests in outside activities.

Both John and Ellen learned to recognize the differences in their career needs and to see John's style of work commitment not as a character flaw but as a preference. In fact, they recognized how complementary their styles were. John remained available to attend to their children's needs, carpooling them to school, taking them to doctor's appointments, and staying at home when they became ill. He continued to respect and admire Ellen's career drive, but no longer saw it as the yardstick by which to measure himself. He did in fact have a creative job and both partners now recognized themselves as highly motivated individuals with different styles of setting priorities.

Case 3 M4F2(2)

Elizabeth is 35 and Peter is 36. They have been married for 12 years and have two children, ages 10 and 8. She is a lawyer and he is a partner in an accounting firm.

Elizabeth has begun to feel bored, unchallenged, and uninterested in the legal research work she had been performing for the past five years. She sought counseling assistance to help her deal with her disillusionment. Counseling revealed that Elizabeth's disinterest with her work reflected a mismatch between her achieving style and values and her current position. Counseling sessions focused on clarifying her career values and skills and exploring the options and opportunities available to her. Elizabeth expressed her dissatisfaction with researching legal issues for others and not being able to follow a case to termination. Although she had initially enjoyed a sense that she was contributing in a meaningful way, lately she felt that this kind of piecemeal work was unrewarding. Elizabeth had been offered the opportunity to perform legal defense work, managing legal cases, and arguing them in court, but had declined. Because this position frequently required traveling, she decided that meshing such demanding work with the needs of her family was just not feasible.

After exploring many options in counseling Elizabeth determined that what would fit best with her achieving style, values, and skills was doing legal defense work within her firm. She still felt, however, that this not compatible with her family's needs. These needs were explored in counseling. Because Peter was central to the beliefs that blocked a career change, he was invited to join the sessions. Elizabeth found that she was operating on the assumption that Peter would not be willing to assume more household and child tasks. When Elizabeth broached this topic with him, she found that this was not the case.

Peter had recently been promoted to the partner level in his firm. He realized that he would not have been able to put as much time and effort into his work, and probably would not have become a partner, if Elizabeth had not assumed the household and child tasks. He was feeling that he "owed" her this new opportunity. Also his new position allowed him more flexibility in time scheduling.

Elizabeth was hesitant at first to believe this. Counseling uncovered her difficulty in letting go and allowing others to do for her. Parallels were seen in her need for this skill as she moved forward in her career also. Elizabeth and Peter negotiated the sharing of responsibilities, as well as Elizabeth's ability to accept the "new" ways in which some of these tasks might be performed. Her firm was more than accommodating and assigned her several cases shortly after she discussed her new plans with her manager.

Peter was able to assume more of the task revolving around the children. These included running carpools, helping them with homework, and cooking. He enjoyed having a more balanced life style and having more time to spend with their children. Peter's involvement allowed Elizabeth to direct more of her efforts toward her work. She found that she enjoyed working with a case from beginning to end, as well as arguing cases in court. She now aspires to the partner level in her law firm.

SUMMARY

It becomes increasingly clear that career counselors deal with career issues that often cannot be viewed in isolation from family stage development and dual-career couple dynamics. Although not all career issues require conjoint counseling, it is a new approach that should be considered in working with clients from dual-career families.

REFERENCES

Berman, E., Sacks, S., & Lief, H. (1975). The two-professional marriage: A new conflict syndrome. *Journal of Sex and Marital Therapy, 1,* 242–253.

Blood, R.P. (1976). The husband-wife relationship. In F.I. Nye and L. Hoffman (Eds.) *The employed mother in America* (pp. 282–305). Westport, CT: Greenwood Press.

Blood, R.O., & Wolfe, D.M. (1960). *Husbands and wives: The dynamics of married living.* Glencoe, IL: Free Press.

Burke, R., & Weir, T. (1976). Relationship of wives' employment status to husband, wife and pair satisfaction and performance. *Journal of Marriage and the Family, 38,* 279–387.

Dalton, G.W., Thompson, P.H., & Price, R.L. (1977). The four stages of professional careers—A new look at performance by professionals. *Organizational Dynamics,* Summer, 19–42.

Derr, C.B. (1980). *Work, family, and the career: New frontiers in theory and research.* New York: Praeger.

Feld, S. (1976). Feelings of adjustment. In F.I. Nye & L. Hoffman (Eds.), *The employed mother in America* (pp. 331–352). Westport, CT: Greenwood Press.

Feldman, H., & Feldman, M. (1973). *The relationship between the family and occupational functioning in a sample of rural women.* Ithaca, NY: Department of Human Development and Family Studies, Cornell University.

Graves, J.P., Dalton, G.W., & Thompson, P.H. (1980). Career stages: In organizations. In C.B. Derr (Ed.), *Work, family, and the career: New frontiers in theory and research* (pp. 18–37). New York: Praeger.

Gross, H.E. (1980). Dual-career couples who live apart: Two types. *Journal of Marriage and the Family, 42,* 567–576.

Hall, F.S., & Hall, D.T. (1979). *The two-career couple.* Reading, MA: Addison-Wesley.

Hester, S.B., & Dickerson, K.G. (1982). The emerging dual-career lifestyle: Are your students prepared for it? *Journal of College Student Personnel, 23,* 514–519.

Holmstrom, L.L. (1972). *The two-career family.* Cambridge, MA: Schenkman.

Jackson, D. (1957). The question of family homeostasis. *Psychiatric Quarterly Supplement, 31,* 79–90.

Masnick, G., & Bane, M.J. (1980). *The nation's families: 1960–1980.* Cambridge, MA: Joint Center for Urban Studies of MIT and Harvard University.

Rapoport, R., & Rapoport, R.N. (1971a). *Dual-career families.* Middlesex, England: Penguin Books.

Rapoport, R., & Rapoport, R.N. (1971b). Further considerations of the dual-career family. *Human Relations, 24,* 519–533.

Rapoport, R., & Rapoport, R.N. (1978). Dual-career families: Progress and prospects. *Marriage and Family Review, 1,* 1–12.

Satir, V.M. (1967). *Conjoint family therapy.* Palo Alto, CA: Science and Behavior Books.

Schein, E. (1978). *Career dynamics: Matching individual and organizational needs.* Reading, MA: Addison-Wesley.

U.S. Department of Commerce, Bureau of the Census (1981). *Statistical abstract of the United States 1981.* (102nd ed.). Washington, DC: U.S. Government Printing Office.

Weingarten, K. (1978). Interdependence. In R. Rapoport & R. Rapoport (Eds.), *Working couples* (pp. 147–158). New York: Harper & Row.

CHAPTER 13

Counseling Adults in Midlife Career Transitions

Philip Abrego
Independent Practice
Seattle, Washington

Lawrence Brammer
Department of Educational Psychology
University of Washington
Seattle, Washington

The purpose of this chapter is to provide a framework for understanding and counseling adults in midlife career changes. First, adult development and career development theories are drawn upon to understand the context of midlife career changes. Next, counseling approaches for assisting adults in managing their midlife career changes are explored. Then illustrative programs that serve midlife career changes are described.

The nature and extent of midlife career change are complex and not well researched. It had been commonly assumed that by age 35 individuals were settled in their careers and no longer trying out various possibilities. Yet, presently people are involved in a variety of career changes well into upper middle age. In reviewing studies of midlife career changes, Waltz (1978) suggested that as many as 25% of men and 30% of business managers between the ages of 35 and 55 are involved in career changes and experience major personality and behavior changes. Because many current research studies include only men, it is difficult to estimate the number of women making midlife career changes.

Fascinating questions are raised as the nature of midlife career change is considered. How is midlife career change a part of the larger process of change and growth during adulthood? How is career change related to reestablishing self-definitions during middle life? How is career change related to satisfaction or distress in other adult roles? What is the meaning of work beyond providing a livelihood? When does career reflect continued growth and development, and when might it involve turning away from personal growth? How do people integrate and express new self-potentialities as they mature in adulthood (Osherson, 1980)? These are some of the questions counselors face as they seek to understand adults in midlife career transitions.

Adding to the complexity of midlife career change is the fact that career changes can take a variety of forms. Some are voluntary, whereas others involve involuntary terminations. Many career changes take place within organizations through a change of roles; others involve interorganizational or interprofessional transitions. Some adults at midlife shift the meaning of their work without altering their job roles. As the nature of midlife career change is explored, the types of changes will be contrasted and their unifying elements synthesized. This will provide a framework for counseling adults across a variety of career transactions.

As a preliminary step to discussion of midlife career change, it is necessary to define some of the terms used frequently. Although the concept of career has been expanded recently to include maturation and change in all aspects of living (personal growth, family life, civic and occupational roles), a more limited definition will be used to provide consistency with the other chapters in this book. *Career change* is defined as changes of an individual's thoughts, feelings, and behavior over the life span in relation to the individual's work role. *Work* includes, but is not necessarily restricted to, paid employment. *Midlife* refers to the period approximately between ages 35 and 55. *Transitions* are events in which an individual: (a) experiences a personal discontinuity in life, and (b) must develop new assumptions or behavioral responses because the situation is new or the required behavioral adjustments are novel (Hopson & Adams, 1977). Transitions need not be career-related, but may also include relocation, marriage, divorce, or disability.

THEORIES RELATED TO MIDLIFE CAREER CHANGE

Until midcentury, it was commonly assumed that little personality change took place following adolescence. Most developmental and vocational researchers focused on childhood and adolescent changes. Carl Jung and Erik Erikson were two exceptions. Jung (1933) described the process of "mid-life individuation" that begins about age 40 and continues through adulthood. Erikson's *Childhood and Society* (1950) described his theory of the human life cycle. Levinson (1980) noted later that it is a "charming irony" that a book with Erikson's title would provide the basis for the next generation's study of adult development.

Levinson (1980) offered a tapestry as being a useful metaphorical image of adulthood. Each person's life is like a huge tapestry threaded by interrelated roles around occupation, friendships, career networks, family relationships, and leisure activities. The meaning of each thread or role depends on its place in the total design of the tapestry. Adult development research and theories have focused on different aspects of this tapestry. Some, such as Levinson, Darrow, Klein, Levinson, and McKee (1978), Erikson (1950), and Gould (1978) have studied the tapestry over time. Super (1957) and Shein (1978) focused primarily on the single-career thread of the tapestry. Still others, such as transition theorist Schlossberg (1981, 1984), Hopson and Adams (1977), and Pearlin and Schooler (1978), described individual responses to major life transitions. Each perspective illuminates a particular aspect of adulthood, yet each is incomplete in itself.

To understand the process of midlife career change, the interwoven contributions of adult development, career development, and transition theorists need to be examined. Five representative adult and career development theorists have been selected for review: Erikson, Levinson, Gould, Super, and Holland. Their contributions to understanding adult career development will be used as a context for transition theory, which will provide a background for describing our assumptions about counseling midlife changers.

Erikson

Erik Erikson's (1950) framework for understanding adult development has been one of the most influential descriptions of human development across the life span. Erikson described three developmental stages corresponding to periods of adulthood. Late adolescence until early middle age is considered a period when an individual must meet the developmental task of achieving "intimacy versus isolation." Erikson refers to intimacy as "the ability to share with and care about another person without fear of losing oneself in the process" (Elkind, 1977). Intimacy includes the relationship between friends, but it need not involve sexuality. If a sense of intimacy is not established with friends or a partner, the result, in Erikson's view, is a sense of isolation. The individual ends up alone without anyone for mutual sharing or caring.

Middle age is characterized by the task of "generativity versus self absorption." Generativity refers to an individual's concern for others beyond the immediate family—future generations and the world in which those generations will live. This task often involves mentoring and being aware of social needs. Failure to establish this sense of generativity results in absorption with one's own personal needs and comforts.

Erikson's final stage of old age is described as "integrity versus despair." The sense of integrity arises from the individual's ability to look back on life with satisfaction. At the other extreme is the individual who looks upon life as a series of missed opportunities and missed directions. Now in the twilight years the individual realizes that it is too late to start again. For such a person the inevitable result is a sense of despair at what might have been (Elkind, 1977).

Erikson's stages of development are hierarchical so that each stage builds upon preceding stages. Nevertheless, an individual who has difficulty mastering the tasks of one stage may find new solutions to them at a later stage.

Levinson

Levinson and his colleagues (1978) developed a descriptive framework of male adult development involving a sequence of four life stages based on common social events. Each stage is separated by a short, and usually unstable, transition period. Levinson's model is more invariant than

Erikson's, but is similar to his in that it characterizes the adult life course as involving flux and discontinuity.

Levinson's concept of life structure involves the patterning of one's sociocultural world, participation in social roles, and self-expression in a developmental process. This life structure evolves through stable and transitional periods. Stable periods allow a person to make crucial choices, build a life structure around them, and then seek to attain particular goals and values within this structure. The primary developmental task of a transitional period is to terminate the existing structure and to work toward the initiation of a new structure. Each stable and transitional period has its own distinctive tasks reflecting its place in the life cycle. Periods are defined according to these tasks rather than to specific external events or inner states.

The early adult transition, lasting roughly from ages 17 to 22, bridges childhood and adulthood. The first task of this period is to start moving out of the preadult world. This involves questioning the nature of one's place in it, modifying existing relationships with important persons and groups, and reappraising the self. The second task is to explore the possibilities of the adult world and to test some preliminary choices for adult living.

From ages 22 to 28 the shift of an individual's life from child to "novice adult" involves creating an adult life structure. During this early adult period, an individual is confronted by the antithetical tasks of exploring the possibilities of adult living while creating a stable life structure. This period often involves making initial choices regarding occupation, love relationships, life style, and values.

Levinson refers to these four issues as having central importance during early adulthood. Visions of future life styles, or "the Dream," often involve development of a mentor relationship with an older adult who will support and facilitate the realization of the dream. The mentor serves as a teacher, sponsor, exemplar, and counselor. The young adult forms an occupation through a variety of routes over the entire novice period. Marriage often takes place during this period. Some men marry what Levinson terms "the special woman" who functions like a mentor in that she is connected with the man's dream. Seventy percent of Levinson's sample experienced crises as they worked to create a balance between keeping options open and arriving at a crystalized definition of themselves as adults.

The age thirty transition, lasting about five years, provides a time of reappraisal and a second chance to create a more satisfying life structure. This transition may be hardly noticeable or may lead to a personal crisis where the person's entire future may be in doubt. Only 18% of Levinson's sample experienced a smooth transition. The period between ages 30 and 40 is considered a settling-down period in which a man's tasks are to establish a niche in society and to advance in efforts to build a better life. Roughly half of the sample experienced smooth advancement whereas others declined, were unable to find stability, or broke out to find a new life structure. The late 30s are suggested to be the period of "becoming one's own man." Levinson's men often severed relations with mentors and sought to become more independent of other individuals and institutions while still seeking affirmation in society.

The midlife transition from ages 40 to 45 provides an opportunity to reappraise the life structure of the settling-down period. There tends to be a time shift associated with one's realization of mortality. During this period many aspects of the dream are recognized as "illusions." Many men began to question long-held assumptions and beliefs about themselves and the world. Eight percent of Levinson's sample experienced crises during this period. Men reported feeling older, coming to a greater sense of generativity, and realizing the gap between the dream and what they had become. This either led to regrets or a determination to close the gap in a final burst of renewed career activity. The questioning of this period often leads to reassessment of the dream, marriage, and relations with young adults. The "de-illusionment" and resulting modifications of the life structure provide the commitments for middle adulthood and beyond.

Levinson's age periods overlap in spite of being age-linked and occurring in a fixed sequence. Levinson describes this overlap metaphorically as a long-distance traveler who changes vehicles, passengers, and baggage, but whose past does not disappear. He believes that his developmental stages have a biological, psychological, and social basis. Through the current unpublished work of his students, Levinson is shown to believe that women experience similar age transitions involving different developmental tasks.

Gould

Gould (1978) described periods of flux and satisfaction during adult years in terms of changes in major assumptions. Gould's framework described what he terms a change from " childhood consciousness" to "adult consciousness" as an individual moves through late adolescence and adulthood. He believes that as individuals grow older they eliminate childhood distortions that restrict life. They move from an orientation of "I am their" (referring to parents) to "I own myself." The emerging adult strips away various false assumptions at each stage of the life cycle, then reevaluates his or her life style according to inner values. The final result is a shedding of childhood fantasies about simplicity and control during midlife, and realization of inner directness and self ownership in later life.

Each adult era becomes associated with dominant self-descriptive themes. Late adolescence, for example, involves issues of separation from family and exploration of the adult world. During the 20s the individual establishes increased independence and views the world from a more complex perspective. The early 30s tend to be a time of personal reassessment. There is often a turning away from the active social life of the 20s and a new focus on child rearing. During the late 30s and 40s, the individual is confronted with commitments toward work choice, well-being, and money. There is also an awareness of progressive deterioration due to aging. The 40s thus involve an unstable period of personal reassessment and discomfort followed by a general stabilization of changes started in the 30s. In the 50s one begins to feel less responsible for one's children and shows increased concern for health and retirement.

Middle age is often accompanied by a shift in time perspective. The realization of being in "the second half of life" (Levinson et al., 1978) may bring about a shift toward greater generativity and concern about others. Yet, it may bring distress and crisis. Individuals often become concerned with their life progress in relation to an idiosyncratic or normative "schedule" of life accomplishments. They may feel "behind" in reaching a dream they held or "off time" with respect to their peers.

Middle age is a time when men tend to become more sensitive and nurturing, more interested in love than power, and more dependent. Women often move in the opposite direction—away from a nurturing position and dependency on others (Brim, 1976). In this sense, both men and women evolve toward an interdependence that balances needs for independence and dependence.

Although researchers disagree on the existence of age-related stages, most authors believe that adult development is characterized by a repetitive cycle of stable and fluctuating periods. Levinson's metaphor of the life course as "seasons of the year" seems apt. It is not uncommon for someone experiencing transition to feel confused and doubtful about her or his life course. Vaillant (1977) found that every individual (including the best adjusted) in his research sample reported experiencing a crisis in adult life to the extent that he or she would have benefited from psychiatric help.

Periods of adult development seem to vary by cultural, sexual, and social class variables. Because of the great variability in the role expectations for social subgroups, it is difficult to adequately describe phases of adult development. There seem to be some universal issues of adult life, but the socially preferred ways of confronting these issues vary.

CAREER DEVELOPMENT THEORIES

Various career development researchers have focused on the importance of developmental career stages. Their theories "specify that individual development proceeds through a series of stages, each of which requires the mastery of developmental tasks and/or resolution of developmental issues unique to that stage. Movement to subsequent stages is viewed as contingent upon the satisfactory completion or resolution of previous stages" (Campbell & Heffernan 1983).

Super

Super's (1957, 1977) writings provide the core assumption of most developmental theorists. He described career development as an evolutionary process occurring over the life span. Super's theory emphasizes that as an individual moves through the life cycle, each stage of that cycle calls for a different kind of vocational behavior. Adolescence is a period of preparation in which the individual crystallizes his or her ideas about appropriate work and makes relevant educational choices. During the late teens and early 20s, young adults must narrow their vocational directions and begin to implement a vocational preference by completing appropriate training and entry employment. After a young adult becomes established, the task of middle age is to stabilize and consolidate one's career. The final stage of career development is retirement, although it is increasingly considered as an opportunity for a new or continued career.

Several writers have further developed Super's framework and related it to adult career development. Shein's (1978) list of career-related developmental tasks for early and middle adulthood involves primarily career entry and advancement in the early and middle years. Then career decline or voluntary renewal characterize later middle age. The final tasks are disengagement from work-related satisfactions and finding new sources of fulfillment.

Campbell and Heffernan (1983) have adapted Super's developmental tasks and applied them to individuals involved in midcareer change. Midcareer changers as well as young people encounter the "preparation" tasks of career development. These tasks involve decisions regarding vocational direction and implementation of the choices. Midlife workers must also complete "establishment" tasks that involve becoming oriented and adapted to the organizational environment. Additional tasks are establishing harmonious relationships with coworkers, learning the requirements of the position, and demonstrating one's competence. In this stage, individuals need to examine their job satisfaction, consider advancement opportunities, and develop future career plans. To manage midlife careers satisfactorily, individuals must be able to succeed at "maintenance stage" career tasks that involve adjusting to changing organizational needs as well as reevaluating work performance goals. Problems with any of these tasks might lead to additional midlife career changes.

Holland

Holland's (1973) theory of career choice provides another important perspective on midlife career change. This theory emphasizes the importance of congruence or fit between one's personality pattern and demands of the work environment. Holland suggests that an individual most resembles one of six types of people: realistic, investigative, artistic, social, enterprising, or conventional. In the same way, work environments may also resemble these six types. Each work environment is dominated by a given type of personality. For example, social environments are dominated by social personalities, realistic environments by realistic personalities, and so on. People and congruent work environments seek each other. Individuals search for work environments that will let them express their personalities and reward them for their skills and values. Environments search for people who are congruent with their dominant type through friendships and recruiting practices.

Holland believes that lack of congruence or fit between people and their work environment is the primary factor accounting for career change. He states that stable career patterns are most likely to occur when one's work environmental patterns resemble one's personality pattern. When these patterns are congruent, the person receives selective reinforcement for her or his behavior. A discrepancy between one's personality pattern and work environmental pattern, however, results in career dissatisfaction. This dissatisfaction is resolved by changing oneself, restructuring one's current work environment, or changing careers. Holland also suggests that an undifferentiated or inconsistent personality pattern can also contribute to a poor fit with one's work. Various counseling instruments such as the Strong Campbell Interest Inventory and the Self-Directed Search can be used to identify an individual's personality pattern according to Holland's codes.

TRANSITION THEORIES

Transition theories describe the process of coping with life transitions. They consider similarities and differences among transitions and the varieties of coping strategies that are utilized. Schlossberg (1981, 1984), Hopson and Adams (1977), and Pearlin and Schooler (1978) are representative of research investigators using this framework to understand life transitions.

Transition theories describe responses to transitions in terms of loss and reattachment. The experience of tangible or symbolic loss often leads to a reorganization of self-concepts and the need to use a wide range of coping skills to resolve the loss. The reorganization of self involves development of new assumptions and beliefs about oneself and the world. For example, a woman who becomes aware that she will no longer progress in her organization may experience a loss of role. No longer a "climber," she may need to develop a new set of beliefs about herself and her career. She might also need new skills for coping with her career standstill. Brammer and Abrego (1981) suggested a taxonomy of basic coping skills for life transitions. These skills include attitudinal responses to transitions, developing and utilizing external and internal support systems, managing emotional and physical distress, and skills for planning and implementing change.

Transition theories are most useful when nested in the broader context of developmental theories. In this way, attention is given to the immediate process of midlife career change, and yet such a change is viewed in relation to earlier life history and long-range implications. Additionally, midlife career change is viewed in relation to other developmental events occurring simultaneously. These might include divorce, death of a parent, or children entering school or leaving home. Osherson (1980) used this developmental approach in studying a small group of male midlife career changers. The approach in this chapter to counseling adults in midlife career change leans heavily on transition theories placed in a larger developmental context.

Several important assumptions are made here about midlife career change. First, midlife career change (particularly voluntary change) cannot be isolated from the developmental issues of midlife. There seems to be a continuum on which midlife developmental issues and career changes are intertwined. For some individuals a midlife career change represents a strategy for coping with the developmental task of individuating or becoming more of a "whole person." Such a person may be searching for ways to become more generative, nurturing, or independent. For others, career change is linked more to specific job-related factors such as poor relationships with supervisors.

For many people, such as dual career couples, one's gender, friendship, spouse, parental, and leisure life roles are not simply complementary but central to maintaining a career and are importantly intertwined with career decisions (O'Neil, Fishman, & Kinsella-Shaw, 1987). Many family developmental factors such as timing of a marriage and childbearing are closely related to career factors such as career promotions, satisfaction, and salience. These various life roles and developmental tasks may come into conflict with career development needs or may enhance career development.

Second, midlife career change involves an attempt to find a better fit between one's midlife self-identity and a work environment that provides an opportunity for integrating dreams and goals. For some people, career transitions may be attempts to cope with the discrepancy between the anticipated self of young adulthood and the perceived self at midlife. This discrepancy may precipitate or be precipitated by a career change and will result in an experience of loss and grief.

Third, when career change becomes a strategy for coping with developmental issues, it can be either growth-oriented or may represent a retreat. It becomes growth-oriented when it offers an opportunity to integrate more of one's total personality into one's life style. This kind of career change enables the individual to better manage other midlife developmental tasks. Career change can also represent a retreat from facing fearful developmental issues and may prematurely foreclose important midlife tasks.

Fourth, the process of coping successfully with midlife career transitions is facilitated by broad, flexible coping skills for managing life transitions, and career transitions in particular. Metaphorically, it is useful to think of coping strategies as "tools in a tool box" or "arrows in a quiver." If something must be fixed or a bull's-eye must be hit, there will be more possibilities of success than with only one tool or arrow.

MIDLIFE CAREER CHANGE AS A TRANSITION

Various researchers have studied the causes of midlife career change. It is obvious that there are multiple reasons for people to change their careers. Some motivation comes from broad social changes affecting individuals. Entine (1977) cited the rise of the women's movement as increasing the entry and reentry of women into the work force. Technological changes have prematurely ended careers for some people and opened opportunities for others. A changing life expectancy and new retirement policies lead people to seek more satisfactions from their work.

There are also internal motivations for midlife career change. Internal conflicts over developmental issues may lead to new goals, the desire to satisfy higher-level needs, and the desire for new purposes and aspirations. Sinick's (1977) list of motivations for career change includes:

1. initial career not person's own choice;
2. dead end in advancement;
3. desire to implement avocational interests;

4. disproportion between prescribed and discretionary duties;
5. lack of variety;
6. excessive work pressure;
7. excessive physical demands;
8. dissatisfying employer policies;
9. personality conflicts;
10. lack of social status;
11. low earnings;
12. co-workers divergent in values and life styles; and
13. incongruence with vocational interests.

There are various types of midlife career changes as well as multiple motivations. Louis (1980) developed a typology of career transitions that includes interrole and intrarole categories.

Interrole transitions involve taking on a new and different career role. There is career *entry transition*, such as a homemaker entering a new job in business. *Interprofessional transitions* involve shifting from one profession to another. A less radical career change occurs when a person transfers from one department to another within the same organization, termed an *intraorganizational transition*. The final interrole transitions in Louis's typology are the *exit transitions*, which may be voluntary exits such as child care leaves and sabbaticals, or involuntary terminations.

Intrarole transitions involve an individual's internal change of attitude without actually altering the job role. Some employees want change, but do not want to change organizations or job roles because of personal constraints (e.g., loss of pension plans). Pearlin and Schooler (1978) found that these dissatisfied employees coped with work frustrations by changing their attitudes. One such coping mechanism was the use of positive comparisons such as "count your blessings" or "we're all in the same boat." Current frustrations may then be evaluated as being an improvement over the past or as a forerunner of an easier future. "Selective ignorance" was a second method for attending to the positive qualities of the experience. A third strategy for changing the meaning of one's work was to change one's hierarchy of priorities, devaluing unavailable rewards and substituting others (e.g., devaluing money and intrinsic work reward and valuing rewards extrinsic to work). Whereas midlife career changes are typically active strategies to cope with career frustrations, these strategies represent more subtle forms of midlife career change. It is possible for individuals to cope with career crises by changing the internal meaning of their work rather than the actual job itself.

FACTORS AFFECTING PERSONAL REACTIONS TO A MIDLIFE CAREER CHANGE

Motivation

Motivation for career change is an important consideration in how a career transition is experienced. Voluntary midlife career changes are generally less stressful than are involuntary changes, and may require different counseling approaches. For example, the voluntary career changer may primarily need support or help in managing fear of failure. An involuntary career changer may be more strongly affected by loss, grief, anger, and threatened self-esteem. Another factor affecting the experience of career change is the degree to which the transition was perceived as predictable. Sometimes the grief of involuntary career change is lessened when the employee has anticipated a possible termination for some time. For example, one middle-aged bank officer said when terminated, "I saw this coming; I should have resigned five years ago."

Magnitude

The magnitude of the transition and the rate of change may also affect the career changer's experience. A sudden transfer across the country away from supportive friends is likely to be more stressful than a more gradual, less disruptive transfer.

Support

The environment, particularly the human environment, can reduce the impact of a career change. A supportive human environment often has a reservoir of social resources (e.g., family, friends, clergy, agencies) from which an individual can seek support in time of transition. Lowenthal and Haven (1968) suggested that the presence of an intimate relationship serves as a buffer against social losses such as those accompanying career changes.

Control

Two important characteristics affecting the experience of a stressful transition are one's perceived control over threatening situations and one's ability to manage anxiety. To the extent that people judge themselves to have control in a situation, the probability is that they will be less likely to perceive that situation as threatening and, in turn, less likely to manifest adverse reactions. When individuals believe they have little control over their circumstances, they are more likely to develop a negative expectancy about the future. This expectancy can result in feelings of helplessness, depression, frustration, anxiety, hostility, or disinterest.

Anxiety

The second important personality factor affecting the experiences of career transition is one's ability to manage anxiety. Sarason (1974) suggested that under stress highly anxious people become preoccupied with themselves. They respond to threats by retreating into fantasy and only attending to annoying, angry, or anxious thoughts. Self-preoccupation generates physiological arousal that interferes with information processing and planning strategies.

TYPICAL INDIVIDUAL REACTIONS TO
MIDLIFE CAREER CHANGE

It is important to recognize that each person has a unique response to career transitions. It is not helpful for anyone to be pigeonholed into "model experiences" that they are supposed to fit. It is annoying for a counselor to suggest that they are in a "midlife-crisis" because it minimizes the unique experience of their transition. Yet, it is helpful for counselors to realize that career transitions have much in common with other life transitions. It is for this reason that we present a process model of transitions described by Hopson (1981). Hopson stated that not everyone's transition fits the model and that "even where an experience does follow the model's flow, it is rarely smooth or continuous as the curve suggests. Progress typically is more of the two steps forward, one step back variety" (p. 37).

Hopson developed a process model for phases of a transition that is useful for discussing intervention strategies. The phases are related to one's emotional or mood experience and are plotted in Figure 1.

Phase 1: Immobilization and Shock

Immobilization describes the beginning awareness that one has entered a transition, whether perceived as desirable or undesirable. Both good news and bad news typically produce an absence of feeling as the person appraises the meaning of the situation. The degree of immobilization varies with the intensity, predictability, and voluntary/involuntary nature of the transition. Immobilization is followed quickly by an emotional response. A positively perceived career change is usually followed by positive feelings, ranging from mild pleasure to elation. A negatively perceived career change is typically followed by a mood reduction.

Phase 2: Minimization

Minimization is a term denoting both regret and denial. When people make a positive career change, they often experience relief and good feelings at first. Then they begin to question what they have done and often experience remorse about leaving their former roles. Consequently, good feelings are lowered as they begin to experience doubts about whether their new career roles will live up to their expectations. When people are told that they have been terminated their usual despair is often followed by denial. This denial reaction provides important stop-time to give the person relief from suffering and the necessity to do something prematurely to adjust. Denial may help the person feel better, and this phase may last for a long time.

Phase 3: Self-Doubt

Hopson (1981) states that following minimization "a period of self-doubt often begins and the person will not emerge out of this until he

Figure 1

Seven-Phase Model of Stages Accompanying Transition.

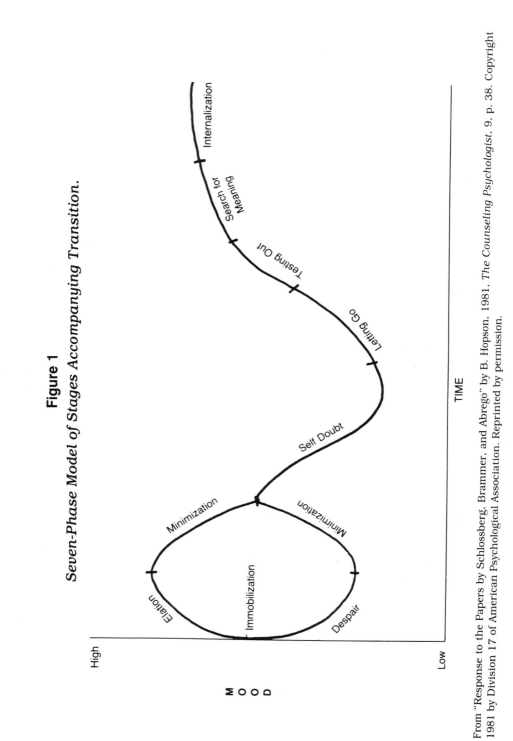

From "Response to the Papers by Schlossberg, Brammer, and Abrego" by B. Hopson. 1981. *The Counseling Psychologist*, 9, p. 38. Copyright 1981 by Division 17 of American Psychological Association. Reprinted by permission.

246

or she has successfully recognized and dealt with any negative feelings that have occurred of loss, anger, jealousy, frustration, disappointment, etc. Letting go of these and old expectations is literally and usually (in the model) 'turning the corner' and an upward mood swing takes over" (p. 37). Some people experience intense sadness early in this phase, and they may show signs of depression.

Phase 4: Letting Go

A critical point is reached in dealing with self-doubts about career changes when people let themselves go into the feeling (i.e., experience it deeply). This permission may lead to tears and expression of anger, or it may evoke a cognitive experience of letting go of their resistance to change and their commitments to the past work. Then they will flow with the new experience.

Phase 5: Testing Options

When the reality of the experience of loss comes clearly into awareness and the past is released, a person typically begins to tentatively explore new options. In this phase, a person might be exploring various career change possibilities.

Phase 6: Search for Meaning

Reassessing commitment to one's values and life style is a central aspect of making career transitions. As one tests new options for living, these choices call into question one's previous values as well as future commitments. This period of active reflection may lead to a change in one's values or a recommitment to old values. A new perspective on one's previous career path often emerges.

Phase 7: Integration and Renewal

In this phase new assumptions, behaviors, and decisions are integrated into a changed life style. Personal renewal is often experienced, although reflection on one's career transition may still generate anxious feelings. There is a sense that the transition is completed and that the transition experience will have a salutary influence over future directions.

COUNSELING MIDLIFE CAREER CHANGERS

In this section the process of counseling adults in midlife career change is discussed. Some general principles for counseling these individuals and various counseling formats are described.

Counselors who have provided services to young adults as well as to middle-aged persons know that there are some unique pleasures in counseling midlife adults. Their maturity gives them better judgment about their motivations, priorities, and commitments. They often have wider work experience and thus have more data about their career interests and abilities. Middle-aged adults are less likely to expect a "test them and tell them" experience from a counselor. They tend to realize that the answers to their longings are to be found within themselves rather than from an expert or a vocational interest test.

Middle-aged career changers also provide some unique challenges to counselors. These challenges come in the form of subtle biases that may be related to conceptions about appropriate age behavior, sexual stereotypes, risk taking, important work values, and more. Rather than generate a long list of such possible biases, a few relevant assumptions for counseling midlife adults will be discussed.

Counseling Goals

It is of primary importance to consider the counseling process as more than "matching people with jobs." Career counseling is aimed at helping adults to: (a) assess their values, abilities, and interests; (b) enhance their general coping and career decision-making skills; and (c) implement choices where more of their self-concept can be expressed in their life styles.

Job Satisfaction

A second principle is the importance of recognizing that one's job does not have to be inherently satisfying. Counselors may set up frustrating expectations for their clients if they assume one's job satisfaction necessarily determines life happiness. Loughary and Ripley (1976) suggested a helpful framework for categorizing a career into three components; job, vocation, and leisure. *Job* refers to activities that contribute to basic survival needs (e.g., making a living); *vocation* refers to activities that provide a sense of fulfillment, self-worth, and meaning; *leisure* activities contribute to recreational and aesthetic pleasures. For some people roles overlap considerably, whereas for others there is little overlap between job, vocation, and leisure. For individuals who do not necessarily want, or cannot find, a job with inherent meaning, there are possibilities of finding satisfying vocational and leisure activities that would provide meaning and fun.

Career Mobility

A related principle is that career mobility is not necessarily available to everyone. Many career counselors assume that there exists a free and open labor market and that people have an array of choices about their careers. Barriers to the labor market, particularly for the disabled, women, and racial minorities, exist because of discrimination, social and economic factors (e.g., availability of child care resources), and personal skills. But job changers from the majorities may also have limited mobility in a society where economic conditions have led to considerable underemployment.

Career counselors might also be aware of their biases about upward career mobility in terms of achieving increased socioeconomic status, prestige, and responsibility. Many organizations have a pyramidal organizational structure in which there are fewer people at the top than at the bottom. As a result, ambitious individuals may become very frustrated if they simply "try harder" to reach the top. It is important for counselors to recognize that some people would rather devote their energy to other areas of life, such as family or leisure, than to continue to pursue career advancement. Others may wish to give up some of their income or prestige to satisfy other pressing midlife interests.

Gender Role Bias

In this era of vocal men's and women's liberation movements, it is easy for counselors to assume that they no longer hold sex-linked occupational stereotypes. Because many counselors continue to hold these stereotypes, they should at least explore the possibility that they possess these biases.

Risking Change

A final assumption that counselors often make is that midlife adults should become "career changers" when they are dissatisfied with their careers. It may be tempting for counselors to subtly and vicariously live out their own fantasies by encouraging a client's career change. Counselors may become disappointed or discouraged if clients do not want to take this risk. It is important to allow clients to make their own decisions regarding the extent of their career changes.

COUNSELING FORMATS

Counseling services for midlife career changers take a variety of forms. Many private services exist for comprehensive career planning help. A growing number of larger businesses, for example, are adding programs called outplacement, inplacement, career counseling, and management succession to their human resource management offices. A few school districts and governmental units are experimenting with pilot programs also.

Outplacement counseling is provided for terminated or about-to-be terminated employees. Outplacement consists of a combination of crisis, grief, family, and career counseling (Brammer & Humberger, 1984). The goal is to have the person placed in a new job, often a new career, in a reasonably short time. With executives, for example, this process takes as long as 10 months to a year. Both individual and group counseling are available and usually start with a self-assessment process followed by instruction in goal-setting and job-seeking skills.

Inplacement counseling, on the other hand, is performed within the organization for employees the company wants to retain, but on the condition that they change their behavior in some significant area. This includes counseling for the marginal employee who may be headed for lateral or downplacement, rehabilitation for the troubled employee, or "refitting" for those who no longer perform up to expectations. Occasionally this counseling involves some retraining for those with obsolete skills, or it may mean planning changes in the way the employee relates to people. Often inplacement counseling involves a change of career direction or planning for early retirement. In any case, businesses are finding that such career counseling is cost-effective in dollars as well as in human terms (Brammer & Humberger, 1984). Such programs have been developed in large corporations such as Citicorp, AT&T, Weyerhauser, and government organizations such as Livermore Laboratories and Goddard Space Flight Center.

A number of corporations have instituted career planning programs that help employees plan long-term career development in that organization. They can find their best fit now and obtain a glimpse of their potential growth through such programs. The Tektronix example, described later, is such a program.

Midlife career counseling is often done in group formats. These groups provide a setting isolated from daily hassles to reexamine one's personal values, life goals, and directions. Typical groups are composed of 8 to 10 individuals meeting weekly over a six-week period. Groups may also meet in a weekend workshop. These groups generally are facilitated by a trained counselor.

Midlife career planning groups involve various self-assessment strategies intended to help participants increase awareness of significant values, priorities, and goals. Lurie (1977, p. 878) indicates this self-assessment includes many life areas:

1. influences that have shaped a person's self-image, including experiences in education, career, family, and other interpersonal influences, introversion and extroversion, fantasies, and previous experiences in seeking employment;
2. a systematic analysis of the participants' work (including volunteer work and hobbies), work skills, specialized knowledge, natural abilities, and accomplishments;
3. current life situation, involving an assessment of values and activities that decrease or increase anxiety, destroy or build self-esteem, produce pleasure or pain, exhaust or energize, and narrow or expand horizons;
4. current time expenditures, past goals, friendships, health and energy, and potential or contemplated goals;
5. long- and short-term goals and an analysis of what they would mean for the participant and his or her family, economic activities, self-concept, and life style. (p. 878)

These groups provide a developmental perspective by using readings by writers on adult development such as Levinson et al. (1978), Sheehy (1976), and Gould (1978). Some groups will teach various transition-coping skills to manage stress, maintain self-esteem, make decisions, and gain employment. Groups often provide a strong network of support and offer the opportunity to learn from the experiences of other participants. The group's main drawback is its inability to tailor information to the particular needs of each individual. Groups generally operate on the assumption that all midlife adults need similar experiences. They may not have time to allow for a complete assessment of each participant's needs. Little screening is done for these groups, so some individuals whose midlife transition is not career-related may be diverted from looking at their more primary transitions. Some of these drawbacks can be alleviated by offering individual, client-centered counseling. The client will not get the support or learn from other group participants involved in a similar transition, however.

An example of groups to help midlife career changers are the "Forty Plus" clubs that sprang up in major cities during the budget cutbacks of the early 1980s when many midmanagers and technical personnel members were terminated. These groups were largely of the self-help type that organized to give one another emotional support, but more importantly to share job search information and experience.

Marital and family counseling are often overlooked in dealing with midlife career change. Marital counseling is often a useful adjunct to individual or group counseling because the career decisions of one person affect his or her spouse. Couples counseling is especially useful for dual-career couples or people experiencing a home/career conflict. These persons find marital counseling helpful in negotiating their needs with one another. Robbins (1980) describes many individuals who would have considered midlife career changes but felt unsupported by their spouses. Marital counseling can thus increase the emotional support a career changer receives from his or her spouse. It is also important to note that groups often treat a career changer as though the decision to change careers is a totally independent decision, whereas for many couples it involves a joint decision.

Family counseling can also be useful in cases where a career change affects the entire family. These include situations where the standard of living is likely to drop, or the family is required to make a geographical move. In these transitional situations, family counseling can mobilize mutual support among family members.

Some counseling assumptions and typical counseling formats for helping individuals encountering midlife career transitions have been described. The next section will describe some model programs designed to assist these individuals.

INSTITUTIONAL PROGRAMS FOR MIDLIFE CAREER CHANGERS

In recent years numerous programs have been developed within governmental, educational, and private institutions to assist midlife individuals to make career changes. Several programs will be described briefly and then some general issues raised in developing these programs will be discussed.

Midlife career counseling is becoming more important in private industry. This is attributed in part to discontinuation of mandatory retirement policies and the move in more companies toward providing guaranteed employment. When the decision to retire becomes a matter of negotiation between the employee and management, it is possible for many employees to work as long after midlife as before. Some individuals may experience several careers within an organization. As employees stay within a company for longer periods, it becomes economically as well as psychologically desirable to provide career counseling. This counseling assists each individual to develop a career plan that considers both the individual's and the company's needs and interests. The outplacement and inplacement counseling described earlier are examples of programs to accomplish mutual goals.

Tektronix, an Oregon-based electronics firm, provides inplacement career planning based on a general commitment to career mobility (Ferrini & Parker, 1978). Tektronix employees are encouraged to learn other jobs in the company through extensive company educational programs. Additionally there is a tuition refund program that provides full reimbursement for job-related courses and half reimbursement for other courses taken by employees at educational institutions in the community. Degree programs are offered at plant facilities in cooperation with educational institutions. Tektronix also offers a management training program, educational counseling, and educational loans. Middle-aged employees as well as others are able to explore new career directions through these programs.

Many educational institutions have developed women's resource centers and reentry programs for women reentering college and work outside the home. The University of British Columbia's Center for Continuing Education, Women's Resource Center (Ironside & Buckland, 1979) successfully offers 80 short-term programs annually for women in management and reentry women. Career and life planning as well as peer counseling services are provided. Core courses at the University of British Columbia and other institutions generally focus on developing self-esteem, a stronger identity as a woman, communication skills, career planning, and job seeking skills.

A related type of program is exemplified by the Mid-Career Counseling Program at the State University of New York at Stony Brook (Entine, 1977). This program offers three noncredit workshops each term—a basic midcareer course, a workshop for women who are coping with midlife adjustments, and an intensive 16-hour weekend workshop on job search strategies. Additionally, vocational and educational counseling services were established in 12 local libraries in a two-county area. This midcareer counseling service has been staffed by counselor interns from several counselor education programs and a midlife assessment program at the SUNY at Stony Brook. Services are supported by grants and course fees.

Various questions are important to consider in developing programs for midlife career counseling. Is it preferable to create special midlife career programs (such as those at SUNY at Stony Brook) or should existing career services be expanded to meet the needs of midlife adults? Will adults participate in programs anticipating midlife concerns or must we settle primarily for services to people already involved in midlife transition? How can midlife counseling programs become economically self-sustaining? Are there possible cooperative efforts with business, government, and educational institutions? Should counseling services include significant others as well as the individual involved? The answers to these questions will come as new and existing programs are better evaluated.

SUMMARY AND NEEDED RESEARCH

In this chapter we have discussed the theoretical bases and several strategies for counseling midlife career changers. People in midlife are diverse in personal style, coping skills, and counseling needs. Many research questions remain that, if answered, would strengthen our basis for understanding and counseling midlife adults. Examples are: What is the effect of mentoring on both the mentor's and the protégé's career development? What effect would removing resource barriers (e.g., money for education, child care) have on the decision to change careers? How is a person's ability to cope with transitions related to the person's productivity and creativity? What educational formats and combinations of skills are most effective for producing coping behavior? How can people be attracted to learn coping skills in a preventative framework? Are different components of career choice (e.g., values clarification) important at different developmental periods of adulthood?

Although many unanswered questions remain, it is encouraging to find a growing interest in midlife career development among counselors, human resource development specialists, and research specialists in education, government, and private industry.

REFERENCES

Brammer, L., & Abrego, P. (1981). Intervention strategies for coping with transitions. *The Counseling Psychologist, 9*, p. 2.

Brammer L., & Humberger. D. (1984). *Inplacement and outplacement counseling.* Englewood Cliffs, NJ: Prentice-Hall.

Brim, O. (1976). Theories of the male mid-life crisis. *The Counseling Psychologist, 6*(1), 2–9.

Campbell, R.E., & Heffernan, J. (1983). Adult vocational behavior. In W.B. Walsh & S. Osipow (Eds.), *Handbook of vocational psychology* (pp. 223–262). Hillsdale, NJ: Lawrence Erlbaum Associates.

Elkind, A. (1977). Erik Erikson's eight stages of man. In L. Allman & D. Jaffee (Eds.). *Readings in adult psychology: Contemporary perspectives* (pp. 3–11). New York: Harper & Row.

Entine, A. (1977). Counseling for mid-life and beyond. *Vocational Guidance Quarterly, 25*(4), 332–336.

Erikson, E. (1950). *Childhood and society.* New York: Norton.

Fernini, P., & Parker, L.A. (1978). *Career change: A handbook of exemplary programs.* Cambridge, MA: Technical Education Research Center.

Gould, R. (1978). *Transformation: Growth and change in adult life.* New York: Simon & Schuster.

Holland, J. (1973). *Making vocational choices: A theory of careers.* Englewood Cliffs, NJ: Prentice-Hall.

Hopson, B. (1981). Response to the papers by Schlossberg, Brammer, and Abrego. *The Counseling Psychologist, 9*(2), 36–39.

Hopson, B., & Adams, J. (1977). Toward an understanding of transition. In J. Adams & B. Hopson (Eds.). *Transition: Understanding and man-*

aging personal change (pp. 3–25). Montclair. NJ: Allenhald & Osmund.

Ironside, A., & Buckland, C. (1979). Women's resource center: A coordinated approach to programs and services for women in mid-life change. In A. Knox (Ed.), *Programming for adults facing mid-life change.* San Francisco: Jossey-Bass.

Jung, C.G. (1933). *Modern man in search of a soul.* New York: Harcourt, Brace & World.

Levinson, D.J. (1980). Toward a conception of the adult life course. In N. Smelser & E. Erikson (Eds.), *Themes of work and love in adulthood* (pp. 265–290). Cambridge: Harvard University Press.

Levinson, D.J., Darrow, C.N., Klein, E.B., Levinson, M.H., & McKee, B. (1978). *The seasons of a man's life.* New York: Knopf.

Loughary, J., & Ripley, T. (1976). *Career and life planning guide.* Chicago: Follett.

Louis, M. (1980). Career traditions: Varieties and commonalities. *Academy of Management Review, 5*(3), 329–340.

Lowenthal, D., & Haven, C. (1968). Interaction and adaptation: Intimacy as a critical variable. *American Sociological Review, 33,* 22–30.

Lurie, H.S. (1977). Life planning: An educational approach to change. *American Journal of Psychiatry, 134,* 878–882.

O'Neil, J.M., Fishman, D.M., & Kinsella-Shaw, M. (1987). Dual-career couple's career transitions and normative dilemmas: A preliminary assessment model. *The Counseling Psychologist, 15,* 50–96.

Osherson, S. (1980). *Holding on or letting go.* New York: Free Press.

Pearlin, L., & Schooler, C. (1978). The structure of coping. *Journal of Health and Social Behavior, 19,* 2–21.

Robbins, P. (1980). *Successful mid-life career change.* New York: AMACOM.

Sarason, I. (1974). Anxiety and self-preoccupation. In C. Spielberger & I. Sarason (Eds.). *Stress and anxiety: Vol. 2.* Washington, DC: Hemisphere Publications.

Schlossberg, N. (1981). A model for analyzing human adaptation to transition. *Counseling Psychologist, 9*(2), 2–18.

Schlossberg, N. (1984). *Counseling adults in transition.* New York: Springer.

Sheehy, G. (1976). *Passages: Predictable crises of adult life.* New York: E.P. Dutton.

Shein, E.H. (1978). *Career dynamics: Matching individual and organizational needs.* Reading, MA: Addison-Wesley.

Sinick, D. (1977). *Counseling older persons: Careers, retirement, dying.* New York: Human Sciences.

Super, D.E. (1957). *The psychology of careers.* New York: Harper & Row.

Super, D.E. (1977). Vocational maturity in mid-career. *Vocational Guidance Quarterly, 25,* 294–302.

Vaillant, G. (1977). *Adaptation to life.* Boston: Little, Brown.

Waltz, G. (1978). *Searchlight: Relevant resources in high interest areas. M.D. career change: An overview of counseling practices and programs.* Ann Arbor, MI: ERIC Clearinghouse on Counseling and Personnel Services. (ERIC Document Reproduction Service No. ED 160 905).

CHAPTER 14

Career Counseling for the Mature Worker

Geraldine M. Horton
The Development Center, Garland, Texas

Dennis W. Engels
Department of Counselor Education
University of North Texas, Denton, Texas

Jill was 95, and Harold was 96. They had both shared their lives and worked together for more than 60 years in a loving marital and business relationship. He ran the independent business, and she kept the books and cared for their home. Over time, physical changes intruded somewhat. She had always been diabetic and required daily injections, and he had always been there to help with the injections when needed. However, his vision began to fail, to a point where he could scarcely see, and she became his eyes, reading the company books and eventually even helping him drive (although she had never taken driving lessons) by telling him where to turn on their brief midday trips to the neighborhood store. It seemed they were always together, Jill and Harold, and they always seemed happy and at peace with each other and with the world. Then it happened—on a Saturday. They both agreed that Jill needed more help with her medications and injections than Harold could give her, and therefore, they decided she needed full-time care in a home for the aging. They had thought about this before, but had always managed. Now the time had come. They checked her in about 4:00 in the afternoon. With much anxiety, sadness, love, and resignation, they parted, with a warm farewell, until the next morning. But that next morning saw them both deceased. When Harold got home, he felt chest pains and called for assistance. He died within two hours of the modest heart attack which claimed him. But Jill never heard of his passing. She died in her sleep that night. After over 60 years together in life, they died within about eight hours of one another.

Janice worked all her life, first as an outstanding student, then as a teacher, and for most of her formal career as an elementary school principal. She retired at age 65 and continued her career development by teaching reading part-time at a local business school and part-time at the county jail, helping inmates learn to read and to appreciate the value of reading. She never married, but she influenced many elementary school children, teachers, parents, and all the others she took the time to share with. At 85, physical impairments interfered with her teaching, and she moved to a fully supported environment where she had the freedom to provide for herself and the security to have any health and personal services she needed.

At the 1990 National Career Development Association's (NCDA) second national conference, "Empowering Work and Workers," in Scottsdale, Arizona, two of our own NCDA pioneers and current senior citizens, David Tiedeman and C. Gilbert Wrenn presented a program (Richmond, Tiedeman and Wrenn, 1990) wherein they shared their views on career development and life after 65. What they said was moving and quietly profound, befitting the status and grandeur of their respective career accomplishments and contributions to our field and echoing the opening remarks of part of Betty Friedan's (1990) presentation, "From the Feminine Mystique to the Aging Mystique." What they did not say, however was as moving as their spoken message. There were two of the most significant figures in our field, sharing their views, ideas, and visions, through the wise eyes of advanced maturity, encouraging the audience to think beyond the moment (and this century) and to work to help clients empower themselves in life and career. One got the distinct impression that both men were at peace and were continuing their long record of mentoring.

John Rothney, eminent counselor, educator, and researcher, said he and his wife, Ruth, consciously chose to retire and stop most formal scholarly work at age 65, opting instead for travel, adventure, and more sharing with one another until John's ill health pushed him near death, a death which proved a long time in coming. In spite of considerable pain and suffering, Rothney afforded us a poignant perspective of readiness for death.

"I know that the time is coming pretty soon now when I won't be around, but that is just part of life. It's just like being born. Dying is part of life, so you just take it in stride. It's inevitable. You know that the world will get along well without you and always has." (Engels, 1986, 139)

If Erik Erikson had not used the term, integrity, to describe a final and positive state of life in his theory of human development, anyone who knows or knew Jill and Harold, Janice, John and Ruth, David or Gilbert would have had no problem grasping the concept of a time of considerable integration, congruity, peace, altruism, and love in the long lives of these heroes and heroines. Each of these biographical snapshots provides a personalized definition of work and retirement, all noble, good, and worthy of emulation. In the differences of the respective operational definitions of work and retirement in each case, one can come to heightened appreciation of the importance of differences, not merely interpersonal differences, but intrapersonal differences, as well.

This chapter is offered as a discussion of the importance of counseling and career counseling with and for the elderly and is based on an assumption of fundamental and important differences between and within people. We are all always changing. We are all unique, each of us defying age and stage categorizations, and each of us worthy of the dignity and uniqueness cited in the Preamble of the Ethical Standards of the American Association for Counseling and Development (AACD, 1988). With this underpinning in mind, the focus of this chapter is on issues, concepts, and practices in career counseling with older workers.

SOCIAL AND ECONOMIC CHANGE

Accelerated, volatile changes in U.S. and global economics, technical breakthroughs in all areas of science, medicine, product development, aerospace technology and travel, communications, and production have spurred a flurry of changes in business and industrial organizations resulting in many changes for workers. Phased-out jobs, involuntary displacement, changes in job definitions requiring new skills or training, and opportunities in new occupations requiring additional education or training, all point to increasing demand for the services of counselors to facilitate adult development in these changing times (Engels & Muro, 1986; Sinick, 1984; Striner, 1984). Career development programs, outplacement, and individual, group, and family counseling are needed, especially in the mid-life years and 50-plus age groups extending to the 80-plus brackets. Loss of job and unanticipated career changes can catapult workers, especially the elderly, into crises, with strong needs for help in retirement planning, self assessment, career development, employability skills, and job placement.

DEFINING THE MATURE WORKER

Sinick (1984) notes that aging is a universal and life-long process. While we are all aging, we may age quite uniquely. Mature adults form a heterogeneous group with wide diversity in stages of aging and development, attitudes, physical and mental health, and economic conditions (Hayslip & Panek, 1989). A popular wave of interest in physical and mental fitness, and the proliferation of programs, seminars, health clubs, and self-help books and videotapes, have led to better nutrition, body-weight control, and preventive medical care for many older persons.

Not *all* mature and old adults are fit, active, or in good economic condition, however. Diverse conditions and needs are apparent, ranging from the human and economic prosperity of those cited at the start of this chapter to older adults beset with illness, poor nutrition, poverty, involuntary unemployment, depression, and physical disabilities. The plight of those in this latter group is amply documented and described in Mowsesian's *Golden Goals, Rusted Realities* (1985), with its panoramic view of the negative conditions confronting so many elderly Americans, for whom the American dream is actually a nightmare, where "social workers" prowl urology wards advising patients as to what asset must be liquidated (sic.) next for continued treatment. For some, the omnipresent bleak message is, if you live very long, you will eventually lose all you possess. Doeringer (1984) cites four groups of elderly—involuntarily displaced workers, ethnic minorities, women living alone, and displaced workers—as having the most severe employment difficulties.

Many elderly Americans have significant needs which are not being met by existing personal, familial, institutional, and societal resources. The major implication for career counseling with those in dire circumstances may be appropriate referral for mental health assistance along with appropriate career counseling and/or placement assistance. Also, lobbying for favorable public policy is an implication for counseling, human development, and related professional organizations.

CHANGING DEMOGRAPHICS

The U.S. Census Bureau reports that America's 65-plus population is growing at the rapid pace of 2.4% annually and will increase by 105% in the next 40 years (AARP, 1989; U.S. News and World Report, 1988; OOH, 1989). Workers aged 16 to 25 will decline in number (− .04%) as the overall size of this same group declines. The population of workers in the 25 to 54 age group (which includes the baby-boom generation) will increase. Workers 55 and older will be more numerous because of increases in this age population and because of the business and industry sector offering flexible job opportunities to offset some labor shortage (OOQ, Fall 1989; Crystal, 1988). In addition, the percentage of women in the labor force will increase faster than the percentage of men (22% compared to 11.1% for men). As more mothers and homemakers go to work, child care needs will increase, and the elderly may find work opportunities in child care which afford them financial and altruistic rewards.

Although the number of whites entering the work force will be greater than all other groups, percentage increases of white workers will grow more slowly than percentages of black, Asian, and other ethnic groups. Hispanic growth will be rapid, adding over 5 million workers, representing a 27% change from 1988 to 2000 (AARP, 1989b; OOH, 1989). Young blacks and Hispanics presently experience higher unemployment (NAB, 1985). Contributing factors are high numbers of school drop-outs, lack of guidance and counseling (College Board, 1987), lack of appropriate training, decreasing numbers of unskilled jobs, and cyclical (multi-generational) poverty. The National Alliance of Business (NAB, 1985) reports that because many older minorities (suffering discrimination during their lives) had limited educational and employment opportunities and were kept in low wage positions, it may be very difficult for them to find and keep work in their later years.

Older women workers face the general problems of all older workers with added special difficulties of previous low earnings and interrupted employment for child birth, child care, and homemaking. Traditional occupations generally filled by women offered limited training and less flexibility for career development. A critical issue for women is their longer life span and consequent potential widowhood in the later years (Roundtable, 1986). Due to inflation and the escalating costs of medical care, some women are extending their work life because of concerns for maintaining an income and need for employee benefits. Additionally, some women are working longer as a means of staying active and productive.

Some older workers face barriers other than discrimination and labor market policies. Some adults have personal limitations restricting their capacity and capabilities in the workplace. They may be physically handicapped or have poor health and diminished physical strengths that make less skilled work difficult. Some may need upgraded skill training and may lack the educational background necessary for retraining. However, the biggest employment barrier for older workers is still age discrimination, which will be discussed later.

Many of the problems encountered by elderly people seeking work can be counteracted through career counseling and learning employability skills, such as resume writing, job hunting, and interviewing techniques. Concepts, issues, and approaches to career counseling with these mature workers will be discussed in following sections on career counseling practices and techniques.

TRENDS AND LAWS

The last two decades saw a trend toward early retirement due to various factors: availability of pension and other retirement income; ability of companies to withhold accrual of pension after age 65; legislation that required employers to make private health care available for retired workers if they provided the same coverage for other employees; and the Social Security earnings test (Moon & Hushbeck, 1989). Increased pressures on Social Security and pension systems, health care, and social services by our aging population have become a concern for all, especially employers, the elderly, and policy makers.

The federal Age Discrimination in Employment Act (ADEA) set age 70 as the mandatory retirement age and provided protection against discrimination in various ways for older workers. Many states have established stricter standards and eliminated mandatory retirement. Attorneys are helping the elderly and their employers understand the rights and responsibilities of mature workers (MW) (Goldstein, 1990; Mackaronis, 1986; Ventrell-Monsees & Mackaronis, undated). Congress has enacted additional laws such as the Employment Retirement Income Security Act and the Tax Equity and Fiscal Responsibility Act (NAB, 1985) to provide and protect pension and health care plans. While laws and rules will likely deter some hiring of mature workers 65 and over because of soaring health care costs of this age group, it may not dampen hiring of older workers for small business firms whose benefit packages are not usually as extensive as those of large business (Yankelovich, Skelly & White, Inc., 1988). The American Association of Retired Persons (AARP, 1989a) has developed an "Age Equity Checklist for Employers" and numerous other materials such as, "How to Manage Older Workers" (AARP, 1987).

With estimated life expectancy at 81 years (for Americans who reach age 65), payroll costs and pensions for this group are rising, and we could see a 200–400% increase in costs for health insurance (AARP, 1989c). More companies are developing flexible retirement programs which will encourage mature workers to remain in the job market. NAB (1985) and AARP (1989c), note a growing trend by employers to hire older workers, with part-time work favored by both the employer and the older worker.

259

Active elderly employees, too, have noticed that many retirees are adrift in planning their leisure time, are bored, and, most of all, miss the contacts and sense of accomplishment they had while working. There are changes, too, in the attitudes of the MW toward retirement. These attitudinal and awareness shifts present a great opportunity for counselors to help MW set new goals and learn ways to enhance their lives. A process of self-assessment, listing priorities, analyzing personal resources, and interests and building action plans with target dates for completion can be helpful and will be further discussed in the section on counseling practices.

TRAINING PROGRAMS AND OPPORTUNITIES

In our world of rapid and massive change, learning and training for the older adult are needed, and, yet, because of fewer opportunities for training in the past, older adults may feel their learning skills are obsolete. They may also be less willing to take risks. Some employers may think the investment will be too costly if the older adult is near the end of his/ her employment. However, training sessions for elderly workers can be very cost effective when compared to the high rate of turnover of younger workers who also receive training (Goddard, 1987). Companies want people who can contribute to corporations immediately and, because of their work and human relations experience, mature workers may be more adept at this than inexperienced young employees.

In order to recruit and keep the MW, some organizations are developing a variety of work options with flexible hours, scheduling, and work patterns, such as: full-time, 30–40 hours/week; part-time, under 30 hours per week; seasonal; reduced hours; reduced pay; flextime and job sharing; compressed time, 40 hours in four days; expanded and reduced hours; scheduled hours/flexible tasks; and job rotation (Goddard, 1987).

Many companies' individual option plans are described in a pamphlet, "Using the Experience of a Lifetime" (AARP, 1988e). Kelly Services, Inc., ". . . has a special recruitment effort geared toward older persons and retirees because it found they often prefer the flexibility of part-time and short-time assignments" (AARP, 1988b, 7). Many part-time employees in Kelly's technical division are retirees who return to their former employers for temporary work. McDonalds' Corporation started their "McMasters' " program to train employees over age 55, with a special "job coach" who closely trains eight to ten employees per month. This program has retained approximately 71% of the McMasters employees. Minnesota Title Financial Corporation has a staff of "Interoffice messengers" and "foot messengers" averaging 67 years of age, who perform pickup and delivery work throughout the Minneapolis-St. Paul area. Their workforce includes former executives and others who want low stress work. In targeting retirees who were relocating into Arizona, the Western Savings and Loan Association actively hired retirees between the ages of 60 and 75 for full time employment in positions at all levels from tellers to branch managers and recognized a strong positive gain in rapport with elderly customers (AARP, 1988a; 1988c; 1988d).

EMERGING VIEWPOINTS AND OPPORTUNITIES

Multitudes of mature adults, 50 years and older, with longer life-spans than ever before are making transitions to new attitudes, and new life styles with new goals and activities (Dychtwald & Flower, 1989). Many retired adults are finding numerous reasons for reentering the work force. Longer life-expectancies, for example, may render previous financial plans for retirement inadequate for many of these older adults. Besides financial concerns, many of them want to be productive in new ways, continue to learn, be part of a group effort, and feel they are contributing to society.

Many of these adults return to the marketplace, choosing new career opportunities based on their interests, choice of work environment, and scheduling flexibility. Some are finding purpose and satisfaction in volunteer work for institutions and social causes.

To date, the marketplace has been recognizing this surge of re-entry mature workers with some ambivalence. Some businesses are feeling the pressure of high benefit costs for mature workers, while some mid-size and smaller companies with less extensive benefits packages are turning with interest to the mature experienced adult. A wide variety of options and flexible work plans and scheduling attractive to these workers can be cost effective for the employer. Mature workers can also choose contract projects or consulting work.

CAREER DEVELOPMENT RESOURCES

With today's global climate of change and substantial occupational shifts due to technology, economics, and other factors, people may need and can be helped to see numerous options. Changing times present a fertile field for career counselors to stimulate and facilitate transitions while fostering continuing growth for mature adults. Through guided self-assessments, identification of meaningful work options matching interests and values, and mastery of employability skills, with the career counselor as facilitator, the mature client can find meaningful employment. The senior author has found this group of clients stimulating, eager to learn, and highly motivated. Mature workers are a large and increasing market for counselors to serve.

A wide variety of career counseling and career development services are available to mature workers in numerous settings, through associations, churches, state employment services, continuing education, community colleges, and universities with career centers and counselors on staff. Career counselors in private practice, Job Service settings throughout the United States, and others working in-house in businesses and industries constitute other services available to mature workers seeking help.

CAREER COUNSELING ISSUES AND APPROACHES

Of all the areas requiring attention in working with the mature workers, no issue seems of greater importance than "ageism," implicit and

261

explicit discrimination against people on the basis of age (Butler, 1969; Hayslip, 1988; Cavanaugh, 1990). Unfortunately, ageism continues in spite of the existence of the Age Discrimination in Employment Act (ADEA) of 1974, as amended in 1976 and 1978) prohibiting discrimination in hiring, recruiting, discharge, remuneration, and related areas on the basis of age for people between the ages of 40 and 70. Hoyt's (1977) concept of psychosclerosis ("hardening of the attitudes") seems both an apt description and explanation of the outrageous barrier of ageism. That ageism knows no chronological boundaries is manifest in Hirsch's (1990) note that many elderly workers resent having to take orders from younger managers and thus, inadvertently, foster ageism. Ageism, replete with all its myths and attitudinal barriers, needs to be addressed at every opportunity. The elderly also need to know their rights and the human and financial costs of exercising legal redress to combat ageism.

Probably the greatest assistance any counselor can provide for the aging is stimulating awareness of ageism, and the importance of combating it on all quarters. Perhaps the worst practitioners of ageism are elderly people themselves, who unwittingly fall victim to ageism by assuming the truth of negatively slanted myths about the elderly and, in turn, by "living down to" the expectations of such myths as equations of aging with ill health, poor work habits, feebleness of mind and body, and accident proneness (Yankelovich, Skelly & White, Inc., 1985).

There may have been strong confidence and self-esteem during peak work years; but if a mature adult had been terminated in a job or had a suspended absence from the marketplace, he or she may have succumbed to the concept of the "elder within" (Dychtwald & Flower, 1989). Besides the "child within" made up of childhood memories, adults may also have an image of their later years. Adults may imagine ill health, loneliness, loss of competence, and loss of respect from younger adults. Counselors working with adults with this negative bias toward the later years will need to facilitate growth of self-esteem along with other attitudinal changes. If adults expect a long active life of fulfilling projects and contributions to the work world and to society, *that* can become their older experience. Older adults living successfully and contributing socially and to the work world invariably attribute their success to "attitude" and keeping mind, body, and spirit active (Dychtwald, 1990). As our society ages, biases about the elderly may begin to subside.

We believe that everyone has untapped multipotentiality. We further believe that a healthy self-esteem is one of the most important elements to be brought into or developed within the counseling process for career development and growth. Individual sessions, group sessions, seminars, programs, and course work, can include exercises to raise self-esteem as an essential ingredient of every session. The senior author has found in her practice that the mature adult with work and living experience is often a good candidate for this kind of personal growth.

As in any counseling, a major area of emphasis needs to be helping clients notice possibilities for choice. The sooner one becomes aware of choices, the sooner one can choose to exercise opportunities for choice. The immediate implication for counselors is to help clients notice they have choices, and to help clients learn to intelligently exploit or otherwise prudently handle choice. A crucial ingredient in this area is decision-making, and counselors can do much to help clients learn decision-making, risk-taking, and problem-solving strategies and processes so that when the times come to make important decisions, the clients are better able to make them than they would have been had they not had counseling. Looking back to the less fortunate and/or the most at risk elderly populations, the need for early planning, especially financial planning, and deciding is acute. Counselors need to help at risk elderly clients help themselves *before* they cross the line into poverty, with all its attendant problems and debilitating conditions.

INFORMATION RESOURCES

Perhaps the single best information and advocacy resource for counselors and the elderly is the American Association for Retired People (AARP). With over 27 million members and a large and multifaceted staff of paid and voluntary professionals, AARP conducts research, produces a multitude of publications, sponsors numerous programs, and lobbies on behalf of senior citizens. AARP can be a highly fruitful resource for information related to a myriad of topics, and counselors wanting to serve the ever burgeoning elderly population need to know about AARP and its resources.

CAREER DEVELOPMENT PROGRAMS

One unique pilot program being offered by the AARP Workers Equity Department is called AARP WORKS (AARP, 1988a; 1988b; 1988c; 1988d). It is in its third year and has been received with enthusiasm from the participants ranging in age from 50 to 65 years of age. Participants have included minorities, and men and women (more women than men), with a range of educational backgrounds. The program has had good attendance for a total of eight 3 hour sessions. The average age of participants has been 57.

The AARP WORKS program is set up to answer needs of the growing number of mid-life and older people seeking employment services including self-assessment and employability skills. AARP WORKS is attracting women returning to work without recent work experience and those seeking employment for the first time. Some of the participants have retired but want, and some need, meaningful employment. Still other participants are in transition, wanting to change jobs, or find new alternatives in existing jobs, such as flexible hours and different work settings. Some participants are dislocated workers needing information about retraining or recareering (AARP, 1988a).

The eight session AARP WORKS program consists of guided self-assessments; identifying interests, skills, and values; examining and targeting job options; identifying roadblocks to employment and strategies to deal with them; focusing on work-environment preferences; and collecting occupational information. Lessons on resume writing and developing several appropriate resumes are also included. Instruction in job interview skills and role-playing practice are important segments of the seminars. Leader and participant manuals developed by leaders in career counseling and other specialized experts include homework exercises for the participants. Large group and small group work, role-playing, and networking contribute greatly to the success of the program. Seminars with similar goals and career planning sessions are also offered by some state employment commission Job Service Offices. Depending upon the location and needs, there may be white collar seminars for professionals and blue collar seminars for trade workers and skilled workers.

Often, experienced executives have rusty employability skills because they have not used the skills for years. They need help in resume writing as well as strategies for the job hunt and other aspects of career development such as values and priorities assessments. Many agencies, organizations, churches, universities, military bases, and non-profit organizations offer career planning and counseling, assessment, and job hunting strategies. Job Clubs all over the United States offer group help, networking, and moral support (National Employment Weekly, 1990).

Richard Bolles (1990a), offers many suggestions and options to those in the mid-life to older years:

- Ease into retirement, slowly reducing requirements;
- Work vigorously for a final promotion;
- Try for a major achievement in the arena of your choice;
- Work through a job transition;
- Retire early with all the bonuses and benefits you can collect;
- Start your own business;
- Be creative with other ideas and possibilities. (36–43)

Bolles' message seems to be: widen the parameters of the belief system, get creative, investigate, gather information, analyze the benefits and risks, set goals, and start action!

In guiding mature adults in the process of career development, job matches, and the job hunt, the senior author frequently gives instruction on the body language of success (Delmar, 1986). She has participants practice alert, active youthful posture, energetic walking, warm handshakes, sitting in and rising from a chair with ease as they role-play scenes to develop self-confidence. Upon asking personnel directors and job interviewers about their impressions of a mature applicant during a job interview, the senior author was told by most that they did not make judgments on the basis of mere chronological age information in the application. Instead, they paid attention to the applicant's keen interest and non-verbal communication in seeking workers who seem physically fit and active.

There are numerous opportunities for counselors to work in programs for the mature adult. Continuing education programs at community colleges, colleges, and other schools, professional, social and service organizations, churches, and military bases, provide opportunities for teachers, counselors, consultants, or volunteers.

Some sources of information valuable for use in this type of work can be obtained from the National Occupational Information Coordinating Committee (NOICC) and respective State Occupational Information Coordinating Committees (SOICC). Resources include Department of Labor publications (*Occupational Outlook Handbook, Dictionary of Occupational Titles*, plus supplements), area job outlook reports by state economic research and analysis departments, state labor market reviews, county employment patterns, worker trait dictionaries, chamber of commerce newsletters, business and industry reports, and numerous library references on career fields. NOICC'S *Using Labor Market Information in Career Exploration and Decision Making* (NOICC, 1986) is another excellent resource guide.

There are many computer-based systems focused on occupational information, training and education, schools and colleges, such as Choices, Coin, Discover, GIS and SIGI Plus. The National Older Workers Information System (NOWIS) (AARP, 1989c) offers resources for mature workers and work seekers. There are numerous programs and printed guides and a growing body of information and guidance for the mature and elderly population. Blocker, in *Career Actualization and Life Planning* (1986), presents a life-planning work book for mature people in transition. In an eight-step program, including self-assessment, clarifying values, motivation, developing goals with an action plan, implementing self-management, coping with stress, problem-solving, and decision-making, the reader can work through the process on his or her own or with a group.

FORECASTING

An exciting time for the increasing numbers of mature workers is beginning. An awareness of the growth of this age group is evident in politics, marketing, education, health care, physical fitness programs and products; leisure, travel and entertainment services; housing; transportation; communications; security systems; family and extended family relationships; and product service development, to name just a few areas. As the numbers of mature people increase, society will be evaluating the liabilities and assets of an aging population. There will be many costs in emotional pain, stress, strained relationships, and monetary costs of health care for the elderly. Many assets of mature people will surface as they contribute to productivity and services in the marketplace in paid or volunteer work.

Corporations and small businesses are finding "gold" in these mature workers who apply their motivation, patience, dependability, conscientiousness, and understanding of human nature to their work. Many flexible plans and options are being woven into the fabric of the work world to accommodate this segment of society.

With 21 million new jobs coming into being by the year 2000, and fewer qualified replacement workers in the 16 to 24 age group, mature workers can contribute positively to the nation's economy (OOQ, 1989). Their experience can add strength and flexibility as America rolls up its sleeves to compete globally. Although the number of mature workers between ages 55 and 64 will decrease through the early nineties, at some point between 1995 and 2000, this age group will be the fastest growing segment of the labor market. Besides many creative options and flexible plans attractive to the older worker, temporary "projects" may be enticing to semi-retired professionals. A unique temporary service, *Prime Timers in Dallas, Texas*, for example, serves mature workers over 50. A wide range of temporary projects as well as temporary conventional office and service work are offered.

Many companies have a "job bank" of their own retirees who wish to work part-time or on special projects. Over 44 percent of present-day employers use part-time help today in a wide variety of task and job description levels (Dychtwald, 1990; AARP, 1989c). Many companies include in this part-time force a large number of mature workers.

Forecasters are predicting changes in the structure of work—with a wide variety of settings and flexible pension plans (AARP, 1989c; Dychtwald, 1990; Dychtwald & Flower, 1989; Ruhm, 1990). Besides flextime, there is also flexplace, an alternative worksite to the home office which can be attractive to many workers from executives to computer data operators and clerical workers. Alternative work sites can be in homes, recreational areas, or satellite offices near homes of most employees. Arrangements can include alternating, part-time in the home office and part-time in the alternative site. Time can be saved, avoiding high stress in freeway peak-traffic travel. The concept of the hour bank is similar to flextime, setting the required number of hours to work over a given time, and then saving extra hours of work with the privilege of drawing on them for leisure hours. Other versions include time-banked against dollars or bartered for other benefits. These flexible work schedules provide all workers, especially mature workers, with more options.

Portable pension plans that the worker can carry with him or her as he or she changes jobs and employers are valuable to the mature worker. Changes in work and leisure time, delays in retirement, a cyclical life style, looping from work to education, to work, to leisure, to retirement, and back again to work, will become more prevalent.

Mature workers with varied experiences, education, and wisdom will become more and more valuable in future diverse work situations to understand and work harmoniously with others (Goddard, 1987). For the mature worker, the extended work life can be one of quality and giving to future generations as well as one of continued self-development. Career counselors can play a major role in facilitating growth and development for mature workers. With greater awareness, more opportunities for choice, and some help, more and more seniors can enjoy and share their work and lives as have Jill, Harold, Janice, John, Ruth, David, and Gilbert.

REFERENCES

American Association for Counseling and Development. (1988). Ethical Standards. Alexandria, VA: AACD.

American Association of Retired Persons. (Undated). AARP WORKS. Fact sheet. Washington, DC: AARP Worker Equity, D12821.

American Association of Retired Persons. (1989a). Age equity in employment: A checklist for employers. Washington, DC: AARP Worker Equity, D13825.

American Association of Retired Persons. (1989b). Coming to America: Special issue on older minorities in work and retirement. *Working Age, Special Issues*, 1–10.

American Association of Retired Persons. (1989c). A look to the future: Home is where the office is. *Working Age, 5*. November-December, 3.

American Association of Retired Persons. (1988a). America's changing work force. Washington, DC: AARP Worker Equity, D12633.

American Association of Retired Persons. (1988b). How to manage older workers. Washington, DC: AARP Worker Equity, D13288.

American Association of Retired Persons. (1988c) How to recruit older workers. Washington, DC: AARP Worker Equity, D13279.

American Association of Retired Persons. (1988d). How to train older workers. Washington, DC: AARP Worker Equity, D13287.

American Association of Retired Persons. (1988e). Using the experience of a lifetime. Washington, DC: AARP Worker Equity, D13353.

American Association of Retired Persons. (1986). Roundtable on older women in the work force. Washington, DC: AARP Worker Equity, author.

Blocker, D. (1986). *Career actualization and life planning.* Denver: Love Publishing.

Bolles, R.N. (1990a). The decade of decisions. *Modern Maturity*, February-March 36–46.

Bolles, R.N. (1990b). *What color is your parachute?* Berkeley, CA: Ten Speed Press.

Butler, R.N. (1969). Ageism: Another form of bigotry. *The Gerontologist, 9*, 243–246.

Cavanaugh, J.C. (1990). *Adult development and aging.* Belmont, CA: Wadsworth Publishing Company.

Cetron, M., and Davies, O. (1989). *American renaissance: Our life at the turn of the 21st century.* New York: St. Martin's Press.

Commission of Precollege Guidance and Counseling. (1986). *Keeping the options open: Recommendations.* New York: The College Board.

Crystal, S. (1988). Work and retirement in the twenty-first century. *Generations.* San Francisco, CA: American Society on Aging, Spring, 60–63.

Delmar, K. (1987). The body language of success: Winning moves. Cassette series. Chicago, IL: Nightingale-Conant Corp.

Dychtwald, K., and Flower, J. (1989). *Age wave.* New York: Bantam Books.

Dychtwald, K. (1990). How to play the aging game to win . . . big. Privileged Breakthrough Information. New York, NY: Boardroom Reports, Inc., January 1.

Engels, D., and Muro, J. (1986). Silver to gold: The alchemy, potential and maturing of ACES and *CES. Counselor Education and Supervision, 25*, 289–305.

Friedan, B. (1990). From the feminine mystique to the aging mystique. Unpublished speech. Scottsdale, AZ: National Career Development Association Conference, January.

Goddard, R.W. (1987). How to harness America's gray power. Costa Mesa, CA: *Personnel Journal*, May, 1–5.

Goldstein, C. (1990). The not so obvious signs of wrongful termination. Privileged Breakthrough Information. New York, NY: Boardroom Reports, Inc., February, 15.

Hayslip, B., and Panek, P.E. (1989). *Adult development and aging*. New York: Harper and Row.

Hirsh, J.S. (1990). Older workers chafe under young managers. *Wall Street Journal*, 26 February, B1.

Hoyt, K.B. (1977). Career education. Arlington, TX: Unpublished address to the Texas Vocational Guidance Association.

Kiernan, M. (1989). Best jobs for the future. *U.S. News & World Report*, September 25, 60–62.

Mackaronis, C.G. (1986). The U.S. Age Discrimination in Employment Act. *Aging International 13*, Washington, DC: International Federation on Aging, 15–16.

Moon, M., and Husbeck, J. (1989). Options for extending work life. *Generations*. San Francisco: American Society on Aging, Spring, 27–30.

Mowsesian, R. (1986). *Golden goals, rusted realities: Work and aging in America*. Far Hills, NJ: New Horizon Press.

National Alliance of Business. (1987). Invest in experience: New directions for an aging work force. Washington, DC: author.

National Employment Weekly. (1990). Friday Feature Section. *Wall Street Journal*.

Richmond, L.J., Tiedman, D.V., and Wrenn, C.G. (1990). Current thinking on empowering individuals through career development. Unpublished presentation. Scottsdale, AZ: National Career Development Association Conference, January.

Ruhm, C.J. (1990). Bridge jobs and partial retirement. *Journal of Labor Economics, 8*, 482–501.

Sinick, D. (1984). Problems of work and retirement for an aging population. In N. Gysbergs, et al., *Designing careers*. San Francisco: Jossey-Bass.

Striner, H.E. (1984). Changes in work and society, 1984–2004: Impact on education, training and career counseling. In N. Gysbers et al., *Designing careers*. San Francisco: Jossey-Bass.

United States Department of Labor. (1990). Tomorrow's jobs. In *Occupational Outlook Handbook*. Washington, DC: U.S. Government Printing Office, 8–13.

United States Department of Labor. (1989). The labor force. *Occupational Outlook Quarterly, 33*, 4–12.

Ventrell-Monsees, C. and Mackaronis, C.G. (Undated). The legal A,B,C's of hiring older workers. Washington, DC: AARP Worker Equity.

Yankelovich, Skelly and White, Inc. (1986). Washington, DC: AARP Worker Equity, D12429.

CHAPTER 15

Preretirement Programming: Needs and Responses

Bruce R. Fretz
Psychology Department
University of Maryland
College Park, Maryland

Marilyn W. Merikangas
Independent Practice
Silver Spring, Maryland

THE SCOPE OF PRERETIREMENT NEEDS

A 42-year old man: "The job offer was really terrific and I know I would be a lot happier with the challenge there than with my present work. But if I stay here, in 13 years I can retire; if I take the new job I will have to wait at least 20 years or more."

A 39-year-old woman: "Even though I really liked working in the health food store, and the wages were enough for me to get by on, I woke up one day and realized that here I was, a divorcee in a job that would never lead to any pension and only minimal levels of social security. Scared? You bet! I had my resume typed by the end of that day."

A 46-year-old lieutenant colonel: "Well, I'm not sure I want to call it retirement. I've got more than 20 years, and it's clear that I'm not going to go any higher up. I'm single and I've made some good investments and actually could retire. Stay, get out, start a new career—what should I do?"

A 54-year-old woman: "I've never thought much about retirement. But now this early retirement, lump-sum offer seems really attractive. I have just three months to make up my mind. I guess I'll retire since it's an offer I may not get again. I'll just get another job if it turns out not to be enough money."

A 58-year-old man: "I took early retirement because I never really had liked my work. But, what with inflation and my wife's medical bills, we're just not making it. I've got to find some kind of paid work; what am I going to do? Who is going to hire me at this age?"

A 68-year-old woman: "Retire? Me? Never! My husband retired five years ago, and he hasn't done anything worth a hoot since then."

A 79-year-old man: "Retirement? Best thing that I ever did. If I had it to do over, I'd take early retirement."

For most people, the term retirement conjures up the image of gray-haired elders. The preceding examples demonstrate that almost every stage of career development, from initial choice onward, may be affected by retirement issues. In this chapter, first presented will be the shifting meanings, theories, and data about what leads to a retirement decision. How that decision potentially affects both the final years of one's paid career and the adjustments of retirement itself will then be briefly discussed. The second and major part of this chapter will complement this knowledge about retirement and career decision-making with practical experiences gained from conducting psychologically-oriented retirement preparation programs. Each of the phases of approaching and experiencing retirement seems to come with its own special needs and resistances.

The number of people becoming eligible for retirement in almost any organization is a staggering figure. The percentage of persons surviving into their 60s and beyond is rapidly approaching 20%. The typical retiree will now spend 20% of his/her life in retirement, as compared to just 3% in 1900 (Dennis, 1989). This increasing life span, combined with the increasing possibilities for and acceptance of early retirement (Parnes, 1981, 1989), often results in a fourth of the work force in many organizations being eligible for retirement.

How does retirement eligibility affect the job performance and career choices of workers? How can companies keep older workers who have special contributions to make? How can companies assist stagnated workers with retirement planning? How satisfied are a company's retirees compared to those from other companies? Does the satisfaction of a company's retirees affect current company image and employee performance? Can steps be taken to maximize performance and good will of employees eligible for retirement? Obviously, these are questions to which any career development specialist in an industrial setting would like to have answers. For practitioners working with retirees in educational and community-based service settings, the focus will be on the kinds of career and social support services that maximize adjustment to the retirement.

The questions are easy to ask. The beginnings of answers are found in the growing amount of literature on both retirement planning (Dennis, 1984, 1989; Migliaccio & Cairo, 1981; Kragie, Gerstein, & Lichtman, 1989) and the consequences of retirement (Palmore, Fillenbaum, & George, 1984; Palmore, Burchett, Fillenbaum, George, & Wallman, 1985), and the increasingly positive evaluations of preretirement counseling programs (Glamser & DeJong, 1975; Morrow, 1981; Shonksmith, 1983; Kamouri & Cavanaugh, 1986). The latter authors were able to show that retirees who had participated in preretirement programs became more satisfied in retirement while nonattendees became less satisfied. This empirical knowledge, combined with the experiences of career development specialists who have company resources to develop and test different approaches to retirement preparation, can provide much useful information for planning preretirement programs. Moreover, such data can provide a promising foundation for programs to help both those preretirees suffering from pervasive anxiety *and* the approximately one-fifth (Parnes, 1981) of all retirees who will come to regret having made the decision to retire.

MEANINGS OF RETIREMENT AND IMPLICATIONS FOR CAREER SERVICES

Company Perspectives

Career development specialists working with retirement issues usually have to reconcile the diverse meanings attributed to retirement by their employers (the companies) and their constituents (the employees whom they serve). The fit is seldom an exact one and is often an uncomfortably oppositional one. Certainly the potential support from a company for retirement programming is related to its own perspectives and attitudes toward retirement. Although retirement has been described from an organization's viewpoint as a necessary and positive process (Donahue, Orbach, & Pollak, 1969; Walker & Lazer, 1978), at the individual company level retirement is often seen, along with health insurance costs, as one of the inevitable penalties of running a company. The rapidly escalating costs of pensions and the high cost of maintaining experienced workers in the absence of legal mandatory retirement systems, all combine to make some employers want to avoid the retirement issue altogether. Simultaneously maintaining profitability, good employee morale, and positive public image often seem an impossible goal. Career development specialists may contribute to the development of retirement programs in their own settings by education of their company managers regarding the benefits of such programs for current employees and company image, as well as for new retirees. Several useful resources that demonstrate the value of employers' involvement in retirement preparation are Fleisher (1981), Kalt and Kohn (1975), Montana (1986), "Retirement Preparation" (1979), Shaw and Grubbs (1981), and "What IBM Retirees Think of Retirement" (1981).

Public Attitudes

Approximately two decades ago, retirement was viewed as about as acceptable as being a welfare cheat. Graebner's (1980) book *A History of Retirement* and empirical research over the past 20 years (Goudy, Powers, Keith, & Reger, 1980; Karp, 1989), charts an amazing shift to much more positive attitudes toward retirement. Workers currently eligible for and entering retirement are doing so in the most positive context in the history of the industrial world. Of course, the reverse side of the coin is that the increased number of people retiring has made retirement *costs* a major social issue as we look ahead to the twenty-first century. This creates the cruel irony that just as retirement becomes a clearly acceptable action, more and more companies (and the government) are making changes that make it less possible financially at the current modal age level, the early 60s.

271

Although the general shift in the public's view can be well-documented, this shift must not be allowed to conceal the tremendous range of views toward retirement that still exists on the individual level. Although significant numbers of people look forward to retirement in terms of freedom and activity, many still fear retirement as a period of passivity, monotony, and death. Identifying and understanding one's own attitude toward retirement is a major step in preparing for retirement. What leads to positive versus negative attitudes about retirement has been investigated again and again, yet the data remain quite inconclusive. Health and finances are most frequently cited as the major contributors to a satisfying retirement (Parnes, 1981). Other studies have found these factors to be less important than career factors (e.g., attitudes toward one's job) (Kamp, 1989; Fretz, Kluge, Ossana, Jones, & Merikangas, 1989). Not surprisingly, a less positive attitude toward one's job leads to a more positive attitude toward retirement. Recently, Fretz et al. (1989) found that anxiety and depression about retirement were *best* predicted by lower levels of planfulness and self-efficacy. More and more, the data suggest that psychological variables may be more critical than money and health in making the transition to retirement (Ekerdt, 1989).

Along with the general trend toward a more positive view of retirement is the seemingly contradictory phenomenon that a given individual's view toward retirement changes as retirement approaches. Although the view of retirement tends to be positive in early middle age, it becomes less positive as the actual retirement approaches (Ekerdt, Bosse, & Mogey, 1980). Kemp (1989) and Fretz et al. (1989) both recently found that high levels of job satisfaction and "unfinished" agendas at work are related to less positive views about retirement.

Changing attitudes toward retirement have been accompanied by an increase both in the percentage of those planning to retire by age 65 (Sheppard, 1981b) and in the variety and complexity of the actions that constitute retirement. Again, up until the last decades, retirement was largely synonymous with a withdrawal from the work force. Theories of disengagement were predominant (Morgan, 1980). The belief was that most people would withdraw not only from work but also from the friends and activities of their working years. More recent research shows disengagement occurs for only a small portion of retirees. Even in earlier decades, substantial portions of retirees who totally withdrew from the work force maintained high levels of avocational, recreational, and altruistic activities. As will be described in the community-based retirement programs section of this chapter, services that help a person stay involved in activities following disengagement from work are the most promising interventions for satisfactory retirement adjustments and increased longevity.

Diversity of Options

The increased good health of many persons in their 60s and 70s, plus the increasing number of persons in their 50s eligible for retirement pensions, has created an entirely new form of retirement. It might more properly be called "late-life career change," in contrast to the already popularized "midlife career change" (e.g., Levinson, Darrow, Klein, Levinson, & McKee, 1978). Certainly there are many similarities between the information and decision-making needs for late-life career changers and those outlined for midlife changers. A very major difference that makes late-life career change a more flexible and exciting exploration is the economic security (pension) underlying this change. The pension guarantees minimal income and may provide sufficient income to maintain the current life style; new work is chosen primarily for noneconomic reasons. Parnes' data (1981, 1989) and other studies suggest that 10 to 33% of all retirees engage in some kind of paid employment. Of those who do choose a "second career," a recent survey (Bird, 1989) indicates some 53% working full time, with a third of these "working retirees" planning to retire from these jobs by the age of 70. Nearly half have no plans at all to retire; the remainder plan to work on into their 70s and 80s. The current economic situation, a larger number of early retirees, and better health in later years may all be contributing to these trends. Parnes (1989) and Sheppard (1981a) both review data that suggest that even a greater percentage of retirees would work if more part time, decently paid opportunities were available. Whatever the reason, preretirees and recent retirees may begin to use career information services as much as employees in early stages of career development.

Part time employment in one's current job constitutes a special form of "career change." Where shortages of skilled personnel exist, part time employment in the same career after retirement is an increasingly popular option. Continuing part time work in the present job is the most popular work option of retirement eligible persons (Usher, 1981). The high percent preferring that option surprised employers and researchers alike. There is a growing interest among some companies in providing these opportunities rather than having the worker retire and find part time work with competing companies. Theoretically, companies can benefit from such policies in two ways. First, workers not maximally productive relative to their current salary will be working less than full time, thereby reducing company expenses. Second, outstanding employees who would choose full retirement over full time work might choose to work when offered the possibility of continuing on a part time basis. Various forms of part time retirement and trial retirement may well receive more attention in the 1990s.

It would not be appropriate to end this section without acknowledging another "retirement option" available—not to retire. Retirement eligibles who have not retired demonstrate the poignancy of the adage "not to decide is to decide." Choosing to work means no time for the activities and interests that retirees pursue alone or with their families. Work can alleviate fears of change, boredom, depression, loneliness, or increased intimacy. Interestingly, just over 20 years ago a retiree was considered a "loafer." Now the nonretiree may be looked upon as some sort of neurotic workaholic or an old codger who keeps young fresh blood from entering the company. In short, services may be needed for the "unretired but eligible-for-retirement" just as much as for those planning to act upon their eligibility.

Transition

Ultimately, retirement in any form is a major transition that calls for new roles and competencies. Seibert and Seibert (1986) aptly describe some of the retirement transition challenges in their article "Retirement: Crisis or Opportunity." Although "winging it" may work in well-established roles, the same behavior often leads to painful crashes in new roles. The management of transitions from a counseling viewpoint has been well articulated in a special issue of *The Counseling Psychologist* (Brammer & Abrego, 1981; Schlossberg, 1981). It defines cognitive information, social support, and a planning scheme as critical elements in effective transition interventions.

The next section provides critical information that retirees need to manage this transition. The concluding sections are devoted to descriptions of interventions and programs that help provide planning and social support at various preretirement and retirement phases.

AGING AND RETIREMENT: THE RELUCTANT MARRIAGE OF TWO SETS OF MYTHS

Aging Myths

It is hardly a secret that our older years are not viewed as the prime era of life, even though they are often referred to as the golden years. Palmore (1977, 1981) identified 50 facts of aging that are poorly known by almost everyone from younger people to middle-aged and aged people (see Table 1). Preretirees and anyone planning to work with preretirees, need to become familiar with these facts. Misunderstandings about these facts constitute a set of myths that have tremendous impact on attitudes toward retirement. Reichard, Livson, and Peterson showed, as early as 1962, that those with better attitudes about aging made the best adjustments to retirement. Because retirement comes only after many years of service, it is, of course, synonymous with being "older" in the minds of many preretirees. Even though retirement from work has gained many positive attractions, fears of aging such as fear of a decline in mental and physical health and well-being may pervasively color and overbalance any positive views about retirement itself.

With so little well-established information about retirement, it is not surprising that there are myths about retirement as well as myths of aging. The professional experiences of the present authors with preretirees have led to the specification of 10 myths about retirement. When asked questions related to these 10 myths, the typical retiree answers only an average of three of the items correctly; moreover, the correct answers are distributed across the items. In the following paragraphs, each myth and its folklore is described and then the appropriate evidence is cited to counteract the myth.

As will be seen, each of the myths has a "grain of truth." For a few individuals, retirement, *like any other stage of life,* may be a period of poor health, poor finances, radical changes in life style, or radical changes in personal relationships. Unfortunately, selective perception of these few instances has led to the development of many negative views about retirement. These views have been strangely resistant to contrary data published again and again in the last 10 to 20 years. In examining these myths, it will become clear that preretirement attitudes have perhaps *the* most potent influence on what happens in retirement. Until people are cognizant of these retirement myths, they may enter retirement with perceptual handicaps.

Retirement Myths

Dissatisfaction. Myth 1: Approximately one-half of all retirees find retirement less enjoyable than they expected (false). Surveys of *preretirees* often find the majority thinking that retirement will be a less desirable time than preretirement. However, when surveys are conducted of *actual* retirees, 80% or more report that their preretirement expectations have been fulfilled or exceeded (Palmore, Fillenbaum, & George, 1984, 1985; Parnes, 1981, 1989). In the 1960s, retirees were reporting high levels of satisfaction if they were in good health (Streib & Schneider, 1971). Parnes most recently (1989) provided data showing that men who retired voluntarily were happier than comparable men still working full time.

Table 1
Items from Palmore's Facts on Aging Quizzes

(Underlined answers are the correct ones)

T F̲ 1. The majority of old people (past age 65) are senile (i.e. defective memory, disoriented, or demented).

T̲ F 2. All five senses tend to decline in old age.

T̲ F̲ 3. Most old people have no interest in, or capacity for, sexual relations.

T̲ F 4. Lung capacity tends to decline in old age.

T̲ F̲ 5. The majority of old people feel miserable most of the time.

T̲ F 6. Physical strength tends to decline in old age.

T̲ F̲ 7. At least one-tenth of the aged are living in long-stay institutions (i.e. nursing homes, mental hospitals, homes for the aged, etc.).

T̲ F 8. Aged drivers have fewer accidents per person than drivers under age 65.

T̲ F̲ 9. Most older workers cannot work as effectively as younger workers.

T̲ F 10. About 80% of the aged are healthy enough to carry out their normal activities.

T̲ F̲ 11. Most old people are set in their ways and unable to change.

T̲ F 12. Old people usually take longer to learn something new.

T̲ F̲ 13. It is almost impossible for most old people to learn new things.

T̲ F 14. The reaction time of most old people tends to be slower than the reaction time of younger people.

(Table 1 continued)

T	F	15.	In general, most old people are pretty much alike.
T	F	16.	The majority of old people are seldom bored.
T	F	17.	The majority of old people are socially isolated and lonely.
T	F	18.	Older workers have fewer accidents than younger workers.
T	F	19.	Over 15% of the U.S. population are now age 65 or over.
T	F	20.	Most medical practitioners tend to give low priority to the aged.
T	F	21.	The majority of older people have incomes below the poverty level (as defined by the federal government).
T	F	22.	The majority of old people are working or would like to have some kind of work to do (including housework and volunteer work).
T	F	23.	Older people tend to become more religious as they age.
T	F	24.	The majority of old people are seldom irritated or angry.
T	F	25.	The health and socioeconomic status of older people (compared to younger people) in the year 2000 will probably be about the same as now.
T	F	26.	A person's height tends to decline in old age.
T	F	27.	More older persons (over 65) have chronic illnesses that limit their activity than younger persons.
T	F	28.	Older persons have more acute (short-term) illnesses than persons under 65.
T	F	29.	Older persons have more injuries in the home than persons under 65.
T	F	30.	Older workers have less absenteeism than younger workers.
T	F	31.	The life expectancy of Blacks at age 65 is about the same as Whites.
T	F	32.	The life expectancy of men at age 65 is about the same as women's.
T	F	33.	Medicare pays over half of the medical expenses for the aged.
T	F	34.	Social Security benefits automatically increase with inflation.
T	F	35.	Supplemental Security Income guarantees a minimum income for needy aged.
T	F	36.	The aged do not get their proportionate share (about 11%) of the nation's income.
T	F	37.	The aged have higher rates of criminal victimization than persons under 65.
T	F	38.	The aged are more fearful of crime than are persons under 65.
T	F	39.	The aged are the most law-abiding of all adult groups according to official statistics.
T	F	40.	There are two widows for each widower among the aged.
T	F	41.	More of the aged vote than any other age group.
T	F	42.	There are proportionately more older persons in public office than in the total population.
T	F	43.	The proportion of Blacks among the aged is growing.
T	F	44.	Participation in voluntary organizations (churches and clubs) tends to decline among the healthy aged.

T <u>F</u> 45. The majority of aged live alone.

<u>T</u> F 46. About 3% more of the aged have incomes below the official poverty level than the rest of the population.

<u>T</u> F 47. The rate of poverty among aged Blacks is about three times as high as among aged Whites.

T <u>F</u> 48. Older persons who reduce their activity tend to be happier than those who remain active.

T <u>F</u> 49. When the last child leaves home, the majority of parents have serious problems adjusting to their "empty nest."

<u>T</u> F 50. The proportion widowed is decreasing among the aged.

Note. From "Facts on Aging: A Short Quiz" by E. Palmore, 1977, *The Gerontologist, 17,* p. 315–320. Copyright 1977 by the Gerontological Society of America. Adapted by permission. Also from "The Facts on Aging Quiz: Part Two" by E. Palmore, 1981, *The Gerontologist, 21,* p. 431–437. Copyright 1981 by The Gerontological Society of America. Adapted by permission.

As noted, a minority of dissatisfied retirees are apparently sufficient "evidence" for many to believe that most retirees are dissatisfied. In seminars when retirees have been brought in to talk to preretirees about their own adjustments and satisfaction, sometimes the preretirees have made accusations that program organizers specifically sought out happy retirees. Similarly, researchers are often amazed at the degree of satisfaction among some retirees who are actually quite impoverished financially or who are experiencing significant health problems.

Critical adjustment periods. Myth 2: The most difficult time to adjust to retirement is during the first few months (false). Folklore about the stress of leaving the work setting and adapting to a new life style in retirement leads many to believe that the first few months will be the crisis-laden ones. Ironically, quite the contrary may be true. The first few months (even the first or second year) of retirement is what Atchley (1976) called the honeymoon period. Reichard, Livson, and Petersen (1962) reported that retirees were immensely surprised by how much they enjoyed the first few months of retirement.

Income and satisfaction. Myth 3: Happiness in retirement is strongly related to the amount of retirement income received (false). Although one often assumes that the more money one has, the happier one will be in retirement, at best this relationship is only true for the lower socioeconomic levels. Once retirement income is above the basic subsistence level, the relationship between amount of retirement income and happiness disappears. In other words, although retirees with an income of $20,000 may be twice as happy as those with an income of $10,000, it is not true that an income of $40,000 will make them twice as happy as those with an income of $20,000. Reichard, Livson, and Petersen (1962) and Streib and Schneider (1971) obtained data that demonstrate that *anxieties* about financial status are related to adjustment to retirement. The actual dollar amounts, however, are not nearly as critical. Many very poor retirees, even those who have to change their life styles significantly to live on half their prior income, are quite satisfied. At the other extreme, some very wealthy retirees become obsessed with worries about inflation and "impending" needs for major life style changes.

Averages that provide some crude guidelines for financial planning for retirement are suggested by studies of income patterns in retirement. The average reduction in income ranges from 20% to 50%, depending on the study. There is also reasonable evidence (Atchley, 1976) that feeling poor may be a more critical factor in adjusting to retirement than actually being poor. There is probably considerable merit in preretirees' realizing (1) that more than a quarter or a third reduction in income will result in their having to make significant changes in current life style, and (2) that they may also find themselves relatively disadvantaged compared to other retirees in their social circles.

If a one-third income reduction brings a retiree below the U.S. published figures for subsistence levels, hard life realities will make adjustment to retirement very difficult unless a retiree is willing to receive some governmental assistance for housing or food costs. Although these subsistence figures may seem low, if a couple is living on one non-professional worker's Social Security, they may well fall below the subsistence level. There are also hundreds of thousands of retirees, generally women, who have typically not had as many working years to accumulate large pensions. If they elect or are forced by health reasons to take early retirement, they will fall below subsistence levels.

Health. *Myth 4:* Retired persons are less healthy than persons of the same age who are still working (false). Again, despite evidence to the contrary for over 20 years (Reichard, Livson, & Petersen, 1962) and reaffirmation of the good health of retirees as compared to similarly aged workers (Palmore, Fillenbaum, & George, 1984), many still focus on the few retirees they know with significant health problems. Again, there is simply inadequate attention to the "base rate" (i.e., how frequently illness is occurring in all persons in the age group of retirees). As indicated earlier by Palmore (see Table 1), while older persons do have a greater accumulation of *chronic* health problems, there is no increase in the rate of acute health problems.

Almost never cited is the evidence of Strieb and Schneider (1971) that retirement actually *improved* the health of a number of workers who retired in relatively poor health. Although this finding may be inexplicable from a standard medical viewpoint, it will come as no surprise to those in the field of behavioral medicine. Their work demonstrates repeatedly the positive health effects of changes in life style.

Early death. *Myth 5:* Retirees are more likely to die prematurely than persons still working (false). It is all too easy to point to persons who die within a couple of years after retirement while many of their age mates still live. "Evidence" of this sort was cited in the 1970s to argue against mandatory retirement. Palmore, Fillenbaum, and George (1984) have presented convincing data that when one compares people who retire *in good health* with those of similar age who do not retire, there is no evidence of a relationship of retirement to age of death. In short, it is state of health, not retirement, that predicts age of death. Selective perception maintains the myth, as we well remember the "tragedy" of the retiree who dies and "forget" to note the worker of similar age who died on the job.

Workaholics. *Myth 6:* Persons who are workaholics most often have the hardest time adjusting to retirement (false). This myth is based on the assumption that people heavily involved in their work will experience an identity crisis when leaving work (Burgess, 1960). Atchley (1976) clearly demonstrated in his study of retirees that work-oriented people could adapt well to careers of leisure. As with all the other myths, there is a grain of truth in this one. Some workers do very much miss their jobs and consequently experience more difficulty in adjusting to retirement. Others may succumb to the "busy ethic" just as they did to the "work ethic," filling time with activity as an expected role rather than as a desired role.

Research by Johnson and Strother (1962), Glamser (1976, 1981), Goudy, Powers, and Keith (1975) and Fretz et al. (1989) all shed some light on who is at risk for experiencing difficulty when leaving the work force. Those who are involved in and enjoy their work primarily because of the interpersonal interactions seldom experience difficulty. They seem readily able to replace those interactions in retirement. On the other hand, those whose involvement in work comes from a fondness for the work itself may have a more difficult time. This is especially true if they do not readily replace that work activity with some other "all-consuming activity" in retirement.

Atchley (1976) found that many workaholics carried their same patterns of high activity level into new retirement activities and thereby made very successful adjustments. The work of Goudy, Powers, and Keith (1975) suggests that attitudes toward retirement are another critical factor. If the workaholic sees retirement as a good thing, he or she is very likely to make a good adjustment. According to research, the person at highest risk is one who is heavily involved in work and does not want to retire but is forced to do so.

Relocation. *Myth 7:* Approximately half of all retirees move to another state sometime during their retirement (false). The inducements of sunny Florida, Arizona, and retirement communities across the Sun Belt engender the belief that great numbers of retirees move to these sunny climates. Extensive studies of the moving patterns of retirees have produced results that surprised even the researchers. Lawton (1980) found that from 1975 to 1978 only about 5% of the retiree age group moved. This was the *lowest* percentage moving for any age group measured between the ages of 20 and over 75. Furthermore, of the very small percentages that did move, only 17% moved to another state. More than two-thirds actually moved within the same county. When working with groups of preretirees, it becomes evident that major moves are in the plans of relatively few.

Lawton's (1980) book, *Environment and Aging,* is highly recommended as background reading for anyone working with preretirees and retirees. He provides an outstanding summary of the advantages and disadvantages of various kinds of residences and geographical locations both by

279

regional and by urban-rural differences. Perhaps the most surprising finding to the age group now approaching retirement and currently in retirement is the higher life satisfaction levels in more urban as compared to rural areas. Lawton's explanation is the much higher level of services in urban areas. Unless good health and significant financial resources abound, rural living can prove to be more difficult for retirees. This finding is a somewhat cruel irony if one reviews the retirement books in the 1950s. They were oriented primarily toward retiring to farms and rural areas.

Marital problems. *Myth 8:* Marital problems usually increase in retirement (false). It is easy to point out what seem to be stable marriages that fail in retirement. A marriage with poor communication and bickering that may have survived during the working years finds retirement the "straw that breaks the camel's back." However, Friedmann and Orbach (1974) cited a long series of studies that provided evidence that ". . . suggests no shock or crisis with retirement, but rather a high degree of continuity of activities and relationships and an enlarged and heightened relationship between spouses in many instances" (p. 626). Vinick and Everett (1989) report that 60% of retirees see some improvement in their marriages. Lee and Sheban (1989) found less positive results, especially in terms of retired husbands with still working wives. For the minority of couples who do experience new strains on the marriage brought on by retirement, Leland and Martha Bradford's (1979) *Retirement: Coping with Emotional Upheavals* provides outstanding reading. For the usual issues (e.g., wife's feeling that her husband is infringing on her turf, husband switching from the independent producer to the dependent consumer role), the Bradfords provide numerous suggestions and strategies for coping and the relationship skills needed. Both Vinick and Ekerdt (1989) and Lee and Shebey (1989) found that a husband's increase in his share of household duties was the *best* predictor of enhancement of a retirement marriage. They suggest that husbands seldom include these "turf" and responsibility issues in their thinking about retirement and that wives are well-advised to initiate relevant discussion *before* retirement occurs.

Family relationships. *Myth 9:* Retirees generally have more interactions with their immediate family (e.g., children, siblings) than persons the same age who are still working (false). This myth is related to aging myths that assume there is much dependence of the elderly on younger children. Again Friedmann and Orbach (1974) summarized the myth and its disconfirming data: "this (myth) has involved two interrelated suppositions: (1) we are dealing with an emotionally charged, disruptive event that destroys prior continuity of life patterns, (2) the occupational role system largely controls the nature of the family role system; it is essential to personal and family role identity; and its loss is 'functionally' irreplaceable" (p. 626). Citing Streib and Schneider's (1971) study, they summarize data that show a high degree of continuity in family relationships. Interestingly enough, Streib and Schneider found increased interactions between retirees and children, *if* the children were more successful than the parents in terms of occupational or financial status.

Because of the longer life span, nearly one-third of all retirees have at least one parent still living. Many of these parents may need some supervision as they are up into their 80s or 90s. In short, we are seeing significant changes in the generational relationships during retirement years. Moreover, for economic reasons such as housing prices and sociological reasons such as divorce rates, numerous retirees find themselves with dependent adult children as well. Vinick and Ekerdt (1989) point out that these responsibilities, plus other adjustment problems of retirees' parents and children, are often perceived as "spoiling" retirement. Thus, the issue for retirement planning is not whether retirees will spend more time with family but how issues like finance, relocation, and activities might be affected by perceived family "responsibilities."

Social relationships. *Myth 10:* Retirees generally have fewer friends and social relationships than similarly aged persons who are still working (false). This item reflects the disengagement theory of retirement (Havighurst, Neugarten, & Tobin, 1968). Unfortunately, this position has received wide attention over the past two decades and readily fits into the prevailing negative perceptions about retirement. Atchley (1976), Friedmann and Orbach (1974), Mutran and Reitzes (1981), and Kunkel (1989) have all produced evidence that there are very few effects of retirement on *patterns* of social activities. Obviously, there is a notable change in *time* spent at work and with friends from work, but otherwise there are surprisingly few changes.

PRERETIREMENT PROGRAMS: CONCEPTS AND REALITIES

At best, the marriage of the two sets of myths on retirement and aging has created a cloudy image of life on the other side of the retirement event. Thus, the primary task counselors and career development specialists in organizations face is creating an environment in which individuals can understand the authentic rather than mythical issues of retirement living. Despite increasingly positive attitudes toward retirement, there is no corresponding increase in retirees' planfulness. Nearly one-third of all retirees do not accurately foresee their date of retirement (Ekerdt, Vinick, & Bosse, 1989). The vast majority of all retirees do not systematically plan for retirement with regards to any area except finances (Fretz, et al., 1989; Kragie, Gerstein, & Lichtman, 1989). Moon and Hushbeck (1989) found that of those choosing early retirement, only eight percent had planned for retirement. Getting people to plan for retirement remains a major challenge of counselors. Regretfully, the low percentages of persons taking part in retirement programs suggest little change since Greene (1969) described "resistors" to some of the earliest preretirement programs. The challenge in preretirement programming is to facilitate a process for the individual to undertake. In contrast to a program which emphasizes only information about finances, as do all too many retirement programs (Dennis, 1989), the need is for programs to prepare the individual to pass through this major life transition with as few emotional scrapes and bruises as possible, and to be equipped with clear values and life direction with which to face future changes.

Remote Phase Program: Seldom-Met Needs

Discarding the role of worker and taking on the role of retiree is normally experienced over a span of time. The retirement celebration may mark the event, but the retirement process within the retiree begins years before (Karp, 1989). Atchley (1976) spoke of a remote phase of preretirement during which the employee is just becoming aware of approaching eligibility and wondering how to begin decision-making and planning. During this stage the two questions generally paramount in the individual's thoughts are: "Can I afford to retire?" and "What will I do with my time?" The ideal retirement preparation, both within and outside of organizations, should begin during the remote phase some three to eight years before retirement. Today, however, adequate remote-phase preparation is almost always left to individuals and not to programmers within organizations. In practice, organizational programs typically combine the content of both "remote" and "near" phases into one intervention, usually a seminar. These seminars are then offered for both individuals nearing or having achieved retirement eligibility. Such proximity to the time of retirement provides little opportunity for making explorations that might be suggested as part of good retirement planning.

Money management.   One obvious need of the employee in the remote phase is to develop a firm financial foundation. Yet one of the greatest challenges facing a career development specialist preparing individuals for retirement is to motivate employees to come to grips with their retirement financial situation. Knowing financial realities is critical for two reasons. First, it provides a foundation for decision making around major retirement issues including: timing (when to retire); housing (present home, smaller home, apartment, warmer climate, a state with lower taxes); life style (can what is desired be reconciled with what is affordable); and employment (part-time/volunteer). Without feeling control over the financial future, the preretiree in a seminar setting cannot focus serious attention on other critical areas of retirement readiness that may significantly influence satisfaction and adjustment in retirement.

In the typical company retirement seminar, the financial planning address is given by professional financial consultants or investment brokers. Their presentations to preretirees often enhance anxiety about financial matters rather than reduce it. Consultants often talk about options that, although understood, often require cash resources not available to many participants. Although someone who has effectively managed previous finances may have from $20,000 to $50,000 or more in liquid investments that can be moved around to add significantly to retirement income, many participants have few assets other than a home, which is not liquid capital. Consequently, the presentations may not only be irrelevant for their finances, but are often threatening to preretirees who may feel inadequate because they have not amassed the liquid assets that the financial consultants suggest should be part of their portfolio.

Responding by questionnaire to one presentation of this type, one-half of the participants said they planned to hire the professional to do their financial planning. They were ready to turn control over to someone else and incur more expenses even when their resources were meager.

The ideal program provides preretirees the incentive to juxtapose their present use of money (e.g., budget) with a projected retirement budget. In this way they look at the differences, decide on the adequacy of what they see, project that into the future for 10 or 15 years indexed for inflation, and then begin to think with more realism about the timing and activities of retirement. Thus, the optimal situation would be to live on the projected retirement budget before retirement. In other words, rehearse the retirement life style while building a nest egg. Financial experts have noted that 5 to 8 years of such planning and saving are necessary to develop appreciable supplemental retirement resources.

Use of time. In addition to the need for money management in the remote phase of preretirement and the challenges to programmers that this presents, a second major question uppermost in many preretirees' thoughts is: "What will I do with my time?"

A widely held fantasy of retirement is that it is an extended vacation. This fantasy is understandable because most people are accustomed to the rhythm of working 5 days, resting 2—working for 11 months, playing for 1. This kind of rhythm is established from the earliest days at school. In seminars when some preretirees look at retirement life, they see total freedom (e.g., wonderful leisure, no decision-making). However, individuals who are already retired (Bradford & Bradford, 1979; Willing, 1981) report quite a different situation. Retirement is not a perpetual vacation. Rather, it is a major life transition that necessitates the development of new roles, or the enlargement of present roles other than that of worker. For this to happen preretirees must have a clear sense of self at their present stage in the life cycle. From this sense of self will then flow the roles to assume or enlarge and knowledge of what to do with time. Retirement programmers do well to rephrase the question, "What will I do with my time?" to "Whom do I choose to be?" When the preretirees understand the uniqueness of their potential contribution to life outside the work context, as well as their personal self-worth and needs, new roles and a list of activities will fall into place.

There are particular difficulties associated with the experience of leaving the work role. These are often denied consciousness, yet are crucial to the satisfying use of time in retirement. Bradford and Bradford (1979) identified a series of psychological needs that are filled inadvertently by most organizations:

- a sense of belonging to a group outside the family network;
- the opportunity to socialize with fellow workers, colleagues, and associates;
- an area of physical and psychological space (title, status, responsibility, image, sense of usefulness, work space, desk, equipment, tools);
- time structure routines;
- goals; and

- achievement, power and influence, affirmation, validation, valued knowledge, and skills.

Few employees realize the extent to which they have these needs, let alone realize that the needs have been filled by the work role. Even the most independent high-level executives who routinely set goals for themselves and their organization do so because of the responsibilities they have agreed to shoulder. When they leave work, they will leave those goals for another person to set. The most basic routines of our day, of the season, and of the year are dictated by one's identity as worker: (a) when to rise, (b) what to wear, (c) what to eat (light breakfast for sedentary workers/ heavy breakfast for manual laborers), (d) what to read, (e) with whom to socialize, (f) when to take a vacation, (g) whether to celebrate a holiday (who gets off Columbus Day?), and (h) when to do the laundry.

Most of us are affirmed largely by our work. Our worth is validated through the use of our knowledge and skills. We exercise power and influence. We experience a sense of accomplishment. To leave these inner benefits at retirement is to lose some of the major psychological props of well-being. Good preretirement programs must examine these issues with the goal of replacing the salient losses with retirement activities that will ensure the continuity of a sense of self-esteem and value. A key question for preretirees to ask is, "What activities in my retirement life style will ensure that my psychological needs filled by work will also be met in retirement?"

The task of facilitating such a self-examination can be challenging, depending on the particular culture of the organization. A highly technical and scientific population will react differently than a highly social population to introspective activities. It can and must be done, however, even in the most challenging settings.

The authors, in a scientific and technical setting, use both content and process to reduce the initial resistance to introspective activities that typically occurs in a retirement age cohort. Content that challenges established myths of retirement leads easily into examining personal values and needs in light of the reality of retirement. Activities that do not *require* self-disclosure, yet promote group sharing, help to establish a social climate of acceptance of the task. Some individuals report that the greatest benefit of a seminar is participating in open discussion about some of the "feeling" issues involved in retirement planning.

In the authors' work, three modules are designed to stimulate thinking around topics that feed into the question of time use: Work and Retirement, Time and Retirement, and Self and Retirement. The programmer's goal is to foster the development of inner control and direction for the future and to forestall a lack of goals and direction that many retirees report. One seminar participant summed it up thus: "Up to now in my life I have just let things happen. Now I see that I can control the direction of my life in retirement." All too often, typical retirement programs simply provide a list of possible activities and a discussion on volunteerism. Such steps are of little help to preretirees looking to feel satisfied about their use of time in retirement. Individuals must come to grips with the direction of their life when life is not structured by work.

Near Phase

When an employee becomes eligible to retire (according to company regulations), the question of when to retire and the accompanying decision-making can precipitate significant anxiety. Atchley (1976) noted that as the retirement time draws near, attitudes toward retirement become more negative for many, probably because of the many unknowns regarding what life will be like in retirement. It is a time when individuals begin to separate themselves psychologically from work. For employees who have planned in the remote phase, nearing retirement is likely to be positive because they have prepared themselves financially and set in place a direction for retirement activities.

A key factor for satisfying retirement adjustment is establishing a realistic concept of retirement life. It is a time to be practical as well as idealistic. Those individuals who see retirement *only* as a time to "do what I want to do, when I want to do it" or to spend the days on a golf course will be ill-prepared for retirement realities (e.g., when family members require their time or there is no partner for the game).

What can the career development specialist do to facilitate reality-based planning in the near phase of the retirement transition? The authors' program focuses on the individual's needs for information, social support, and a concrete plan of action (Schlossberg, Troll, & Leibowitz, 1978).

Information. Information needs of the preretirees are highly practical. Often there is a need for personal pertinent facts, not general information. For this reason it is more useful for leaders to facilitate the participants' own information gathering activities rather than to provide too many details on many topics. One example is Social Security. What preretirees need to know is: (1) the amount of their individual benefit (not general information on the history of the Social Security Administration), and (2) the necessary details involved in applying for the benefit. First, the preretirement programmer should provide necessary phone numbers and addresses of local Social Security offices and information on procedures for applying for benefits. Second, to motivate preretirees to gather information, a discussion could be facilitated on the skills required to deal with bureaucratic institutions.

Similar to the Social Security information is information needed from the organization's benefits officer: (a) the amount of the annuity pension; (b) how and when to begin retirement procedures; and (c) the decisions (e.g., health and life insurance/the optimal time in the year to leave) that need some prior thought. Often, just meeting the benefits officer, having that phone number, and generally understanding the retirement procedure are enough to reduce anxiety.

Another area in which to generate information-gathering activities rather than presenting general information is relocation. Unless an audience is composed of individuals with no family ties, a general talk on the best location in the country to retire based on taxes, cost of living, or climate will be entertaining, but not practical. Of more value to the preretiree is a method for gathering specific information on quality of life in the locations of their choice. Suggestions might be to visit the area during the off-season, live there for a while, subscribe to the local newspapers, interview the local clergy, mayor, and storekeepers, and look at post-retirement activity plans to determine whether resources are available to carry out activities after relocation. Practical suggestions for reality-based information facilitate deciding whether to relocate.

The issue of family adjustment is another area in which the quality of postretirement life will be enhanced with preretirement information gathering. The individual whose retirement dream is to design and build a solar home in a remote area would do well to discuss the plan with his or her spouse who may have conflicting needs and desires to be close to children and other family members. Retirement is a family affair that will affect each member of the family, not only the person retiring. Yet, as noted earlier, all too often there is a lack of communication between spouses about feelings, hopes, and plans for a mutual retirement life style.

Information gathering for family adjustment can take the form of communicating at home with a spouse and other family members. If the spouse is present in the seminar, the work will be easier because of mutual exposure to content; however, communication between spouses will still need to take place in the privacy of their own home.

The final content area necessary to include in a preretirement seminar is health and aging. As noted before, much of the retirement anxiety is linked to misconceptions about normal aging, illness, and death. The health and aging module should include a thorough discussion on normal aging, with special attention to health practices that promote optimum health. Although this module emphasizes content more than information-gathering activities, it needs to include some self-review and decision-making regarding normal health and life style. Because the retirement cohort is often struggling with its own parents' illness, dependency, and pending death, an open discussion about issues involved with very old age (Neugarten, 1968) and death of the spouse is often difficult. However, the cathartic experience of such a discussion can free participants to make decisions about their own health and life style. "Now we are really preparing for retirement," is a response often heard after working with this topic.

In summary, although the seminar leader presents information through the various modules to the seminar participants, the emphasis is not on providing information as much as on teaching and facilitating skills for individual information gathering. Dennis' (1984) book on *Retirement Preparation* provides a listing of numerous topics and resources that can be explored by both counselors and preretirees.

Planning schema. It is important to include within the seminar setting a structure for individualized planning. Without a structure that includes specific activities designed to teach and practice planning skills, participants are not likely to summarize their learning into a practical step-by-step action plan. Such a plan, along with the knowledge, skills, confidence, and motivation needed to create it, will provide the preretiree with an increased feeling of control over the pending change.

Social support. The role of social support provided by career development centers, social service agencies, families, and friends is finally earning its place in an understanding of coping with transitions (House, 1981; Russell & Cutrona, 1984). Kimmell, Price, and Walker (1978) showed that voluntary retirees with more positive feelings about retirement had more family support for the decision to retire. Based on the emerging literature about the role of social support in coping with, for example, unemployment, AIDS, and change of schools, it seems highly likely that other forms of social support will also contribute to one's well-being in retirement. Effective planning calls for an identification of how social support will be obtained during the retirement years. To the extent that fellow workers have been a source of social support, the need for a consideration of new sources of social support is clearly the greatest. The preretirement seminar leader should be perceived as a source of supportive information (someone to go to with questions when needed). Seminar participants themselves will support each other by sharing feelings, ideas, and fears they have in common. When the seminar format includes former employees and colleagues who have retired from the organization, these retirement veterans will also be perceived as a source of support. Retirement clubs linked to the organization by ties of collegial friendship and mutual service are yet another work place source of social support.

Preretirement Planning for Women

Because the percentage of *career* women was relatively small until recent decades, almost all the earliest studies of retirees were of men. The 1980s saw the publication of many articles to rectify this imbalance, although there is still a relative paucity of empirical research to guide specialized planning (Behling, Kitty, & Foster, 1983). Whether homemakers or careerists, women are greatly affected by the retirement transition. Gratton and Hauge (1983) concluded that more recent research shows most women effectively adjusting to retirement in contrast to some earlier studies showing women having a more difficult time adjusting (often because of impoverished finances). Unfortunately, Kragic, Gerstein, and Lichtman (1989) still find women, as compared to men, considering it less important to plan for retirement. Fretz et al. (1989) found some evidence to indicate that single women were more like men in their preretirement attitudes and behaviors. It was married women who were not concerning themselves with retirement issues. The rapidly changing percentages of women who have long-term work experience and primary responsibility for their own retirement will require careful study in the 1990s. For programs for women who are currently retiring, the work of Szinovacz (1982) on *Women's Retirement* is a major resource. Further, since women are most often the single persons in retirement, Keith's (1989) *The Unmarried in Later Life* and Salwen's (1975) *Solo Retirement* are crucial resources.

PROGRAMMING OPTIONS IN THE ORGANIZATION AND COMMUNITY

Organizationally based preretirement programs must respond to the need of the retirement-eligible employee for: (1) information and skill development to identify and locate information; (2) social support from fellow employees, former employees, and information experts; and (3) a planning structure that will focus learned information into action steps. Individuals who design these programs need to be aware of the psychological needs and requirements of participants during the various phases of the retirement transition. Seminars are only one method of intervention, however, albeit the most widely employed intervention serving the preretirees (Benjamin, 1978; Migliaccio & Cairo, 1981; Dennis, 1989). Some organizations back up seminars with individual or couple retirement counseling using trained psychological counselors. Seminars may be offered for specialized populations such as all women, or all couples. Resource centers containing self-paced retirement preparation materials, a small library of retirement literature, or retirement preparation programs by computer can be established. The American Association of Retired Persons has provided a variety of basic resource materials to serve as a start. Because organizations possess unique cultures, however, prewritten programs will not best meet the needs of every organization. The authors have found that even in organizations with the same basic professions and types (Holland, 1973), because of differing geographic locations and work forces, programs are more effective when adapted to a particular agency.

Given that career decision-making assistance has always been provided in this country in educational or industrial settings, it is not surprising to find almost a complete absence of community-based programs for preretirement and retirement (see Jones, Marion, & McIntire, 1983, for a rare exception). Formal preretirement programs in education settings are also extremely rare, but do exist (e.g., Bynum, Cooper, & Acuff, 1978). The absence of more community-based programs is particularly lamentable on three counts. First, there are innumerable workers whose companies do not provide any preretirement seminars or retirement planning assistance. Second, even where companies do provide programs, some employees are hesitant to participate for fear of the consequences of declaring their interest in retirement. Will they be passed for promotions, for inservice training, for new projects or possibly forced out before they want to be? Such questions keep workers from taking part until they are absolutely ready to declare their retirement time. In many cases it is then too late to achieve maximal benefits from retirement plans. For most aspects of retirement, planning should take place minimally a year and a half to three years ahead of time. For financial aspects, planning and investment management should begin four to eight years before retirement time. Finally, for the retirement period itself, the presence of community-based programs has a strong positive effect on the well-being of both men and women in retirement (Mutran & Reitzes, 1981).

In some educational settings there are programs that admit senior citizens free to courses on a space-available basis. Although this process does not give retirees specific preparation for retirement, it does make available the library and career development and placement center of a campus. There is no existing evidence on retirees' use of these services. Also it has not been determined whether these services have appropriate materials and staff to be of assistance to preretirees or retirees.

How can career development specialists be of use in meeting these needs? Is this not the province of the community's office of aging, public health, or mental health services? Although such agencies are the logical providers of community-based services for preretirees and retirees, their staff almost never have the appropriate expertise. Career development specialists are located almost exclusively in educational and industrial settings. The programs described here for preretirees, however, can be offered in the community as well as in the work place. As noted, there are distinct advantages to offering such programs in the community. Public schools, libraries, senior centers, and civic centers are all locations that might welcome such programs, given appropriate staff. Career development specialists are encouraged to reach out from their school and industrial settings into community settings. These relationships may extend to providing participants access to informational resources available in a work setting (e.g., occupational information library).

Industries and universities that employ career development specialists may be amenable to allowing some release time for providing community services. There is a great deal of good will to be gained from such offerings. In return, the career development specialist has the unique challenges and rewards of working with new populations with new problems. Because there are so few opportunities for preretirees and retirees to participate in these kinds of programs, they are especially appreciative. Again and again, the statements and letters from program participants are deeply moving when they report how much their lives have been affected by the information and self-examination.

Model of a Preretirement Seminar

This chapter will close with an outline of a typical 18-hour seminar. The 10 modules take one to two hours each. They have been arranged, at times, into six weekly three-hour sessions, at other times, into three full days. As noted previously, programmers must make adjustments to accommodate the unique needs of the organization. The topics and objectives are the most critical parts of this description. The actual arrangement can vary according to the availability and interests of the seminar leaders.

1. *The Retirement Experience*
   Objective:
   To offer participants an opportunity to:
   a. examine individual expectations for life in retirement;
   b. identify desirable and undesirable aspects of life in retirement; and
   c. provide a focus for exploring and learning through individual goal setting.

2. *Retiring from Your Agency*
   Objectives:
   To offer participants an opportunity to:
   a. meet the organization's retirement benefits officer;

    b. become aquainted with areas for decision making such as timing of retirement, survivor and insurance options; and

    c. learn what is necessary to estimate one's approximate annuity.

3. *Social Security and Retirement*
   Objectives:
   To offer participants an opportunity to:
   a. learn what is needed to apply for benefits as well as necessary addresses and phone numbers; and
   b. question a Social Security representative.

4. *You and Retirement*
   Objectives:
   To offer participants an opportunity to:
   a. identify what needs and values are currently fulfilled by their work; and
   b. develop a self-profile in relation to preferred activities, competencies, commitments, surroundings, hobbies, people, and things.

5. *Time and Retirement*
   Objectives:
   To offer participants an opportunity to:
   a. examine their current use of time; and
   b. integrate a review of their self-profile with a projected use of time in retirement in order to plan a set of activities that they will find fulfilling.

6. *Life Style Implications for One's 70s and 80s*
   Objectives:
   To offer participants an opportunity to:
   increase awareness of the health and environmental issues involved in planning for their later years.

7. *Financial Planning*
   Objectives
   To offer participants an opportunity to:
   a. examine their present financial situation as it relates to financial management in retirement; and
   b. develop a retirement budget based on reasonable projections of income.

8. *Your Spouse, Family, and Retirement*
   Objectives:
   To offer participants an opportunity to:
   a. consider issues in spouse and family adjustment to retirement that have been shown to affect overall satisfaction in retirement; and
   b. identify useful communication skills for discussion of problem areas.

9. *Work and Retirement*
   Objectives:
   To offer participants an opportunity to:
   a. explore the varieties of paid work experiences in retirement;
   b. consider salient aspects of their work experience and self-profile that might lead to exploration of work opportunities; and

c. understand some of the threats to self-esteem for an "older" job applicant; e.g., low salary offers, treatment as "outdated" in terms of today's technology.

10. *Your Retirement Plan*
Objectives:
To offer participants an opportunity to:
integrate all information gained during the seminar into a reality-based action plan for retirement preparation.

REFERENCES

Atchley, R.C. (1976). *The sociology of retirement.* New York: Wiley.

Behling, J.H., Kilty, K.M., & Foster, S.T. (1983). Scarce resources for retirement planning: A dilemma for professional women. *Journal of Gerontological Social Work, 5*(3), 49–60.

Belgrave, L.L. (1989). Understanding women's retirement. *Generations, 13*(2), 49–52.

Benjamin, L. (1978). *Preretirement counseling.* Ann Arbor, MI: ERIC Counseling and Personnel Services Clearinghouse.

Bird, C. (1989, November). The jobs you do. *Modern Maturity,* pp. 40–46.

Bradford, L., & Bradford, M. (1979). *Retirement: Coping with emotional upheavals.* Chicago: Nelson-Hall.

Brammer, L., & Abrego, P. (1981). Intervention strategies for coping with transitions. *The Counseling Psychologist, 9*(2), 19–36.

Burgess, E. (1960). *Aging in western societies.* Chicago: University of Chicago Press.

Bynum, J.E., Cooper, B.L., & Acuff, F.G. (1978). Retirement reorientation: Senior adult education. *Journal of Gerontology, 33,* 253–261.

Dennis, H. (Ed.) (1984). *Retirement Preparation.* Lexington, MA: Lexington Books.

Dennis, H. (1989). The current state of retirement planning. *Generations, 13*(2), 38–41.

Donahue, W., Orbach, H.L., & Pollak, O. (1969). Retirement: The emerging social pattern. In C. Tibbits (Ed.), *Handbook of Social Gerontology* (pp. 330–406). Chicago: University of Chicago Press.

Ekerdt, D.J. (1989). Introduction: Retirement comes of age. *Generations, 13*(2), 5–6.

Ekerdt, D.J., Bosse, R., & Mogey, J.M. (1980). Concurrent change in planned and preferred age for retirement. *Journal of Gerontology, 35,* 232–240.

Ekerdt, D.J., Vinick, D.H., & Bosse, R. (1989). Orderly endings: Do men know when they will retire? *Journal of Gerontology, 44,* S28–35.

Fleisher, D. (1981). Alternative work options for older workers: Part IV. *Aging and Work, 4,* 153–159.

Fretz, B.R., Kluge, N.A., Ossana, S.M., Jones, S.M., & Merikangas, M.W. (1989). Intervention targets for reducing preretirement anxiety and depression. *Journal of Counseling Psychology, 36,* 301–307.

Friedmann, E.A., & Orbach, H.L. (1974). Adjustment to retirement. In A. Silvano (Ed.), *American handbook of psychology* (pp. 607–645). New York: Basic Books.

Glamser, F.D. (1976). Determinants of a positive attitude toward retirement. *Journal of Gerontology, 31*, 104–107.

Glamser, F.D. (1981). Predictors of retirement attitudes. *Aging and Work, 4*, 23–29.

Glamser, F.D., & DeJong, G.F. (1975). The efficacy of preretirement preparation programs for industrial workers. *Journal of Gerontology, 30*, 595–600.

Goudy, W.J., Powers, E.A., & Keith, P. (1975). Work and retirement: A test of attitudinal relationships. *Journal of Gerontology, 30*, 193–198.

Goudy, W.J., Powers, E.A., Keith, P.M., & Reger, R.A. (1980). Changes in attitude toward retirement. *Journal of Gerontology, 35*, 941–948.

Graebner, W. (1980). *A history of retirement.* New Haven: Yale University Press.

Gratton, B., & Hauge, M.R. (1983). Decision and adoption: Research on female retirement. *Research on Aging, 5*, 59–78.

Greene, M.R. (1969). Preretirement counseling, retirement adjustment and the older employee. *Resources in Education,* Document #ED 042996.

Havighurst, R.J., Neugarten, B.L., & Tobin, S. (1968). Disengagement and patterns of aging. In Neugarten, B.L. (Ed.), *Middle Age and Aging* (pp. 161–172). Chicago: University of Chicago Press.

Holland, J.L. (1973). *Making vocational choices: A theory of careers.* Englewood Cliffs, NJ: Prentice-Hall.

House, J.S. (1981). *Work stress and social support.* Reading, MA: Addison-Wesley.

Johnson, L., & Strother, G.B. (1962). Job expectations and retirement planning. *Journal of Gerontology, 17*, 418–423.

Jones, H.R., Marion, U.V., & McIntire, R.H. (1983). Developing community retirement planning services. *Aging and Work, 6*, 291–300.

Kalt, N.E., & Kohn, M.H. (1975). Preretirement counseling: Characteristics of programs and preferences of retirees. *Gerontology, 15*, 179–181.

Kamouri, A.L., & Cavanaugh, J.C. (1986). The impact of preretirement education programmes on women's preretirement socialization. *Journal of Occupational Behavior, 7*, 245–256.

Karp, D.A. (1989). The social construction of retirement among professionals 50–60 years old. *Gerontologist, 29*, 750–756.

Keith, P.M. (1989). *The unmarried in later life.* New York: Praeger.

Kimmel, D.C., Price, K.F., & Walker, J.W. (1978). Retirement choice and retirement satisfaction. *Journal of Gerontology, 33*, 575–585.

Kragie, E.R., Gerstein, M., & Lichtman, M. (1989). Do Americans plan for retirement? Some recent trends. *Career Development Quarterly, 37*, 232–239.

Kunkle, S.R. (1989). An extra eight hours a day. *Generations, 13*(2), 57–60.

Lawton, M.P. (1980). *Environment and aging.* Monterey, CA: Brooks/Cole.

Lee, G.R., & Shehan, C.L. (1989). Retirement and marital satisfaction. *Journal of Gerontology, 44*, S226–230.

Levinson, D.J., Darrow, C.M., Klein, E.B., Levinson, M.H., & McKee, B. (1978). *The seasons of a man's life.* New York: Knopf.

Merikangas, M. W. (1983). Retirement planning with a difference. *Personnel Journal, 62*(5), 420–427.

Migliaccio, J.N., & Cairo, P.C. (1981). Preparation for retirement: A selective bibliography. 1974–1980. *Aging and Work, 4*, 31–41.

Montana, P.J. (1986). Pre-retirement planning: How corporations help. *Personnel Administrator, 31*(6), 121–128.

Moon, M., & Hushbeck, J. (1989). Employment policy and public policy. *Generations, 13*(2), 27–30.

Morgan, J.N. (1980). Antecedents and consequences of retirement. In M.S. Hill, D.H. Hill, & T.N. Morgan (Eds.), *Five thousand American families.* (pp. 207–240). Ann Arbor, MI: Institute for Social Research.

Morrow, P.C. (1981). Retirement planning programs: Assessing their attendance and efficacy. *Aging and Work, 4*, 244–251.

Mutran, D., & Reitzes, D.C. (1981). Retirement identity and well-being: Realignment of role relationships. *Journal of Gerontology, 36*, 733–740.

Neugarten, B.L. (Ed.) (1968). *Middle age and aging.* Chicago: University of Chicago Press.

O'Brien, G.E. (1981). Leisure attributes and retirement satisfaction. *Journal of Applied Psychology, 66*, 371–384.

Palmore, E. (1977). Facts on aging. *Gerontologist, 17*, 315–320.

Palmore, E. (1981). The facts on aging quiz: Part two. *Gerontologist, 21*, 431–437.

Palmore, E.B., Burchett, B.M., Fillenbaum, G.G., George, L.K., & Wallman, L.M. (1985). *Retirement: Causes and consequences.* New York: Springer.

Palmore, E., Fillenbaum, C.G., & George, L. (1984). Consequences of retirement. *Journal of Gerontology, 39*, 109–116.

Parnes, H. (1981). *Work and retirement.* Cambridge, MA: MIT Press.

Parnes, H.S. (1989). Post retirement employment. *Generations, 13*(2), 23–26.

Reichard, S., Livson, F., & Peterson, P. (1962). *Aging and personality.* New York: Wiley.

Retirement preparation: Growing corporate involvement. (1979). New York: Research & Forecasts. (Abstracted in *Aging and Work, 3,* 1–13.)

Russell, D., & Cutrona, C. (1984, August). New strategies for measuring social support: Development of the Social Provisions Scale. Paper presented at the annual meeting of the American Psychology Association, Toronto.

Salwen, J. (1985). *Solo retirement.* New York: Dodd, Mead, & Co.

Schlossberg, N.K. (1981). A model for analyzing humans' adaptation to transition. *The Counseling Psychologist, 9*(2), 2–18.

Schlossberg, N.K., Troll, L., & Leibowitz, Z. (1978). *Perspectives on counseling adults: Issues and skills.* Monterey, CA: Brooks/Cole.

Seibart, E.P., & Seibart, J. (1986). Retirement: Crisis or opportunity. *Personnel Administrator, 31*(8), 43–49.

Shaw, J.B., & Grubbs, L.L. (1981). The process of retiring: Organizational entry in reverse. *Academy of Management Review, 6,* 41–47.

Sheppard, H. (1981a). NCOA aging survey shows pronounced preferences for part-time work. *Aging and Work, 4,* 221–223.

Sheppard, H. (1981b). Retirement decisions shift. *Aging and Work, 4,* 202–203.

Shouksmith, G. (1983). Change in attitude to retirement following a short preretirement planning seminar. *Journal of Psychology, 114,* 3–7.

Streib, G.F., & Schneider, C.J. (1971). *Retirement in American society.* Ithaca: Cornell University Press.

Szinovac, M. (1982). *Women's retirement.* Beverly Hills, CA: Sage.

Torres-Gil, F. (1984). Retirement issues that affect minorities. In H. Dennis (Ed.), *Retirement preparation* (pp. 109–129). Lexington, MA: Lexington Books.

Usher, C. (1981). Alternative work options for older workers: Part 1. *Aging and Work, 4,* 74–80.

Vinick, B.H., & Ekerdt, D.J. (1989). Retirement and the family. *Generations, 13*(2), 53–56.

Walker, J.W., & Lazer, H.L. (1978). *The end of mandatory retirement: Application for management.* New York: Wiley.

What IBM retirees think of retirement (1981). *Aging and Work, 4,* 191–196. (Originally appeared in *Think* magazine published by IBM.)

Willing, J.E. (1981). *The reality of retirement: The inner experience of becoming a retired person.* New York: Morrow.

SECTION IV:

SETTINGS

IN A VARIETY OF PLACES...

CHAPTER 16

Career Planning and Development in Organizations

Peter C. Cairo
Teachers College
Columbia University
New York, New York

In recent years there has been increasing interest among organizations in programs intended to promote the career development of their employees. Several factors account for this surge in popularity. From the organization's point of view, career planning and development programs are intended to enhance job performance, help employees use personnel systems more effectively, and improve the organization's ability to utilize employee talent. Among the other reasons frequently cited for sponsoring career planning and development programs are to reduce turnover, to conform to affirmative action and equal employment opportunity requirements, to encourage employees to take greater responsibility for their own careers, and, finally, to respond positively to employees' expressions of interest in such programs (Cohen, 1977; Griffith, 1980; Gutteridge & Otte, 1983; Keller & Piotrowski, 1987; Lancaster & Berne, 1981; Morgan, Hall, & Martier, 1979). When these lofty ambitions are combined with employees' recognition that work strongly influences the overall quality of their lives, it is not surprising that career planning and development programs of all kinds have emerged in so many organizations.

Yet even the most ardent proponent of career planning and development in organizations would concede that it is unclear to just what extent many activities have achieved their objectives. Opinions regarding the effectiveness of various types of career planning and development programs vary widely from organization to organization. In addition, there is a notable dearth of systematic research on the impact of such programs (Brooks, 1984; Cairo, 1983; Hall & Lerner, 1980).

Despite the absence of evaluative evidence, much attention has been devoted to adult development, including issues adults confront in managing their careers. An increasingly large body of literature is devoted to describing career development in organizations and specific efforts to implement various career planning and development programs. A review of this literature suggests that several key issues bear directly on the success of any organization's effort to mount such programs. Before identifying these issues, however, this chapter will begin with a discussion of several concepts and definitions relevant to the understanding of career development in organizational settings, followed by a brief description of current practices.

CONCEPTS AND DEFINITIONS

Much attention has been devoted to understanding the salient developmental tasks which are confronted during adulthood (Gould, 1978; Levinson, 1978; Lowenthal, Thurnhuer, & Chiriboga, 1975; Neugarten, 1976; Schlossberg, Troll, & Leibowitz, 1978; Vaillant, 1977). Some of these approaches have enhanced our understanding of the issues in which adults engage during the course of their careers. Recently, Cytrynbaum and Crites (1989) proposed a model for integrating adult development concepts with career dynamics to understand more fully the process of career adjustment. These theories, and others that focus more specifically on career development, are reviewed in greater detail elsewhere (see Chapters 1–3). This section will describe briefly the concepts associated directly with careers in organizations.

The literature on careers in organizations reveals that the term *career* means different things to different people. For some, career is synonymous with advancement or vertical mobility, whereas for others it is regarded as a lifelong sequence of work-related experiences and attitudes regardless of their direction (Hall, 1976). Adding to the confusion is the frequent absence of any clear distinction between such practices as career planning, career pathing, career counseling, career ladders, and career management. In an effort to bring some order to this disarray, Gutteridge and Otte (1983) proposed a model that distinguishes between institutional and individual processes within the organization. They refer to the former as *career management* processes and include activities such as recruitment and selection, human resource allocation, appraisal and evaluation, and training and development. The latter are referred to as *career planning* processes. Generally intended to respond to individual needs, these activities include occupational choice, organizational choice, choice of job assignment, and career self-development. Gutteridge (1986), in an overview of organizational practices concerned with career development, described how career management and career planning programs can be integrated.

Schein (1978) proposed a similar, though more elaborate, model based on the notion that human resource activities must be congruent with both organizational needs and individual needs to maximize organizational effectiveness while at the same time enhancing individual satisfaction. In his view, traditional personnel functions such as job analysis, selection, performance appraisal, and so forth should be intended to meet not only the present and future human resource demands of the organization, but the developmental needs of the individuals who are a part of the organization. For example, the success of an assessment center intended to evaluate employee potential would be contingent not only upon the extent to which it responded effectively to the organization's need to anticipate future human resource needs. It would also be judged on the extent to which it could be used to promote the development of individual participants, perhaps by helping them identify skills needing improvement, the positions most likely to maximize their strengths, or methods for integrating assessment results within a larger framework of overall career planning.

In a further elaboration of the organizational career, Schein (1978) suggested that each individual develops what he referred to as a "career anchor." Based on a small sample of business school alumni, he observed that from the early stages of a career employees acquire important self-knowledge that gradually shapes their occupational self-concept. Career anchors are composed of persons' self-perceived *talents and abilities, motives and needs,* and *attitudes and values.* Developing on the basis of actual work experiences in which these various self-perceptions are tested, career anchors become more stable as persons acquire more and more feedback from their work environment.

On the basis of his limited research, Schein (1978) identified five career anchors that he labeled *managerial, technical/functional, security, autonomy,* and *creativity.* He concedes, however, that these categories may not be inclusive of all employees in all organizations. More research is needed to validate existing anchors and to determine whether or not others should be added.

Driver (1979) offered a typology of career patterns that takes into account individual aspirations as well as certain organizational structures. He identified four career concepts:

- *Transitory* careers are characterized by movement from job to job with no particular pattern.
- *Steady-state* careers involve the selection of a particular field or job that becomes one's work role for life (e.g., lawyer, electrician).
- *Linear* careers are most common among corporate managers who, having selected a field early in life, develop and implement a plan for upward movement.
- *Spiral* careers involve development in one field for a period of time, then movement on to another area, either related or unrelated, on a cyclic basis.

Dalton and Thompson (1986) proposed a model of careers based on interviews of professionally trained employees (i.e., engineers, scientists, and professors) whom they identified as high or low performers. Their analyses suggested a four-stage model. Stage one is described as an apprenticeship during which the employee depends on the directions of others and is involved principally in learning from more senior members of the organization. During stage two the individual establishes independence, becomes an individual contributor, and establishes credibility by taking on greater responsibility. In stage three the individual assumes responsibility for others by assuming formal supervisory responsibility and/or serving in the capacity of mentor. Finally, the central activity in stage four is to provide direction for the organization. The authors contend that although some aspects of each stage are present in others, there are central issues that make each stage unique.

Another of their observations was that within most organizations there were informal and often unstated expectations about crucial activities (and relationships) that determined both formal and informal rewards. For example, although achieving career success and satisfaction might involve becoming an effective mentor, nowhere is this expectation formally communicated to employees in the organization. They argue that not only can discussion of these so-called informal expectations be helpful to people in planning their careers, but that they should become a formal part of performance appraisal and training curricula.

CURRENT PRACTICES

Perhaps as result of the rapid proliferation of career development activities in organizations in recent years, it is difficult to determine accurately the current "state-of-the-art." In part, this confusion stems from a tendency to refer to similar activities by different titles and different activities by the same titles. Brooks (1984) observed that, although *career planning program* is perhaps the most widely used label for programs intended to promote career development, there does not seem to be any consensus on precisely what career planning means. After careful review she concluded that there were four commonalities among several definitions of career planning: first, career planning is an active, not passive, process; second, it generally involves some method of fostering individual self-assessment, career exploration, occupational choice, goal setting, and planning; third, career planning is intended to bring about movement and growth; and fourth, it is a practice that is useful at various points throughout one's life. In an organizational context methods for facilitating career planning vary widely, from special programs devoted exclusively to career planning to the incorporation of career planning concepts in existing human resource functions.

There have been several efforts to determine the extent and type of career planning activities in organizations. Griffith (1980) conducted a survey of the career development practices provided by the Fortune 500 companies. Because only 23% of the companies contacted responded to his questionnaire, it is unclear to what extent his results are representative of business and industry as a whole. Nevertheless he found that approximately 30% of the organizations offered counseling to facilitate career exploration and planning, 43% provided job separation (i.e., outplacement) counseling; and 56% had some form of retirement planning program.

A larger and more representative sample was surveyed by Walker and Gutteridge (1979). Among the 225 companies studied there was strong support for the concept of career planning. There seemed, however, to be a wide gap between what was desired and what was practiced. This was reflected by the finding that the two most common types of career planning assistance available to employees were informal counseling by personnel staff or supervisors and dissemination of information about related services such as educational assistance, equal employment opportunity programs, and affirmative action. Most companies viewed career planning as a serious need, not simply a fad, and an important part of overall employee development.

Gutteridge and Otte (1983) conducted a series of structured telephone interviews with representatives of 40 United States organizations to determine their career development practices. These organizations were selected because they were known to have career development programs; in addition, they varied in size, geographic location, and type of industry. The two most common approaches were career planning workshops and career counseling/career discussions. Each of these approaches was found in approximately three-fourths of the organizations surveyed.

More recently, Keller and Piotrowski (1987) investigated the status of career development programs in Fortune 500 companies. Only 50 companies were found to have programs in place. Programs tended to be of short duration (typically workshops lasting several days), were targeted to middle and upper level management, were initiated and/or sponsored by senior management, and considered effective by the human resources professionals who responded to the survey.

Despite the number of surveys that have attempted to determine just how extensive career planning programs are, the answer to this question remains elusive. Most surveys have reported response rates of less than 25%; it is possible, perhaps likely, that the failure of the "other 75%" to respond was due, at least in part, to the absence of any comprehensive and systematic career planning activities in their organizations. Furthermore, because most investigators have studied primarily large organizations, the extent and type of activities present in small and mid-sized organizations is unclear. Only Walker and Gutteridge (1979) are known to have made an effort to identify a large representative sample of organizations based on size, industry, and location.

In 1979, Walker and Gutteridge concluded that, despite increasing interest in career planning, it remains for most companies a largely informal, experimental, and fragmented activity. Their conclusion seems as fitting today as it was then, over ten years ago. At the same time, however, among those organizations that have made a strong commitment to career planning, the most common types of activities are individual counseling, group workshops, and self-directed materials (Brooks, 1984). Individual counseling is provided in many forms, sometimes by external or internal consultants and sometimes by supervisors. Lancaster and Berne (1981) described a program at Disneyland in which a career planning orientation is followed by an individual consultation with a counselor to discuss employee educational objectives and career goals. Follow-up sessions with the counselor are available as often as desired.

Group workshops are another common form of career planning activity. Hanson (1981) described a comprehensive career/life planning workshop developed at Lawrence Livermore National Laboratory. Participants are exposed to a variety of techniques and instruments that help them assess their interests, values, goals, and vocational choices. Workshop leaders also guide participants through a series of activities intended to help them identify their *motivated skills*, that is, the skills and abilities they enjoy and perform well. Individual counseling, self-directed workbooks,

300

and a career resource center are available to participants who want to supplement workshop activities.

In recent years the marketplace has been flooded with self-help books of all kinds. Among them are some designed to promote career planning. The most widely known is Bolles' (1988) *What Color Is Your Parachute?* Many organizations have developed their own self-directed workbooks that take employees through a set of career planning exercises. Employees are generally encouraged to work through the exercises independently and at their own pace, though frequently they are encouraged to share the results with their immediate supervisor or someone else in the organization from whom they can get feedback.

Finally, DISCOVER, an interactive computer-based career planning system originally targeted for college-age audiences, has been used in organizational settings. Employees are led through a five-step process: (1) understanding career development and change, (2) self-assessment, (3) gathering information, (4) making decisions, and (5) taking action. Other widely used interactive computer-based systems designed for organizations include *Careerpoint* and SIGI.

There is increasing evidence of interest in adapting some traditional human resource functions to meet individual career development needs, although this is not among the most common forms of career planning. Cairo and Lyness (1988), Gilbert and Jaffee (1982), and Hart and Thompson (1979) described how assessment centers, in particular, can be used for facilitating career planning and development. The data that are collected during assessment represent a rich source of information about a person's skills and abilities that have direct implications for training, next assignments, education, as well as finding one's appropriate organizational "niche." Similar outcomes can be envisioned for performance appraisals. Past work performance could be evaluated in light of short-term and long-term career goals. Despite the uneven quality and frequency of the performance appraisal process in most organizations (Hall, 1976), it is nevertheless a common human resource activity that also has the potential for assisting individuals in their career planning.

Regardless of what method is used to facilitate individual career planning and development, several key issues will influence the success of such efforts. The next section is devoted to a discussion of these issues and their practical implications.

ISSUES IN DEVELOPING CAREER PLANNING PROGRAMS

Recent interest in career development in organizations has brought tolight several important elements that affect all efforts to implement successful programs. Some of these elements are indigenous to organizations and reflect the inherent tensions between organizational and individual needs. Other elements have grown from the haphazard and unsystematic proliferation of programs over the past 10 or 15 years and from the effort to translate concepts, principles, and practices directly from the traditional contexts of career counseling to large business organizations.

301

Employee Expectations

Some organizations resist sponsoring career planning programs for fear of creating unrealistic expectations of advancement among employees. Yet the extent to which these expectations exist is unclear. A survey of 56 Chicago-based companies led Morgan, Hall, and Martier (1979) to conclude that many employees see promotion as the most likely and desirable outcome of career development programs, and are likely to be disappointed if no new position awaits them. In contrast, Walker and Gutteridge (1979) concluded that raising employee expectations was not considered a significant problem among the companies they surveyed. Despite this apparent confusion, it is safe to assume that for at least some employees the term career development is synonymous with upward movement in the organization and can create the expectation that participation will lead directly to advancement.

The presence of these expectations can undermine the potential success of any program. In addition to fostering resistance from upper management who fear career development programs might lower morale among employees who are not soon promoted, there are other problems. Associating career development entirely with advancement diminishes employees' perception of the value of career planning and development activities during times of limited expansion of opportunities or when an organization is undergoing major changes that cloud the future. Ironically, it is at times such as these when career planning activities may be needed most. One of the desired outcomes of career planning is to prepare people to respond effectively to changing circumstances by applying their competencies to whatever opportunities are available. The rationale is simple. If, for example, two departments in the same company are merged, creating many new positions, the individual who has acquired basic career planning competencies will be in a better position to make choices based on clear preferences than the one who hasn't. On the other hand, when an organization is forced to contract and positions are being eliminated, enlightenment about their capabilities and aspirations can equip employees to be more flexible about using their skills to take advantage of what opportunities do exist.

Another problem associated with the expectation of advancement is the tendency for employees to ignore other potentially valuable career goals. These goals might include anything from finding a different type of work to making more effective use of leisure to managing dual-career family situations to enriching one's current position. Such activities may not lead to promotion, but might well enhance overall career satisfaction in other ways.

Avoiding the problem of unrealistic expectations may be a matter of simply providing realistic and up-to-date information about career opportunities and increasing employees' awareness of options other than promotion that can enhance their satisfaction. Hall and Lerner (1980) have suggested that realistic information about promotional opportunities coupled with realistic feedback on potential will alleviate the problem of unrealistic career expectations. This is consistent with the literature on recruitment that reveals that when organizations communicate realistic expectations to recruits, the turnover rate among the people eventually hired is lower than for those who have unrealistic expectations. Furthermore, communicating both the positive and negative aspects of the organization does not hurt overall recruiting efforts (Wanous, 1973). These findings would seem to provide additional support for the notion that employees should be given accurate and realistic information about career opportunities if career planning and development efforts are going to be successful.

Responding to Diverse Career Development Needs

It comes as no surprise that increased attention to the career development of adults has led to the conclusion that there are considerable differences among individuals with respect to what they need. Campbell and Cellini (1981) developed a diagnostic taxonomy of adult career problems that included four common tasks, or types of problems, that occur across developmental stages. These tasks include career decision making, implementing career plans, organizational/institutional performance, and organizational/institutional adaptation. Each of these major categories is further divided and subdivided into more specific types of problems that adults might confront.

Yet an examination of career planning and development programs in organizations suggests there is little recognition of the diversity and complexity of the career problems of adults. Although strategies and techniques may vary, most programs have as their primary objective helping employees acquire, in one form or another, the same basic career planning competencies (i.e., self-appraisal, career exploration, goal setting, and planning). For many employees, particularly those at an early stage in their career who have not had prior career planning assistance, this approach is extremely valuable. For others, who have different needs, it can miss the mark. For example, employees with previous work experience may already have achieved a satisfactory level of competence in career planning. Individual and institutional needs change over time, and organizations must be able to respond in a manner consistent with these needs and resist offering a standard solution to different problems. The implication is that an important step in establishing any career planning and development program is to analyze carefully the needs of the people for whom it is intended. Although this is an obvious point, Gutteridge and Otte (1983) reported that most of the organizations included in their survey indicated that they should have had a better understanding of employees' needs prior to program development.

The work of Ference, Stoner, and Warren (1977) and Bardwick (1986) on the phenomenon of "career plateauing" illustrates further the importance of understanding clearly employees' career development needs. Plateau, defined as "the point in a career where the likelihood of additional hierarchical promotion is very low" (Ference, Stoner, & Warren, 1977, p. 602), is regarded as a function of organizational conditions (e.g., limited number of openings at higher levels) or personal factors (e.g., lack of ability or motivation). One of the most important implications of this phenomenon is that the career development needs of employees who have reached a plateau will differ according to what factors are impeding promotion. The individual who is unable to move to higher levels because of restricted opportunities could be encouraged to take special projects or rotational assignments to enhance specific skills or broaden experience. Individuals limited by personal factors might be encouraged to explore career goals that do not involve advancement but that will allow them to be recognized by the organization for the contributions they continue to make.

It is also evident that the career development needs of "plateaued" performers will be different from those for whom the possibilities for promotion are still very much alive (Bardwick, 1986). The challenge for the organization is to differentiate among employees on the basis of their specific career development needs and match them with the most appropriate type of career planning and development activity.

Developing and Improving Skills

Central to any comprehensive approach to career planning and development is some form of self-appraisal. Often this involves an examination of work-related skills and abilities through the use of tests, work simulations, or structured exercises eliciting self-estimates. Whatever method is used, employees who participate in career planning programs are normally encouraged to review their skills and, in addition to noting their strengths, identify skills they need to improve. Although there is a certain logic to this approach, it also presumes that any skill can be acquired or improved given the right kind of training or work-related experience.

London and Strumpf (1982) have pointed out, however, that evidence suggests that not all skills, and in particular managerial skills, can be acquired. In a longitudinal study of the careers of AT&T managers, Bray, Campbell, and Grant (1974) found that some very important managerial skills did not change over time and were very difficult to improve substantially. Managers either had them at an early point in their careers or they didn't have them at all.

At a minimum, then, any effort to recommend methods for acquiring managerial skills must recognize that some skills are much easier to develop than others and that some skills might be nearly impossible to acquire. For example, shortcomings in oral communication skills might be easily remediated through a formal training program in one-to-one and group presentations skills. On the other hand, a person's lack of ability to interpret complex information may be largely affected by aptitude and, as such, be less amenable to change regardless of the follow-up actions taken.

Although some factors affecting skill acquisition in the work setting are attributable to individual characteristics such as aptitude or ability, others may be related to aspects of the work situation itself. Examples of such factors include interpersonal relationships, budget constraints, degree of autonomy, and quality of feedback. It is somewhat puzzling that, in view of the frequency with which assignments are labeled "developmental," so little is known about the effectiveness of such assignments (that is, by whom and under what conditions specific skills are acquired).

Importance of Information

A comprehensive approach to career planning and development must also include some effort to provide individuals with relevant career information. This is particularly important for adults. Herr and Cramer (1984) have suggested that, in view of their previous experience, most adults are likely to be more aware of their values, needs, skills, abilities, and other personal characteristics than adolescents who seek career planning assistance. Consequently, they are likely to have a greater need for pertinent career information than perhaps any other aspect of career planning. Too often, however, good information about career opportunities is missing from career planning and development programs (Gutteridge & Otte, 1983).

Walker (1977) described the kind of career information that organizations should provide to employees. He expressed the view that effective career planning was contingent upon receiving descriptions of career paths, job requirements, training and development resources, appraisal systems, and job posting. Similar types of information were identified by Leach (1980), who also suggested that if employees are to be managers of their own careers, the organization must provide them with up-to-date, accurate, and accessible information about career opportunities. Information about career paths can be particularly useful. Although many positions do not have clearly defined career paths, information about those that do can help employees identify objectives, understand what will be required of them, and enhance their understanding of how work activities can further their professional development.

The Supervisor's Role as Career "Coach"

Discussions of career planning and development in organizations invariably turn to the issue of who provides employees with the guidance they need. Although many organizations use group formats in which the leader is at least nominally a specialist in career development, most rely on supervisors to play the role of counselor, adviser, or coach on an ongoing basis when the employee has returned to the job. Whether or not supervisors are motivated or adequately equipped for this role is another matter. Walker and Gutteridge (1979) reported that most supervisors did not feel that career counseling should be part of their job. Moreover, 87% of the human resource professionals surveyed reported that, in their judgment, few supervisors possess the necessary skills to perform in this role. These findings are particularly troublesome because the supervisor, in many organizations, is in the best position to influence employee career development. Even those individuals who have participated in workshops or completed self-contained career planning materials require follow-up that could be provided by a skilled supervisor.

Hall (1976) has stressed the importance, for career development purposes, of accurate feedback on performance and potential. Of even greater value would be a discussion of job performance in the context of overall career goals and plans. This could include a review of performance dimensions in light of other factors, such as values, needs, interests, family circumstances, and economic conditions, which also play an important role in career decision making.

To realize the potential value of the supervisor's role as career development "coach," three conditions are necessary. First, there must be an incentive for supervisors to perform this role. In many organizations, supervisors are rewarded for keeping, rather than developing, employees (Miller, 1981). Organizations that expect their supervisors to play a central role in fostering the career development of subordinates must be willing to reinforce and reward these activities. Second, supervisors must have specific knowledge, skills, and attitudes in order to be effective coaches. Miller, in connection with his description of a training program for managers, suggests that they should:

- know about organizational policies and practices that bear on career development issues;
- know the information resources available to support career planning;
- have the skills and techniques required to facilitate career planning discussions with employees;
- have a broad perspective on career development with respect to its importance to the company and what can and cannot be done; and
- have struggled successfully with some of their own career concerns.

The literature contains descriptions of other training programs intended to accomplish similar objectives (Leibowitz, Farren, & Kaye, 1986). Finally, and somewhat paradoxically, another strategy for making supervisors more effective counselors is to train subordinates to be more active in seeking guidance from their bosses. This is not intended to suggest a shift in responsibility away from the supervisor, but rather to emphasize the joint responsibility involved in career planning and the need to encourage employees to take as much initiative as possible in planning their careers. Whatever career planning discussions occur between supervisors and subordinates, the outcomes will be enhanced if both are adequately prepared. For the subordinate this might mean initiating a career development discussion rather than waiting for the supervisor to take action, requesting feedback on specific skills that might be consistent with but not limited to those contained in the normal performance appraisal, identifying specific questions about the organization and existing career opportunities, and getting feedback on the viability of specific career goals and plans. Clearly, the organizational climate must be conducive to this type of self-initiated activity, and the supervisor must have the skills necessary to respond effectively, but such actions by the subordinate seem an obvious extension of the active planning and goal setting that are nearly always a central element of career planning and development programs.

Monitoring Career Plans

One of the ironies of programs intended to promote career development is that employees are encouraged to look at their work from a "life span" perspective, setting long-term and short-term goals and generating plans for achieving them, yet few, if any, programs try to help individuals monitor the eventual success (or failure) of their efforts. There are too many factors outside the control of the individual to expect that goals and plans formulated at one point will remain unchanged over time. An important question, however, is how individuals cope with the inevitable barriers and discontinuities which they encounter. How should they? Storey (1981) suggests emphasizing "controllables," that is, those factors that the individual who is managing his or her own career can influence. Although this is important, an individual can learn a great deal about career planning by examining how he or she copes with discontinuities. Yet there is little evidence in the professional literature of any successful efforts to facilitate the acquisition of this skill, despite the fact that organizations seem particularly well suited to helping individuals acquire the ability to monitor their career plans. Ideally, an integrated and coordinated career development system could incorporate methods involving employee review of earlier goals and plans in light of changing organizational circumstances and evolving personal characteristics, of barriers encountered and how they were negotiated, what was learned, and how all of this could impact future planning and goal setting.

Evaluating Program Effects

The recent popularity of career planning and development programs in organizations represents a triumph of good intentions over careful inquiry. Several years ago, Super and Hall (1978) pointed out that "in view of the great number of training activities in industry specifically devoted to career planning, it is disappointing that there is so little published research on their effectiveness" (p. 360). Cairo (1983) came to a similar conclusion in a more recent review and went on to argue for more carefully conceived program evaluations. Although the call for this kind of effort is common in connection with career planning and development interventions in any context, the absence of program evaluations in organizations is especially evident (Leibowitz, Farren, & Kaye, 1986; Storey, 1979).

Several articles have summarized research on career counseling outcomes and offered recommendations for further inquiry (Holland, Magoon, & Spokane, 1981; Myers, 1986; Spokane & Oliver, 1983). They report, for the most part, the results of career interventions outside specific organizational settings. Many of their observations and conclusions, however, are directly relevant and should be considered carefully by persons responsible for evaluating career planning and development programs in organizations.

Although it is not the intention here to summarize all of the conclusions made in these earlier reviews, three specific points are worth mentioning in connection with the issues discussed above.

1. Because so many different types of programs are referred to as career planning and development, it is essential that program evaluators specify precisely the characteristics of the intervention. This should include descriptions of the nature, content, and duration of the activity being evaluated.

2. More clarity regarding goals and objectives is also needed, including specific criteria for evaluating effects. Moreover, multiple criteria should be considered, for example, to identify particular behaviors, knowledge, and attitudes that are expected to result from a career planning and development activity.

3. Studies comparing different types of helping strategies would also be useful. Although this is potentially expensive and time consuming (and rather idealistic), such efforts would help us determine the types of activities that are most effective in facilitating career development in organizations.

Although it is much easier and less expensive to evaluate career planning and development programs on the basis of their good intentions and popularity among participants, more rigorous evaluations are needed. Such efforts should ultimately become an integral part of every organization's program planning process.

SUMMARY

Recognizing that the absence of evaluative data makes any conclusions tentative, the following recommendations are offered for the design and implementation of career planning and development programs in organizations.

1. Program development should be preceded by a systematic and thorough assessment of the career development needs of the target population. This should include some effort to distinguish between employees who require help in obtaining the standard career planning competencies and those with different, but equally important, career development needs.

2. To avoid the problems associated with employees' unrealistic expectations of career planning and development programs, information about career opportunities should be honest, accurate, and up-to-date. Wherever possible, this element of a program should include information about job requirements, career paths, training and development resources, and promotional possibilities.

3. Efforts to facilitate employees' appraisal of work-related skills must include the recognition that some important skills might be extremely difficult, perhaps even impossible, to acquire regardless of subsequent developmental activities. In such cases, employees might be encouraged to focus on finding positions that maximize strengths and minimize weaknesses rather than searching for developmental activities that, in reality, have little potential of success.

4. Organizations that expect supervisors to take a central role in the career development of their subordinates should provide incentives and rewards for these efforts and should insure that supervisors possess, or acquire, the knowledge, skills, and attitudes required to be effective helpers.

5. Methods for helping employees monitor their career plans should be a part of every program. This will require coordination among other career-related activities to provide employees with ongoing

opportunities to review earlier goals and plans and modify them in light of any new information or circumstances.

6. Finally, there is a clear need for more and better program evaluations. Given the large number of existing career planning and development programs and the likelihood of continued growth in the area, it is important that we begin to examine carefully the effects of our efforts.

REFERENCES

Arthur, M.B., Hall, D.T., & Lawrence, B.S. (1989). *Handbook of career theory*. Cambridge: Cambridge University Press.

Bardwick, J.M. (1986). *The plateauing trap*. Toronto: Bantam.

Bolles, R.N. (1988). *What color is your parachute?* (6th edition). Berkeley, CA: Ten Speed Press.

Brooks, L. (1984). Career planning programs in the workplace. In D. Brown & L. Brooks (Eds.), *Career choice and development* (pp. 388–405). San Francisco: Jossey-Bass.

Bray, D.W., Campbell, R.J., & Grant, D.E. (1974). *Formative years in business*. New York: Wiley.

Cairo, P.C. (1983). Counseling in industry: A selected review of literature. *Personnel Psychology, 36*, 1–18.

Cairo, P.S., & Lyness, K.L. (1988). Stimulating high-potential career development through an assessment center process. In M. London & E.M. Monc (Eds.), *Career growth and human resource strategies* (pp. 183–193). New York: Quorum.

Campbell, R.E., & Cellini, J.V. (1981). A diagnostic taxonomy of adult career problems. *Journal of Vocational Behavior, 19*, 175–190.

Cohen, B. (1977). *Career development in industry: A study of selected programs and recommendations for program planning*. Princeton, NJ: Educational Testing Service.

Cytrynbaum, S., & Crites, J.O. (1989). Adult development theory and career adjustment. In M.B. Arthur, D.T. Hall, & B.S. Lawrence (Eds.), *Handbook of career theory* (pp. 66–88). Cambridge: Cambridge University Press.

Dalton, G.W., & Thompson, P.H. (1986). *Novations: Strategies for career development*. Glenview, IL: Scott Foresman.

Driver, M. (1979). Career concepts and career management in organizations. In C.L. Cooper (Ed.), *Behavioral problems in organizations* (pp. 79–139). Englewood Cliffs, NJ: Prentice-Hall.

Ference, T.P., Stoner, J.A.F., & Warren, E.K. (1977). Managing the career plateau. *Academy of Management Review, 2*, 602–612.

Gilbert, P.J., & Jaffee, C.L. (1982). The assessment center method: An effective strategy for human resource development. In G.R. Walz (Ed.), *Career development in organizations* (pp. 99–134). Ann Arbor, MI: ERIC/CAPS.

Gould, R. (1978). *Transformations: Growth and change in adult life*. New York: Simon and Schuster.

Griffith, A.R. (1980). A survey of career development in corporations. *Personnel and Guidance Journal, 58*, 537–543.

Gutteridge, T.G. (1986). Organizational and career development systems: The state of the practice. In D.T. Hall and Associates, *Career development in organizations* (pp. 50–94). San Francisco: Jossey-Bass.

Gutteridge, T.G., & Otte, F.L. (1983). Organizational career development: What's going on out there? *Training and Development Journal, 37* (2), 22–26.

Hall, D.T. (1976). *Careers in organizations.* Santa Monica, CA: Goodyear.

Hall, D.T., & Lerner, P. (1980). Career development in work organizations: Research and practice. *Professional Psychology, 11*, 428–435.

Hanson, M.C. (1981). Career counseling in organizational groups. In D.H. Montross & C.J. Shinkman (Eds.), *Career development in the 1980s: Theory and practice* (pp. 379–392). Springfield, IL: Charles C. Thomas.

Hart, G.L., & Thompson, P.H. (1979). Assessment centers: For selection or development. *Organizational Dynamics, 7*(4), 63–77.

Herr, E.L., & Cramer, S.H. (1984). *Career guidance and counseling through the life span: Systematic approaches* (2nd ed.). Boston: Little, Brown.

Holland, J.L., Magoon, T.M., & Spokane, A.R. (1981). Counseling psychology: Career interventions, research, and theory. *Annual Review of Psychology, 32*, 279–305.

Keller, J., & Piotrowski, C. (1987). Career development programs in Fortune 500 firms. *Psychological Reports, 61*, 920–922.

Lancaster, A.S., & Berne, R.R. (1981). *Employer-sponsored career development programs.* Columbus, OH: ERIC Clearinghouse on Adult, Career, and Vocational Education.

Leach, J.J. (1980). Career development: Some questions and tentative answers. *Personnel Administrator, 25*(10), 31–34.

Leibowitz, Z., Farren, C., & Kaye, B.L. (1986). *Designing career development systems.* San Francisco: Jossey-Bass.

Levinson, D.J. (1978). *The seasons of a man's life.* New York: Knopf.

London, M., & Strumpf, S.A. (1982). *Managing careers.* Reading, MA: Addison-Wesley.

Lowenthal, M., Thurnher, M., & Chiriboga, D. (1975). *The four stages of life: A comparative study of women and men facing transitions.* San Francisco: Jossey-Bass.

Miller, D.B. (1981). Training managers to stimulate employee development. *Training and Development Journal, 35*(2), 47–53.

Morgan, M.A., Hall, D.T., & Martier, A. (1979). Career development strategies in industry—Where are we and where should we be? *Personnel, 56* (2), 13–30.

Myers, R.A. (1986). Research on educational and vocational counseling. In S.L. Garfield & A.E. Bergin (Eds.), *Handbook of psychotherapy and behavior change* (3rd ed.). New York: Wiley.

Neugarten, B.L. (1976). Adaptation and the life cycle. *The Counseling Psychologist, 6*, 16–20.

Schein, E.H. (1978). *Career dynamics: Matching individual and organizational needs.* Reading, MA: Addison-Wesley.

Schlossberg, N.K., Troll, L.E., & Leibowitz, Z. (1978). *Perspectives on counseling adults: Issues and skills*. Monterey, CA: Brooks/Cole.

Spokane, A.R., & Oliver, L.W. (1983). The outcomes of vocational interventions. In W.B. Walsh & S.H. Osipow (Eds.), *Handbook of vocational psychology* (pp. 99–136). Hillsdale, NJ: Erlbaum.

Storey, W.D. (Ed.). (1979). *A guide for career development inquiry*. Madison, WI: American Society for Training and Development.

Storey, W.D. (1981). Strategic personal career management. In D.H. Montross & C.J. Shinkman (Eds.), *Career development in the 1980s: Theory and practice* (pp. 353–362). Springfield, IL: Charles C. Thomas.

Super, D.E., & Hall, D.T. (1978). Career development: Exploration and planning. *Annual Review of Psychology, 29*, 333–372.

Vaillant, G.E. (1977). *Adaptation to life*. Boston: Little, Brown.

Walker, J.W. (1977). Personal and career development. In D. Yoder & H.O. Heneman, Jr. (Eds.), *Training and development, ASPA handbook of personnel and industrial relations* (Vol. 5) (pp. 57–64). Washington, DC: Bureau of National Affairs.

Walker, J.W., & Gutteridge, T. (1979). *Career planning practices: An AMA report*. New York: AMACOM.

Wanous, J.P. (1973). Effects of realistic job preview on job acceptance, job attitudes, and job survival. *Journal of Applied Psychology, 58*, 327–332.

CHAPTER 17

A Coming of Age: Addressing the Career Development Needs of Adult Students in University Settings

Dennis L. Keierleber
L. Sunny Hansen
University of Minnesota
Minneapolis, Minnesota

The university historically has been the province of youth, representing the beginning stage of the career and life aspirations of young adults. Today, however, the university is home to persons of all ages in all stages of development over the lifespan. The increasing numbers of adult, non-traditional students on campus, predicted in the early 1980s (Dearman & Plisko, 1982), have arrived. Of the projected 12.9 to 13.4 million students enrolled annually in colleges and universities between the years 1990 and 2000, an estimated 40 to 50 percent each year will be 25 years or older ("Projection of College Enrollment," 1990; U.S. Department of Education, 1989).

The concept of "adult student" goes beyond any age-based definition. It includes students who have been away from formal education for several years or who have stopped out of college, who attend college part-time, who hold full-time or part-time jobs, who have established their own homes, and who have assumed primary life roles other than that of student (Polson, 1989). By the mid-1990s, an estimated 60 percent of undergraduate students alone will be these nontraditional adult students (Pew Higher Education Research Program, 1990).

A new, diverse clientele is on campus, and, as Johnson (1986) suggests, they require something different. Higher education institutions and their employees, faculty, staff, and administrators may in the past have been more accustomed to assisting primarily traditional-aged students in career decision-making. Today, they may not have the services, the skills, or the knowledge to help this large group of adult students. Rather than a simple restructuring of current practice to address adult students' needs, a whole new perspective is necessary to assist adults with their educational, career, and life decisions.

In this chapter, we examine adult career development from the perspective of adult students, their interactions with the university, and the institutional philosophy and practices that influence the career and educational development of these students. We conceptualize the whole of the university as a career services network with almost every employee—faculty, administrators, professional staff, support staff—functioning in some way as a career service provider. We discuss the multiple roles that career service providers play in meeting the needs of adults on campus. In the last section we discuss several issues and trends for the future. The term, "university," in this chapter is defined as four-year and graduate-level universities and colleges.

CAREER AND ADULT DEVELOPMENT MODELS

From the many different models and theories of career and adult development, three concepts relate particularly to the issues of adults as university students: life roles, concepts of age, and transitions.

Life roles. Adulthood is characterized by a complexity of life roles. Super (1980, 1990) conceptualizes that adults, at any one time over the lifespan, may play simultaneously the roles of child (including son/daughter), student, parent, worker, spouse, homemaker, leisurite, citizen, retiree, and others. Life stage theories with sequential roles designated at chronological ages no longer seem to apply (Cross, 1981; Neugarten & Neugarten, 1987; Schlossberg, 1984). The linear model, in which one goes to school, goes to work, marries, has children, and retires, has been replaced by Cross' (1981) "blended life pattern," a fluid life plan that involves moving in and out of education, work, family responsibilities, retirement, and other roles over the lifespan.

Adult students play multiple roles. They must function as students. At the same time, they may have to meet the responsibilities of their jobs. At home, they balance roles of parent, citizen, spouse, and others. For adult students, role involvements influence decisions to pursue education, to what degree, and in what manner. Mohney and Anderson (1988) found that most women attributed their decisions to enroll in college to changing role demands (such as having children now in school, having fewer work demands, or leaving a job). Universities must acknowledge the increased and varied complexity of life roles that adult students bring to the classroom.

Concepts of age. With little biological basis for most age-related behaviors, adults often are directed and constrained primarily by age-related historical and social influences on behavior (Neugarten & Neugarten, 1987). Age-related educational and career expectations are still deeply rooted in adult perceptions, and reinforced by tradition, stereotypes, and popular stage models of adult development (see, for example, Levinson, Darrow, Klein, Levinson, & McKee, 1978; Sheehy, 1976). Statements such as, "Adults should be settled down and on a career track by their late 20s," and, "As a 50 year old woman, I'm too old to go to graduate school," express still common beliefs that lead adults to restrict their growth opportunities. Age restrictions are also externally imposed; they come from university admissions committees, faculty, employers, and families (Schlossberg, 1984). Universities must directly confront the problem of ageism as lifelong learners become the norm on campus.

Transitions. Aslanian and Brickell (1980) believe that adults seeking further education are in the process of transition. Schlossberg (1984) defines transition as an "event or nonevent that results in change of relationships, routines, assumptions, and/or roles within the settings of self, work, family, health, and/or economics" (p. 43). Aslanian and Brickell (1980) apply the concept of transition more specifically to education as a movement from one status in life to another that requires the learning of new knowledge, new skills, and new attitudes or values.

More recently, Schlossberg, Lynch, and Chickering (1989) refined the concept of transition further in the context of adult students in higher education into three phases: moving in (e.g., learning the institution's rules and norms), moving through (e.g., balancing student and other life roles), and moving on (e.g., preparing for roles beyond college). Adults in higher education experience transitions as a process over time. The needs of adult students differ depending on where they are in the transition process. To meet the needs of adults, universities must address the process of transition as inherent to the educational process of adults.

THE ADULT STUDENT

Individuality and commonality. Adult students are characterized above all by their individuality (Cross, 1981; Heffernan, 1981; Schlossberg, Lynch, & Chickering, 1989). They vary on all dimensions: life styles, interests, self-concepts, self-esteem, achievement motivation, risk-taking, goals, civic involvements, learning styles, support systems, and demographic characteristics. Diversity characterizes persons of any age, but as adults have more experiences over the lifespan, they are characterized by a "fanning out," or an increased differentiation, variability, and individual uniqueness with age (Neugarten, 1976).

As Schlossberg and associates observe, when addressing the concept of the adult student, a focus on age as a main variable often results in a disregard of other important characteristics, as well as the individuality of adult learners. A misleading assumption is that age provides understanding of people's thoughts, feelings, and behaviors. Educators frequently view adult students as if they form a recognizable entity with a set way of learning and for whom there is a set way of teaching (Schlossberg, Lynch, & Chickering, 1989).

At the same time, adult students as a group do have special needs and characteristics that distinguish them from traditional-aged students. Miller and Musgrave (1986) have noted that career service providers often become so engaged in working with and perceiving clients individually that they overlook the importance of analyzing the group characteristics of their adult clientele. Several research reviews (Cross, 1981; Heffernan, 1981; Hughes, 1983) and national surveys (Aslanian & Brickell, 1980, 1988) provide a general picture of some of the needs and characteristics of adult students.

Demographic characteristics. Compared with the general population, adults who participate in organized learning tend to be in their mid-twenties to mid-forties, better educated, employed, and in better-paying jobs. Adult degree-seeking students frequently come from working class backgrounds and might best be described as "upwardly mobile" from their parents' socioeconomic level (Cross, 1981). Adult learners include a greater percentage of women than men. They tend to be those for whom organized education has worked in the past, and they continue to use it (Goldstein, 1984).

Career concerns. Adults seek further education primarily for career reasons. In an extensive review of client inquiries at adult educational resource centers, Heffernan (1981) found vocational concerns were primary. Educational concerns typically were expressed in relation to career and job development concerns. A nationwide survey of why adults seek further learning found that over half the adults reported a career-related need as the main reason (Aslanian & Brickell, 1980). The occupational motive outweighed all other motives combined, with family concerns a distant second. In a recent national study, Aslanian and Brickell (1988) found that, for adults studying for college credit, 70 percent of the courses taken were in career fields. About 80 percent of adults studying for degrees were taking them in career areas, such as business, computer science, engineering, education, or health.

Career concerns in these studies include primarily occupational, job, and work-related concerns. However, others (Lewis, 1988; Schlossberg, Lynch, & Chickering, 1989) note that reasons for returning to college also fit a broader definition of "career." For many adults, educational goals include learning about life and the world, achieving personal satisfaction, helping solve personal and community problems, sharing knowledge, or meeting new people. The pursuit of higher education for adult students often involves a complex set of individual goals.

Barriers to learning. Several educators have identified barriers to further learning for adults (Cross 1981; Heffernan, 1981; Hughes, 1983; Lewis, 1988). Cross (1981) identified three general categories of barriers: situational, dispositional, and institutional. Situational barriers reflect everyday life conditions, such as lack of money, limited time, demanding home and job responsibilities, needs for affordable child care, limited means of transportation, and lack of support from family and friends. Funding for adults' education often is viewed as a discretionary income cost, not as an investment or obligation as is a younger person's college expenses. Adults are often limited to educational institutions in their immediate geographical area. Job, family, community, and other responsibilities take priority over educational activities. As a result, formal education is often intermittent, sporadic, and part-time.

Dispositional barriers include self-perceptions and attitudes of the person as an adult student. Adults may believe they are too old and have too limited energy for school. Because they frequently are out of practice in academic skills, they are uncertain about their abilities and tend to overestimate or underestimate their capacities as students. Adults may have ambivalent feelings about the university as a result of bad past experiences, lack of familiarity with a university culture, or doubts about a university's willingness to respond to their individual situations.

Institutional barriers are those institutional policies and practices that hinder adult learners, such as inappropriate admissions criteria, restricted class offerings, unavailability of classes other than during daytime hours, or biased attitudes of university staff members. A more detailed review of these conditions follows in our discussion of the university.

Adult student needs. The nationwide study by Aslanian and Brickell (1988) of adults enrolled in college courses for credit emphasizes some basic needs of adult students on campus. Students were asked to indicate what services they most wanted colleges to offer to help with their college experience. Most wanted services by adult students were: convenient registration (e.g., by mail or phone), adequate parking, financial help (e.g., grants, loans), help with obtaining off-campus jobs, practical application labs for class material, and academic and career counseling.

Moderately desired services included campus facilities (e.g., cafeterias, library desks), study assistance (e.g., tutoring services, study groups, study skills classes), deferred payment of tuition, and on-campus jobs. Lowest rated services for colleges to offer included organized social activities, personal conveniences (e.g., personal lockers or mailboxes), and public transportation.

Student ratings in this study reflected the practical side of student needs. Adult students want help with managing their limited available time and finances, focusing on career goals, and balancing competing demands of their on-campus and off-campus lives. Surveys conducted for specific institutions (see Bodensteiner, 1989; Hughes, 1983) report similar results.

Strengths of adult students. Even facing many obstacles, adult students are successful in their educational pursuits because they bring many strengths to campus. They have had more, and more varied, experiences in life than their younger counterparts. They have a richer array of ongoing experiences and developed skills, preferences, and values. They have greater self-determination and acceptance of responsibility (Lynch & Chickering, 1984).

As Heffernan (1981) notes, many adult students have positive attitudes about themselves and their possibilities for change. These students may be frustrated, unprepared, and tentative about change, but they are willing to try. Some may be hesitant to embark on further learning and a new career; others bring a fierce determination to the process (Brademas, 1990). Once they begin, adult students typically are self-directed and forward-moving. They are willing to make changes under difficult circumstances when stability, not change, is the perceived norm for their age group.

316

CONCERNS OF SPECIFIC POPULATIONS

The future of higher education and its success in serving adult students will require major action to address the needs of at-risk groups of current and prospective students. The preceding section presents only part of the picture. As educators, we need to look further to those persons who have not participated in higher education, who have been ill-served in the college environment, and who will be the significant population forces of the future. Such specific populations include persons of color, women, persons with disabilities, immigrants, the elderly, the economically disadvantaged, gay/lesbian individuals, and other persons who have not been accepted fully into the mainstream of higher education or society. For illustrative purposes, we focus here primarily on minority groups and women within higher education, but the problems discussed apply to a wide range of disadvantaged persons.

Minority groups. As the 21st century approaches, persons of color will become a significantly larger part of this country's general population, work force, and prospective college student population. Hodgkinson (1985) presents a comprehensive summary of these demographic trends. By the year 2000, one of every three people in the United States will be a person of color. These increases will result from both the number of minority children currently being born and growing up through the school system and the continued flow of immigrants into the country.

Aslanian (1990) reports that minority group individuals will make up over 30 percent of the new entrants into the work force, twice their current percentage, between now and the year 2000. Immigrants, especially Asian-Americans and Hispanics, will make up the largest share of the increase in the work force since World War I. Native born white males, who currently make up almost half of the workforce, will constitute less than one-third of new entrants to the labor force in the future (Fullerton, 1989).

Prospects for persons of color are both positive and pessimistic. Minority individuals will cover a broader socioeconomic range than ever before. They will have increased access to good jobs, their own businessess, and political leadership. Increasing demands for workers in certain occupations may improve the opportunities for minority groups to access areas that have not been open to them in the past (Hodgkinson, 1985; McDaniels, 1989). At the same time, disproportionate numbers of minority workers will remain in low-status occupations and earn substantially less than white workers (Hotchkiss & Borow, 1990).

Persons of color still face pervasive bias and discrimination that limit both the perception and reality of their career options. Learning experiences that would lead to entrance into certain occupations, and occupational success, have been restricted for minority groups. They are blocked from learning the skills necessary to break the cycle of poverty and discrimination (Mitchell & Krumboltz, 1990). Many minority youth acquire a perception that they are entering a work world that is essentially unmanageable. They have a burden of negative self-images, feelings of inadequacy as workers-to-be, and a disbelief in the efficacy of rational career planning (Hotchkiss & Borow, 1990).

317

Within educational settings, Hodgkinson (1985) warns that coming through the educational system is a group of individuals approaching adulthood who are poorer, more ethnically and linguistically diverse, and have more handicaps to affect their learning. There will still continue to be large numbers of persons of color who do not complete high school, recurring declines in the already small number of minority individuals who apply to college, and a persistently high dropout rate among minority college students.

At the same time, Wolfman (1990), focusing on African-American college students, states that the majority of such current students are middle class. They come from a variety of types of secondary schools, have a record of accomplishment in academic and extracurricular activities, and have family and community expectations to achieve. She expresses concern that on college campuses, as well as in the national consciousness, there is a pervading, single-dimensional concept of African-American students that ignores their individual differences and talents.

Though minority student enrollments in college reached a new high in Fall 1988, minority groups are still greatly underrepresented among college students (Evangelauf, 1990). Of minorities attending college, a disproportionate number, especially African-American and Hispanic students, attend community colleges, not four-year schools (Aslanian & Brickell, 1988; Hodgkinson, 1985). Further, there appears to be limited movement from community colleges to four-year colleges and, therefore, limited educational advancement that the latter institutions could provide these students. A recent study (Lee & Frank, 1990) indicated that few minority community college students with poor academic and economic backgrounds go on to four-year institutions. Those who do go on generally have had greater academic preparation and financial resources to begin with.

Persistence in the college environment for persons of color is an extremely fragile reality. A study of national college attendence (Wilson, 1990) reported that within four-year colleges, only 24 percent of African-American students and 29 percent of Hispanic students graduated with a bachelor's degree after six years. Over half of the Hispanic students and 63 percent of African-American students had permanently dropped out of college within that time. Thus, persons of color, the groups with the greatest demographic growth potential, are the least likely to attend college and to complete a bachelor's degree.

Hodgkinson (1985) raises the basic question of why higher education does not seem to appeal to persons of color in America. Whether the causes are lack of relationship between a college degree and a good job, declining financial aid, inadequate high school counseling programs, or plans to attend higher education a few years after high school, little is known about why a larger number of minority high school graduates is producing a smaller number of college students. Access has no meaning if persons do not seek out that to which access is available.

Aslanian (1990) suggests that minority students might avoid college because they expect to be uncomfortable there, and they may feel uncomfortable if they ever get there. Wolfman (1990) believes some minority students may be concerned about being assimilated into the campus culture and estranged from their family and community bonds. Because of their unique status on campus, minority students may feel they do not belong. They are labelled "minority" and are unsure if they are accepted on campus because of merit, affirmative action, special dispensation, or lowered standards. Minority groups place a high value on education (Hotchkiss & Borow, 1990; Wolfman, 1990), yet, as Hodgkinson (1985) concludes, the current pattern of college enrollment casts doubt on the idea that higher education is an essential part of the American dream for an increasing number of students of diverse racial and ethnic backgrounds.

Women. A number of trends and issues for the career and educational development of women parallel those described for minority groups. Aslanian (1990) reports that, in the 1990s, still more women will enter the labor force. By the year 2000, over 60 percent of women of working age will have jobs. In this time period, women will account for 62 percent of the net increase of new entrants into the labor force (Fullerton, 1989). Demands for workers in certain occupations may improve opportunities for women to work in areas from which they have been restricted in the past. However, as a group, women are still more limited in their occupational choices than men, are underrepresented in a variety of fields and professions, and tend to enter lower-paying, lower status occupations (Brooks, 1990).

As Mitchell and Krumboltz (1990) indicate, women's career choices have been and continue to be strongly directed by cultural influences regarding acceptable career paths. Such influences have a major effect on whether women are allowed the opportunity for learning experiences that lead to nontraditional career choices. Pervasive socialization processes perpetuate rigidly defined sex roles that limit career options.

Various theoretical and conceptual models of women's career development (e.g., Gottfredson, 1981; Hackett & Betz, 1981; Hansen & Biernat, in press; Sundal-Hansen, 1984) have explored how cultural influences limit women's perceptions of their career capabilities, of the likelihood of career success, and of accessibility of opportunities. Many women have not received guidance or encouragement to develop a strong sense of career orientation or accomplishment. Others have been accustomed to having their decisions made for them, with a limited self-concept of being able to choose, plan, and balance work and other life roles. Still others may have married early, have little or no occupational history, and have little confidence and knowledge, but much anxiety, about the career development process.

Significant numbers of adult women do participate in higher education. Almost 60 percent of adult, nontraditional college students are women (Aslanian & Brickell, 1988), and this enrollment trend is expected to continue well into the 1990s (Pew Higher Education Research Program, 1990). This extensive participation is impressive considering that gender-biased cultural influences are strongly evident in the sphere of higher education.

Many of the situational and dispositional barriers for adult learners, discussed earlier, apply especially to women returning to college (Lewis, 1988). Women have doubts about their abilities to perform academically because of limited or negative prior school experiences, often many years in the past. Financial strains and changing roles as mothers and wives may set finite time limits to accomplish goals or may generate feelings of guilt that accompany a return to school. Child care becomes a tremendous concern. Displaced homemakers and single parents often are already struggling financially, lacking the funds to pay for child care and other basic costs of living, as well as for their educations.

Adult women students also appear to have difficulty in connecting with important, needed assistance on campus. In reviewing several research studies on adult students, Hughes (1983) summarizes that returning women often are in greater need of services. Lewis (1988) reports, however, that studies comparing returning women to other nontraditional students find that women are less likely to use such support services. Lewis concludes that many women feel they must manage the transition back to school and all that such a move entails by themselves. Support services are avoided, with many women believing they are for traditional students. Yet the need for services, such as orientation, counseling, financial aid, and child care are critical for successful reentry and continued academic accomplishment.

Individuality and diversity. Understanding the problems of these specific populations is a complex process. The individuality and diversity that characterize adult learners in general also characterize every individual in these groups. It would be a great error to assume that problems and situations among Native Americans, African-Americans, Hispanics, and Asian-Americans are the same. Gay and lesbian individuals experience different kinds of problems and discrimination in education and work. Of returning adult women students, one will find minority group members, older women, displaced homemakers, disabled women, single parents, women from rural areas, and women with financial hardship— all with different backgrounds, situations, and needs.

The career and educational development problems of ethnic groups, and also of other specific populations, are especially complex because many influential factors such as race, gender, social class, economic conditions, and others are intertwined (Brooks, 1990; Mitchell & Krumboltz, 1990). Problems compound for many of these individuals. Persons of color, those with disabilities, and single-parent women must not only cope with the discrimination found in society and in higher education, they frequently must also struggle with economic hardships which limit their access to higher education. Women of color often struggle with the compounded influences of race, gender, and socioeconomic class. The diversity among these groups of individuals is great; their situations necessitate many different solutions.

THE UNIVERSITY

Very slowly, the university is adapting to its new constituency. Some institutions have been designed specifically for adult students (e.g., Empire State College in New York; Metropolitan State University in Minnesota). Others have been recognized nationally for their efforts to meet the needs of adult students (Apps, 1988). Many universities have continuing education units with primary responsibility for serving adult students. Continuing education for women (Adam & Lindoo, 1989) and returning women's programs (Copland, 1988) are well established. However, development of substantive programs, services, and practices for adult students is not the norm. The university still has a limited orientation toward the educational, career, and life needs of its adult students (Brademas, 1990; Giczkowski, 1990; Pew Higher Education Research Program, 1990; Schlossberg, Lynch, & Chickering, 1989).

Traditional student orientation. The pervasive value orientation among universities is still toward youth. The student stereotype is of young adults with limited maturity and life experiences who are passive learners dependent on expert guidance of faculty and administrators. In contrast, adult students beyond (and many within) traditional college age typically have had extensive life experiences. They play the major roles of adulthood—employees, parents, citizens—at work, at home, and in the community. They are accustomed to being in charge of their own and others' lives. They can, and prefer to, direct their lives independently but must function in a system that expects and fosters dependence. The adult student is a paradox; when the adult and the student come together, the university tends to emphasize the student and ignore the adult (Schlossberg, Lynch, & Chickering, 1989).

Adult students often face obstacles to what Aslanian (1990) calls "psychological access" to colleges and universities. Older students may sometimes be viewed as having too few productive years left for a program or for a professor to invest in training them. As Lewis (1988) suggests, part-time students are sometimes considered to be less serious about education or peripheral to an institution. Such students may be seen as uncommitted or frivolous rather than as taking their studies in earnest.

Women especially encounter many such obstacles. They sometimes face the stereotype that they are not career-oriented; educators often question an adult woman student's seriousness about pursuing her education. In academia, adult women students encounter few women role models and mentors, lack of encouragement and reinforcement, discrimination in both sex and age, sexual harassment, and other attitudes and behaviors that adversely affect their self-concepts, self-expectations, and performance. The many subtle ways in which women are discriminated against and discouraged from accomplishment, the "chilly climate for women on campus," have been documented by Sandler and Hall (Hall & Sandler, 1982; Sandler & Hall, 1986). They describe how conscious and nonconscious attitudes and behaviors of many university staff communicate negative messages about women being in higher education—that they are second-class citizens, that their opinions are not central, and that their presence is not significant.

Organizational practices. University organizational structure and practices are also oriented toward the young student: one who attends school full time during the day, lives on campus, is enrolled in a degree

321

program directly out of high school, and whose primary life role is that of student. Admission criteria, for example, such as high school test scores and college grade point averages from many years ago, are inappropriate for adult students because the criteria do not relate to current capability or performance. Traditional admissions policies may not allow an adult student to reenroll to establish a current successful record of academic accomplishment. Complicated procedures for admissions to a program or simply for course registration can consume much time, require days off from work, create child care problems, and discourage an adult from attending college.

Citing national census bureau statistics, Lewis (1988) notes that the average American moves almost 13 times during a lifetime, and half of the nation's population moves every five years. This situation often leaves adult students unable to show an orderly progression in their educational pursuits. Women often have to move because their husbands' professions require a change of location. Single parents may have to move to find jobs. Many women find it difficult to put together a college education in the face of continual disruption (Schlossberg, Lynch, & Chickering, 1989). Residency requirements, time limits to finish a degree, and the discounting of "old" credits leave both women and men returning adult students at a disadvantage.

Courses and services are often offered on campus during the day only, with few if any evening, weekend, and late afternoon hours or off-campus sites for working, part-time students. Part-time students not on campus are often disadvantaged because they do not learn of programs and services available to them. Financial aid is often limited to full-time students, or full fees are charged for part-time attendance. Often women cannot apply for financial aid independent of their husbands' incomes. Adults from families with moderate incomes often exceed the limits to qualify for aid.

Need and prospects for change.   The need for change is evident as adult students, in their daily experiences, are placed on the periphery of the academic community. The structure, policies, and practices of the university frequently do not fit with the life situations of adult learners. Adult students are continually sent messages that they do not fit in with the university culture, that they are atypical, and that they do not belong. They are treated as marginal students in a system not adapted to their backgrounds, needs, and goals (Schlossberg, Lynch, & Chickering, 1989).

Yet, adult students are a significant part of the university's present and future. As Hodgkinson (1985) notes, for the future, adult education is the only growth component possible in postsecondary education. The prospects for change, though hopeful, also reflect a reluctance to change. Changes in areas such as admissions requirements may be viewed as jeopardizing the academic quality of the institution. Program modifications, more varied course scheduling, new services, and other changes require additional work and inconveniences to university faculty, administrators, and staff accustomed to a routine designed to fit their preferences and life styles. The reward system, especially at larger research universities, does not encourage effort toward such changes.

The university is still a major source of postsecondary education in this country and offers much for adult students: a great diversity of programs and perspectives, the only available training for many occupational areas, the credentialing and credibility needed for different career fields, and critical life coping skills. It offers persons of color and other at-risk groups the opportunities to improve their economic situations and life satisfaction. If the university is to remain a major resource for educational and career development in the future, it must become more flexible, accessible, and adaptive to the needs of adult students.

PROVIDING CAREER SERVICES FOR ADULT STUDENTS

The growing number of adult students on campus requires a more encompassing view of career development services for the university. Several organizational perspectives provide a framework for such a view. Within this framework, we conceptualize the whole of the university as a career services network and outline some key roles of career service providers addressing adult student needs..

Organizational perspectives. The career needs of adult students at the university require an *ecological perspective* in conceptualizing, designing, and providing services (Schlossberg, 1984; Schlossberg, Lynch, & Chickering, 1989; Walz & Benjamin, 1984). The university, its faculty, administrators, staff, and students form a system of interdependent, dynamic parts. Career services go beyond assisting students in career development, counseling, or student services only. They involve coordinating and intervening with the university at several levels, in several areas, through a variety of university personnel.

An ecological perspective on human services is not new, but the continuing call for such an approach by educators and practitioners in career, educational, and adult development indicates that the translation of model to practice in these areas has been limited. Implementation of the ecological perspective requires a much greater awareness on the part of higher education institutions of the multipotentialities and talents of adult student populations.

The *educational brokering perspective* was developed in the 1970s to provide community educational and career resources for adults seeking further education. The perspective, as described by Heffernan (1981), extends beyond the simple connotation of "broker" as intermediary between adult students and educational resources. It incorporates a combination of established ideas and practices familiar to counselors, educators, and others who work in universities. The core functions or roles *include* providing information, assessment, counseling, referral, advocacy, and outreach. The educational brokering concept has as its mission the empowerment and self-determination of adults to make informed choices, use educational resources, and increase their capabilities to improve their work and personal lives.

The *transitions perspective* of adult learners (Schlossberg, Lynch, & Chickering, 1989) provides another model for organizing services. The "Moving In" phase of the model suggests clustering together services such as admissions, reentry orientation programs, financial aid assistance, academic advising, registration, and assessment of prior learning. The "Moving Through" phase incorporates services such as career development services, regular educational programs, health and wellness programs, adult learner associations, support groups for special populations, and developmental mentoring programs. The "Moving On" phase encompasses services such as internships and cooperative learning, a culminating course for soon-to-graduate students, transition groups, and placement services. As part of this service model, the authors recommend the creation of an entry education center to coordinate and house the "Moving In" services and the establishment of a culminating education center for the "Moving On" services.

NETWORK OF UNIVERSITY CAREER SERVICES

Student needs and university services. University student services are often organized along functional lines with little integration of services or communication between offices. Students with complex problems are frequently faced with fragmented information from different student service offices (Schlossberg, Lynch, & Chickering, 1989). As an example, an adult part-time evening student has taken prerequisite courses for several years with the goal of admission to a university's college of business administration. The student has received marginal grades and has just been put on probation, jeopardizing the student's financial aid. What are the problems? Where does the student go to resolve them? Adult students' lives and their career and educational needs cut across organizational and functional lines of the university.

Creating a services network. A comprehensive, physically and organizationally integrated set of career and educational services is a desirable goal. At many smaller schools such integrated service units have been established as formal career development programs. At larger universities, services have been integrated across functions to help some students, such as in centers for specific groups (women, minority students, older adults, disabled students, international students) and in career centers. The "one-stop" career and educational services unit, however, may not be practical or possible at many universities because of historical, political, or financial reasons. Also, adult student needs often extend across a wider range of services than can be formally integrated.

Though university services units may be functionally different and physically separate, they can work together to develop a more comprehensive service delivery system for adult students' career needs. Each unit should be viewed as part of an interrelated network with a common goal of assisting adult students with their career and educational development. A network of career services for adult university students includes the range of offices that provide services spanning the student's length of stay at the university: preadmissions and admissions, departmental and collegiate level advising, financial aids, registration, academic and student affairs administration, extension and continuing education units, advisory committees, student boards, placement centers, alumni organizations, and others. Faculty and their academic departments are very much a part of this career services network through the daily enterprise of educating students. The full corps of university employees, as career service providers, plays the key role in establishing the connecting relationship between the offices.

Intervention points. Translating these perspectives into action appears to be a major task. On a daily basis, service providers are restricted by assigned job responsibilities, time, funding, administrative and colleague support, institutional policies, and other constraints. Individual service providers and units need to target the parts of the system they can affect. University employees can start with examining their own attitudes, stereotypes, knowledge base, and practices that affect adult students. Offices can look at their units' assigned responsibilities, practices, and policies to better meet adult student needs and reduce barriers. Beyond any one office is the development of a coordinated effort between offices to provide problem solutions relating more to students' needs and less to organizational boundaries. At the institutional level, service offices and academic departments can band together to modify institutional policies and practices that affect adult students.

Using an imperfect system. Though service providers have a responsibility to intervene and assist adult students, Walz and Benjamin (1984) emphasize also that service providers need to help adult university students learn and adapt in an imperfect world. The challenges of overcoming barriers, managing stresses, and solving situational problems help students to develop the coping skills they need for life. The development of independence and self-determination requires students to learn how to best use the system, its people, and its resources to make progress. A university's policies and practices may be unfair and restrictive for some, but students must work with and through the system and not let it deter them from their central mission of furthering their career and educational development. The institution must do its part to adapt to its new constituency, but nontraditional students must also accept the university as a special place with a unique mission and set of goals (Giczkowski, 1990).

ROLES OF CAREER SERVICE PROVIDERS

University employees must function in a variety of roles to provide career services to adult students. A number of roles have been identified as important for the behavioral repertoires of helpers (Herr, 1984; Heffernan, 1981; Schlossberg, 1984). Several such roles, following Heffernan's (1981) model, are discussed here. Whether faculty, counselors, advisers, admissions officers, or administrators, all university staff members should examine their different roles that influence the career and educational needs of adult students.

Networking. Both career service providers and adult students need to create networks for themselves. The development of a network among service providers requires effort toward planned, regular communication between practitioners. A coordinated, collaborative network can be informal, with each unit maintaining its own identity but benefiting from jointly developing and sharing resources. Service offices might share information about adult student characteristics and needs, training and resource materials, and comparative practices that have or have not worked in planning and management of student services. At higher levels, an informal network of service offices can promote the career and educational needs of adult students to policy-makers on campus and beyond. Concerned professionals can provide input at the state level to affect relevant programs, such as state-based occupational information systems and financial aid programs.

Adult students need to establish a network among themselves at the university. They often have no vehicle to share common concerns, experiences, knowledge, and resources and to build a sense of community within the university. Career service providers can be the facilitators to bring adult students in contact with one another. Networking devices might include special orientation programs addressing campus life, academic survival skills, and other concerns of adult students. Support groups can be developed around common issues or target populations, such as veterans, reentry women, single parents, displaced workers, or men changing careers. A lounge or general meeting place with weekly programs addressing adult student issues can also put students in touch with each other. There are a number of ways to bring adult students together to create networks among themselves, but career service providers need to assist in providing a reason and a place for adult students to establish contact with one another.

Information. The greatest need among adult students is access to information. Adult students need information about themselves, their values, skills, interests, and life situations. They need work-related information on occupations, training and credentialing requirements, necessary skills, and employers. They need information on career and adult development, such as perspectives on career and life roles, the process of career planning, career socialization, and the process of transitions and change. They need to be aware of the interactive effects of work on family and of family on work. They need information about the changing and more diverse workplace as well as about the changing family patterns in society (Hansen & Minor, 1989). In general, adult students need information to understand the nature of their development, to understand the environmental factors which affect their growth, and to act on their environment to move forward developmentally.

Adult students need basic institutional and educational information about courses, programs, degrees, university procedures, and financial aid, as well as information about the educational culture of the university. They need to know about services and resources available both on and off campus, such as counseling, student employment, special student centers, support groups, and child care services.

Adult students need general occupational information, but such information must also be adult-relevant. Adult students often want information on occupations beyond the entry-level. They seek options that can use their prior experience, supplemented with further education, to advance or change directions. People with limited paid employment experience, such as returning women, may need information about occupations and job areas in which they can begin, but these students also express interest in information on advanced-level positions that they can move into in time.

The process of providing occupational information must be free of gender bias. Educators often unintentionally perpetuate traditional sex-role stereotypes in educational and occupational options. Career service providers need to familiarize educators and others who work less frequently with occupational information toward a gender-neutral approach to such options.

Adult students' occupational information requests often require more detailed responses about the gains and losses in choosing one occupational area versus another (including the client's current occupation). The costs of further education, including time, money, and effort, as well as impact on current life style, need to be balanced and evaluated against gains in salary, advancement, work conditions, and future life style. For adults, educational and career information are closely tied; adults require a direct, practical translation of how different education and career options relate to one another.

Because they are frequently bound to a locale by job and family, adult students need regionally-based occupational and job information. Traditional information resources, such as the *Occupational Outlook Handbook*, may be inexpensive and readily accessible but are less useful without supplemental information on local labor market conditions, employers, industries, and further training.

Adults need information about the changing labor market. McDaniels (1989) provides an excellent summary of occupational forecasts for the 1990s and beyond. He stresses the necessity that career service providers help students be fully aware of the different possible trends for the future of work. Scenarios range from a "futurist" approach (an increase in newly emerging careers created by rapidly developing technologies); to a more moderate perspective of change, with many current traditional career areas continuing as such during the coming years; to a pessimistic forecast of high levels of unemployment and underemployment due to continued elimination of jobs and downscaling of corporations and industries.

Besides scanning the traditional occupational environment to choose from what is out there, adult students need to be introduced to entrepreneurial planning and ways to "create your own" careers. McDaniels (1989) stresses the need for career service providers to become better equipped to discuss with clients what he calls the "wild cards" of the future of work: entrepreneurial ventures, small businesses, and work-at-home jobs. He views these career options as special opportunities for women and persons of color. These options allow these individuals to build their own businesses and to have less of a struggle with an entrenched bureaucratic structure, the "old boys' network," and pervasive discrimination.

Adult students need information on a broad base of educational options both within and outside the university. A particular university may not have appropriate offerings or be practical for a student's knowledge needs and situational constraints. Career service providers should become familiar with a variety of other learning opportunities, such as local schools and community resources, alternative programs for adults, short-term workshops and conferences, internships, and self-study options.

Accessibility of information is a problem for adult students because they generally spend limited time on campus. In addition to traditional sources of information, such as college bulletins, U.S. Department of Labor publications, and in-person group presentations, career service providers will need to rely more on nontraditional sources. Methods of information delivery might include readily available telephone advising and information tapes; self-managed slide, videotape, and audiotape programs; computer-assisted guidance systems; columns specifically for adult students in the university newspaper; announcements in local and community newspapers; television and radio announcements and programs; and computer information and guidance packages. Career service providers should stress a balance of personal contact and other methods of information delivery to involve adult students fully in the university community.

Beyond helping adult students identify and gain access to information is the critical task of helping them use the information. Adults may have little sense of how the educational and career information relates to their lives and goals. They often do not know what questions to ask. They are unaware of the complexity of the response that an initial question can bring. Their ability to process and interpret information is sometimes limited because of their unfamiliarity with university structure and practices or their narrow view of career planing. To help students understand the nature of the career development process, career service providers must rely especially on their empathic skills and continually seek feedback from the students.

Assessment.   The role of assessment is also basic to most career service providers. Assessment begins at first contact to determine students' particular needs and problems. It continues with assisting students with clarification of their life roles, values, skills, personal and family circumstances, work and learning experiences, and other areas. Assessment for adult students often draws more heavily on their life experiences than for younger students. Many adults have reality-tested their life values and capabilities that can suggest new directions. Their major need is translation of their personal qualities and assets developed from past experiences into terms relevant to work and other life roles for the future. From this base, career service providers can determine what further learning experiences are needed to achieve students' career goals.

A variety of formal and informal assessment methods are needed in working with adult students. Methods may include interviewing and questioning, written worksheets and exercises, or self-help career/planning books. Computerized career guidance systems for adult learners are well developed. Traditional standardized tests and assessment inventories are still in demand among adult students. Generally, for adults, standardized methods for assessment of relevant experiences for career and educational planning do not easily tap the full complexity of adults' experiences. Assessment must often rely on more subjective methods to evaluate the personal characteristics and situational conditions that will be important for such planning; it simply requires more time, effort, and extensive analysis.

Regarding specific populations of concern, Miller (1986) stresses that, for women, career assessment cannot rely simply on such personal dimensions as values, interests, and abilities. It must also focus on such areas as perceptions of sex-role behavior with regard to a career, the extent to which occupational stereotyping is influencing career choices, and the types of occupational role models available. Brown (1990) further emphasizes that standardized methods of assessment, such as tests and inventories, should be selected carefully and used judiciously to avoid invalid, discriminatory information. Criticisms have been raised about use of achievement measures with minority students and interest inventories with women, for example. Use of such measures by skilled professionals can provide valuable information for students, but it must be guided by ethical, moral, and legal considerations.

Counseling. For our purposes here, counseling is broadly defined to include, beyond traditional counselor functions, such roles as advising, consulting, coaching, instructing, and mentoring (Schlossberg, 1984). Its methods may involve one-to-one interviewing, workshops, support groups, courses, correspondence, computer-assisted guidance, and other structured programs. Counselors might be adult student peers or psychologists, although a variety of university personnel perform counseling kinds of functions. Counselors help with a number of student needs, such as support, goal-setting, identification of alternatives, strategy planning, career/life planning process information, coping and instrumental skills, evaluation, and feedback.

For adult students, the counseling process should start at the client's current level of development and stage in the career planning process. An individual student can be at any of several stages in career and educational planning, from initial assessment of self and situation, to implementation of a choice already made, to searching for a job for which the student is already prepared. Many adult students do not need all the steps of a general career and educational planning procedure. They do, however, need to learn the whole of the decision-making process, so that when faced with future transitions and decisions, they will be able to apply the process to the new situation. Again, counselors need to rely on a thorough initial assessment of the particular adult student's needs and adapt a problem-solving strategy or program according to the student's particular stage in the process.

Many adult students carry a full array of personal and mental health issues with them as they consider and pursue further education. Family and other relationships, substance abuse, sexual abuse, depression, self-esteem, and other problem areas are present and require the attention of counseling services. Professional counselors have the added tasks of assisting adult students with undoing influences of the past, helping them manage their present situations and barriers, and building a preventive stance for effective planning of the future.

Referral.   Another role of career services providers is referral, or putting adult students in touch with other resources. Individual university staff and offices cannot meet all students' needs. Within a career services network model, service providers need to develop cooperative relationships with and rely on the breadth of other offices and agencies to help solve students' problems. Full use of available resources helps maintain quality of services, meet students' needs, and limit the burden on any one service provider. The use of a referral network also helps adult students increase their knowledge of available resources, gain understanding of the broader university system in which they must function, and develop skills for more autonomous use of the system in solving their problems throughout their stay in college.

Ideally, career service providers should have an extensive knowledge of the range of available services for career, educational, and supportive needs. Services should include those within the university (e.g., career information libraries, the financial aid office, the disabled student services office, minority student centers) and outside the university (e.g., services for displaced homemakers, neighborhood agencies for low income persons, agencies for specific ethnic groups, community financial assistance agencies, local churches sponsoring job hunting support groups). Career service providers should have evaluative information about other services, such as the quality of services or the kind of treatment students can expect from another office. They are also on the receiving end of referral. Each office should make its service offerings clear to other referring units, encourage referrals, and seek evaluative feedback on how other service units and students perceive the quality and practices of the office.

Advocacy.   As advocates, career service providers intervene within and outside the university to remove obstacles for adult students both as individuals and as a collective group. An individual adult student might need help with designing a special program, working through a complication in admissions, receiving consideration for special circumstances affecting financial aid, gaining access to a service not normally available to the student, pursuing a nontraditional educational or career field, or redressing discrimination or harrassment within the university. A complex, atypical problem may require the waiver of a rule or procedure. The service provider is an advocate to work through an individual's special situation that does not fit normal policies and practices and that is an obstacle to the development and implementation of the person's educational and career plan.

The advocacy role also involves intervention in policies and practices that affect adult students collectively. Career service providers can play an educative, developmental function. They can provide information to increase the visibility of both the special needs and the characteristics of adult students among university staff. For example, university career development specialists who work with adult students can make faculty aware of services available for adult students, develop programs to help university personnel examine stereotypes of adult students, and represent adult student concerns in the university governance.

Service providers can also work to improve services and conditions and to change practices that are restrictive for adult students. Career service providers can lobby for special services for adult students, programs for different adult student groups, child care on campus, or evening hours for service offices. Intervention is also needed to reduce restrictions on part-time adult students involving registration, scheduling, financial aid, access to courses and services, fees, and other areas.

In attempting change, all administrators, faculty, and other university staff who can help make the change a reality must be involved. Advocates need to identify a clear target for change, indicate what can be done, and document adult student problems. They can assist key people in making good decisions about programs and services. They can relate the needed changes for adult students to issues such as the mission of the institution, recruitment, and retention. As advocates, career service providers need to show how the change will benefit both adult students and the university.

Outreach. Outreach includes increasing adults' awareness of career and educational services, increasing accessibility of services, and promoting the legitimacy of adult career development. A primary barrier to further learning among adults is not knowing the services available to help them. Career service providers need to promote their services widely to their clientele and encourage adults to use the resources available.

Personal contact is an important part of promotion to establish relationships with other helpers and with the target groups of adult students. Service providers can make informal presentations to referral sources for better understanding of services available and the kinds of people that can be helped. Presentations can be made in settings such as community centers, churches, synagogues, shopping centers, community colleges, vocational-technical schools, and advocacy centers for women, persons of color, the disabled, the elderly, and other special interest groups.

The type of outreach effort for promotion also applies to service delivery. Where possible, services should be provided off-campus with, for example, periodic evening hours at community centers, libraries, and schools to increase accessibility. Career specialists can also work as consultants on campus with departmental and collegiate advising offices, orientation and recruitment programs, special student centers, student unions, continuing education units, and other offices that sponsor university-wide information and development programs for students.

Beyond promotion of services is the promotion of adult career development itself. Many adults still believe there is something abnormal about desires to change careers, to have more balance between work and non-work roles, or to return to the university at midlife. Service providers need to increase public awareness about the issues of career and adult development and help the public realize that continuous examination, planning, and change in career and life is an inevitable part of growth over the lifespan.

TRENDS AND ISSUES FOR THE FUTURE

Adult students, with a broad range of educational, career, and life needs are an established part of the university community. The annual numbers of adult students expected on campus for the rest of this century are already on campus today. Yet, it seems that the university has just begun to respond to their presence. In this final section, we note a few issues and trends—some long standing, some newly emerging—for adult students. As university employees, whether faculty, staff, or administrators, we are all career service providers. We face continuing challenges and have the responsibility to help the university reach its potential as a significant, positive contributor to adult and career development over the lifespan.

1. As we have emphasized throughout this chapter, the university and its staff must focus strongly on active recruitment and support of adult students at-risk in the university community and society—persons of color, single parents, disabled persons, economically disadvantaged individuals, displaced homemakers, and others. As Hodgkinson (1985) notes concerning persons of color, the increasing numbers of the minority population are a fact. Educators need to make a commitment that all students in higher education have the opportunity to perform to their academic potential. There will be barriers of language, color, and cultural attitudes as Spanish-speaking students join those from Thailand and Vietnam in the college classroom. More than ever before, increased effort and commitment are needed among educators to offer these individuals the educational opportunities which will better prepare them for equal roles in a democratic society.

Schlossberg and her colleagues (Schlossberg, Lynch, & Chickering, 1989) stress the need for a preventive orientation among administrators, faculty, and student development professionals. They must become increasingly proactive in using their skills and experience to identify and design intervention strategies for vulnerable target subpopulations. Individuals considered at-risk, disadvantaged, or underrepresented need support in changing a social system, including the university, that perpetuates barriers to career and educational opportunities.

2. Career service providers must give increased attention to the unique needs and differential socialization of female and male students for life roles and choices. Differences exist in prior experiences and expectations for career and education, and in experiences in the university setting. Especially for women, the university can be an inhospitable learning environment. Sex bias, stereotyping, discrimination, harrassment, and many other such attitudes and behaviors, whether deliberate or unintentional on the part of educators, discourage learning and accomplishment.

Career service providers must be aware of biases in testing, sexual harrassment policies, discrimination laws, sex-fair counseling practices, and other relevant regulations and practices to insure equity in education and careers. Adult women will be an even greater force in the labor market and on the college campus of the future. The university can no longer ignore the long-standing inequities of the past if the potentials of these individuals are to be developed for the benefit of themselves and society.

3. Some emerging trends suggest that the changing face of today's college student extends beyond the adult student. Based on her recent work, Aslanian (1990) notes that the characteristics that typically have distinguished the younger, traditional college student and the older, non-traditional student are melding together more and more each day. One trend she observes is that younger students are acting more like adults. Aslanian believes there is a newly developing group of students on campus who come from the large number of students who did not graduate in the upper academic ranks of their high school class, and who did not go right on to college. While their higher-ranked high school class peers went to college, this group went to work, got married, had children, established themselves in their communities, and built a complex life off-campus. Now they are coming to college, attending part-time, taking evening classes, working part-time, commuting to class, and occasionally stopping out for a year.

Another trend Aslanian observes is that some older students are acting more like younger students. There is an increase in adult students studying on campus, full time, during the day, in degree programs. Who these adult students are is unclear; Aslanian speculates these persons may be men and women who gave up their jobs, involuntarily or voluntarily, and have come back to college to learn for new occupations. They may include women whose children are either in school during the day or have grown up and left home. Together, these developments reinforce the notion that the historical concepts of the "traditional" and "nontraditional" college student no longer apply.

4. With the changing nature of college students, the myth of the four-year undergraduate college degree must be dispelled. The university must alter its policies and attitudes based on the myth. A national study of 1980 high school graduates (Wilson, 1990) found that only 15 percent of students attending four-year colleges graduated in four years, with fewer than half graduating within six years. For minority students, less than a quarter had completed bachelor's degrees within six years.

This trend may be greater currently, but as Hodgkinson (1985) noted several years ago, studies done over the previous 20 years affirm the central finding that of every 100 students admitted to a four-year bachelor's degree program, fewer than half graduate in four years from the institution in which they started. Students drop out, transfer to other institutions, or come back to school at a later time. He stresses that the model for undergraduate education, completion of 8 semesters or 12 quarters, full time, through to graduation, at the same institution, has not been the path of even a simple majority of students for many years.

A typical university system is still based on the four-year model. The model dictates the bounds of such organizational practices as standards of academic progress and financial aid requirements. The university's response to older and part-time students with job and family responsibilities has been to criticize their potential, motivation, and commitment rather than allow for a variable length of time for degree completion. Of students who leave school for reasons other than academic failure, Hodgkinson (1985) suggests these persons often are not "drop-outs" but "stop-outs;" they may have bills to pay or other tasks to accomplish before they resume their studies. Most adult students do not fit the mold of the four-year college degree; they are continually hindered by a standard that no longer reflects reality.

5. With the continued trend toward downscaling organizations, an increasing number of workers in all areas—white collar executives, blue collar employees, rural workers—are being displaced (McDaniels, 1989). College has much to offer these people for developing and reshaping careers, but many of these individuals may not have participated in higher education before or are many years distant from their college experiences. The needs of and diversity among these individuals represent a new challenge for university educators. Joint ventures between business and labor for training and retraining have been developed to serve as an impetus for these workers. One example is the PATHWAYS to the Future program created by US West Communications, the Communications Workers of America, and the Council for Adult and Experiential Learning (PATHWAYS to the Future, 1990). In 14 states, over 42,000 regular employees, regardless of employment status, have access to funds annually for tuition, books, student fees, assessment, and counseling. As more of these kinds of workers enter universities and as these kinds of programs expand to new companies, universities will need to become partners with business and industry to better meet the career and educational concerns of these adults in whom they share a common interest.

6. Career service providers should acknowledge and encourage new ways of knowing and learning as part of the university. Several scholars have suggested that society is moving away from the old Newtonian/Cartesian model of knowledge, on which traditional universities are based, to new ways of perceiving and knowing. The old ways are rational, competitive, logical, objective, compartmentalization of knowledge that have characterized university departments and disciplines and have been acknowledged as a male "agentic" model. The new ways are described as more holistic, cooperative, compassionate, caring, integrative, and "communal"—characteristics associated with women (Capra, 1982; Ferguson, 1980).

The research of Belenky and colleagues (Belenky, Clinchy, Goldberger, and Tarule, 1986; Tarule, 1988) describes new ways of learning based on an extensive study of adult women. Their work elaborates on Gilligan's (1982) thesis that women speak in a "different voice." Tarule (1988), in her discussion of women returning to higher education, summarizes some basic concepts. Women tend to employ different strategies in dialogue for learning than does the majority culture. They have a sensitivity to engage in conversation that is exploratory rather than decisive. Though completed ideas may be the norm for conversations in the academic setting, women students enter the educational environment with well-developed abilities to hold their opinions while they question other people about theirs; to engage in narrative conversations that trace the details; and to remain sensitive to how well a message is received by checking with the listener. As connected learners, women focus on understanding and acceptance of an idea to precede, if not replace, the typical approach of assessment and criticism. Cooperative, collaborative discussions about ideas are preferred over debates. Connected knowing is respectful of personal, firsthand experience in becoming knowledgeable. The process emphasizes relationships: between oneself and the material, between oneself and the teacher, and between what one learns and how one is living one's life.

At the institutional level, the scientific method and empiricism still dominate the production of knowledge in large research universities. There is also, though, a growing professional recognition of alternative ways to obtain knowledge as well as ways of using it. Qualitative methodology is becoming more respected as a way to new and emerging knowledge in career psychology and adult development as in other fields.

7. The university must also encourage its staff to develop new ways of teaching to fit the needs, diverse learning styles, and developmental levels of adult students. The traditional methods of teaching—lecturing, note-taking, testing—with the professor as expert in a superior-subordinate relationship are being challenged by adult students who expect a more humane environment in which to learn, grow, and make decisions. Though educators specializing in the area of adult learning conclude that no one teaching method is necessarily preferable (Apps, 1988), there is a need to make education a more active enterprise. Various methods suggested by educators include short talks by the instructor followed by discussion in which students ask and answer questions; collaborative learning, such as panel presentations or small discussion groups; and journals and reaction papers to reading. There should be an emphasis on such processes as self-directed learning, open discussion, interdisciplinary perspectives, and problem-solving to bring the connected learner into a relationship with the course content (Brademas, 1990; Tarule, 1988; Watkins, 1990). From the broader view of a philosophy of education, such methods suggest that the traditional agentic model should be replaced by an agentic-communal model in which the best of both perspectives are integrated into a model encompassing a balance of independence and connectedness.

New ways of teaching must account for the varied learning styles and developmental levels of adult students. The work of Kolb (1981) suggests that adults learn differently, some through concrete experience, some by reflecting, some by abstract conceptualization, and others by active experimentation. The Myer-Briggs Type Indicator (Myers & McCaulley, 1985) explores the different ways individuals perceive and process information. Models of integrating developmental theory into curriculum offer promise for the development of adult students. For example, Tarule (1988) applies the perspective of "developmental position" to women returning to higher education. Belenky and colleagues (Belenky, Clinchy, Goldberger, & Tarule, 1986) found five epistemological positions from which women view the world, ranging from "silence" (experiencing self as voiceless and powerless) to "constructed knowing" (experiencing self and others as capable of creating knowledge). An expectation of independent learning assumes an adult learner is ready and able to participate in the collaborative construction of knowledge, though the individual student's developmental position currently might not be at that level in the particular area of learning. In sum, these trends suggest that adult students of tomorrow need a wider menu of environments in which they can learn, of learning styles from which they can freely choose, and of teaching methods which best fit a diverse group of learners.

CONCLUSIONS

The major transformations to improve the quality and conditions of university life for adult students will require the involvement of faculty, administrators, and staff across the university campus. Noteworthy, however, is that student development professionals often have the most direct responsibility for many of the educational and service missions presented here (Schlossberg, Lynch, & Chickering, 1989). Student development professionals are in a position to be most knowledgeable about the processes of career and adult development and the concrete concerns of adult students. It is a major responsibility, but student development professionals also have behind them the power of an inevitable movement. Adult students, and the issues of adult career development over the lifespan, are on campus now, and they are here to stay.

REFERENCES

Adam, K., & Lindoo, S.J. (1989). Continuing education programs for women: Current status and future directions. *Continuing Higher Education Review, 53*, 11–25.

Apps, J.W. (1988). *Higher education in a learning society*. San Francisco: Jossey-Bass.

Aslanian, C.B. (1990, May). *Back from the future*. Paper presented at the meeting of the National University Continuing Education Association, New Orleans, LA.

Aslanian, C.B., & Brickell, H.M. (1980). *Americans in transition: Life changes as reasons for adult learning*. New York: College Entrance Examination Board.

Aslanian, C.B., & Brickell, H.M. (1988). *How Americans in transition study for college credit*. New York: College Entrance Examination Board.

Belenky, M., Clinchy, B., Goldberger, N., and Tarule, J. (1986). *Women's ways of knowing: The development of self, voice, and mind*. New York: Basic Books.

Bodensteiner, J. (1989). A profile of nontraditional college students and recommendations for continuing educators. *Continuing Higher Education Review, 53*, 87–98.

Brademas, J. (1990, May 2). Universities must treat adult education as a fundamental part of their mission. *The Chronicle of Higher Education*, pp. B1, B3.

Brooks, L. (1990). Recent developments in theory building. In D. Brown and L. Brooks (Eds.), *Career choice and development* (2nd ed.) (pp. 364–394). San Francisco: Jossey-Bass.

Brown, D. (1990). Trait and factor theory. In D. Brown and L. Brooks (Eds.), *Career choice and development* (2nd ed.) (pp. 13–36). San Francisco: Jossey-Bass.

Capra, F. (1982). *The turning point: Science, society, and the rising culture*. New York: Bantam Books.

Copland B.A. (1988). Returning women on campus: Higher education takes notice. In L.H. Lewis (Ed.), *New directions for continuing education: No. 39. Addressing the needs of returning women* (pp. 35–47). San Francisco: Jossey-Bass.

Cross, K.P. (1981). *Adults as learners*. San Francisco: Jossey-Bass.

Dearman, N.B., & Plisko, V.W. (1982). *The condition of education, 1982 Edition*. Washington, DC: U.S. Department of Education, National Center for Education Statistics.

Evangelauf, J. (1990, April 11). 1988 enrollments of all racial groups hit record levels. *The Chronicle of Higher Education*, pp. A1, A37.

Ferguson, M. (1980). *The Aquarian conspiracy: Personal and social transformation in the 1980s*. Boston: Houghton Mifflin.

Fullerton, Jr., H.N. (1989). New labor force projections, spanning 1988 to 2000. *Monthly Labor Review, 112*(11), 3–12.

Giczkowski, W. (1990, April 4). Colleges must cope with market-oriented adult students. *The Chronicle of Higher Education*, p. B2.

Gilligan, C. (1982). *In a different voice*. Cambridge, MA: Harvard University Press.

Goldstein, H. (1984). Changing structure of work: Occupational trends and implications. In N.C. Gysbers (Ed.), *Designing careers* (pp. 54–77). San Francisco: Jossey-Bass.

Gottfredson, L. (1981). Circumscription and compromise: A developmental theory of occupational aspirations [Monograph]. *Journal of Counseling Psychology, 28*, 545–579.

Hackett, G., & Betz, N.E. (1981). A self-efficacy approach to the career development of women. *Journal of Vocational Behavior, 18*, 326–339.

Hall, R.M., & Sandler, B.R. (1982). *The classroom climate: A chilly one for women?* Washington, DC: Project on the Status and Education of Women, Association of American Colleges.

Hansen, L.S., & Biernat, B. (in press). Daring to dream: Career aspirations in childhood and adolescence. In J. Lewis, L. Bradley, & B. Hayes (Eds.), *Counseling women over the life span*. Denver, CO: Love Publishing.

Hansen, L.S., & Minor, C.W. (1989). Work, family, and career development: Implications for persons, policies, and practices. In D. Brown and C.W. Minor (Eds.), *Working in America: A status report on planning and problems* (pp. 25–42). Alexandria, VA: National Career Development Association.

Heffernan, J.M. (1981). *Educational and career services for adults*. Lexington, MA: D.C. Heath.

Herr, E.L. (1984). What an ideal counseling/support program for the adult learner should look like. In G.R. Walz & L. Benjamin (Eds.), *New perspectives on counseling adult learners* (pp. 27–44). Ann Arbor, MI: ERIC Counseling and Personnel Services.

Hodgkinson, H.L. (1985). *All one system: Demographics of education— kindergarten through graduate school.* Washington, DC: Institute for Educational Leadership.

Hotchkiss, L. & Borow, H. (1990). Sociological perspectives on work and career development. In D. Brown and L. Brooks (Eds.), *Career choice and development* (2nd ed.) (pp. 262–307). San Francisco: Jossey-Bass.

Hughes, R. (1983). The non-traditional student in higher education: A synthesis of the literature. *NASPA Journal, 20,* 51–64.

Johnson, C.S. (1986). New perspectives on career counseling for adults. In J. V. Miller & M. L. Musgrave (Eds.), *New directions for continuing education: No. 32. Issues in adult career counseling* (pp. 5–13). San Francisco: Jossey-Bass.

Kolb, D.A. (1981). Learning styles and disciplinary differences. In A.W. Chickering (Ed.), *The modern American college* (pp. 232–255). San Francisco: Jossey-Bass.

Lee, V.E., & Frank, K.A. (1990). Students' characteristics that facilitate the transfer from two-year to four-year colleges. *Sociology of Education, 63,* 178–193.

Lewis, L.H. (1988). Ingredients of successful programming. In L.H. Lewis (Ed.), *New directions for continuing education: No. 39. Addressing the needs of returning women* (pp. 5–17). San Francisco: Jossey-Bass.

Levinson, D.J., Darrow, C.N., Klein, E.B., Levinson, M.H., & McKee, B. (1978). *The seasons of a man's life.* New York: Knopf.

Lynch, A.Q., & Chickering, A.W. (1984). Comprehensive counseling and support programs for adult learners: Challenge to higher education. In G.R. Walz & L. Benjamin (Eds.), *New perspectives on counseling adult learners* (pp. 45–73). Ann Arbor, MI: ERIC Counseling and Personnel Services.

McDaniels, C. (1989). *The changing workplace: Career counseling strategies for the 1990s and beyond.* San Francisco: Jossey-Bass.

Miller, J.V. (1986). Helping adults balance career and family roles. In J.V. Miller & M.L. Musgrave (Eds.), *New directions for continuing education: No. 32. Issues in adult career counseling* (pp. 45–58). San Francisco: Jossey-Bass.

Miller, J.V., & Musgrave, M.L. (1986). Quality issues in adult career counseling. In J.V. Miller & M.L. Musgrave (Eds.), *New directions for continuing education: No. 32. Issues in adult career counseling* (pp. 95–99). San Francisco: Jossey-Bass

Mitchell, L.K., & Krumboltz, J.D. (1990). Social learning approach to career decision-making: Krumboltz's theory. In D. Brown and L. Brooks (Eds.), *Career choice and development* (2nd ed.) (pp. 145–196). San Francisco: Jossey-Bass.

Mohney, C., & Anderson, W. (1988). The effect of life events and relationships on adult women's decisions to enroll in college. *Journal of Counseling and Development, 66,* 271–274.

Myers, I.B., & McCaulley, M.H. (1985). *Manual: A guide to the development and use of the Myers-Briggs Type Indicator.* Palo Alto, CA: Consulting Psychologists Press.

Neugarten, B.L. (1976). Adaptation and the life cycle. *The Counseling Psychologist, 6*(1), 16–20.

Neugarten, B.L., & Neugarten, D.A. (1987). The changing meanings of age. *Psychology Today, 21*(5), 29–33.

PATHWAYS to the Future. (1990, February). Three year contract awarded to CAEL for new 14 state training/retraining program. *The PATHWAYS Sign Post*, p. 1.

Pew Higher Education Research Program. (1990). Breaking the mold. *Policy Perspectives, 2*(2), 1–8.

Polson, C.J. (1989). Adult learners: Characteristics, concerns, and challenges to higher education—a bibliography. *NACADA Journal, 9*(2), 86–112.

Projections of college enrollment, 1990–2000. (1990, September 5). *The Chronicle of Higher Education Almanac*, p. 14.

Sandler, B.R., & Hall, R.M. (1986). *The campus climate revisited: Chilly for women faculty, administrators, and graduate students.* Washington, DC: Project on the Status and Education of Women, Association of American Colleges.

Schlossberg, N.K. (1984). *Counseling adults in transition.* New York: Springer.

Schlossberg, N.K., Lynch, A.Q., & Chickering, A.W. (1989). *Improving higher education environments.* San Francisco: Jossey-Bass.

Sheehy, G. (1976). *Passages: Predictable crises of adult life.* New York: Bantam Books.

Sundal-Hansen, L.S. (1984). Interrelationship of gender and career. In N.C. Gysbers (Ed.), *Designing careers* (pp. 216–247). San Francisco: Jossey-Bass.

Super, D.E. (1980). A life-span, life-space approach to career development. *Journal of Vocational Behavior, 16*, 282–298.

Super, D.E. (1990). A life-span, life-space approach to career development. In D. Brown & L. Brooks (Eds.), *Career choice and development* (2nd ed.) (pp. 197–261). San Francisco: Jossey-Bass.

Tarule, J.M. (1988). Voices of returning women: Ways of knowing. In L.H. Lewis (Ed.), *New directions for continuing education: No. 39. Addressing the needs of returning women* (pp. 19–33). San Francisco: Jossey-Bass.

U.S. Department of Education. (1989). *Digest of educational statistics* (25th ed.) (NCES 89–643). Washington, DC: U.S. Department of Education, National Center for Education Statistics.

Walz, G.R., & Benjamin, L. (1984). Synthesis and a look to the future. In G.R. Walz & L. Benjamin (Eds.), *New perspectives on counseling adult learners* (pp. 75–87). Ann Arbor, MI: ERIC Counseling and Personnel Services.

Watkins, B.T. (1990, August 1). Growing number of older students stirs professors to alter teaching style. *The Chronicle of Higher Education*, pp. A1, A12.

Wilson, R. (1990, February 21). Only 15% of students graduate in 4 years, a new study finds. *The Chronicle of Higher Education*, pp. A1, A42.

Wolfman, B.R. (1990, September 21). College leaders must act firmly to end racial resegregation on their campuses. *The Chronicle of Higher Education*, pp. B1, B3.

CHAPTER 18

Community-Based Adult Career Counseling

Jane Goodman
Dept. of Leadership and Counseling
Eastern Michigan University
Ypsilanti, Michigan

Elinor Waters
Continuum Center
Oakland University
Rochester, Michigan

The focus of this chapter is on organizations which provide career development services to adults who may not be affiliated with the sponsoring organization. The key is open access. While many organizations who employ adults, and educational institutions who teach adults, have career development programs, most do not. In addition, many adults who are self-employed, unemployed, or work for no monetary compensation as homemakers or volunteers have no institutional affiliations. A school district, college, or university may have an adult career development program, but it would be considered community-based only if it were open to non-students. In addition, a new type of sponsor for career development services has emerged in recent years—joint union-management programs. Although not strictly open access, they have broader constituencies than single organization programs. Therefore, we have described one such program as a case study.

In this chapter we identify some parameters that program planners need to consider in developing their community-based approaches. We look at the needs of adults related to entering, moving within, re-entering, and leaving the work force. We present several case studies of programs in Michigan; some briefly, some in more detail, to provide a clearer picture of different approaches to community-based programs.

NEEDS OF ADULTS

Over the years the concept of what constitutes career development for adults has changed and expanded. Many of these changes have come in response to an increasingly rapidly changing society where "future shock" is indeed a present reality. Also important are the changing notions of the meaning of work and expectations of the work environment. Employers expect workers to be able to manage their own personal and career development. "As it [the workplace] constantly changes form, appearing and disappearing with economic circumstances, the commitment between individuals and specific institutions declines. With this new, more temporary institutional 'format,' employees must be more responsible for their own career development and job security." (Carnevale, Gainer, & Meltzer, 1988, p. 4)

Sometimes the approach of community-based counseling represents a blending of the stated desires of adult clients with the perceptions of career counselors as to their needs. Typically adult clients, particularly those whose career change is not voluntary, want help in finding a job. Arbeiter, Aslanian, Schmerbeck and Brickell (1978) found the primary career service requested by adults to be lists of available jobs. Adult career counselors, on the other hand, usually believe in teaching the career development process and often insist that clients take a long-range view.

A National Career Development Association commissioned Gallup poll found that about 7% of adults *in any one year* (emphasis added) wanted help in "selecting, changing, or getting a job." (NCDA, 1990) It also found that only about 41% of adults used a systematic process in "getting started in their present career." Clearly, the need is there. What is being done to address that need? Both the immediate needs of the clients and their longer-range interests *can* be served. The traditional adage "Give me a fish and I'll eat for today; teach me to fish and I'll eat for the rest of my life" needs to be amended. If you feed people while you are teaching them, they are apt to learn better.

Recent data indicate that the average person changes careers 5 to 10 times during a lifetime, and changes jobs far more often. This clearly supports the need for adults to learn decision-making and job-seeking processes. At the same time, adult career counselors must understand the sense of urgency many adult clients experience when they seek help with their careers. In an increasing number of cases this sense of urgency stems from real survival needs, as laid off and displaced workers experience long-term unemployment and exhausted benefits. In such situations, career counselors may need to become advocates for their clients. They need to know about survival resources (i.e., where to get food, clothing, and shelter) as well as occupational and educational resources. Even when poverty and unemployment are not a reality, adults anticipating or experiencing a change may feel a sense of panic. This could be related to a sudden perception of running out of time to make and implement career decisions. To meet both these short term and long term needs, it is important that counselors have an overview of the whole career development process. Such an overview is provided by the guidelines described below.

ADULT CAREER DEVELOPMENT COMPETENCIES

The National Occupational Information Coordinating Committee has developed a series of career development competencies (undated). The 12 competencies for the adult level are:

Self Knowledge:
Skills to maintain a positive self-concept.
Skills to maintain effective behaviors.
Understanding developmental changes and transitions.

Educational & Occupational Exploration:
Skills to enter and participate in education and training.
Skills to participate in work and life-long learning.
Skills to locate, evaluate, and interpret career information.
Skills to prepare to seek, obtain, maintain, and change jobs.
Understanding how the needs and functions of society influence the nature and structure of work.

Career Planning:
Skills to make decisions.
Understanding the impact of work on individual and family life.
Understanding the continuing changes in male/female roles.
Skills to make career transitions.

Each of these competencies implies a number of activities and counseling interventions. For example, the last mentioned, "skills to make career transitions," includes some intangible emotional components. Transitions often engender a grieving process which arouses such emotions as denial, anger, panic, and acceptance. A model for assisting people to cope with transitions has been developed by Schlossberg (1984). This model identifies a number of attributes of the situation, the person, and his or her support system which both predict and can be used to enhance the successful navigation of a particular transition. In developing programs, adult career counselors should consider how each of these competencies will be achieved, and develop an action strategy based on that analysis.

WHAT'S OUT THERE?

By its very nature, community-based adult career counseling is delivered in many ways to a wide variety of clients. In this section a schematic way of looking at an array of services will be presented, along with several illustrations of how components of this array can be put together.

In Table 1, programmatic components are listed, using four basic parameters of program planning: organizational sponsor, clientele, services provided, and method of delivery. Program planners may view this table as a "menu"—choose at least one appetizer, main course, dessert, and beverage. The lists in each category are not exhaustive, but hopefully they are comprehensive enough to be useful for program planning. Used with the NOICC guidelines, they can help service providers plan a comprehensive program rather than simply offer an array of services.

Program planners usually do not have a choice as to their organizational sponsor, because this is generally where they begin. In most cases planners also have little choice regarding clientele. That is often fixed by funding sources or by the basic mission of their organization. Choices are more likely to exist with respect to services provided and method of

Table 1

Programmatic Components

Organizational Sponsor	Clientele	Services Provided	Methods of Delivery
Private agencies	All adults	Formal assessment	Individual
Business and industry	Women	Emotional support	Group
Unions	Minorities	Self-assessment	Face-to-face
"Y"s	Older people	Decision-making skills	Telephone
Public agencies e.g., vocational rehabilitation	Displaced workers	Job seeking information	Television
Schools	Physically or emotionally disabled	Job retention techniques	Computer
Colleges and universities	Prisoners and ex-offenders	Retirement planning	Professional/ paraprofessional

delivery. Program planners who wish to include one or more vocational guidance instruments among their services may find Kapes and Mastie's (1988) guide to be a useful resource.

To illustrate the way in which the "menu" approach to planning works, three "meals" are described below.

DIFFERENT APPROACHES TO PROGRAM PLANNING

The three case studies represent different decisions made by program planners with respect to the components listed in Table 1. Although all three programs operate in southeastern Michigan they differ markedly in terms of sponsorship, clientele, services, and methods of delivery.

Jewish Vocational Service

The first case study, and the oldest of the organizations profiled here, JVS is a private nonprofit organization that has been providing vocational services for close to 50 years. During the 1988–89 fiscal year, JVS served over 5,000 people in the metropolitan Detroit area. (Jewish Vocational Service 1988–89 Annual Report).

Organizational sponsor. JVS, a member agency of the Jewish Welfare Federation and the United Foundation, receives funding from the Allied Jewish Campaign and the United Foundation Torch Drive and serves people on a non-sectarian basis. JVS receives funds from the public and private sector, as well as through fees for services. In 1988–89, for example, major funding came from state and county mental health boards, and other governmental agencies such as the Department of Social Services, Department of Labor, and Area Agency on Aging, and from contracts with Job Training Partnership Act and with union-management groups.

Clientele. According to its brochure, the mission of JVS is to "help people achieve success and fulfillment in their working lives." Toward that end "JVS offers a broad range of vocational services on a non-sectarian basis to individuals and businesses in the metropolitan Detroit area. Among those assisted are: people at career transition points, unemployed and displaced workers, physically, mentally and emotionally disabled adults, persons with industrial injuries, senior citizens, and students seeking educational loans or their first job."

Services. The career services offered by JVS are broad. Under- or unemployed adults or people seeking a new challenge may sign up for individual counseling and get help with self assessment, exploration of available jobs, and assistance in the job search process. JVS offers a computerized job placement service that helps match individuals with employers.

In addition to individual and group career counseling, JVS operates a number of programs targeted to a particular clientele. For example, the Displaced Homemaker Program, funded by the Michigan Department of Labor, Office of Women and Work, is designed for people who have lost

344

their source of economic support though widowhood, divorce or disablement of a spouse. The program offers in-depth vocational assessment, training in job seeking skills, and an ongoing job club. The job club, based on the Azrin and Besalel (1980) model, meets two mornings a week to provide ongoing support.

Another JVS program, designed to meet the needs of disabled adults, is a community workshop where participants learn work skills and appropriate work behavior while performing assembling, collating, and packaging tasks. Participants in this workshop are paid piece-rate as they work under close supervision. They are also provided with an array of individual and group counseling services. Participants are prepared for the job market by learning life skills (i.e., how to socialize with co-workers and cope with criticism). The community workshop is also used for assessment purposes in evaluating the aptitudes, skills, and degree of disability of persons who are physically disabled.

The Rehabilitation Case Management Services provided by JVS are vocational rehabilitation services for injured workers referred by insurance companies and private industry. This program uses evaluation, case management, counseling, and vocational preparation to help injured workers return to gainful employment.

JVS also offers special programs for older people—both those who need help and those who wish to give it. The Senior Adult Workshop provides people over 60 with a work environment where they can find a useful job, new friendships, and support services. Built into this workshop experience are health maintenance activities and group counseling. Door-to-door transportation is provided, if needed. The Senior Service Corps is designed for older adults who have time and skills to donate. Corps members are assigned as volunteers to a variety of community agencies. The group meets weekly with a counselor to discuss work-related and personal issues. Career counselors assign people to agencies based on their interests and abilities and lead the weekly group discussions.

Method of delivery. The typical career counselee is seen weekly and receives assistance in both career decision-making and job seeking. JVS maintains an extensive library of occupational and educational information as well as lists of job openings. Fees for individual counseling are based on ability to pay. The job placement service is free to both job seekers and employers.

THE CONTINUUM CENTER OF OAKLAND UNIVERSITY

The second case study is an example of a university affiliated, community-based program. Founded in 1965 as a women's center, the Continuum Center over the years has diversified its clientele so that it now serves men and women from young adulthood to old age. While the Center offers a variety of personal and professional development programs, only its career-related programs are described here.

Organizational sponsor. Oakland University, a medium-sized state institution, includes the Continuum Center as part of its community service function. Although the center's offices are located on campus, its programs are geared to nonuniversity affiliated adults. Some Center programs are held on campus, others at hotels, churches, and community centers in the metropolitan Detroit area. Continuum Center staff also offer career planning and outplacement services on a contractual basis. These programs are typically held on-site or near the former workplace, if the business has closed. The Center's funds are derived from fees for service and from grants.

Clientele. The center's career counseling clients are men and women who are in the process of change. This group includes re-entry women, dislocated workers, and others who by choice or necessity are looking for new educational, vocational, or leisure options. Modest fees are charged for both individual and group career counseling offered directly through the Continuum Center. Some of the clients are employees of organizations which hire the Center staff to provide career development services. In this way Center staff may have an opportunity to reach displaced workers and employees who would not normally have the financial ability and/or motivation to seek career counseling on their own.

Services and method of delivery. Throughout its 25 years, the Center has assisted adults with career planning. In many ways, the Continuum Center's career services have developed along the lines described in the introduction to this chapter. In its early years, when it helped women make decisions about returning to work, school, or volunteer activities, the focus was on self assessment (weighing interests, values, priorities, and desires) and programs had titles such as Investigation into Identity. As more women entered the work force, and as men expressed more interest in increasing their satisfaction with their work and their lives, a program for working people entitled Careers in Transition came into being. That program combined self assessment with occupational and educational information, decision-making techniques, and some job seeking skills.

The program described above is targeted to adults who want help in career planning—in identifying paid and unpaid work opportunities. Center staff also offer individual counseling and workshops for people who know what they want to do or "be," but need assistance in putting the plan into action. To meet this need, Center staff have developed a workshop using the workbook, *Opening Doors: A Practical Guide for Job Seekers* (Goodman & Hoppin, 1990) which teaches participants how to identify their strengths and abilities, analyze an employer's needs, and attempt to identify a fit. This competency-based program follows a six step model of self assessment, decision-making, planning the job campaign, communicating with employers, interviewing, retaining the job, and preparing for the next one. (The complete competency list is provided in the appendix).

Over the years the Center has increased its impact by training professionals in career planning and employability skills for adults. These trainings use *Opening Doors* and its Leader Guide (Goodman & Hoppin, 1990), and *Directions for Change* (Goodman & Hoppin, 1986), a workbook which focuses on the decision-making aspects of career development.

346

THE ALLIANCE

Our third case study is a joint union management program, the Alliance for Employee Growth and Development. It is a national program funded under a negotiated labor agreement, and it also seeks external funding, particularly to support programs for at-risk and dislocated workers. It is organized for the education, training, and development of AT&T's union represented workers. These kinds of programs are designed to be a "win/win" situation for workers and company. As workers take advantage of career planning and tuition assistance programs, the company gains a better educated work force and workers improve their career position. In a situation of downsizing such as that experienced recently by AT&T, workers can be better prepared to move to other positions within AT&T or to seek new employment.

Organizational sponsor. The Alliance is a joint program of the American Telephone and Telegraph Corporation, The Communications Workers of America, and the International Brotherhood of Electrical Workers. With headquarters in New Jersey and regional offices in Georgia and Texas, it is a national program, with services wherever there are union represented AT&T workers.

Clientele. The men and women who work for AT&T in bargaining unit positions represent a wide variety of work areas. Many are operators and service technicians or work in other areas which are becoming technically obsolete. Before deregulation, AT&T was a very stable organization. Many employees have worked for the company for a long time—often since graduation from high school. The necessity to upgrade skills and/or leave the company has left many feeling betrayed by the organization, formerly known as "Ma Bell," and frightened about their own future. The services offered by the Alliance help to address those feelings.

Services. Development of a Career Action Plan (CAP) is the cornerstone of the Alliance's career planning services. Before workers can take advantage of the Alliance's educational benefits they need to have developed a CAP. This requirement increases the likelihood that the education will lead in directions productive for the employee. The purpose of career planning and assessment is to help participants make appropriate decisions about their career goals and understand the steps necessary to reach those goals. It should help them define realistic career goals by assessing their interests, aptitudes, skills, and experience and matching them with appropriate occupational choices based on reliable labor market information about employment opportunities. Its outcome is a personalized CAP which defines career goals, specifies the steps necessary to achieve them, and lays out a plan, with timelines, for the employee to follow.

Other services provided may include stress management, training for returning to learning (study and test taking skills), job seeking skills, including resume writing, and placement for dislocated workers.

Method of delivery. The Alliance contracts with educational institutions and community agencies to deliver the services described above.

Each organization delivers its service in its own way, but most use a combination of individual and group counseling, workshops, and individual consultation. In Michigan, one provider uses a computerized aptitude assessment in combination with paper and pencil interest and personality inventories. The state occupational information system is also used to provide up-to-date localized labor market data and information about educational opportunities and requirements.

JVS, the Continuum Center, and the Alliance programs have been described in some detail to demonstrate the process that planners can follow in designing their programs. The following three mini-case studies are provided to give an example of the range of services which can be found in a typical community.

Computer-Based Adult Career Counseling

Oakland University's adult career counseling center in Rochester, Michigan is "staffed by" four microcomputers outfitted with DISCOVER for Adults, SIGI PLUS and the Michigan Occupational Information System. Graduate students, under the supervision of Howard Splete, a member of the Counseling faculty, meet with clients for an initial consultation, help them through the program which best meets their needs, and meet with them again for a brief follow up. At this follow up they may refer the client to other University counseling services, academic advising, job seeking programs, or other agencies as needed. All of these services are free to interested adults. The program has been used by laid-off auto workers, welfare recipients, returning homemakers, midlife career changers, or others who are interested in rethinking their career goals.

Operation Able: An Older Worker Program

While the definition of when a person qualifies as an older worker varies from one government agency to another, it seems clear that older adults have some special problems in identifying new careers and/or seeking new jobs. Barclay and McDougall (1990) note that the average length of unemployment for an older job seeker is up to twice as long as for the general population. To help address this problem, the Mott Foundation has funded a national network of organizations designed to promote awareness of the qualities of older workers, inform older citizens of employment services and programs, link employers with older job seekers, and coordinate and strengthen older worker programs.

Operation ABLE of Michigan, a part of this network, operates a statewide job hotline, conducts client assessments, provides skill training, offers opportunities for on-the-job-training, provides computer based job leads, and conducts seminars on job-seeking techniques. Barclay and McDougall (1990) believe that client assessment is the most important part of their operation. "The process of uncovering skills, interests, and values over decades takes skillful interviewing. Focusing on past employment and life experiences, with emphasis on success and achievements, not only identifies transferable skills for the client but helps in the important tasks of building self-esteem" (p. 53). They report that skill training is most effective when it is jointly sponsored by an employer who needs employees with specific skills and agrees to hire qualified older workers who successfully complete the training.

The Working Channel

Sponsored by Wayne State University and WTVS, the public television station in Detroit, Michigan, The Working Channel devotes 24 hours a day of programming to the job hunting, retraining, and family survival needs of the unemployed in the Detroit metropolitan area. Programs include Michigan Employment Security Commission job announcements, job club information, labor issues, a motivational series, GED, learn to read, and basic skills programs, and other relevant adult education offerings.

The method of delivery is perhaps the facet of The Working Channel which most merits attention. People with a cable hookup can access its programming, free of charge, in the privacy of their home, at any time of the day or night. Referrals to additional assistance are frequent; in this way the channel serves as a conduit between the general public of unemployed workers and the sector funded to serve them, for example, Job Training Partnership Act programs, adult education programs, etc. The Working Channel concept has been replicated in several other states and in Canada.

IMPLICATIONS FOR PROGRAM PLANNERS

Program planners have a challenge! They are often asked to develop the best program for the least money in the shortest time for the most people. How can the necessary decisions and compromises be made to ensure good programs, at an affordable cost, in a reasonable time, for a sufficient number of people? We recommend returning to what we, as career counselors, know about decision-making. Tiedeman and O'Hara's (1963) paradigm of exploration and clarification seems a good schema to use in deciding about services to offer and method of delivery. This is to assume that organizational sponsor and clientele are "givens." If not, these principles, with some translation, apply there as well.

Selection of Services

The first step is gathering information or expanding possibilities. This is the crucial "pie in the sky" stage. As a program planner, what if everything you wish could be offered to your clients? You may wish to ask questions such as: What are their needs? What is the nature of the social-political-economic environment? What services are already available? Look through the list of "services provided" in Table 1 and the competencies discussed in the beginning of this chapter and in the appendix and decide on the ones you wish could be provided.

The next step, narrowing to a focus in Tiedeman and O'Hara's (1963) paradigm, might be compared to zero-based budgeting. What is necessary to meet the mission and goals of your organization? From "what is the most you can do," it is important to look at "what is the least you can do." Real program planning consists of a compromise between these two positions.

At this point, you may have chosen several services to provide. You may wish to repeat the expand-then-narrow process in relation to each component. For example, in planning a job search workshop you may want to begin with a competency list such as the one in the appendix and then narrow it down to those skills most needed by your group.

Method of Delivery

In deciding upon a method of delivery, a series of decisions must be made. Some of the choices and the rationale for each are presented below.

Individual versus group counseling. Working with individuals provides the most flexibility of programming. Each individual's personal requirements are addressed. For some people, the confidentiality of individual sessions is crucial. Furthermore, participants can progress at their own pace. Groups, however, provide an opportunity for support and caring confrontation that is difficult to match in an individual session. In addition, the group can provide a richness of resources, ideas, contacts, and connections that no individual helper could master. A further consideration is the efficiency of service. Groups use less staff time.

Face-to-face versus technological intermediary. Direct personal contact with clients is certainly the mode with which most of us are comfortable. The advantages are (a) familiarity for both counselor and client, (b) the ability to use nonverbal communication and to give feedback on nonverbal behavior (e.g., in rehearsing an interview), (c) the ability to change and modify a program based on changing client needs, and, most intangible but perhaps most important, (d) the personal support conveyed by a counselor.

The advantages of technological approaches are also many. Television is anonymously accessible to most clients without travel. This may be particularly useful for the disabled, homemakers with young children, and people with severely limited incomes. It can provide information efficiently to large numbers of people. This information can be delivered by skillful presenters in a form to which the American public has become accustomed.

The computer, with its interactive properties, offers other advantages. It can store large amounts of information and retrieve it on command. Through its branched design capabilities, it can allow a client to determine the direction of exploration or information. It can provide on command a written record of all transactions. Also, it never gets tired, bored, or takes a vacation!

Professional versus paraprofessional counselors. Ideally, professional counselors have expertise in counseling and group work, along with the ability to make presentations and give feedback. They also have a storehouse of career development information and knowledge of how to access the rest. They have the capability to administer and interpret tests. For all of these reasons, they are usually the "method of choice."

Paraprofessional counselors may or may not have all of these skills, but they have one distinct advantage. Whether paid or volunteer, they are often peers or close to being peers of the clients. Therefore they can serve as role models and have a credibility that professionals sometimes lack. If an ex-con says you have to get that high school diploma, the person on probation may believe it. If Dr. Jones says it, "The Man" is telling the client what to do, and what does he know about the streets? Similarly, a 58-year-old widow who has recently reentered the work force may have more impact on a newly displaced homemaker than would a young PhD. Under the supervision of counselors, paraprofessionals can provide extremely effective service delivery.

SUMMARY

In all of the foregoing we have only touched on the plethora of different programs that exist for adults in the community at large. This variety is exciting yet it also contributes to a confusion as to what is best in setting up new programs or evaluating existing programs. It has been our aim to provide some dimensions to use in decision making and some examples of the range of possible alternatives. The examples cited will, we hope, provide practitioners with some new ideas or possible resources.

Appendix
Competencies Needed by Job Seekers

Developed by the Continuum Center
Oakland University*

A. Self Awareness/Assessment

Participants will:
1. Understand the psychological impact of looking for work
2. Identify and list accomplishments and achievements
3. Identify and list their technical skills
4. Identify and list their transferable skills
5. Realistically assess their strengths
6. Realistically identify weaknesses, develop strategies to correct them, and minimize their effect on the job campaign
7. Realistically assess liabilities, identify those that can be overcome, and develop an action plan for doing so
8. Specify values and prioritize them
9. Define interests
10. Know techniques for reducing stress related to the job hunt
11. Combine self-assessment information and match to potential job target

*Under a grant from the State Board of Education, Michigan Department of Education, Vocational-Technical Education Services

B. Decision Making

Participants will:
1. Identify individual realities and practicalities
2. Be able to set long/short term goals.
3. Know appropriate decision-making strategies for job search process
4. Assess relocation, self-employment, civil service, and military service as alternatives

C. Planning Job Campaign

Participants will:
1. Be able to demonstrate knowledge of the sequential nature of the job hunt process
2. Know sources of occupational/educational information
3. Know how to establish, expand, and utilize an information and support network
4. Be able to locate employers who hire in their occupational area(s)
5. Be able to identify job openings or potential openings
6. Be able to conduct an information interview
7. Have knowledge of information relevant to their identified area(s) of work
8. Define alternative ways of gaining needed experience and training and know nonformal aspects of the job search
9. Set-up and maintain a record-keeping system

D. Communication
    1. Oral
       Participants will:
       a. Be competent in assertive communication techniques as applied to the job search process
       b. Be able to gather information and market themselves over the telephone
    2. Written
       Participants will:
       a. Compile a personal data inventory including previous work experience, educational/training history, military and community service activities
       b. Be able to complete a job application correctly
       c. Know how to write an effective resume
       d. Know how to write an effective business letter including cover and follow-up letters

E. Interview Skills

Participants will:
    1. Know what to expect from a job interview
    2. Be able to translate self-assessment into an interview presentation
    3. Be able to state clearly occupational goals

352

4. Know how to rehearse answers to both typical and problematic interview questions
5. Know legal rights in interview situation
6. Be able to demonstrate knowledge of organization and job responsibilities and ask relevant questions
7. Know how to dress appropriately
8. Be able to implement effective non-verbal behavior
9. Know how to develop an interview plan and apply it in the actual interview
10. Know appropriate time to ask questions regarding pay and fringe benefits
11. Be able to utilize appropriate closing and follow-up techniques

F. Job Retention

Participants will:
1. Learn how to assess the expectations of the work environment
2. Be able to ask for on-going evaluation
3. Be able to ask questions to enhance knowledge of job and organization
4. Know employer's expectations regarding punctuality, reliability, quality, and quantity of work
5. Be able to realistically self-evaluate and point out achievements at performance evaluation
6. Know how to gather information and make decisions regarding occupational future

REFERENCES

Arbeiter, S., Aslanian, C.C., Schmerbeck, F.A., & Brickell, H.M. (1978). *Forty million Americans in career transition: The need for information.* New York College Examination Board.

Azrin, N.H., & Besalel, V.A. (1980). *Job club counselor's manual: A behavioral approach to vocational counseling.* Baltimore: University Park Press.

Barclay, T. and McDougall, M. (1990). Older worker programs. *Generations, 14,* 1, 53–54.

Carnevale, A.P., Gainer, L.J., and Meltzer, A.S. (1988). *Workplace basics: The skills employees want.* Alexandria, VA: American Society for Training and Development.

Goodman, J. & Hoppin, J.M. (1990). *Opening doors: A practical guide to job hunting.* (2nd ed). Rochester, MI: Oakland University, Continuum Center.

Goodman, J. & Hoppin, J.M. (1986). *Directions for change: A career development workbook.* (4th ed). Rochester, MI: Oakland University.

Jewish Vocational Service and Community Workshop. (1988–89). *Annual report.* Oakland County Branch, 25900 Greenfield Road, Suite 242, Oak Park, Michigan 48237.

Kapes, J.T. & Mastie, M.M. (1988) *A counselor's guide to career assessment instruments* (2nd ed.). Alexandria, VA: The National Career Development Association.

National Occupational Information Coordinating Committee (undated). *The national career development guidelines.* Washington, D.C.

Schlossberg, N.K. (1984). *Counseling adults in transition: Linking practice with theory.* New York: Springer.

Tiedeman, D.V., & O'Hara, R.P. (1963). *Career development: Choices and adjustment.* Princeton, NJ: College Entrance Examination Board.

CHAPTER 19

Career Counseling Adults in a Community College Setting

Patricia Haskell
Career Counseling Services
Rockville, Maryland

Nancy Wiener
Montgomery College
Rockville, Maryland

Adult and career development theories encompass rich and varied concepts that can help community college counselors understand and better meet students' needs. On the other hand, limitations of adult career development theories are exacerbated by the nature and scope of the community college and its students.

COMMUNITY COLLEGE DEMOGRAPHICS

The community college is a comprehensive, public, postsecondary institution with an open-door admissions policy offering both credit and noncredit courses. Community colleges offer one-year certificates and two-year degrees in technical and semiprofessional occupational areas, academic programs for those transferring to four-year institutions, and developmental education for precollege students with marginal skills (Chernow & Chernow, 1981).

The students in community colleges are as diverse as the programs. Consider Montgomery College, a three-campus community college in Maryland, where the student enrollment pattern is similar to that of many other community colleges. Of the 20,000 students, 91% are county residents and 45% are Montgomery County public school graduates. Fifty-six percent of the students are women, 25% are ethnic minorities, and 16% are from foreign countries. The average age for students is 28 years. About 54% are employed full time, whereas 19% hold part-time jobs. Fifty-four percent of the students attend day classes, 32% attend evening classes, and 14% attend both day and evening classes. Fifty-eight percent intend to transfer to a four-year college. More than 300 students take courses by television. Forty-one percent are enrolled in occupational programs (Office of Institutional Research, 1984). Thus, the nontraditional student—women, minorities, international students, older students, part-time students, full-time workers, evening students, commuter students, and students in occupational programs are increasingly the typical students in community colleges.

ISSUES FOR COMMUNITY COLLEGE COUNSELORS

Despite the diversity of students and programs the community college counselor consistently encounters three categories of interrelated issues: transitional, self-concept, and logistical.

The characteristics of a transition as described by Schlossberg (1981) include the following: (a) role change, (b) positive or negative affective changes, (c) internal focus of control versus perceived lack of control in one's life, (d) on time versus off time with respect to an event being age relevant, (e) gradual or sudden onset of change, and lastly, (f) the degree of stress. Some examples of transitions include: reentering the job market, changing careers, returning to college to earn a degree, and retiring.

Self-concept pertains to the worth of self in relation to others and the empowering of self to make choices and accept responsibility for those choices. Some of the self-concept issues encountered in the community college setting involve low self-esteem resulting from poor past performance in an educational setting, a fear of being too old to learn, and feelings of inadequacy due to a lack of information about how to negotiate the community college environment or the job market. Particularly, self-concept issues are exhibited in the forms of:

- "A syndrome" where many adults believe that they must receive an "A" grade in courses or they have failed. This seems to be generally true of adults returning to school after a number of years away.
- "Role conflicts" where there is difficulty in integrating two different roles. Some examples are: retiree versus worker; wife/mother versus career woman; discontented but secure worker versus career changer; student versus worker; and married person versus divorcee.
- "Identity crisis" with the loss of support systems and uncertainty about self-image. An example of this might be a woman in her second year of study who loses the encouragement and understanding of family members and friends. As she begins to develop a new sense of self, conflicts may arise with family members and friends.
- "Nontraditional labeling" where discomfort is created because adult students are considered different from the traditional student population. They are sometimes assigned the status of an appendage to youth (Barton, 1982).
- "Gender-role and occupational stereotyping" where either college advisors or adults themselves limit their behaviors and occupational choices due to their internal stereotypes of gender-appropriate behaviors and occupations.

Logistical issues are feasibility issues. Adults are concerned about child care resources, ease of parking, hassle free registration, availability of a suitable class schedule to fit in with child care and employment needs, and financial aid. In addition, adult community college students want to know that, if they take classes or get a degree, job placement services will be available at the end of the program.

Some of the services available within the community college to address these logistical needs are: weekend college (classes offered all day Saturdays); open child care centers; evening career advising; and extended hours for career resource centers.

These issues are "reality" issues that must be taken into account in judging the usefulness of adult career development concepts in the community college setting. A theory-based interest inventory that indicates engineering technology as a possible occupation is of little use if the student's occupational stereotypes and math anxiety are not addressed. Also, that adult student may never graduate if required classes cannot be scheduled to fit in with employment needs. These key issues need to be explored and resolved by the career counselor and adult learner together. The role of the career counselor must be to develop programs and approaches that focus on these reality issues as well as those of career development theory.

COMMUNITY COLLEGE CAREER PROGRAMS

Career counseling programs and services at community colleges are designed to meet the diverse needs of adult students. Some of the characteristic programs and services that will be discussed are: the career resource center, individual career counseling, student development courses, career and educational workshops, cooperative educational courses and programs with business and industry, and computerized occupational choice and information services.

The focal point of many community college programs is the career resource center. Career resource centers in the community college setting are usually open 12 hours a day and feature a variety of materials and services for adults. These include written information and books on job hunting and changing careers; audiovisual materials on job search; occupational or company information career files on a variety of occupations; "how to" stations; computerized college and job search systems; college transfer information; and job placement services.

Community college career resource centers also generally have a series of self-managed career/life planning activities to answer the needs of adults who do not participate in courses or workshops. After individual consultation with the career counselor, adults work independently on a wide range of issues. These activities generally take place in work stations organized around: self-assessment (skills, values, and interests); occupational exploration (library research, networking, informational interviewing); and refining job search skills (resume writing and job interviewing).

Individual career counseling is a valuable service provided in the community college setting to assist adults as they reenter college, seek job upgrading, make midlife/career decisions, and plan for the use of their leisure time during retirement. At some small campuses, all new students are interviewed by a career counselor to define career goals and select the appropriate curriculum. Often, career counselors use a host of career inventory and personality assessment instruments for diagnostic purposes. Some of the major assessment instruments used in the community college setting are: Strong-Campbell Interest Inventory; Myers-Briggs Type Indicator; Self-Directed Search; VIESA Career Guidebook; and ACT Career Planning Program (adult series).

Student development courses offered at many community colleges are designed to help adults meet their educational and vocational needs. For example, at the Rockville campus of Montgomery Community College, adults can choose from a group of courses all taught by the counseling faculty. The course, "Options for Women," offers women over age 25 training in the following skills: time management, assertiveness, decision-making and goal setting, networking, and career/life planning. In the course, "Career Development, Dynamics and Application," students learn to plan, establish, or change a career. Three courses address the need for academic skills: "Study Habits Development," "College Survival," and "Memory Development."

Workshops are also generally offered on career and educational issues. For example, "Career Life Assessment Skills Series" (Curtin & Hecklinger, 1981) is offered at Northern Virginia Community College. It is a group of eight noncredit workshops covering the following topics: Your Unique Self, Job Market Investigation, Job Campaign Strategies, Job Keeping and Revitalization, the Federal Employment Process, Academic Survival Skills, Mid-Life and Career Transition, and Pre-Retirement. The workbooks and audiovisual materials developed for these topics also may be used by career counselors with individuals and groups outside the workshops.

Cooperative programs with business, government, and nonprofit institutions represent a growing trend used for student placement, especially for older students. For example, "Jobs for Older Women" at the College of the Emeriti, San Diego Community College District, assists women entering the job market by use of a mentor network of volunteer business and professional women. Job applicants are recruited and advised and are offered services from the college's counseling center and community agencies. Individual mentors provide advice and modeling. (Aronson & Eccles, 1980).

Cooperative education courses are offered on a number of community college campuses. At Montgomery College, Germantown Campus, career counselors advise adults who have met prerequisites to choose from a series of courses, with learning taking place in the work setting. Courses are offered in accounting, computer science, electromechanical technology, and business. The courses help link adult students with employers. Thus, adults are given the opportunity to integrate classroom theory with real life work applications. The student earns academic credit and is evaluated by the employer.

Other community college programs and services include career information, outreach activities, and employment services. Career information is provided by various means. One approach to occupational information is through the use of a computer system such as INFORM (a local and nationwide career information delivery system) or COIN (College Occupational Information Network). At Montgomery College, Rockville Campus, a faculty member is selected and given time to be an occupational program specialist. In this role, the faculty member serves as liaison with the occupational program coordinator and the career counselors. The occupational program specialist conducts needs assessments, suggests career development interventions and strategies, plans and coordinates career fairs, and updates curricular and employment information. Another approach to providing career information is for career counselors to maintain alumni banks of graduates as referrals to provide occupational information. In addition, newsletters are used to inform adults about employment trends, job information, occupational profiles, career development events, and related adult career development issues such as test anxiety, time management skills, and stress coping skills.

In providing outreach, the role of the career counselor is expanding. Community college career counselors speak to homemaker groups, county organizations, civic clubs, government agencies, unions, and employers about employment trends, the career/life planning process, and resources of the community college. In rural areas, adults are served by mobile career vans equipped with occupational literature, filmstrips, cassettes, and self-help career/life planning stations.

Employment or placement services at the community college's career center take many forms. The range is from bulletin boards with job listings to computerized data banks of local job opportunities to elaborate systems of matching students' credential files to employer needs from the on-campus interviewing program. The emphasis is generally on employment and employer information.

CHANGING ROLE OF THE COMMUNITY COLLEGE CAREER COUNSELOR

In developing programs and approaches, the career counselor at the community college assumes many roles. One role may be that of a personal counselor who must deal with personal issues and their immediate effect on the student. Another role may be that of a career development skills instructor. Still another may be the role of program developer and manager. A fourth role is that of an immediate problem solver. Finally, there is the role of community referral agent.

In today's rapidly changing college and work environment the nontraditional student of the past is becoming today's traditional student. Career development services must reflect a multidimensional perspective, rely on theoretical foundations, but incorporate key reality issues. Career development resource centers, courses, workshops, self-managed activities, cooperative programs, information, and outreach and employment efforts are but a few examples of career development services. The goals of any career development program should be to meet the diverse needs of the target population, to promote a rewarding life style, and positive self-concepts. The diversity and complexity of community college students make the provision of career services in community college settings a more complex challenge than in more traditional settings.

IMPLICATIONS FOR CAREER COUNSELING TRAINING

Listed below are some training implications for career counselors perparing to work in community colleges.

- At the graduate school level, career counselors planning to work with adults should take required courses in adult and career development (with emphasis on gender role socialization).
- Materials used in career counselor training should include diverse client populations and be carefully reviewed for bias.
- A practicum should be required in career counseling of adults in a community college setting

Some implications for practicing community college career counselors are:

- Career counselors should have periodic inservice training on adult development, nonbiased career counseling practices, and job market information.
- Theories of career development need to be reviewed for applicability to diverse, nontraditional student populations.
- Career counselors must examine their attitudes toward diverse client groups (i.e., women, the aged, the handicapped, and minorities).
- Career counselors should be familiar with current literature regarding stereotyping, developmental needs, career/life planning theory, and employment trends.
- Career counselors must perceive themselves as change agents: (a) this includes career counselors taking a proactive role in developing strategies and procedures to deal with transition, self-concept, and logistical isues. Some examples include: job clubs for students, opportunity seminars for entering nontraditional fields, and dress-for-success workshops; (b) it also includes career counselors becoming involved in career curriculum development (i.e., consulting with advisory boards and faculty); (c) finally, it also means that the career counselor must push for change in their own work place (i.e., alternative work patterns, flextime, increased child care options, and job sharing).
- Community college counselors have to concern themselves with the assumptions and technological implications of androgogy, the art and science of helping adults learn (Knowles, 1977).

SUMMARY

The purpose of this chapter has been to describe the demographics of the community college student population, to point out three interrelated reality-based issues confronted by community college students, to describe some typical community college programs and services, and finally, to discuss the diverse roles of the community college career counselor. Although only brief descriptions and elaborations of these areas were possible, it is hoped that the reader has gained a broad overview of career counseling issues and practices in the community college setting.

REFERENCES

Aronson, J., & Eccles, M. (1980). Community college and career education for older adults. *Community and Junior College Journal, 51*, 24–29.

Barton, P.E. (1982). *Worklife transitions, the adult learning connection.* New York: McGraw-Hill.

Chernow, F., & Chernow, C. (1981). *Careers for the community college graduate.* New York, Arco.

Curtin, B., & Hecklinger, F. (1981). *Career life assessment skills series (CLASS).* Alexandria, VA: Northern Virginia Community College.

Knowles, M.S. (1970). *The modern practice of adult education: Androgogy versus pedagogy.* New York: Association Press.

Office of Institutional Research (1984). *Montgomery College student profile, fall 1983.* Rockville, MD: Montgomery College.

Schlossberg, N. (1981). A model for analyzing human adaptation to transition. *Counseling Psychologist, 9*, 2–18.

SECTION V:

TRAINING PROGRAMS

PREPARING OURSELVES . . .

CHAPTER 20

The Career Development Professional of the 1990s: A Training Model

Janice M. Chiappone
John F. Kennedy University
Orinda, California

In the recent past, numerous changes have emerged to affect the career development professional. These include developmental changes, technological changes, economic changes, cultural changes, and demographic changes. With economic uncertainty, diminished resources, increased education and underemployment, higher divorce rates, and increased numbers of women in the workforce, there is a need both to understand the impact of these changes and to help prepare adults for continual change. The one thing that is certain about future employment is change. It will require people who can adapt to a changing environment.

In this chapter, I will examine some of these changes and how they have influenced individuals, organizations, and career development professionals. These changes created a new clientele in different settings and new activities and have led to the need for a new career development professional with new skills. An example of a program designed to train the new career development professional of the 1990s will then be presented (See Figure 1).

CHANGES AFFECTING THE CAREER DEVELOPMENT PROFESSIONAL

Technological Changes

Technological innovations in the workplace represent one of the major changes affecting the careers of adults. The world's technology is doubling every 20 years. Increased automation and robotics are beginning to pervade American life. The number of Americans employed in the industrial sector of the economy is falling sharply, whereas the number of people in the information sector is rising just as sharply. The office is replacing the factory as the center of the economy. In fact, more than-

Figure 1

The Growth of the Career Development Profession

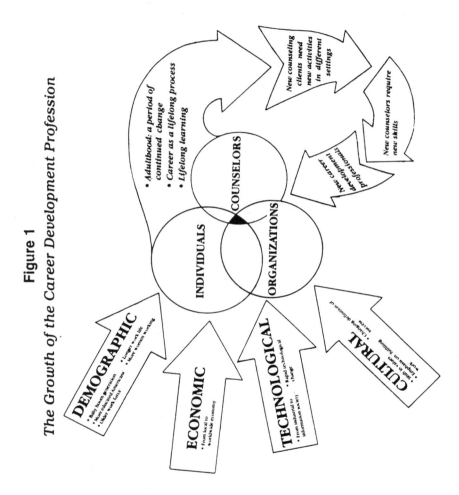

half of the national work force collects, manipulates, and disseminates information.

The skills required for the careers of the 1990s and beyond will continue to shift. Many low-skill, low-education jobs will disappear and many new jobs will emerge, requiring additional training and skills. According to the Bureau of Labor Statistics, rapid growth in jobs for white-collar and professional workers and for service workers is expected to continue through the 1990s, whereas jobs for blue-collar workers and farm workers will continue to disappear.

As manufacturing becomes more automated, workers will continue to shift into new jobs in the information and service sector. This includes banking, accounting, insurance, and real estate; hotels, restaurants, and airlines; medicine, law, and engineering; data-processing, word processing, publishing, and broadcasting.

As the United States continues to move from an industrial society to an informational society, many new positions will emerge. Scientists, mathematicians, engineers, computer analysts, and designers will be in great demand to continually create and advance the expanding technology. More and more paraprofessional technicians will be needed for the high technology industries. Computer repair technicians, computer operators, chemistry and engineering technicians, and biomedical technicians will be in demand to keep the information society running smoothly. Sales, marketing, and training personnel will also be needed to service management information systems and to train people to understand, use, and adjust to the advent of computers in their lives.

These technological changes in the work place mean changes in the ways people are employed, how responsibilities are assigned to them, and what work skills are required of them. These changes are forecast to continue and may require a lifetime of learning and retraining.

Economic Changes

The greatest economic change that has affected the career development of adults is the move from a local economy to a world economy. The United States is increasingly becoming part of a global world marketplace. The economy used to be predominantly local and internal; the United States consumed most of what it produced and produced most of what it consumed. That is changing rapidly. As the United States becomes more of an importer/exporter of basic goods, jobs are disappearing permanently. A total of 90% of the 21 million new jobs will be in service-producing, not goods-producing, industries. Employees from such huge industries as steel and automobiles will be forced to seek retraining to become job marketable in a society that no longer needs the skills they possess.

Global competition, corporate downsizing, and mergers have resulted in drastic cost-cutting programs and huge layoffs. The middle management layer is thinning out and more employees are vying for fewer jobs at the higher levels of the corporation. The prevailing mood in many American companies is one of fear and anxiety. Many employees are facing the loss of a job they once believed would be secure, as well as a shattering of their belief that they would be rewarded for good work with job security.

A growing number of employees are reacting to corporate downsizing by finding new employers, making lateral moves within the company, or beginning their own company. These displaced workers will increasingly seek the services of career development professionals as they deal with the grief of losing their job, reassess their career prospects, and begin a job search.

Cultural Changes

A number of cultural changes have occurred that influence the career development of individuals. Some of these changes are a shift in work values, emphasis on fulfilling work, changing definition of success, growing acceptance of career change, and an increase in dual career couples.

In a world of increasingly rapid change and high mobility, ideas about what makes a successful career and the meaning of work itself are being reevaluated. With a general rise in socioeconomic status and educational levels, more people have rising expectations about what constitutes a happy and fulfilling life. People are questioning their happiness at work and seeking more meaning through their work.

Yankelovich (1979) indicated that the meaning of work has changed for many individuals. These changes include revised definitions of success that place less emphasis on material achievement and more emphasis on personal fulfillment. His research suggests that people are looking for psychological benefits from their work: an opportunity to do a good job; a yearning to find self-fulfillment through meaningful work; the chance to become involved, committed, and challenged in their work, and to have greater participation in decision-making on the job.

A more highly educated work force implies growing interest in jobs that provide opportunities for use of abilities, self-expression, and fulfillment, along with traditional economic and material rewards. People have always worked for economic reasons, but now, in addition to the economic motive, there is a powerful psychological desire for self-actualization. Its effects are a change in work values and an emphasis on the quality of work life.

Along with the emphasis on fulfilling work has been a growing acceptance of career change. In the past, it was assumed that people chose one career that would last all their adult lives until retirement. Today, the average worker will change careers at least three times in a lifetime, and more people are thinking in terms of second or multiple careers. Women who have reared children, along with both men and women whose careers have provided financial security but not a sense of accomplishment, may seek second careers in which they can find fulfillment. There is a growing trend toward job changes in midcareer as people seek career satisfaction and a higher quality of life.

For many, the midlife period may be a time of transition to reappraise lives, values, goals, and careers (Levinson, 1977). This reappraisal may lead to midcareer change. Incompatible interests with a current career, a desire to have more control over the future, and a desire to find more meaningful work influence an individual to change careers (Neopolitan, 1980; Osherson, 1980).

Another cultural change has been the emergence of the dual career couple. More than 50% of married couples in the United States are both pursuing careers. Social indicators suggest that these dual career couples will continue to rise in number. Increasing numbers of women are preparing for careers by continuing their education, and higher levels of education are associated with increasing numbers of women who are entering professional fields. Because professional women are likely to marry professional men, the dual career pattern will become more and more prevalent in this society. This change is forcing husbands and wives to give increasing attention to managing their dual career families (Rapaport & Rapaport, 1976). Balancing work and family roles is stressful for many dual career couples. Organizations often lose valuable professionals because employees are unable to cope with the exacting organizational demands of a career and the strenuous roles of parent and spouse (Taylor, 1986).

Demographic Changes

The United States is becoming a nation of adults. Profound demographic shifts are pushing the average age of the population and work force upward. By the year 2000, the largest age group will be 25–44 year-olds, with a rising curve for 45–64 year olds.

Because of the low birthrate of the 1960s, the numbers of young workers aged 18–24 is expected to decline from 20% in 1986 to 16% in 2000. Due to the baby boom generation there is a sharp increase in workers in the 25–54 age bracket. The proportion of the work force aged 25–54 will constitute about 73% in the year 2000 (Fullerton, 1987).

These factors will have far-reaching consequences for the job market. Individuals in the 25–54 year-old range will undoubtedly face fierce competition for promotions and supervisory positions, and many may face problems obtaining jobs in the professional and managerial arena. Only a limited number of workers will progress to higher positions, competition will be intense, and disappointment widespread. The enormous size of this group will make its career concerns impossible to ignore.

According to the U.S. Bureau of the Census, the population aged 65 and over is more than 29 million in 1990. Also, the number of people aged 55–64 will continue to rise. Between 1900 and 1980 the life expectancy of Americans increased more than 40%. Advances in nutrition, health, and medical care have all contributed to this increase in longevity. This has led to a longer work life for many as well as to more time spent in education, retirement, and leisure. Early retirement programs are becoming numerous, and employees who have retired from one career may consider other part-time careers. Also, extended employment has become more of a possibility for the older worker because of a rise in the mandatory retirement age.

The large-scale movement of women into the labor force is an important and dramatic demographic change. By the year 2000, 8 of every 10 women ages 25–54 are expected to be in the labor force (Fullerton, 1987). The rising number of unmarried women in the population has made it economically necessary for many single, separated, divorced, and widowed women to establish their own careers. Today's female labor force consists of a high proportion of college graduates. Because further education usually means a better chance of employment, the most significant gains have occurred among the highly educated.

Perhaps the most significant recent change in the labor force has involved working mothers. The labor force participation rate of women with children under age six has more than tripled in the past decade. By 1995, almost 70% of those women will be employed. The sharply rising educational levels of women, the acceptance of dual-career couples, and the high incidence of women reentering the work force soon after having children suggest that the increase will continue. As more and more working mothers stay in the work force and obtain management positions, employers will be competing for their services. Child care programs, flexible hours, paid parental leave, elder care, seminars on balancing work and family issues, and job sharing options will continue to grow as companies realize they can no longer deny that employees' personal lives affect their work lives. Many employers are finding that programs such as these foster employee satisfaction and enhance productivity.

Five of every six new labor market employees between 1986 and 2000 will be women, minority persons, or immigrants. In today's labor force, these groups are underrepresented in those occupational areas experiencing the greatest job growth and overrepresented in those areas experiencing the least amount of job growth (National Alliance of Business, 1986).

There has also been a rapid rise of educational attainment in the United States as a result of the dramatic increase in the number of people completing high school and continuing their education. Almost two-thirds of the adults in the United States 17 and older are now high school graduates. Research suggests that the more education people have, the more education they want, and the more they participate in further learning activities (Cross, 1981). A high percentage of new jobs created by the year 2000 will require some post-secondary education. Because of a number of social, economic, and technological changes, the United States is rapidly becoming a "lifelong learning society" where individuals continually need the benefits of education to keep marketable skills, further career change, or enhance self-fulfillment.

All of these demographic changes have created a very diverse labor force which will provide many challenges for the career development professional of the 1990's.

Developmental Changes

One of the major changes affecting adult career development is the recognition of adulthood as a period of continual change and potential development, as opposed to one of stability and certainty. Adults continually experience changes or transitions in different areas of their lives. These changes often cause them to reevaluate their values, goals, and choices and to move for greater growth and development. Changes that occur in adulthood have no absolute timing, although some events are linked to specific ages by social expectation. Different adults experience changes at different times in their lives, and some, not at all. Although adult theorists disagree on how to explain transitions, most agree that adulthood is characterized by periods of stability that are bridged by these transitions. It is the study of these adult transitions that has been the focus of much of the adult development literature and research in recent years.

Career is an important theme in adult development, particularly during adult transitions (Gottfredson, 1977, Schlossberg, 1984). Smelser and Erikson (1980) identified work as one of the two major themes of adulthood. A major portion of an adult's identity and feelings of self worth is often expressed through work, which absorbs a great deal of time and energy.

Along with the shift in the perception of adulthood as a period of continual change is a shift in the view of career development as a lifelong process. Traditionally, the field of guidance or vocational counseling focused on adolescence and was limited to testing and finding one vocation for a lifetime. Given all the changes mentioned earlier, it is no longer feasible for individuals to choose one career in adolescence and continue in that same career for their whole lives. Society and the economy are changing rapidly and forcing people to choose and rechoose many times during their lives and to seek additional training to remain job-marketable.

People are constantly changing, and as they change, so do their career patterns and commitments. Virtually every person's work history is characterized by some kind of change. The days of "one job for life" are fading fast, and there is greater recognition that career choices are required throughout one's life, not simply in adolescence. Job change rather than job continuity is becoming the norm.

Many adults are currently in transition, moving from one career to another. A College Board survey found that of the 40 million Americans in career transition, 60% will seek additional education and many have expressed a need for a variety of career services (Arbeiter, Aslanian, Schmerbeck, & Brickell, 1978). Aslanian and Brickell (1980) found that job or career change is the most common of all adult transitions and the most likely to motivate people to seek new learning opportunities. When adult learners were asked what motivated their learning activities, 83% mentioned some change in their life, and for 56% of them the change was related to a job or career change.

Given the social, demographic, economic, and technological changes mentioned earlier, lifelong learning has also become necessary, desirable, and acceptable for many adults. Change is now so great that no amount of education during youth can adequately prepare adults to meet the changing demands of society. More and more adults are recognizing the need to continue their education and to retrain in order to remain marketable in a society that has undergone tremendous change (Bolles, 1979).

Adults who seek the services of a career development professional bring a variety of psychological issues that impact their career development (Chiappone, 1989). Adults are continually experiencing personal transitions that affect their career and career transitions that affect their personal lives. Even if the major source for the problem is not career, an adult's worklife may be affected to the point that career counseling is needed.

Psychological issues will continue to be important as the workplace continues to downsize and change with more and more adults facing job change, job insecurity, and job loss. Since work is such an important part of identity for many adults, issues of low self-esteem, depression, fear, anger, and grief may result when adults are faced with the threat of change or loss in this important facet of their identity (Chiaponne, 1989). Career development professionals in the 1990s will need to consider the implications of these changes in their work with adults.

CHANGES CREATE NEW NEEDS

Some of the needs these changes have pinpointed for individuals, organizations, and career development professionals of the 1990s are the following:

Individuals

- need to become aware of adult development issues and how these issues affect their lives;
- need to realize that change is the norm in adulthood and learn to become more comfortable with change;
- need to understand the transition process and how to cope with transitions;
- need to be willing and prepared to continually reassess and reevaluate their goals, values, interests, and career decisions;
- need to continually assess their skills and be willing to retrain to stay job-marketable;
- need to develop career decision-making skills;
- need to become more proactive in managing their careers;
- need to stay abreast of changes in the economy and society and know how these changes affect the job market and their career goals;
- need to balance family and work concerns at different stages in their lives;
- need to help employers design programs to reduce tensions that arise when job and family responsibilities conflict;
- need to prepare for the possibility of midcareer changes, second careers, and what may be long retirement years; and
- need to take responsibility for their careers.

Organizations

- need to understand adult development issues;
- need to be aware of and respond to changing employee work values;
- need to improve job-employee match;
- need to provide employees with the organizational mission and policies;

- need to help employees with transition management;
- need to support the roles of managers in the career development of employees;
- need to provide alternatives and opportunities for midcareer, dual career, plateaued, and older employees;
- need to be prepared to help women enter and reenter the work force throughout their lives;
- need to improve human resource planning and development activities;
- need to keep employee turnover at a minimum by creating opportunities within the company;
- need to develop programs to increase productivity and quality of work life such as job sharing, child-care programs, elder care programs, seminars, spousal relocation assistance, flexible benefits, flexible work schedules, part-time jobs, flexible retirement plans, quality control circles, shared decision-making, and flexible career structures;
- need to help managers develop skills to manage the diverse work force;
- need to prepare career planning programs with multiple options for employees;
- need to tie career development activities into the goals of the corporation.

Career Development Professionals of the 1990s

- need to be aware of adult development issues;
- need to view career development as a lifelong process;
- need to stay aware of the changes taking place in the economy, society, and job market;
- need to help clients interpret these changes so they can take charge of their careers;
- need to help clients continually reassess their goals, values, interests, and career decisions;
- need to teach career decision-making skills;
- need to help clients understand transitions and cope with change;
- need to consider how activities related to self, career, and family interact throughout the entire life span;
- need to balance knowledge of career development with an awareness of a client's psychological and developmental needs;
- need to be sensitive to the variety of psychological issues clients bring to the career counseling process;
- need to help clients prepare for retirement years, the possibility of second careers, and a longer work life;
- need to be aware of and educate clients about stereotypes and biases in sex, race, age, and culture;
- need to design and implement human resource planning systems and provide career support to employees;
- need to design organizational programs to help employees successfully manage career transitions;
- need to teach clients skills to manage their careers;

- need to be aware of and provide assistance with all the complexities of dual careers, working mothers, and child care issues;
- need to help men and women prepare for multiple roles throughout their lives;
- need to develop evaluation of their services and programs for accountability purposes.

These changes have also created new clients in different settings as well as new activities, which has led to the need for a new career development professional with new skills. All of these changes have brought many new clients including older workers, disabled workers, plateaued employees, immigrant workers, minority workers, functionally illiterate workers, special interest groups, preretirement individuals, working mothers, and dual career couples. In addition, many organizations have continued to need and expand career development services.

As the clients change, the kinds of activities appropriate to their concerns and needs change, and the settings where these activities take place have expanded from the traditional settings, such as schools, to include new settings, such as business and industry (see Figure 2).

As the problems of clients change, the kinds of activities that are appropriate to a career counseling intervention must also change. Clients may need to be taught **how** to cope with change, **how** to find information, **how** to conduct a job search campaign, **how** to make career decisions, **how** to balance career and family responsibilities rather than to be offered answers to career questions. Career counselors of adults must develop and expand on the model of adulthood as a process of lifelong change. With this model, counselors can help their clients to be more proactive in their work life. In this way, career counselors will become participants and change agents in the dynamic process of career development in the coming decades.

A NEW CAREER DEVELOPMENT GRADUATE PROGRAM

The need for a new counselor equipped with new skills and a thorough preparation in adult and career development has generated a new model for the education of career counselors. Traditionally, programs preparing counselors to work in career counseling have been found in counseling or educational psychology programs. In these programs, students concentrate their studies on becoming a counselor and take only a few courses specifically in career counseling and career development. These few courses seem insufficient training for the career development professional of the 1990s.

John F. Kennedy University decided to change this and created a new program to meet the needs of the new career development professional. In the Spring of 1980, the Master's Degree Program in Career Development was developed in response to the many cultural, demographic, economic, and technological changes in society. A major goal of the program was to train career development professionals with an understanding of adult development to help a diversity of clients cope with these changes and manage their careers.

Figure 2
Career Development: Settings and Activities

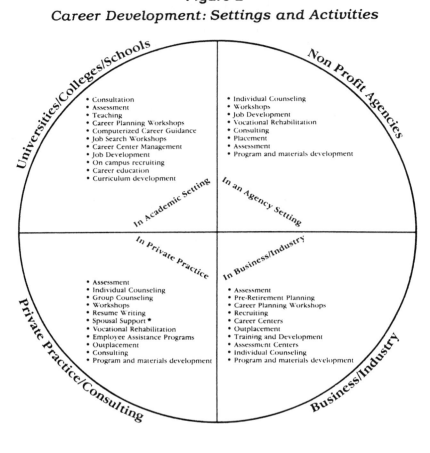

*(In states where career assessment
is allowed in divorce litigation.)

What emerged is a career development program which includes many of the strengths of a graduate program in counseling while adding a core curriculum focused on career development issues. In addition to taking coursework in career development, psychology, and management, students are required to complete a supervised internship, supervised external fieldwork, and a career development project. Emphasizing adult development theories, students receive a solid grounding in the theories and practices useful in helping adults cope with transitions. In response to the need for new career development activities in new settings, the interdisciplinary 60 unit program has drawn on the disciplines of career development, psychology, and management. Graduates of the program are prepared to assist clients, both individuals and organizations, to understand adult and career development and to acquire the skills and the knowledge required to respond to, and cope with, change.

To build a curriculum that included many of the strengths of graduate programs in counseling while adding the focus of career development and adult development, the planning group at J.F.K. University developed a unique curriculum. As a school for adults in midcareer, the upper division and graduate schools at John F. Kennedy University provided support, assistance, and encouragement for the birth of the career development program. Also, the beginning of the graduate program in career development facilitated the formation and staffing of a long-awaited career development center for the J.F.K. University student body.

In creating this program, the following curriculum goals were established:

- to train students in career counseling skills and adult development theories;
- to expose students to a wide range of world of work information;
- to prepare students to be experts in the skills and knowledge of career development;
- to prepare students to work in a variety of settings.

To achieve these goals, John F. Kennedy University established a Master's Degree and Post-Master's Certificate Program in Career Development. After the start of the program, the National Vocational Guidance Association (now the National Career Development Association) developed a list of competencies for the vocational/career professional. These competencies provide a useful model for discussion of the areas covered in the Kennedy graduate program. The six areas are: General Counseling, Information, Individual/Group Assessment, Management/Administration, Implementation, and Consultation. These areas are covered in the graduate program in the following ways:

1. **General Counseling**
   Career Counseling Interview
   (Students learn the career counseling process and develop counseling skills.)
   Career Counseling Practicum
   (Students continue to develop their counseling skills and receive supervision as they counsel at least one client from the Career Center.)
   Career Counseling for Special Populations
   (Students learn techniques and resources for counseling people with diverse backgrounds.)
   Group Process
   Adulthood
   (Students explore individual development, sexuality, family life, and work in adulthood.)
   Psychology of Adult Development
   (Students explore major theories of adult development with an emphasis on career development within adulthood. Students also explore their own adult development and transitions.)
   Personality and Psychotherapy

Clinical Issues in Career Counseling
(Students explore a variety of clinical issues in career counseling, learn how to address these issues with clients, and evaluate their appropriateness for career counseling.)

2. **Information**
Philosophy of Work: Meaning and Mission
(Students explore the historical, multicultural, and personal perspectives of work.)
Theories of Career Development
World of Work
(Students analyze and study the local economy, explore various economic sectors, and develop a model and method for future study of the economy.)
Career Resource Information
Vocational Rehabilitation
(Students learn theories of vocational rehabilitation and review problems of career choice and implementation.)

3. **Individual/Group Assessment**
Assessment Approaches in Career Development
Case Studies in Assessment
(Students learn how to integrate a variety of career assessments in a case study format.)

4. **Management/Administration**
Career Development in Organizations
(Students focus on ways to unite career and personal objectives in the world of work and learn how to design and implement programs for career development within organizations.)
Human Resource Management
Planning, Conducting, and Evaluating Workshops
(Students learn theories and methods of teaching and training adults as well as actually designing a career workshop.)

5. **Implementation**
Career Development Techniques and Practices
(Students explore theories and applications of career development in a series of one day workshops. Topics have included managing career transitions, intuitive decision-making, coping with job loss, dual career issues, Myers-Briggs Type Indicator, etc.)
Supervised Career Center Internship
(Students intern at the Kennedy Career Center where they focus on individual career counseling. They also have individual and group supervisions and case seminars.)
External Fieldwork
(Students have an opportunity to do fieldwork in a variety of settings, including many universities, agencies, and major corporations in the Bay Area, such as Lockheed, Bank of America, and Pacific Bell. Students perform a variety of functions including individual and group counseling, developing career manuals, em-

ployee training, and designing and delivering pre-retirement and career planning workshops.)

6. **Consultation**
   Principles of Organizational Consulting
   Strategic Management of Change
   (Students participate in a change effort in an organization of their choice. They learn contract development, data gathering, problem identification, and implementation.)

Additional programming is provided during the Career Development Summer Institute held annually for three days in late July. During the Institute, for which students may receive academic credit, nationally known career development professionals provide intensive programming. Institute speakers have included Richard Bolles, author of *What Color Is Your Parachute*; Robert Waterman, co-author of *In Search of Excellence*, Howard Figler, author of books on career counseling, Nancy Schlossberg, psychologist and author of books on adult and career development, and Zandy Leibowitz, psychologist and author of books on career development in organizations and adult development. In this format, career development students have an opportunity to learn from career development professionals and to meet Institute attendees from all over the United States and Canada.

In 1986, the Career Development Summer Institute became the nucleus of an external career development master's degree program at John F. Kennedy University. The Career Development Field Studies Master's Degree Program was created to provide an educational opportunity to those individuals who seek training in career development, but who have no local program available to them or are unable to attend a resident graduate program because of job or family responsibilities. The program was designed to meet the changing needs of adult learners by providing independent learning opportunities, supervised internships and fieldwork, and two-week yearly residencies in the San Francisco Bay area. The field studies program is modeled after the resident program to ensure quality and consistency. Because of the high quality of the Master's Degree Program in Career Development at Kennedy and the fact that no comparable programs exist in the country, the Field Studies Program has attracted national and international students. The program continues to grow and provides a quality alternative for training the career development professional of the 1990s.

Effective career counselors need the skills and knowledge to provide service for many different groups of people in many different settings. The skills which form the basis of the program's curriculum include basic listening and counseling, assessment, world of work information, decision-making and the job search. In addition, career development professionals may need the skills to develop, conduct, and evaluate career-related programs, to consult with organizations, and to develop and manage programs. In the 1990s, adult career development professionals will need knowledge of theories of adult development, and theories of organizational change and development, as well as familiarity with specific programs needed by their expanding clientele including: dual career issues, outplacement counseling, spousal relocation services, succession planning, career pathing, training design and implementation, preretirement planning, and human resource management.

The content and structure of the career development graduate program is designed to give students the skills to cope with career concerns of adult clients and the opportunity to try out and test those new skills. The curriculum of the program is continually reviewed and revised to remain state of the art. Graduates of the Master's Degree program at Kennedy have found employment as career development professionals in a variety of settings, including academic, private practice, consulting, agency/nonprofit, and business. As career development activities increase, training programs preparing professionals to design, conduct, and evaluate these programs will also increase. The quality of these training programs has much to contribute to the future of the career development profession.

With all the aforementioned cultural, demographic, technological, and economic changes, as well as the change in accepting adulthood and career development as lifelong processes of change and development, the need to prepare individuals and organizations for the present and future is greater than ever. Consequently, the field of career development is expanding and the role of the career development professional is changing dramatically. Helping clients manage career and life transitions and encouraging continual career renewal are new challenges for the career development professional of the 1990s. Career development has emerged as a way for organizations and individuals to look at these issues in a way that is mutually beneficial. Technological change, job obsolescence, and organizational downsizing are forcing both individuals and organizations to recognize the need for career planning and the development of multiple skills and careers. Organizations are beginning to realize that career development programming may be a way to help increase productivity, reduce turnover, and meet workers' changing values. Individuals may need career planning assistance to learn more about opportunities and changes in society and the labor market, and about skills in career decision-making.

A high percentage of the work force will continue to experience career-related crises and transitions and, because change seems to be a certainty in adulthood and career development, it is important for individuals to learn to cope with changes and transitions in their lives. This has created a need for a new career development professional who can help adults become more comfortable with the inevitability of change and can teach career decision-making skills to cope with these changes and become managers of their own careers.

REFERENCES

Arbeiter, S. Aslanian, C.B., Schmerbeck, F.A., & Brickell, H.M. (1978). *Forty million Americans in career transition: The need for information.* New York: College Entrance Examination Board.

Aslanian, C.B. & Brickell, H.M. (1980). *Americans in transition: Life changes and reasons for adult learning.* New York: College Entrance Examination Board.

Bolles, R.N. (1979). *The quick job hunting map.* Berkeley: Ten Speed Press.

Chiappone, J. (1989). Clinical issues in career counseling of adults: A new challenge. *Career Planning and Adult Development Journal,* Fall.

Cross, K.P. (1981). *Adults as learners.* San Francisco: Jossey-Bass.

Freeman, R.B. (1979). The work force of the future: An overview. In C. Kerr & J.M. Rosow (Eds). *Work in America: The decade ahead* (pp. 58–79). New York: Van Nostrand Reinhold.

Fullerton, H., Jr. (1987). Projections 2000: Labor force projections—1986 to 2000. *Monthly Labor Review.* Washington, DC: U.S. Department of Labor.

Gottfredson, S.D. (1977). Career stability and redirection in adulthood. *Journal of Applied Psychology, 62,* 436–445.

Levinson, L. (1977). The mid-life transitions: A period in psychosocial development. *Psychiatry, 40,* 99–112.

National Alliance of Business, (1987, September 30). A critical message for every American who plans to work or do business in the 21st century. *New York Times Magazine.*

Neapolitan, J. (1980). Occupational change in mid-career: An exploratory investigation, *Journal of Vocational Behavior, 16,* 212–225.

Osherson, S. (1980). *Holding on or letting go: Men and career change at midlife.* New York: Free Press.

Rapaport, R. & Rapaport, R.N. (1976). *Dual-careers reexamined: New integrations of work and family.* New York: Harper & Row.

Schlossberg, N.K. (1984). *Counseling adults in transition: Linking practice with theory.* New York: Springer.

Smelser, N.J., & Erikson, E.H. (Eds). (1980). *Themes of work and love in adulthood.* Cambridge, MA: Harvard University Press.

Taylor, A. (1986, August 18). Why women managers are bailing out. *Fortune,* pp. 16–23.

Yankelovich, D. (1979). Work, values, and the new breed. In C. Kerr & J.M. Rosow (Eds). *Work in America: The decade ahead* (pp. 58–79). New York: Van Nostrand Reinhold.

CHAPTER 21

Training Professionals for Career Development Responsibilities in Business and Industry: An Update

Martin Gerstein
Counselor Education
Virginia Polytechnic Institute
and State University
Blacksburg, Virginia

Why train individuals in adult career development? Can counseling skills be readily transferred and applied in a business setting? What do worker values and expectations have to do with the "bottom line" of a profit and loss statement? These questions and others have been addressed in the career development literature (Bolyard, 1981; Fisher & Gerstein, 1983; Leibowitz & Schlossberg, 1981; Smith, Piercy, & Lutz, 1982; Souerwine, 1981; and Walz, 1982).

Differing views about the efficacy of organizational career development programs have emerged. It is clear that such programs are not cure-alls for personnel woes. Yet, when well designed and implemented, they can be significant contributors to high employee morale and more effective utilization of employee skills.

The experience base for career development programs has widened since a study by Gutteridge and Otte (1983) reviewed the career development practices of 40 major organizations throughout the country. In this study the industrial classifications included: manufacturing, communication, wholesale and retail trade, finance, insurance, service industries, and government. Thus, it seems that a lot of organizational career development is occurring in the world of work. This is a result of both individual and institutional efforts. Efforts by the individual include planning for, entering, and becoming successful in a career. Efforts by institutions include career management systems (recruitment and selection), human resource allocation, appraisal and evaluation, and training and development activities. The institution supports and enhances the individual efforts with the expectation that both the individual and the organization will profit.

Walz (1982) identified a series of characteristics of optimum career development systems in organizations. Central to an optimum system is the leadership of an in-house specialist(s) knowledgeable about and skilled in career development. Extensive data have not been collected about the educational background of training and development specialists responsible for organizational career management programs. Yet, it is assumed that most have come from a college background of personnel administration, business administration, or liberal arts.

Since then several researchers, among them Gysbers and Moore (1987), McDaniels (1989), and Raskin (1987), have reported extensively on counseling strategies and skills and techniques needed by practitioners in career and vocational counseling. McDaniels (1989) in particular presents a comprehensive analysis of tomorrow's workplace, providing career development specialists in the workplace with several alternative scenarios for work in the last decade of this century.

Training professionals to deliver adult career development services should involve emphasis in human resource management, training and development, and counseling. The major professional organization for career development, the National Career Development Association (formerly the National Vocational Guidance Association), has addressed the competencies needed for training career guidance personnel (Phillips-Jones, Jones, & Drier, 1981). The American Society for Training and Development has also addressed this in its recent training and development competencies study (McLagan, 1983). And the Vocational Occupational Information Coordinating Council (NOICC, 1989) has published national career development guidelines which address competencies needed by adults in three significant areas: self knowledge, educational and occupational exploration, and career planning. Guidance training programs at universities around the country are focusing on the preparation of career development specialists for human resource positions in business, industry, and government. Also, more employers are establishing career planning units and counseling and employee assistance arms to improve human resource areas.

The balance of this chapter will focus on the theoretical and conceptual foundations for adult career development (ACD) education, issues related to developing education and training programs in ACD, and elements of graduate degree programs in ACD.

Theoretical and Conceptual Foundations for Adult Career Development

Historically, in the career development literature, the emphasis has been on initial vocational choice (high school years) and implementation of this choice through training or postsecondary education. This concept treats career choice as an event that happens at a point in time, is permanent and irreversible, and has a lifelong effect. Thus, for almost 50 years from the establishment of Breadwinners' College in Boston in 1905 until the launching of the Career Pattern Study at Teachers College,

Columbia University in 1951 (Borow, 1964), career counselors worked almost exclusively with adolescents in a career choice model known as trait-factor. This system assumes that a straightforward matching of an individual's abilities and interests with the world's vocational opportunities can be accomplished and solves that individual's problems of vocational choice (Osipow, 1983).

The model changed slowly over the years. The vocational testing movement grew from the trait-factor point of view. Such commonly used measures in career counseling as the Strong-Campbell Interest Inventory and the General Aptitude Test Battery are based on the trait-factor stream of thought.

The developmental or self-concept model has grown out of the work of Ginzberg, Ginsburg, Axelrad, and Herma (1951) and Super (1957) on the developmental side, and Rogers (1951) on the self-concept side. These theoreticians developed an approach leading to the concept of adult career development. Their central ideas are:

1. Individuals develop more clearly defined self-concepts as they grow older. These vary to conform with the changes of one's view of reality as correlated with aging.
2. Individuals develop images of the occupational world that they compare with their self-images in trying to make career decisions.
3. The adequacy of the eventual career decision is based on the similarity between an individual's self-concept and the career chosen.

The NOICC guidelines (1989) represent a major nationwide effort to foster career development at all levels, including adulthood. They are a competency-based approach to career development that serve as a blueprint for persons who plan career counseling programs. These guidelines represent a professional consensus in three main areas:

- *Adult Competencies and Indicators*
  Recommended adult outcomes are organized around self-knowledge, educational and occupational exploration, and career planning.
- *Organizational Capabilities*
  The structure and support needed for quality programs include administrative commitments, facilities, materials, and equipment.
- *Personnel Requirements*
  Counselors and other staff must have the knowledge and skills to deliver a quality program.

The guidelines represent a synthesis of the research describing the benefits of comprehensive career guidance and counseling programs, and further identify the elements of high quality, comprehensive career guidance and counseling programs. Table 1 summarizes the career development competencies by area at the adult level.

Adult career development means helping people grow and change. One of the primary and most common vehicles for helping people grow and change is learning. In fact, career counseling itself is an *educative* function that teaches processes such as career decision-making, self-representation, and job hunting. (Forney, 1981).

In one-to-one counseling, knowledge of adult development is important. Yet adult career development programs include more than just career

Table 1

Career Development Competencies by Area for the Adult Level

Self Knowledge Area	Educational and Occupational Area	Career Planning Area
• Skills to maintain a positive self-concept	• Skills to enter and participate in education and training	• Skills to make decisions
• Skills to maintain effective work relationships	• Skills to participate in work and lifelong learning	• Understanding the impact of work on individual and family life
• Understanding developmental changes and transitions	• Skills to locate, evaluate, and interpret career information	• Understanding the continuing changes in male/female roles
	• Skills to prepare to seek, obtain, maintain, and change jobs	• Skills to make career transitions
	• Understanding how the needs and functions of society influence the nature and structure of work	

Note: Adapted from *The National Career Development Guidelines*, 1989. The National Occupational Information Coordinating Committee, Washington, DC.

counseling activities. Such elements as career planning workshops, stress management workshops, life planning workshops, preretirement workshops, supervisory and management training in career counseling, and other individual and group developmental activities are included in many programs (Gutteridge & Otte, 1983). These activities require two major areas of competence in which most career counselors lack education or training: (a) knowledge of adult learning theory, and (b) skill in design of adult learning (training) programs.

Adult Learning Theory

Adults differ from children and adolescents in four major respects:

1. Adults' self-concept is one of being a self-directed human being rather than dependent on others.

2. Adults accumulate a reservoir of experience that becomes an increasingly rich resource for learning.
3. Adults' readiness to learn becomes oriented increasingly to the developmental tasks of their social roles.
4. Adults' time perspective changes from one of postponed application of knowledge to immediacy of application. Accordingly, their orientation toward learning shifts from one of subject-centeredness to one of performance-centeredness. (Knowles, 1980)

The adult career developer needs to be aware of the theory of how adults learn (androgogy) and also how this theory is put into practice.

Design of Training (Adult Learning) Programs

Adult learning (androgogy) involves designing training programs that build in the implications of adult learning theory. There are numerous models for designing training in the literature. One general model is depicted in Figure 1. In designing any training program, the adult career developer must be aware of the organization's, institution's, or community's need for such a program. If the need relates to a specific job or task, performance standards may have to be developed. The needs of the individual learners who make up the potential audience for the program must be identified. Then learning objectives can be established, the curriculum developed, the instruction planned, and the training conducted.

Throughout this entire process, the implications for helping adults learn must be integrated into the curriculum to create a meaningful learning experience (Ingalls, 1973). For example, it is important to:

1. set a climate for learning and develop a positive learning environment;
2. establish a structure for mutual planning and collaborate on learning objectives;
3. design the learning and provide ways for participants to be involved in the learning; and
4. evaluate the learning and identify methods for participants to evaluate their own learning.

This is only a brief view of adult learning theory and practice. Much more goes into the art of helping adults learn. What is important to realize is that designing and conducting an effective adult learning program takes more than desire. It also takes competence in the areas mentioned.

ISSUES RELATED TO DEVELOPING EDUCATION AND TRAINING PROGRAMS IN ACD

The prerequisite roles and competencies of adult career development specialists have been recently addressed in two major professional society publications: *Developing Training Competencies for Career Guidance Personnel*, published by NVGA (now NCDA) (Phillips-Jones, Jones, & Drier, 1981) and *Training and Development Competencies*, published by ASTD (McLagan, 1983). The former document focuses on the com-

Figure 1
A General Model for Designing Training

THE TRAINING PROCESS

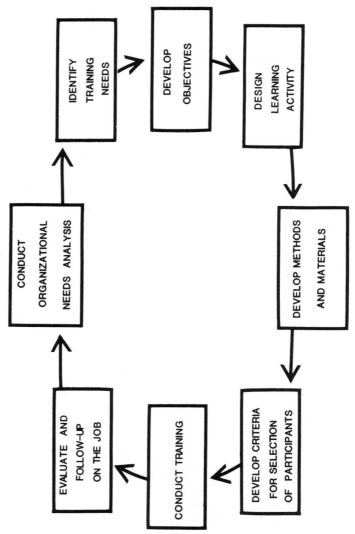

petencies needed by career counselors working with any age level and provides many models (competency domains) for developing training programs. One model, developed by the Illinois Guidance and Personnel Association's (IGPA) Professional Development Program, is presented in Figure 2.

This model resulted from work by a task force of counselor educators and guidance practitioners from 17 institutions. The IGPA planning group identified skills generic across human service areas. These skills were compared with those mentioned in the literature and then converted into competency statements. The nine competency areas that compose IGPA's domain are:

1. counselor as person;
2. counseling services;
3. career development;
4. human environmental assessment;
5. consultation;
6. coordination;
7. research and evaluation;
8. referral; and
9. change agentry.

This group also added three levels of mastery: (a) beginning counselor, (b) professional counselor, and (c) consultant/supervisor/instructor. The competency statements in Figure 2 are called Goal Statements and Objectives.

The ASTD document identifies 31 competencies (see Table 2) important for excellent performance in the training and development field. Each competency is defined, and behaviors illustrate the levels of expertise. As with the NVGA competency model, three levels of expertise are identified: basic, intermediate, and advanced. An example of a competency and the illustrative behaviors follows:

> 7. Counseling Skill (competency) . . . Helping individuals recognize and understand needs, values, problems, alternatives, and goals.
>
> *BASIC*: The training and development specialist uses a career planning kit to help an individual seeking career assistance. She *empathizes with the employee's quandry*. Then, based on the data from interest questionnaires, *helps the employee explore* a variety of suitable new career directions.
>
> *INTERMEDIATE*: A participant in a leadership program is befuddled by survey feedback from people who assessed his leadership style before the program. The program facilitator notices him puzzling over his data and asks if she can help. She *listens to and acknowledges his concerns then helps him interpret* the results and decide on a course of action
>
> *ADVANCED*: The training and development specialist has been asked to help an angry, shocked 50-year-old ex-executive who has just been fired. The specialist *gives him time to vent his feelings and concerns.* Then she *helps channel his energy* into self-assessment, opportunity search. (McLagan, 1983)

In the past, the most common settings for career development programs have been schools, academic institutions, and community agencies. Recently, the work place has emerged as an appropriate setting for the delivery of these services (Leibowitz & Schlossberg, 1981).

Human Resource Development as Career Development Base

Within the work place, the human resource development (HRD) function has emerged as the base for career development. The roles and functions within HRD have undergone extensive changes in recent years. At one time job skill training was the major purpose of HRD in many companies. Later, the emphasis on management and executive programs added another dimension. Recently, the emphasis on matching individual interests and goals with the skills needed and directions anticipated by organizations has created another role for HRD. This rapidly evolving role of liaison between the individual (who needs training and development to achieve personal goals) and the organization (which needs skilled, capable, and prepared employees to accomplish organizational goals) is an increasingly relevant focus of HRD (Gutteridge & Hutcheson, 1984).

With a career development-related HRD system, decision-making about training and development for each employee is shared. The individual has the opportunity to express desired moves and goals. These may be expressed in terms of skills, knowledge, abilities, and desired target positions. The organization has the opportunity to react to those growth-related goals, provide feedback on their operational reality, and assist in identifying learning strategies to reach those goals supported by the organization. The individual's interests, goals, and desired growth strategies are usually formulated in a developmental plan. This developmental plan is an essential part of the information used in planning other HRD developmental activities.

This information sharing offers HRD the opportunity to be responsive to existing and future needs. Program offerings can be planned that are consistent with the perceived needs of employees and their supervisors. Training for the present job and education for a future job are seen as highly beneficial by both participants and supervisors because attendance is designed around both individual and organizational goals.

Because the developmental plan is outcome-based (focuses on the skill, knowledge, ability, or experience desired), it provides a microview of each individual within an organization. Collectively, the developmental plans represent a macroview of the training and development needs within the organization.

In addition to developmental planning, other organizational career development techniques include:

- career planning seminars or workshops;
- career counseling by staff counselors;
- job posting;
- career workbooks;
- skills inventory;
- career pathing;

Figure 2

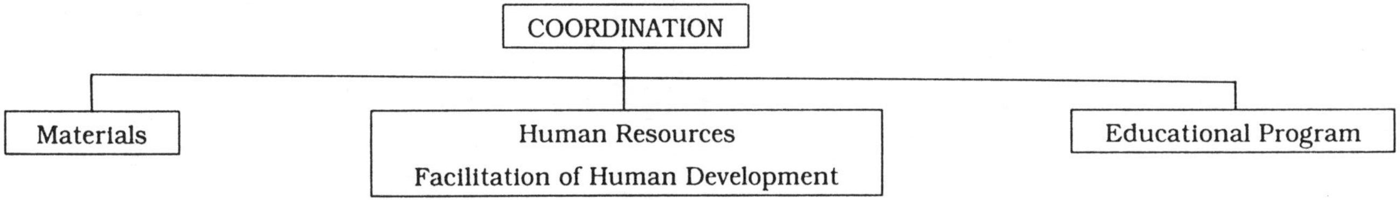

```
                    ┌──────────────┐
                    │ COORDINATION │
                    └──────┬───────┘
        ┌──────────────────┼──────────────────┐
┌──────────┐      ┌─────────────────┐    ┌──────────────────┐
│ Materials│      │ Human Resources │    │Educational Program│
└──────────┘      │ Facilitation of │    └──────────────────┘
                  │Human Development│
                  └─────────────────┘
```

Goal Statement: The counselor must be able to coordinate the various aspects of the total counseling program resulting in a continuous and meaningful sequence of services to individuals, staff, and community.

Objectives	*Implementation and Evaluation*		
The professional counselor must:	The professional counselor provides evidence of competence by:		
	Level 1	**Level 2**	**Level 3**
1. Be able to assess and respond to client needs.	Initiating an assessment of client needs.	Making recommendations based on an assessment of client needs. Implementing the above recommendations.	Demonstrating the ability to teach client needs assessment techniques.
2. Be able to analyze and respond to existing program needs.	Completing an analysis of existing programs.	Making recommendations based upon an assessment of program needs. Implementing the above recommendations.	Demonstrating ability to teach program development techniques.
3. Be able to assess available and potential resources.	Completing an assessment of available and potential resources.	Making recommendations based upon an assessment of available and potential resources. Implementing the above recommendations.	Demonstrating the ability to teach resource assessment and development.

4. Be able to define, detail, and communicate a recommended program by: a) writing specific program objectives; b) specifying activities that would facilitate reaching objectives.	Generating written program goals by: a) Involving community institutions in identifying goals, objectives, and activities. b) writing specific objectives. c) Initiating activities which meet program goals and objectives.	Demonstrating an understanding of existing institutional and community communication systems. Demonstrating the ability to coordinate local programs with systems beyond the local level. Demonstrating the ability to communicate program goals and objectives.	Conducting and reporting ongoing research activities. Demonstrating the ability to teach the writing of specific program goals.
5. Be able to attain program goals through cooperative or independent efforts.	Differentiating similarities and differences between programs. Initiating and/or maintaining cooperative relationships with existing community agencies. Selecting resources which will assist in attaining program goals.	Evaluating program goals with emphasis on recognition of similarities and differences between programs. Generating the means by which additional agencies and programs may support and enhance each other.	Suggesting means by which established cooperative ventures may be maintained. Generating means utilization of community resources in attaining program goals.
6. To establish a public relations program that explains human services to the community.	Identifying specific human services (who, what, when, how). Transmitting the who, what, where, when, and how of the community human services program.	Designing and producing materials that adequately inform the community of available human services.	Analyzing alternative means for disseminating human services information to various populations. Demonstrating the ability to teach techniques of information dissemination.

From *Developing Training Competencies for Career Guidance Personnel* (p. 34–35) by L. Phillips-Jones, G.B. Jones, and H.N. Drier, 1981, Falls Church, VA: National Vocational Guidance Association. Copyright 1981 by National Vocational Guidance Association. Reprinted by permission.

Table 2

Knowledge/Skill Areas Identified as Important for Excellent Performance in the Training and Development Field

1. *Adult Learning Understanding* . . . Knowing how adults acquire and use knowledge, skills, attitudes. Understanding individual differences in learning.

2. *A/V Skill* . . . Selecting and using audio/visual hardware and software.

3. *Career Development Knowledge* . . . Understanding the personal and organizational issues and practices relevant to individual careers.

4. *Competency Identification Skill* . . . Identifying the knowledge and skill requirements of jobs, tasks, roles.

5. *Computer Competence* . . . Understanding and being able to use computers.

6. *Cost-Benefit Analysis Skill* . . . Assessing alternatives in terms of their financial, psychological, and strategic advantages and disadvantages.

7. *Counseling Skill* . . . Helping individuals recognize and understand personal needs, values, problems, alternatives and goals.

8. *Data Reduction Skill* . . . Scanning, synthesizing, and drawing conclusions from data.

9. *Delegation Skill* . . . Assigning task responsibility and authority to others.

10. *Facilities Skill* . . . Planning and coordinating logistics in an efficient and cost-effective manner.

11. *Feedback Skill* . . . Communicating opinions, observations and conclusions such that they are understood.

12. *Futuring Skill* . . . Projecting trends and visualizing possible and probable futures and their implications.

13. *Group Process Skill* . . . Influencing groups to both accomplish tasks and fulfill the needs of their members.

14. *Industry Understanding* . . . Knowing the key concepts and variables that define an industry or sector (e.g., critical issues, economic vulnerabilities, measurements, distribution channels, inputs, outputs, information sources).

15. *Intellectual Versatility* . . . Recognizing, exploring and using a broad range of ideas and practices. Thinking logically and creatively without undue influence from personal biases.

16. *Library Skills* . . . Gathering information from printed and other recorded sources. Identifying and using information specialists and reference services and aids.

17. *Model Building Skill* . . . Developing theoretical and practical frameworks which describe complex ideas in understandable, usable ways.

18. *Negotiation Skill* . . . Securing win-win agreements while successfully representing a special interest in a decision situation.

19. *Objectives Preparation Skill* . . . Preparing clear statements which describe desired outputs.
20. *Organization Behavior Understanding* . . . Seeing organizations as dynamic, political, economic, and social systems which have multiple goals; using this larger perspective as a framework for understanding and influencing events and change.
21. *Organization Understanding* . . . Knowing the strategy, structure, power networks, financial position, systems of a SPECIFIC organization.
22. *Performance Observation Skills* . . . Tracking and describing behaviors and their effect.
23. *Personnel/HR Field Understanding* . . . Understanding issues and practices in other HR areas (Organization Development, Organization Job Design, Human Resource Planning, Selection and Staffing, Personnel Research and Information Systems, Compensation and Benefits, Employee Assistance, Union/Labor Relations).
24. *Presentation Skills* . . . Verbally presenting information such that the intended purpose is achieved.
25. *Questioning Skill* . . . Gathering information from and stimulating insight in individuals and groups through the use of interviews, questionnaires and other probing methods.
26. *Records Management Skill* . . . Storing data in easily retrievable form.
27. *Relationship Versatility* . . . Adjusting behavior in order to establish relationships across a broad range of people and groups.
28. *Research Skills* . . . Selecting, developing and using methodologies, statistical and data collection techniques for a formal inquiry.
29. *Training and Development Field Understanding* . . . Knowing the technological, social, economic, professional, and regulatory issues in the field; understanding the role T&D plays in helping individuals learn for current and future jobs.
30. *Training and Development Techniques Understanding* . . . Knowing the techniques and methods used in training; understanding their appropriate uses.
31. *Writing Skills* . . . Preparing written material which follows generally accepted rules of style and form, is appropriate for the audience, creative, and accomplishes its intended purposes.

Note. From *Training and Development Competencies* (p.36) by P.A. McLagan, 1983, Washington, DC: American Society for Training and Development. Copyright 1983 by ASTD. Reprinted by permission.

- succession planning;
- career discussions by supervisors with employees;
- career resource center; and
- outplacement counseling. (Gutteridge & Otte, 1983)

Ideally, career development would be part of or allied with human resource development. Both would be essential elements of a comprehensive human resource management system.

Traditional graduate counseling programs have generally ignored the significance of organizational career development, the human resource perspective, and organizational theory. An understanding of HRD, internal (and external) consultation, group facilitation, organization and management theory, human resource planning, organization development, and human resource management are vital to adult career developers in organizations. "Organizations are able to grow, change, and adapt to an extent that is at least partially dependent on the ability of its human resources to grow, change, and adapt. Career development is a major means of preparing individual employees for this process." (Gutteridge & Hutcheson, 1984, pp. 30.24.)

Elements of a Graduate Degree Program in ACD

To this point the need to train individuals in ACD has been identified and discussed, the theoretical and conceptual foundations for ACD education have been reviewed, roles and competencies for this new profession have been identified, and career development programs within the HRD function in an organization have been discussed. Now the elements of a graduate degree program in ACD will be considered. This is being offered in an increasing number of universities, particularly in colleges of education (American Society for Training and Development, 1981).

The following courses, seminars, or clinical experiences are common to most programs at the master's degree level:

Career Development Theory: This course reviews basic principles of human growth and development through the life span. The special emphasis is on career development and career development theory. Also considered are the social, economic, political, family, and educational influences on an individual.

Counseling Techniques: The emphasis in this course is on basic counseling techniques for working with adults in the work setting. Extensive practice of counseling skills through role-playing, behavior rehearsal, and audio- and videotaping is included.

Measurement and Assessment: This course emphasizes various group tests and nontest approaches (i.e., inventories and surveys) to help the counselor understand the adult in the work place. Some emphasis is also placed on individual measurement.

Adult Learning and Development: The knowledge of adult human development is generally a core element of a graduate program in adult counseling. But an emphasis on adult learning and its relation to human development is important both to career counseling and to designing career programs for adults. Not only is career counseling a learning process but pursuing career change involves learning new knowledge, competencies, and values.

Training Program Design: As discussed earlier, designing training (adult learning) programs and integrating adult learning theory are important to the adult career developer planning to design and conduct career-oriented workshops, seminars, and computer-assisted instruction.

Consultation: Many career developers are consulting with institutions of higher learning, community agencies, businesses, and government.

They assist in planning and implementing career development programs. In addition, career developers in organizations consult internally with management to help it understand how career development enhances organizational effectiveness.

Group Facilitation: Much of the counseling and learning in career development is performed in group settings. Knowledge of group dynamics and skill in group facilitation is essential for both group counseling and conducting group programs.

Organization Theory: This is a support field or cognate with a mixture of organization behavior, human resource management, organization design, human resource planning, organization development, and human resource development that will provide the "world of work" perspective for those interested in organization-based career development.

Internship/Practicum: Students should have a chance to work in the field to see adult career development in practice within an organizational setting.

Throughout the graduate program, emphasis should be given to such activities as guest speakers, field trips, and informational interviews. This will expose students to the real world of adult career development. In addition, the faculty advisor should act as an educational and career counselor to fully prepare the students for their career choice in this field.

CONCLUSION

Counselor education programs and human resource development programs are well equipped to train professionals for human resource positions in business and industry. To be successful, a close working relationship needs to be established between the departments or colleges that offer the course work and the practitioners in business and industry where internship and practicum experience are offered. Only then will the graduates of these programs be well-rounded professionals who will contribute uniquely to human resource development in organizational settings.

REFERENCES

American Society for Training and Development (1981). *Directory of academic programs in training and development/human resource development.* Washington, DC: Author.

Bolyard, C.W. (1981). Career development: Who's responsible in the organization. In D.H. Montross & C.J. Shinkman (Eds.), *Career development in the 1980s: Theory and practice* (pp. 292–299). Springfield, IL: Charles C. Thomas.

Borow, H. (Ed.) (1964). *Man in a world at work.* Boston: Houghton-Mifflin.

Fisher, P.G., & Gerstein, M. (1983). Considerations when initiating a career pathing program. *Career Planning and Adult Development Journal, 1*(4), 15–20.

Forney, D.S. (1981). The art and science of career counseling: A conceptual framework for counseling the individual. In D.H. Montross & C.J. Shinkman (Eds.), *Career development in the 1980s: Theory and practice* (pp. 185–194). Springfield, IL: Charles C. Thomas.

Ginzberg, E., Ginsburg, S.W., Axelrad, S., & Herma, J.L. (1951). *Occupational choice: An approach to a general theory.* New York: Columbia University Press.

Gutteridge, T.G., & Hutcheson, P.G. (1984). Career development. In L. Nadler (Ed.), *The handbook of human resource development* (pp. 30.1–30.25). New York: Wiley.

Gutteridge, T.G., & Otte, F.L. (1983). *Organizational career development: State of the practice.* Washington, DC: American Society for Training and Development.

Gysbers, N.C., & Moore, E.J. (1987). *Career counseling: Skills and techniques for practitioners.* Englewood Cliffs, NJ: Prentice-Hall, Inc.

Ingalls, M.S. (1973). *A trainer's guide to androgogy: Its concepts, experience and application.* Washington, DC: U.S. Department of Health, Education, and Welfare.

Knowles, M.S. (1980). *The modern practice of adult education: From pedagogy to androgogy.* Chicago: Follett.

Leibowitz, Z., & Schlossberg, N. (1981). Designing career development programs in organization: A systems approach. In D.H. Montross and C.J. Shinkman (Eds.), *Career development in the 1980s: Theory and practice* (pp. 277–291). Springfield, IL: Charles C. Thomas.

McDaniels, C. (1989). *The Changing Workplace.* San Francisco: Jossey-Bass.

McLagan, P.A. (1983). *Training and development competencies.* Washington, DC: American Society for Training and Development.

National Occupational Information Coordinating Council. (1989). *The national career development guidelines.* Washington, DC: Author.

Osipow, S.H. (1983). *Theories of career development* (3rd ed). Englewood Cliffs, NJ: Prentice-Hall.

Phillips-Jones, L., Jones, G.B., & Drier, H.N. (1981). *Developing training competencies for career guidance personnel.* Falls Church, VA: National Vocational Guidance Association.

Raskin, P.M. (1987). *Vocational Counseling: A guide for the practitioner.* New York: Teachers College Press.

Rogers, C.R. (1951). *Client-centered therapy.* Boston: Houghton-Mifflin.

Smith, R.L., Piercy, F.P., & Lutz, P. (1982). Training counselors for human resource development positions in business and industry. *Counselor Education and Supervision, 22,* 107–112.

Souerwine, A.H. (1981). Career planning: Getting started with top management support. In D.H. Montross & C.J. Shinkman (Eds.), *Career development in the 1980s: Theory and practice* (pp. 300–314). Springfield, IL: Charles C. Thomas.

Super, D.E. (1957). *The psychology of careers.* New York: Harper & Row.

Walz, G.R. (Ed.) (1982). *Career development in organizations.* Ann Arbor, MI: ERIC/CAPS.

SECTION VI:

EVALUATION

ESTABLISHING OUR EFFECTIVENESS AND ACCOUNTABILITY . . .

Chapter 22

Evaluating the Effectiveness of Adult Career Development Programs: Key Concepts and Issues

Michael T. Brown
Wayne State University
Detroit, Michigan

Robert B. Bhaerman
Research for Better Schools,
Philadelphia, Pennsylvania

Robert Campbell
The Ohio State University
Columbus, Ohio

For almost 60 years, research and practice in vocational psychology have been preoccupied with the adolescent and young adult. Further, it was assumed that very little of significance occurred after an adolescent or young adult selected and entered an occupation (Campbell & Heffernan, 1983). Within the last 20 years, however, interest in adult career development has swelled. A number of factors are responsible for the increasing attention: the aging of the "baby-boom" generation; the increase in life expectancy; the results of a number of empirical studies indicating that adulthood is not the period of stability it was thought to be; rapid technological change presenting adults with the need for change to avoid the alternative of obsolescence and social-economic displacement; and rapid social change, including change in family patterns and life-styles as well as growing multiculturalism.

These features of today's world have spurred the development of new concepts regarding adult career development and have generated new ideas for its facilitation. Relatedly, though of much shorter history, research on vocational behavior has sought to determine which career development programs, when employed with which of the various adult groups and under what circumstances, are most effective.

In the previous edition of this book, the authors wrote a chapter addressing key observations and conclusions concerning the evaluation of adult career development programs (see Bhaerman & Campbell, 1986). The present chapter substantially supplements the earlier work by presenting important concepts in the design and evaluation of adult career development programs, reviewing the conclusions of various literary and meta-analytic reviews of career development programs, and charting new and needed directions in program evaluation. This chapter is organized around the following questions: 1) What concepts should underlie the construction of adult career interventions and their evaluation? 2) What strategies exist for facilitating adult vocational behavior? 3) What do current evaluation studies show regarding the effectiveness of adult career development programs? 4) What directions should future evaluation studies take in determining what programs when administered under what circumstances best facilitate the career development of what adults?

KEY CONCEPTS UNDERLYING INTERVENTION AND EVALUATION

A primary source of concepts and ideas which should underlie intervention and evaluation efforts are theories of adult career development. A variety of theories dealing with diverse aspects of career development have been formulated. Various career development experts have attempted to synthesize the theories (see Bhaerman & Campbell, 1986; Campbell & Heffernan, 1983; Giroux, 1983; Harmon & Farmer, 1983; Schlossberg, 1981; Tolbert, 1980). The work of Campbell and Heffernan will be briefly presented.

Campbell and Heffernan's Overview

Campbell and Heffernan selected a number of general adult development and career development models to review and synthesize. The models of Erikson (1950), Havighurst (1952), Levinson and McKee (1978), Miller and Form (1951, 1964), Schein (1978), and Super (1963) were found to have a number of features in common. For example, individual development is viewed as proceeding through a series of stages, each of which requires the management of stage-specific tasks or issues. Progress through subsequent stages is viewed as contingent upon satisfactory resolution of earlier stages. Stage progression is also viewed as being unidirectional; each stage is encountered only once and persons do not return to lower stages. The models differed in terms of the number of stages delineated, but each model linked age ranges to its stages; these linkages varied in degree of specificity. Most of the models included tasks that reflected development in psychological, social, and career areas though the number of tasks varied across them. Finally, the models viewed the developmental tasks as universal and assumed that they applied to all persons regardless of generation, sex/gender, ethnicity, and socioeconomic status.

Based on the synthesis of the six career development models, four career development stages were postulated to occur: 1) Preparation—preparation for an occupation or for obtaining a job, 2) Establishment—demonstration of competence in and adjustment to a new work environment, 3) Maintenance—maintenance and/or achievement of one's position in an established occupation, and 4) Retirement—decline in involvement with the workplace. For each stage, Campbell and Heffernan delineated developmental tasks. While not presented here, it should be noted that Campbell and Heffernan also described specific action steps associated with each developmental task.

Preparation Stage

The goal of the preparation stage is to prepare for an occupation and obtain a position in the work force. Key tasks in this stage are: a) assessing personal attributes and the world of work in anticipation of work entry/reentry, b) engaging in decision-making for work entry/reentry, c) implementing plans to prepare for work entry/reentry, d) performing adequately in and adapting to the demands of the organizational/institutional environment during preparation, and e) obtaining a position in the chosen occupation.

Establishment Stage

Demonstrating, initially, one's ability to function effectively in an occupation is the goal of this stage. Individual tasks of the stage are: a) becoming oriented to the organization/institution in which one is hired, b) learning position responsibilities and demonstrating satisfactory performance, c) exploring career plans of personal goals and advancement opportunities, and d) implementing a plan for achievement and position change.

Maintenance Stage

The central focus in this stage is to achieve and maintain a desired level of functioning in one's established occupation. The five tasks of the stage are: a) assessing one's status within one's present position, occupation, and organizational setting, b) deciding on a maintenance plan, c) implementing the plan, d) adjusting to changing personal and organizational events arising during maintenance, and e) achieving and maintaining performance at a level that is considered within organizational requirements and maintenance plan.

Retirement

In this last stage, the individual's goal is to maximize personal options in leaving full-time employment to assume a retirement role. This is done by: a) deciding whether or not to retire full-time or part-time, b) exploring career options for part-time retirement, c) assessing interpersonal relationships, and d) developing and maintaining a retirement plan.

Implication for Intervention and Practice

The synthesis devised by Campbell and Heffernan can be used to create developmentally appropriate intervention strategies. Further, the goals and tasks of the stages can be used to identify assessment and evaluation tools necessary for determining whether the intervention strategies initiated were effective. The clear implication of the model is that both intervention strategy and evaluation method should vary as a function of the stage of development of the adult client; however, such uses of the model constitute yet another new frontier in adult career development.

Other Important Concepts

While the Campbell and Heffernan model can be useful in designing interventions and evaluation programs relevant for adults in different life stages, it lacks a degree of specificity for such purposes. Further, there appear to be commonalities in the tasks across the four stages of the model. To eliminate the redundancy and achieve greater parsimony, Campbell and Heffernan analyzed the 17 tasks and 80 subtasks of the four stages and identified four common tasks:

1. *Decision Making*—Information about self and work environment is gathered, alternatives are evaluated, and choices are made.
2. *Implementing Plans*—Activities based on choices are scheduled and put into action.
3. *Organizational/Institutional Performance*—An acceptable level of performance is reached.
4. *Organizational/Institutional Adaptation*—Individuals adjust in order to effectively take part in the work environment.

Campbell and Cellini (1981) constructed a taxonomy of adult career development problems based on those four common tasks. The taxonomy consists of four major problem categories and a number of subcategories which are further divided into possible causal factors underlying difficulties with the tasks and subtasks. The categories and subcategories are:

1.0 *Problems in career decision-making*
    1.1 Getting started
    1.2 Information gathering
    1.3 Generating, evaluating, and selecting alternatives
    1.4 Formulating plans for implementing decisions

2.0 *Problems in implementing career plans*
    2.1 Characteristics of the individual
    2.2 Characteristics external to the individual

3.0 *Problems in organizational/institutional performance*
    3.1 Deficiencies in skills, abilities, and knowledge
    3.2 Personal factors
    3.3 Conditions of the organizational/institutional environment

4.0 *Problems in organizational/institutional adaptation*
    4.1 Initial entry
    4.2 Changes over time
    4.3 Interpersonal relationships

Of available classification systems, Campbell and Cellini's has been cited (see Rounds & Tinsley, 1984) as having the greatest utility. However, classification systems, including that of Campbell and Cellini, have rarely been evaluated or used in career intervention studies (Rounds & Tinsley, 1984).

Nonetheless, there is pressing need to have and use valid and reliable classification systems. According to Rounds and Tinsley (1984), the field of career development has grown to the state that an increasingly heterogenous array of interventions are applied to an even broader set of vocational problems. Yet, the issue of what interventions work best for specific vocational problems has not been addressed. Rounds and Tinsley further suggest that a reliable and valid vocational problem diagnostic or classification system would help in the identification of which clients or which problems are best suited for particular interventions. Further, such a system would allow more precise determination of why particular interventions worked in particular situations. Such efforts would greatly enhance current intervention and evaluation efforts.

CAREER DEVELOPMENT STRATEGIES

As alluded to above, an almost endless array of strategies and interventions exist. Below is a brief sampling of some of the strategies that could be used and evaluated either singly or jointly. Not all of the 41 items listed will be relevant. It will depend, of course, on the nature of the agency and the agency's clients. However, without the type of diagnostic/classification schema discussed earlier in this paper, counselors and evaluators will find it difficult to select appropriate strategies and effectively evaluate them.

- Job search approaches
- Media—radio and TV—approaches
- Outplacement counseling approaches
- Career resource banks/centers
- Job development programs
- Occupational retraining programs
- Referral systems
- Telephone counseling services
- Computer-assisted programs
- Correspondence courses
- Home study courses
- Job-finding training
- Family counseling
- Assertiveness training
- Support systems
- Consciousness-raising activities
- Work simulation exercises

- Employability skills training
- Follow-up services
- Information on education/training programs
- Information on job opportunities
- Information on credentials
- Information on transferable skills
- Placement services
- Training in coping and adaptive skills
- Child care services
- Classes in communication/language facility
- Financial counseling services
- Formal instructional classes
- Outreach programs
- Peer support groups
- Remedial education programs
- Seminars and workshops
- Transportation services
- Peer counselor and volunteer training
- Professional staff training
- Peer counselors
- Self-help; self-instructional materials
- Volunteers
- Comprehensive, formal guidance systems
- Testing or other means to gather client information

The reader should also refer to Lunnenborg (1983) for a comprehensive review of career counseling techniques.

EVALUATION

This part of the chapter is divided into the following sections: evaluation studies of adult career development programs, literary and meta-analytic reviews of general career development evaluation studies, and directions needed in conducting evaluation studies and reporting their results.

Evaluation of Adult Career Intervention Programs

As indicated by Bhaerman and Campbell (1986), evaluation studies of adult career intervention programs are infrequent. Harrison and Entine (1976) reviewed a national survey of 367 adult career counseling programs. They found that only 20% provided evaluation data that measured specific changes in client behavior as a result of the program. An additional one-third of the programs reported that they collected anecdotal reports of client reactions and success.

Walz and Benjamin (1981) in their review of adult counseling programs also found serious deficits in assessing program effectiveness. In general, they observed that systematic efforts to collect evaluative data were rare. They did not find a single program that used criterion-referenced measures to assess client change in actual attitudes, skills, or knowledge. Walz and Benjamin did note, however, that program staff were convinced that they were successful in helping their clients. This was based on subjective feedback in the absence of hard data. Unfortunately, subjective impressions of effectiveness do not convince budget allocators.

Stump (1982) observed a similar deficit in the evaluation of adult career development programs. He cites a number of reasons why professionals avoid evaluating their programs. These include lack of time and energy, insufficient budget, task difficulty, low response rates, political program decisions, data considered unimportant, disinterest, and inadequate knowledge to evaluate process.

Cairo (1983) reviewed 30 studies on vocational counseling in industry. He also reported limited information on counseling effectiveness.

Nevertheless, in the last five or six years a number of useful intervention studies have appeared in the published empirical literature and these will now be discussed. The earliest studies will be presented first.

Cited by Borgen, Layton, Veenhuizen, and Johnson (1985) in their review of the research literature on vocational behavior published in 1984 as that year's best intervention study, West, Horan, and Games (1984) employed an intervention based on a stress inoculation model to reduce occupational stress in a sample of acute care nurses. Using a component analysis approach to identify the active ingredients of the stress inoculation intervention and perform a multiple analysis of variance, they examined the effects on four treatment groups (plus a control group) of 13 dependent measures of stress. Post-test data and data gathered after four months indicated that coping skills training was the effective component.

Slaney and Dickson (1985) found that a vocational card sorting task, alone or in conjunction with a videotape, did not encourage reentry college women to consider nontraditional occupations. Ferrara, Rudrud, Wendlegass, and Markve (1985) were able to demonstrate that their intervention program increased the vocational knowledge possessed by mentally retarded adults.

Mueser, Foy, and Carter (1986), using an N of 1 design, showed the effectiveness of a social skills training program for a man who was in danger of losing his job repairing office machines because of customer complaints about his temper and rudeness. Slaney and Lewis (1986) randomly assigned a sample of reentry women to a vocational card sort or a Strong-Campbell Interest Inventory treatment program. At three week and six month follow-ups, both treatments were found to be equally effective in reducing career indecision and in impacting other outcomes. Kostka and Wilson (1986) discovered an effective program designed for non-traditional age women who were anxious about a future academic requirement for mathematics and needed to improve their math skills.

Gladstein and Apfel (1987) described a career counseling center for adults based on a developmental perspective which they found to be effective. McDaniels and Watts (1987) found that cooperation was the key to the effectiveness of a career development program for university employees. Kingdon and Blimline (1987) described a program they found successful in facilitating the career development of employed women.

Research Conclusions

The few evaluation studies reviewed above seem to indicate that, in general, career interventions with adults were effective in addressing targeted concerns. However, with the exception of the West et al. (1984) study, those evaluation studies yielded little information for determining why the interventions worked or under what circumstances and with what population of adults the intervention is most effective. In addition, few of the studies were conceptually tied to theoretically based models concerning adult career development. Consequently, the evaluation studies conducted thus far in adult career development are sterile and fail to promote an understanding of adult vocational behavior.

Reviews of General Career Development Evaluation Studies

Because few evaluation studies exist which address adult career development, useful conclusions based on such studies are difficult to determine. Therefore, we will supplement the above review with broader reviews of the career intervention literature. A number of such reviews have been conducted and have taken two forms: the literary review and the meta-analytic review (Rounds & Tinsley, 1984, chap. 4). The first type of review is the more traditional form in which the reviewer critically analyzes the relevant studies, distills his or her analyses of the studies, and then presents the results of this critical analysis. In the meta-analytic approach (see Glass, McGraw, & Smith, 1981; Rounds & Tinsley, 1984; Smith & Glass, 1977), statistical procedures are used to transform the results of individual evaluation studies to a common metric, called effect size, to determine the relationships between the characteristics of different studies and the comparative effects of the interventions. The literary reviews are presented first, followed by the meta-analytic reviews. A section discussing the conclusions to be drawn from the reviews concludes this section.

Literary Reviews

The first review of career intervention studies appeared in 1971 and was written by Myers (1971). The review examined educational and vocational intervention studies, though the number of vocational outcome studies were few. Though problems with the available studies were cited, such as the tendency to regard different treatments and/or different clients as similar, Myers was able to conclude that the literature offered many "tentatively" valid procedures and methods.

Oliver (1978) surveyed career counseling research from 1950 to 1976 and uncovered four major problems with such studies which made results hard to interpret: 1) inappropriate criteria for determining effectiveness, 2) overuse of reactive measures such as self-report questionnaires,

3) infrequent reporting or evaluation of the reliability and validity of research measures, and 4) methodological problems such as the lack of randomization of subjects, inappropriate comparison groups, inappropriate data analyzes.

Reviewing studies published between 1976 and 1978, Krumboltz, Becker-Haven, and Burnett (1979) concluded that, for the most part, career interventions of all types are effective in the improvement of career decision-making skills and career maturity; however, the authors indicated that the literature failed to shed light on how to improve occupational success or satisfaction.

Fretz (1981) concluded in his review that most career interventions seem to result in consistently detectable gains despite differences in treatment approaches; the gains, however, appear small. He offered a number of suggestions for improving career evaluation studies, such as more explicit description of treatment procedures, the clients under study, and outcome measures; determination of treatment costs; comparison of two or more treatments using random assignment of subjects; and use of multiple outcomes.

Holland, Magoon, and Spokane (1981) focused their review on research published between 1978 and 1979. They concluded that, regardless of type, most treatments had a positive effect on clients. They also suggested that this beneficial effect was due to four factors the interventions had in common: 1) exposure to occupational information, 2) cognitive rehearsal of vocational aspirations, 3) acquisition of some cognitive structure of organizing information about self-occupations and their relations, and 4) social support from counselors or career intervention participants.

Pickering and Vacc (1984) reviewed 47 articles published between 1975 and 1984 that evaluated career interventions with college students. They found that over three-quarters of these studies indicated that treatments were effective with the most frequent outcome variables being career maturity and decision-making skills.

Lastly, Osipow (1987) concluded, based on his review of career intervention studies published since 1984, that most studies have failed to address the concerns of writers such as Fretz (1981) and Oliver (1978).

Meta-analytic Reviews

A number of meta-analytic studies exist and these will be briefly reviewed starting with the earliest review. Smith, Glass, and Miller (1980) surveyed the psychotherapy outcome literature from 1900 to 1977 in which vocational counseling studies were included. The results of meta-analyses indicated that vocational counseling, with an effect size of .65, was largely effective, though its effectiveness did not seem to vary as a function of duration of therapy, diagnosis of client, or experience of therapist as would be expected.

Baker and Popowicz (1983) conducted a meta-analysis of 18 studies of career education intervention with students in kindergarten through the 12th grade. The authors reported an effect size of .50 indicating a moderate degree of effectiveness. However, examining a different set of 52 studies, which excluded dissertations and those studies performed in industrial settings or those using rehabilitation clients and educational interventions, Spokane and Oliver (1983) found that the outcome statuses of clients, regardless of their individual characteristics or type of vocational intervention, were better than 80% of untreated controls; the effect size was .85. Further, those clients in the evaluation studies who received group or class interventions appeared to fare better than those receiving individual forms of counseling, but the authors cautioned that this difference in effectiveness may be due to differences in intervention content and the longer duration of the group approaches.

Rounds and Tinsley (1984) criticized the Spokane and Oliver study because, similar to the Baker and Popowicz report, they failed to investigate which evaluation characteristics were most strongly linked to intervention effectiveness. Recently, Oliver and Spokane (1988), after meta-analyzing the results of 58 evaluation studies, reconfirmed their earlier findings and extended those results to include characteristics that most related to beneficial treatment outcomes. After considering a number of characteristics, including client age, they found that only intensity of treatment (in terms of number or hours and sessions) was significantly related to degree of treatment effectiveness. We should note that while most of the evaluation studies focused on collegiate populations, those studies focusing on non-collegiate, adult populations reported effect sizes comparable to all other client groups. It should also be noted that Fitzgerald and Rounds (1989) have recently criticized the results of the 1988 Oliver and Spokane study indicating that it lacked sophistication in categorization of characteristics of the evaluation studies, and thus failed to find expected relationships between types of interventions, types of clients, types of outcomes, and intervention effectiveness.

EVALUATION CONCLUSIONS, PROBLEMS AND NEEDED DIRECTION

As Rounds and Tinsley (1984) effectively point out, evaluation research to date has, for the most part, sought to address the fundamental question, "Do the interventions work?" The above research review clearly reveals that for all clients, including adults, on a variety of criteria, career interventions are effective. Consequently, such continuing lines of evaluation research would seem somewhat outdated. What is yet to be learned, however, is why a particular intervention works, and, relatedly, under what circumscribed set of conditions does it work. The evaluation studies cited above lack a degree of sophistication to address these concerns, particularly in regard to adult career intervention programs.

A number of noted scholars have offered suggestions for increasing the level of sophistication of evaluation studies (see Bhaerman & Campbell, 1986; Oliver & Spokane, 1988; Rounds & Tinsley, 1983; and Spokane & Oliver, 1983). As we look at the status of evaluating the effectiveness of adult career development programs, at least four issues need to be addressed: measurement, methodology, outcomes, and stimulation of more evaluation.

Measurement

Although a vast array of aptitude, ability, and interest measurement techniques are available to facilitate career development, measurement of client outcomes is very limited (Kapes & Mastie, 1988). Standardized tests to assess outcomes are pretty much limited to vocational maturity, decision-making behavior, and attitude change. Many of the outcomes that need to be assessed are amenable to behavioral sampling and observations (i.e., demonstration of use of career planning and job search skills, supervisory ratings of job adjustment, morale, and productivity). It would be helpful for future evaluations if assessment experts could devise alternative approaches for measuring client outcomes. Perhaps a manual could be developed describing how various outcomes could be assessed.

Methodology

In their review of numerous vocational intervention studies, Spokane and Oliver (1983) and Oliver and Spokane (1988) identified various methodological weaknesses that reduce internal and external validity. They devised a "suggestions" checklist to improve vocational intervention evaluation. The checklist covers four areas: design and analysis, criteria, instrumentation, and reporting. Those who want to improve the quality of assessing program effectiveness could profit from reviewing their checklist before designing evaluation studies. Key suggestions are: use real clients, randomly assign them to treatments, clearly identify client needs for counseling and expected outcomes, and employ interventions relevant to specific client concerns.

Vocational Outcomes

These need to be more explicitly defined for each client. It is a mistake to assume that all clients of a group treatment expect the same treatment outcomes. With that assumption, outcome criteria would be the same for all clients and chances for demonstrating differential effectiveness would be reduced. For example, client outcome expectations for a career planning group may vary from simply confirming a career decision to expanding career options or narrowing choices. It would be inappropriate to use the same outcome criteria for all members of a group. This would suggest, as Spokane and Oliver (1988) and Rounds and Tinsley (1983) recommend, that clients need to be diagnosed more carefully to identify the counseling goals to be used as outcome criteria. Goal attainment scaling is useful as an individualized approach to setting and measuring specific client outcomes. Also, Campbell and Cellini's (1981) diagnostic taxonomy, briefly presented earlier, may also be helpful.

In assessing the effects of a career development program, there is often ambiguity as to what specific outcomes should be assessed. To provide some direction for the range of outcomes that could be assessed, it is suggested that these be classified into two groups: a) client outcomes, and b) program outcomes. Client outcomes represent fairly specific client behaviors that result from counseling and usually reflect client goals. Fretz (1981) classified these as follows:

Career Knowledge and Skills

- Accuracy of self-knowledge
- Accuracy of occupational information
- Accuracy of job-seeking skills knowledge
- Planning and goal selection skills
- Appropriateness of choices (realism)
- Range of choices

Career Behavior

- Career information seeking
- Relevant academic performance
- Seeking initial/new job
- Getting initial/new job
- Job ratings
- Being promoted
- Earnings

Sentiments

- Attitudes toward choices: certainty, satisfaction, commitment, career salience
- Job satisfaction
- Qualify-of-life ratings
- Satisfaction with intervention
- Perceived effectiveness of intervention

Effective Role Functioning

- Self-concept adequacy
- Personal adjustment
- Relapses of career problems
- Contributions to community

Program outcomes represent broader programmatic goals and reflect the overall operations of the program. They also encompass client outcomes in that they represent an index of the total effectiveness of the program. According to Braskamp (1979) these might include:

- The program's outreach, visibility, and liaison activities with other services and agencies within the community
- The quality, recentness, and appropriateness of resource materials, facilities, and equipment
- The management of the services
- The quality and competencies of program staff
- The program's image

- The range of services provided
- The program budget

Stimulating More Effective Evaluation

This is not easy to do in view of some of the constraints mentioned earlier. It is hoped that the many models outlined, however, will help increase the thinking about the possibility of conducting an evaluation. Half of the battle is getting started. Start on a small scale by asking basic questions (e.g., Who wants the information? What information is needed? How can it be obtained?). These questions eventually can be refined into a more sophisticated scheme and used to stimulate program staff's involvement in evaluation.

Possible Types of Evaluation

There exist a great number of evaluation approaches. Different types of evaluations ask different questions and focus on specific aspects of the evaluative function. For example, Raizen and Rossi (1981) reported on the work of a committee of the National Academy of Sciences that has delineated the following types of evaluation: needs assessment, basic research, small-scale testing, field evaluation, policy analyses, fiscal accountability, coverage accountability, impact assessment, and economic analyses. Patton (1982, p. 44) also cited several types of evaluation identified in 1980 by the Evaluation Research Society Standards committee:

- Front-end analysis (preinstallation, feasibility analysis). This takes place prior to installation of a program to provide guidance in planning and implementing the program as well as deciding if it should be implemented.
- Evaluability assessment. This includes activities aimed at assessing the feasibility of various evaluation approaches and methods.
- Formative evaluation (developmental, process). This evaluation is aimed at providing information for program improvement, modification, and management.
- Impact evaluation (summative, outcome). This evaluation is aimed at determining program results and effects. It is used especially for making major decisions about program continuation, expansion, reduction, and funding.
- Program monitoring. These activities vary from periodic checks of compliance with policy to relatively straightforward "tracking" of services delivered and "counting" of clients.

Patton stressed that these types of evaluation are by no means mutually exclusive. Over a period of time a program might be involved in activities from each of the categories. He also pointed out that a) some activities occur simultaneously (e.g., program monitoring, formative evaluation, and impact analysis); and b) numerous types of specific evaluations exist within each category.

408

From Patton's (1982) extensive list (pp. 45–47), a few selected evaluation types that adult career development personnel might wish to explore are summarized in Table 1.

An Illustrative Model

We conclude this chapter with an illustrative model as an aid in developing more effective adult career program evaluations. There are five basic phases to program evaluation: 1) purpose, 2) data collection designs, 3) analysis of data, 4) reporting findings, and 5) acting on findings, decision, and actions. A description of each phase follows:

Phase 1: Purpose. The first phase is the most critical because it sets the stage for the four subsequent phases. The purpose of the evaluation needs to be clearly stated and related questions need to be carefully addressed (e.g., Who needs the data? What information is needed? How soon is it needed? Why do they need the information?)

For example, a community college has invested $100,000 in a computerized career information system. The career center director is asking for an additional $20,000 to expand the system. The president of the college wants to know if this is a worthwhile investment. Clearly, the president wants evidence of how the system has been effective and how the additional $20,000 will make it more effective.

A second example represents a different level of purpose. A program has been teaching job search techniques, but the results are unsatisfactory. The purpose is to conduct a careful evaluation of the job search techniques. This should include evaluating techniques being used, teaching effectiveness, client utilization, and impediments and problems interfering with successful implementation.

Phase 2: Data Collection Design. Although Phase 1 provides direction for the evaluation and the information needed, it does not include methods of obtaining this information. We need a data collection design responsive to such fundamental questions as: How do we obtain the data? When will it be obtained? Who will collect the data? Who will provide the data (respondents)? How long will it take to get it? How much will it cost?

According to Leibowitz and Schlossberg (1981), evaluation data consist of three types: a) reaction, b) learning and c) behavioral and organizational change. The first type, reaction data, is process-oriented; data are obtained about the soundness of the procedures used for program activities. These are usually subjective reactions from clients. For example, was the job search technique clearly communicated? Were the sample materials easy to read?

The other two types of evaluation data are outcome data, assessing the effects of the program on the client and the organization. This includes acquisition of new skills, improved morale, number of job placements, reduced turnover, and job satisfaction. The second type, learning data, is an objective assessment of client learning from an activity. Often standardized tests or other objective techniques are used to measure these results. The third type, behavioral and organizational change data, is,

Table 1
Selected Evaluation Types

- Accreditation (Does the program meet minimum standards for accreditation or licensing?)
- Appropriateness (What services should clients be receiving? To what extent are current services appropriate to client needs?)
- Awareness focus (Who knows about the program? What do they know?)
- Cost-benefit analysis (What is the relationship between program costs and program outcomes expressed in dollars?)
- Cost-effectiveness (What is the relationship between program costs and outcomes where the latter are not measured in dollars?)
- Descriptive (What happens in the program?)
- Effectiveness (To what extent is the program effective in attaining its goals?)
- Efficiency (Can inputs be reduced and still obtain the same level of output, or can greater output be obtained with no increase in inputs?)
- Effort (What are the inputs into the program in terms of number of personnel, staff/client ratios, and other descriptors of level of activity and effort in the program?)
- Extensiveness (How does the present level of services compare to the needed level of services?)
- Goal attainment scaling (To what extent do individual clients attain individual goals on a standardized measurement scale?)
- Goals-based (To what extent have program goals been attained?)
- Goal-free (What are the actual effects of the program on clients— without regard to what staff say they want to accomplish?)
- Impact (What are the direct and indirect program effects on the larger community of which it is a part?)
- Longitudinal (What happens to the program and to participants over time?)
- Outcomes (To what extent are desired client outcomes being attained? What are the effects of the program on clients?)
- Performance (What are the participants actually able to do as a result of participation in the program?)
- Personnel (How effective are staff in carrying out their assigned tasks and in accomplishing their individual goals?)
- Process (What are the strengths and weaknesses of day-to-day operations?)
- Product (What are the characteristics of specific and concrete products generated by or used in a program?)
- Quality assurance (Are minimum and accepted standards of care being routinely and systematically provided to clients?)
- Systems analysis (What are the available alternatives and, given those alternatives, what is the optimum way to administer this program?)

again, objective evidence of outcome after a specified period of time. The data represent long-term changes or results.

Phase 3: Analysis of the Data. The analysis should be organized to answer the original questions in the purpose phase. The answers (findings) should be organized systematically so that the reader can clearly see the relationships between the data and the original questions. For example, in the previous illustration of assessing the clients' reactions to learning and using job search techniques, it might be found that these are not working for various reasons. Possibly some clients cannot read help-wanted ads. Maybe there are not enough telephones to respond to the job openings. It could be that some clients fear job rejections. Also, some may not be receiving job messages due to a breakdown in the communication system.

Phase 4: Reporting the Findings. How should the evaluation data be reported? Optimal media techniques should be used to communicate the findings. Yet perhaps more important is that optional recommendations be given, where appropriate, for subsequent decisions and activities. For example, for job search techniques it might be recommended that a) additional telephones be installed for a specified cost, b) volunteers be used to help record job messages, and c) telephone schedules be developed to distribute the call.

Phase 5: Acting on the Findings (Decisions and Actions). The best way to lose staff enthusiasm for conducting evaluations is for staff to discover that no action was taken as a result of the evaluation and that it was a total waste of time, energy, and dollars. Unfortunately this often occurs. Consequently it is essential that this phase is carefully planned and implemented. Will the right people read the evaluation (those in authority to make decisions)? Are the actions feasible? Was adequate information provided for decisions?

REFERENCES

Baker, S.B., & Popowicz, C.L. (1983). Meta-analysis as a strategy for evaluating effects of career education interventions. *Vocational Guidance, 31,* 178–186.

Bhaerman, R.B., & Campbell, R. (1986). Evaluation: Measuring Effectiveness of Adult Career Development Practice. In Z.B. Leibowitz & H.D. Lea (Eds.), *Adult Career Development: Concepts, Issues and Practices* (pp. 326–340): Alexandria, VA. National Career Development Association.

Borgen, F.H., Layton, W.L., Veenhuizen, D.L., & Johnson, D.J. (1985). Vocational behavior and career development, 1984: A review. *Journal of Vocational Behavior, 27,* 218–269.

Braskamp, L.M. (1979). Program evaluation: Process and product. In R.E. Campbell and P. Shaltry (Eds.), *Perspectus on adult career development and guidance* (pp. 187–197). Columbus: The National Center for Research in Vocational Education, the Ohio State University.

Cairo, P.C. (1983). Counseling in industry: A select review of literature. *Personal Psychology, 36,* 1–18.

Campbell, R.E., & Cellini, J.V. (1981). A diagnostic taxonomy of adult career problems. *Journal of Vocational Behavior, 19,* 179–180.

Campbell, R.E., & Heffernan, J.M. (1983). Adult vocational behavior. In W.B. Walsh, & S.H. Osipow (Eds.), *Handbook of Vocational Psychology,* (Vol. 1, pp. 223–260). Hillsdale, NJ: Erlbaum.

Erickson, E.H. (1950). *Childhood and society.* New York: Norton.

Ferrara, J., Rudrud, E., Wendlegass, P., & Markve, R.A. (1985). Vocational awareness training and job preferences among mentally retarded adults. *Vocational Guidance Quarterly, 33,* 305–314.

Fitzgerald, L.F., & Rounds, J.B. (1989). Vocational behavior, 1988: A critical analysis. *Journal of Vocational Behavior, 35,* 105–163.

Fretz, W.B. (1981). Evaluating the effectiveness of career interventions. [Monograph]. *Journal of Counseling Psychology, 28,* 77–99.

Giroux, R.R. (1983). *Adult career counseling and guidance.* (NATCON Series No. 3). Ottawa-Hull: Canada Employment and Immigration Commission.

Gladstein, G.A., & Apfel, F.S. (1987). A theoretically based adult career counseling center. *Career Development Quarterly, 36,* 178–185.

Glass, G.B., McGraw, B., & Smith, M.L. (1981). *Meta-analysis in social research.* Beverly Hills, CA: Sage.

Harrison, L.R. & Entine, A.D. (1976). Existing programs and emerging strategies. *The Counseling Psychologist, 6,* 45–50.

Harmon, L.W., & Farmer, H.S. (1983). Current theoretical issues in vocational psychology. In W.B. Walsh, & S.H. Osipow (Eds.), *Handbook of Vocational Psychology* (Vol. 1, pp. 39–77). Hillsdale, NJ: Erlbaum.

Havighurst, R.J. (1952). *Developmental tasks and education.* (2nd ed.). New York: Longmans, Green, & Company.

Holland, J.L., Magoon, T.M. & Spokane, A.R. (1981). Counseling psychology: Career interventions, research, and theory. *Annual Review of Psychology, 32,* 279–305.

Kapes, J.T. & Mastie, M.M. (1988). *A counselor's guide to career assessment instruments.* (2nd ed.). Alexandria, VA: National Career Development Association.

Kingdon, M.A., & Blimline, C.A. (1987). Evaluating the effectiveness of career development training for women. *Career Development Quarterly, 35,* 220–227.

Kostka, M.P., & Wilson, C.K. (1986). Reducing mathematics anxiety in non-traditional-age female students. *Journal of College Student Personnel, 27,* 530–534.

Krumboltz, J.D., Becker-Haven, J.F., & Burnett, K.F. (1979). Counseling psychology. *Annual Review of Psychology, 30,* 555–602.

Leibowitz, Z. & Schlossberg, N. (1981). Designing career development programs in organizations: A systems approach. In D.H. Montross & C.J. Shinkman (Eds.), *Career Development in the 1980s: Theory and practice* (pp. 277–292). Springfield, IL: Charles C. Thomas.

Levinson, D.J., Darrow, C.N., Klein, E.B., Levinson, M.H., & McKee, B. (1978). *The seasons of a man's life.* New York: Knopf.

McDaniels C., & Watts, G.A. (1987). Cooperation: Key to employee career development program. *Career Development Quarterly, 36*, 170–175.

Miller, D.C., & Form, W.H. (1951). *Industrial sociology: An introduction to the sociology of work reactions.* New York: Harper & Row.

Miller, D.C., & Form, W.H. (1964). *Industrial sociology: The sociology of work organizations.* New York: Harper & Row.

Mueser, K.T., Foy, D.W., & Carter, M.J. (1986). Social skills training for job maintenance in a psychiatric patient. *Journal of Counseling Psychology, 33*, 360–362.

Myers, R.A. (1971). Research on educational and vocational counseling. In A.E. Bergin, & S.L. Garfield (Eds.), *Handbook of psychotherapy and behavior change: An empirical analysis.* New York: Wiley.

Oliver, L.W. (Ed.). (1978). *Outcome measures for counseling research.* (ARI Technical Paper No. 316). Alexandria, VA: U.S. Army Research Institute for the Behavioral and Social Sciences.

Oliver, L.W., & Spokane, A.R. (1988). Career-intervention outcome: What contributes to client gain? *Journal of Counseling Psychology, 35*(4), 447–462.

Osipow, S.H. (1987). Counseling psychology: Theory, research, and practice in career counseling. *Annual Review of Psychology, 38*, 257–278.

Patton, M.Q. (1982). *Practical evaluation.* Beverly Hills, CA: Sage Publications.

Pickering, J.W., & Vacc, N.A. (1984). Effectiveness of career development interventions for college students: A review of published research. *Vocational Guidance Quarterly, 32*, 149–159.

Raizen, S. & Rossi, P. (Eds.) (1981). *Program evaluation in education: When? How? To what ends?* Washington, DC: National Academy of Sciences.

Rounds, J.B., Jr., & Tinsley, H.E.A. (1984). Diagnosis and treatment of vocational problems. In S.D. Brown, & R.W. Lent (Eds.), *Handbook of counseling psychology* (pp. 137–177). New York: Wiley-Interscience.

Schein, E.H. (1978). *Career dynamics: Matching individual and organizational needs.* Reading, Mass.: Addison-Wesley.

Schlossberg, N.K. (1981). A model for analyzing human adaptation to transition. *The Counseling Psychologist, 9*, 2–18.

Slaney, R.B., & Dickson, R.D. (1985). Relation of career indecisions in career exploration with reentry women: A treatment and follow-up study. *Journal of Counseling Psychology, 32*, 355–362.

Slaney, R.B., & Lewis, E.T. (1986). Effects of career exploration on career undecided reentry women: An intervention and follow-up. *Journal of Vocational Behavior, 28*, 97–109.

Smith, M.L., & Glass, G.V. (1977). Meta-analysis of psychology outcome studies. *American Psychologist, 32*, 752–760.

Smith, M.L., Glass, G.V., & Miller, T.I. (1980). *The benefits of psychotherapy.* Baltimore, MD: Johns Hopkins University Press.

Stump, R. (1982). Evaluating your career development system. *Career Planning and Adult Development Newsletter, 4*,(6), pp. 1–2.

Super, D.E. (1963). Vocational development in adolescence and early childhood: Tasks and behaviors. In D.E. Super, R. Starishevsky, N.

Matlin, & J.P. Jordan (Eds.), *Career development: Self-concept theory* (Research monograph No. 4). New York: College Entrance Examination Board.

Tolbert, E.L. (1980). Career development theories: What help for older persons? *Journal of Employment Counseling, 17,* 17–27.

Walz, G.R. & Benjamin, L. (1981). *Programs and practices in adult counseling.* Ann Arbor, MI: ERIC Clearinghouse on Counseling

West, D.J. Jr., Horan, J.J., & Games, P.A. (1984). Component analysis of occupational stress inoculation applied to registered nurses in an acute care hospital setting. *Journal of Counseling Psychology, 31,* 209–218.

SECTION VII:

FUTURE TRENDS

ANTICIPATING THE FUTURE . . .

CHAPTER 23

Adult Career Development in an Uncertain Future

Donald E. Super
Savannah, Georgia

We look into the future "through a glass darkly"—or perhaps, with the current rate of technological, economic, and social change, we might better say "through a kaleidoscope confusedly!" Looking into the future is indeed a risky endeavor, as labor market forecasting and econometrics have demonstrated time and again. While "The more it changes, the more it is the same thing" remains true, there is a new truth to go with it: "The more it changes, the more it changes!" The rate of change appears to accelerate constantly.

Despite this fact, if we do not look ahead we are sure to miss some trends that can be foreseen. As other chapters in this book examine the present state of career development theory and practice, and as this writer has recently published an updated statement of his principles, methods, and views (Super, 1990), what follows will be, first, a very brief restatement, followed by a more detailed presentation of one person's views concerning the future.

A QUICK LOOK AT ONE PERSON'S MODEL

A Life-Span, Life-Space Perspective

We now generally accept the fact that "career choice" is not an event, but rather a process. Career choices are not made, they emerge. They emerge from the third grader's realization that he or she learns faster and performs better in class than his or her peers, while a classmate who rarely shines in schoolwork concludes that he or she is not a scholar and seeks recognition as an athlete, as a friend, or as a clown. Developing self-concepts are gradually translated into role preferences and occupational plans. Thus one 16-year-old girl, on opening a letter from an Ivy League university just before dinner one summer evening before her junior year in high school, said in wonderment to her father: "You know, these people want me to go there!" The star student and figure skater was beginning to see what a brilliant future was opening up before her in a traditionally male specialty at a traditionally male university.

416

Some fortunate people, some gifted and some not gifted, do their career-, self-, and occupational-exploration early, as did the girl just described. Some do it later, in the labor market, the work force, or in college. One very competent, but not gifted, high-school youth in the Career Pattern Study drifted into a job a few months after graduation, and kept on drifting and stagnating and drifting until he was 28 years old, at which time he learned from a neighbor something about the work of a state trooper. He liked what he heard. And, when interviewed at the age of 36, he was successful, satisfied, and well settled in the occupation which had become his "career." However some people, for reasons of personality, aptitude, opportunity, or circumstances, never do "settle down"; their careers are labelled, by some occupational sociologists, as "unstable" or as "multiple trial," and by some psychologist as "free-form."

After exploration and establishment comes "maintenance"—if all goes according to the model. But a model is, in the sciences, not necessarily the "typical" or "ideal" ("that which should be"); it is a deliberate simplification of that which is often observed in carefully designed studies. In one very real sense a model is that from which people differ in various ways. Some of these divergences from the "model" (the schematic, theoretical, simplification of that which is observed in many people) are "good," some are "neutral," and some are "bad." Maintenance is, again, a generalization, and hence to some degree a misleading term. As noted in the "staircase" model (Super, 1990, p. 214) which examines in a different light the Rainbow Model, "maintenance" may mean just holding one's own, or it may mean stagnating, updating, or even innovating. A comparison with some of the theories described in the second edition of Brown and Brooks' (1990) classic, e.g., that of John Holland's evolved theory, will make clear to the thoughtful reader that "maintenance" and "innovation" can proceed together. In fact, one might go so far as to say that some people's careers involve innovative maintenance until late deceleration and death without retirement (and at this point the naming of names is no longer possible, as history has not yet unfolded to that extent!).

The Theory Turned Into a Method and Applied

This writer's occupational career began as a practitioner. His experience with unemployed young men at the depth of the Great Depression led him to ponder the long-term effects of prolonged unemployment as portrayed in Lazarsfeld's "Unemployed Village" (1932). This led to doctoral study and a career of researching, writing, and teaching, with periodic time out for applications. In recent years applications of theory have demanded increasing attention (Super, 1980, 1983, 1990). The C-DAC Model was the outcome, and is briefly described below.

The Career Development Assessment and Counseling Model (C-DAC). This approach to assessment and counseling postulates that career counseling is improved if one takes into account the level of career development attained by the counselee. Occupational preferences, vocational interest inventories, values, and even aptitudes need to be viewed in terms of career maturity and role preferences. These have generally been assessed subjectively, and thus too often incidentally and unreliably, in interviews only. The Career Pattern Study (Super & Overstreet, 1960; Super & Kidd, 1979) and the Work Importance Study (Super & Sverko, in press) have produced objective measures of traits relevant to developmental career assessment and counseling. These are the Career Development Inventory (Super et al., 1981), the Adult Career Concerns Inventory (Super et al., 1985), the Salience Inventory (Super & Nevill, 1985) and the Values Scale (Super & Nevill, 1986). The postulate (or hypothesis, for it is now being tested in research projects at the Universities of Georgia, North Carolina at Greensboro, and Virginia) is that if work is not as important to a person as, say, homemaking, leisure, community service, or even study, he or she is not likely to be sufficiently well oriented to the world of work (vocationally career-mature) for scores on an interest inventory such as the Strong or the Kuder to mean very much. They may point to areas which might be explored, but are likely to be a poor basis for occupational or even curricular choices. A career maturity inventory can help look into this question more thoroughly. A measure of values, of which there are several on the market (e.g., Super & Nevill, 1986), may also probe more deeply into the goals which a person seeks in life and thus in vocational and in other career activities. The method has been detailed and illustrated in Brown and Brooks (1990, 2nd ed., pp. 244–253 and 256–257) and in workshops at several national conventions and major universities. It is much more briefly illustrated here with another case, a young adult male.

The model and the methods applied. When he came to the counseling center of the university from which he had graduated with a major in psychology, a minor in mathematics, and a *cum laude* degree, this 25-year old man was facing a problem which, although some theories would ascribe it to the early or mid-thirties, was seen fairly often in Career Pattern Study (Super et al., 1957) men of his age. Sam, like some of his peers, was facing an early career "crisis": he was dissatisfied with his way of life, his income, his job, and therefore with his occupation (i.e., his conception of other jobs in the same field). Employed for the previous three years as a teacher of mathematics, assistant housemaster, and football coach in a boys' prep school, he wanted to review with a counselor his plans to enroll in a four-year Law and Business Administration degree program. Thus he could train for an occupation that would pay him (he hoped) considerably more than would the field of education, place him nearer to his parental home, and allow more opportunity for self-expression in "professional or managerial work" than did teaching.

Sam's father was a professor of chemistry in a small college, and his mother was a teacher of home economics. His older sister, a graduate of a selective university, was employed as a fashion designer and doing well in that field. As is often done in career counseling he was given the *Strong Interest Inventory* to assess his vocational interest. To help in the interpretation of these scores, even though he was no longer a student and had been out in the work world for three years, he was also given the *Career Development Inventory* (University Form, Super et al., 1981) be-

418

cause the counselor wondered how vocationally mature he actually was. To supplement this multidimensional developmental measure designed for students, he was given the *Adult Career Concerns Inventory* (Super et al., 1985), a unidimensional career maturity or adaptability inventory designed for adults. The *Values Scale* developed by the Work Importance Study (Nevill & Super, 1986b) was also administered in an attempt to probe more deeply into what he sought in life, and the values that might underly his occupational interests (the means of attaining values). The *Salience Inventory* of the Work Importance Study (Nevill & Super, 1986a) was used as another vocational readiness measure, to compare the relative importance, to him, of the roles of worker, student, homemaker, citizen, and leisurite.

The Strong scores did not agree with Sam's expressed choice of a new occupation: his measured interests were only slightly like those of people in business and law, but were very much like those people in social service and teaching, including school administration. Therefore, it seemed especially important to examine his underlying values, his career maturity, and his life-role involvements.

On the Career Development Inventory (CDI) Sam showed openness to career exploration, but deficiency in career planning attitudes. Furthermore, his knowledge of and ability to apply career decision-making principles and information were only average when compared to college seniors, *and* he had had three years of experience. He knew little about career stages and developmental tasks or about occupations or the world of work, and very little about the field of work into which he was thinking of going. The Adult Career Concerns Inventory (ACCI) confirmed what the intake interview had suggested. He is now much concerned with the tasks of career exploration, with crystallizing and specifying a vocational preference. He is not yet concerned with the tasks of establishment, maintenance, or, of course, disengagement.

The Salience Inventory (SI) reveals a fairly even balance of involvement in the major life roles: study, work, home and family, and leisure are all important to him. Only community service does not rate high because his "community," as a young assistant housemaster in a boarding school is, no doubt, the school itself.

The Values Scale (VS) shows that Sam values highly opportunity to use his abilities, and, with this, personal development and achievement. But economic security is also important to him, along with economic rewards and social relations. He also values altruism and authority, and appears not to be much of a risk taker. Sam wants both a self-fulfilling and a comfortable life.

The Strong and the VS thus appear to contradict Sam's expressed vocational preferences for business and law (especially investment analysis), and to suggest that these goals are manifestations of ignorance of the world of work and of occupations. This is confirmed by the CDI. Sam's willingness to explore and his desire to make a wise choice make him a promising counselee. He was advised to look into ways of moving into a better-paying school situation (perhaps a good public school system), and to put a year into meeting the necessary certification requirements and into finding out more about and preparing for work in school administration. Thus, it seemed to the counselor, Sam could express his interest, attain his values, and build on, rather than jettison, his previous training and experience. The art of counseling enters into the next steps, which are sharing these facts and thoughts with Sam in such a way that he can assimilate them.

This may be easier to do than most counselors realize, for if the client or counselee has had the motivation and the persistence to complete a battery of tests and inventories such as those of the C-DAC Model, he or she usually has what is needed to work through guided self-assessment with the aids of profile displays of the test scores, discussions of what they mean, and their possible implications for action.

One adult, tested in a situation in which an intake interview was followed a few days later by a full day of testing, came in for a discussion of the results after the counselor had done his work-up. He sat down and said: "You know, after taking those tests I've decided maybe I'm not ready to make a decision. . . . I think I need to do a bit of exploring. Let's talk about what and how." The hardest part of test interpretation, of counseling, was thus done by the client himself in between contacts, as a result of what might be called an encounter with simulated reality. It had made him think. Such techniques are not new, and have been discussed in texts and journals for at least forty years (e.g., Super, 1949; 1962, 2nd ed., pp. 605–629). Test data can stimulate discussion of what they mean, of how they relate to bio-data, of what can legitimately be inferred from tests and from bio-data, and of what they portend for the future educationally, occupationally, and perhaps also for other life roles. In such counseling the professional is a guide in assessment, not an assessor; a guide to and through occupational and career (life-stage) data, not the owner-pilot who decides where to go and how to go there!

Another common technique is to give the interest inventory to the counselee at the end of the first interview (during which the procedure has been discussed and agreed to) to fill out alone and bring in for scoring. An appointment is then made for a discussion of the results in the light of the career history as related in the first contact. This discussion of measured interests and of experiences and preferences as revealed so far led, in Sam's case, to the conclusion that it might be well to look into his career maturity (attitudes and knowledge helpful in making good career decisions), his values, and his objective. Thus, when Sam had completed the other C-DAC tests he was ready to rethink his "plans" rather than to merely receive confirmation or negation. He needed to "rethink" with guidelines and ideas about potentially better objectives.

In contemporary career counseling there is no "testing and telling"— no non-directive limiting of counseling to the reflection and clarification of feeling. There is, instead, help in encountering relevant realities in ways that stimulate thought, provide material for thought, and help test the soundness of data, inferences, and conclusions. In the process, of course, there are often expressions of feelings by the client, and a need for appropriate responses by the counselor. There may even be a need for some psychotherapeutic sessions: Sam Stasko (Super, 1955, pp. 219–226) is an example of this type. The exploration of the meanings of developmental data, whether life-history or inventory data, is best done in a joint expedition of counselor and client. This aspect of the present seems likely to persist into the future, even to become more general.

FUTURE TRENDS

Person, Organization, and Society

The focus of clients, and of the professional counselors and psychologists who work with them, tends to be on the individual as a person. As has been well emphasized by some current writers (e.g., Vondracek et al., 1986), the person is too often seen in a near-vacuum: the environment may be mentioned, but is too often not taken adequately into account. Social and organizational psychologists and organizational sociologists, on the other hand, have often been so concerned with the larger entity that they have failed to take the individual adequately into account. Both the individual and the organization must be seen, as political scientists like to point out, in the econo-political context in which they work. The interactions, as in the Vondracek and Associates model (1986, p. 79), become so numerous and so complex that one is inclined to despair of ever being able to take all the relevant variables into account. Holland's (1985) work is a good example of the productivity that can result from simplistic approaches, while my own (Super, 1957, 1980, 1990) may well illustrate, in the reactions of critics, the inadequacies of attempts to place people in their context. Perhaps Vondracek's group, or path analysts such as Card (1978) and other sociologists, will provide a way to handle the more complex models that we now need.

It has been so often pointed out that the person-centered focus on the development of a career may produce different results from an organization-focus that it hardly seems necessary to repeat that fact here. The real issue now is whether we will continue to face this conflict of interest, or if we will find ways to reconcile personal and organizational (and social) interests.

We seem to be living in an age in which people seek, more and more, to achieve self-determination in their careers. The movements for women's rights, for equal opportunities for blacks, Hispanics, and people with divergent sexual orientations, and for the right not to be an "organization man," are examples from the last decade and that which led up to it. We shall, no doubt, see increasing emphasis on self-determination, self-realization, and self-efficacy, while taking social needs such as the preservation of a rapidly deteriorating environment into account. Organizations will, no doubt, have to become more "member-friendly" and more "host-friendly" if they and the Earth are to survive and prosper. The reactions against deregulation as we have known it, and in favor of new types of controls, seem to point this way.

We need to rethink individual, corporate, and societal career development, taking all three into account (see, for example, Super's *Psychology of Careers*, 1957; Kimberly, J.R., Miles, R.H. & Associates' *Organizational Life Cycle*, 1980, or, to cite a true classic, Gibbon's *Rise and Fall of the Roman Empire*, and, let us add, the book that may well be written in the near future, someone's *Rise and Fall of the Russian Empires of 1682–199?*). Such an effort was made when the impact of political and economic events, such as the Great Depression and World War II, on individual and corporate life was assessed by the writer (Super, 1942, Ch.6, and Super, 1957, Ch.18), but without noticeable effect on the field. Since the "social revolution" of the late 1960s and '70s, however, personnel selection and training specialists, aided by career development specialists interested in research, theory, and its applications, have done a great deal to make up for the deficiencies of the past. A few examples, in addition to this volume, are Arthur et al. (1989), Brown and Brooks (1990), Hall et al. (1986), Howard and Bray (1988), Leibowitz et al. (1986), London and Moore (1987), McDaniels (1989), Montross and Shinkman (1981 rev. 1992), and Riverin-Simard (1988).

One of the central, innovative, and yet old, ideas that are now highlighting thinking about career development in the 1990s is the distinction between work, jobs, and careers (Super, 1976). *Work* is the expenditure of effort, which may be *paid* as in employment or self-employment, or *unpaid* as in homemaking, civic activity, or a hobby. *A job* is created when others are willing to pay for a service or a product, and normally means working for an employer or for oneself (it can also mean a task or a contract, such as painting a fence or writing a book). A job may involve one or many *positions*, filled by people doing much the same work. *An occupation* is a group of similar jobs, which may be in different organizations and locations. *And a career*, it seems necessary to keep noting, is the sequence of positions, jobs, and occupations that a person occupies and pursues during the course of a life of preparing to work, working, and retiring from work.

Work can be fulfilling, but can also be debilitating. So, therefore, can a career. One question that is asked with increasing frequency, and that will no doubt continue to be asked, is: "If I pursue the kind of career the Organization wants me to pursue, if I develop in the way they want me to develop, what will happen to the 'real' me?" Thus, a research and development engineer, who was always considered a model "company man" by his corporation, was told by his manager that they wanted him to move to a distant state. At home he was then confronted by a wife and college-student daughter who said that he might move but that they were tired of moving and liked it where they were. In due course he reported back to his company that he had thought things over and was going to resign, keep on living in the small city where he was located, and start his own company to manufacture and market a product he had been dreaming of for some time. Two years later his small company was thriving, as were his home, his marriage, and he himself. He had, like many people today, decided to be his own man. Human resources development as the company saw it was not career development as the pursuer of the career saw it.

More and more corporations have taken note of this fact, and, at the same time that we note pressure on managers to cross from one "career path" to another to become better-qualified top-level managers, we also note that company plans make it possible for the "career" specialist to remain a specialist as long as he or she is willing to forego the significant increases of compensation and authority. But with these plans there is now another type of plan—one which makes it possible, if the specialist so desires, to plan and execute a transition from the corporation to the campus, where a good specialist can rise to the top of his specialty ladder as an independent leader in his or her field. Some of our largest, and leading, corporations now have such policies, and help some employees to implement them.

It has been said that a person's career is his or her most precious possession. Some parents say this in other words when they tell their children that their really important inheritance is the education they have been helped to acquire. If it was indeed an appropriate and good education, it provides the basis for pursuing a satisfying career. Thus an organization that bends a person's career in a way that serves the organization while neglecting important elements in the personality and life of the employee is blighting that precious possession. Career development specialists in business, industry, and government need to be increasingly alert to what they may be doing *to*, as well as *with*, employees.

Careers are sometimes planned well in advance. One young man in the Career Pattern Study said, sixteen years after graduating from college, that he was rather envious of some of his classmates who, unlike himself, had not known what they would do after college. Their lives must have been that much more adventurous than his, for he had known that he would go from college to law school, from law school to clerkship with a judge, and from clerkship into the practice of law in a firm. This he had done. His career was planned and linear. Some of his classmates may have moved along a line that became apparent only as they moved: theirs were what some writers call "emerging careers." The career management skill in such cases lies in seeing what may emerge and in facilitating its emergence "to make the happy accidents happen." This is done also, it should be said, in linear careers, as when a university professor plans, at the end of one sabbatical year, what he would like to do six years later during the next such leave, and makes step-by-step plans for the next sabbatical. Men and women in business and industry sometimes plan ahead in comparable ways. Planned careers can be as "free" and as exciting as "free-form" and "mixed form" careers; the fun is in the game plan and in the player's attitude, and the freedom is in the planning and in the execution of the plan. And, today's informed observers say (e.g. Arthur et al, 1989), the rate of technological change and the shift in industrialized countries from production to service industries will mean that an increasingly high percentage of careers will not be linear (moving from exploration to establishment or maintenance to disengagement), but will be free-form or mixed-form, with recycling and with job changes if not actual occupational changes.

Such changes will be increasingly common, too, as technological, production, and market changes alter and speed up the careers and life cycles of organizations and industries. For we know now that organizations, industries, and empires also have careers: they develop, they prosper, they stagnate, and they decline. In 1987, giving a slide talk about the Soviet Union after a study tour there, this writer used a chart showing the life-spans of some major empires. This chart brought out the fact that the Russian Empire (Czarist and Communist) had already lasted longer than some other major empires such as the French, and raised the question of how much longer the Russian control of Eastern Europe and Northern Asia would last. Little did any of the group anticipate the events of 1989 and the following years!

In a book based on pre-World War II work on career development, the writer (Super, 1942) included a chapter on the psychology and sociology of unemployment. In his second book on career development (Super, 1957), this chapter was omitted because critics considered it irrelevant to that era. But now expert opinion, or at least some important segments of it, holds that we again need to consider periods, yes, repeated periods, of unemployment as part of the normal cycle. It is said by outplacement counselors and "headhunters" that it takes from six months to a year for displaced managers to find new employment, and some displaced skilled and unskilled workers never find new, or even first, jobs.

This emphasizes the importance of the Life-Career Rainbow as a model of careers, and the Salience Inventory (Super & Nevill, 1985) as an assessment instrument, to be considered in education, continuing education, human resources development, and career development programs and counseling. If human resources are not to be allowed to stagnate, if people are to attain life goals and feel self-fulfilled, all types of career outlets must be considered, cultivated, and utilized. The true "worker" works not only on the job, but also at home, in the community, and in a variety of "non-work" workplaces in which the expenditure of effort is intellectually, emotionally, socially, or physically rewarding, and these non-monetary rewards are sufficient.

REFERENCES

Arthur, M.B., Hall, D.T., & Lawrence, B.S. (Eds.) (1989). *Handbook of career theory.* Cambridge: Cambridge University Press.

Brown, D., & Brooks, L. (1990). *Career choice and development.* (2nd ed.) San Francisco: Jossey-Bass.

Card, J.J. (1978). Career commitment processes in the young adult years. *Journal of Vocational Behavior, 12,* 53–78.

Hall, D.T. (1986). *Career development in organizations.* San Francisco: Jossey-Bass.

Holland, J.L. (1985). *Making vocational choices.* Englewood Cliffs: Prentice-Hall.

Howard, A., & Bray, D.W. (1988). *Managerial lives in transition.* New York: Guilford Press.

Kimberly, J.R., Miles, R.H. (Eds.) (1980). *The organizational life cycle.* San Francisco: Jossey-Bass.

Leibowitz, Z., & Lea, D. (Eds.) (1986). *Adult career development.* Alexandria, VA: National Career Development Association.

London, M., & Moore, E.M. (1987). *Career management and survival in the workplace.* San Francisco: Jossey-Bass.

Montross, D.H., & Shinkman, C.J. (Eds.) (1981, being revised for 1992). *Career-development in the 1980s.* Springfield, IL: Charles C. Thomas.

McDaniels, C. (1989). *The changing workplace.* San Francisco: Jossey-Bass.

Nevill, D.D., & Super, D.E. (1986a). *The salience inventory.* Palo Alto, CA: Consulting Psychologists Press.

Riverin-Simard, D. (1988). *Phases of the working life.* Montreal: Meridian Press.

Super, D.E. Note: references antedating 1980 will be found in more recent publications marked with an *, to save space here.

Super, D.E. (1980). A life-span, life-space approach to career development. *Journal of Vocational Behavior, 11,* 282–298.

Super, D.E. (1983). Assessment in career guidance: toward truly developmental counseling. *Personnel & Guidance Journal, 61,* 555–562.

*Super, D.E. (1984). Distinguished scientific award for the applications of psychology: 1983. *American Psychologists, 39,* 274–280.

*Super, D.E. (1985). Coming of age in Middletown: careers in the making. *American Psychologist, 40,* 405–414.

*Super, D.E. (1990). A life-span, life-space approach to career development. Ch. 7 in Brown, D. and Brooks, L. (Eds.), *Career choice and development.* San Francisco: Jossey-Bass.

Super, D.E., & Nevill, D.D. (1985). *The salience inventory.* Palo Alto, CA: Consulting Psychologists Press.

Super, D.E., & Nevill, D.D. (1986). *The values scale.* Palo Alto, CA: Consulting Psychologists Press.

Super, D.E., & Sverko, B. (Eds.) (in Press). Values and roles in cross-cultural perspective: the international work importance study. San Francisco: Jossey-Bass.

Super, D.E., Thompson, A.S., Lindeman, R.H., Jordaan, J.P., & Myers, R.A. (1981). *The career development inventory.* Palo Alto, CA: Consulting Psychologists Press.

Super, D.E., Thompson, A.S., Lindeman, R.H., Myers, R.A., & Jordaan, J.P. (1985). *The adult career concerns inventory.* Palo Alto, CA: Consulting Psychologists Press.

Vondracek, F.W., Lerner, R.M., & Shulenberg, J.E. (1986). *Career Development: A life-span developmental approach.* Hillsdale, NJ: Erlbaum.